Pokémon

VISUAL
COMPANION

Written by: Simcha Whitehill,
Lawrence Neves, Katherine Fang,
Cris Silvestri, and Glenn Dakin

CONTENTS

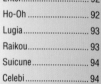

WELCOME POKÉMON FANS!

Welcome to the wide world of Pokémon—a world filled with mystery and adorable creatures known as Pokémon.

What is a Pokémon? Read through this book and you'll discover everything you need to know about Pokémon.

But Pokémon do not live alone. They live in harmony with humans and the world around them. This book will introduce you to many of the brave, sneaky, interesting, and prominent people in the Pokémon world. You will see what it takes to become a Pokémon Trainer (a human that makes Pokémon and human partnerships his or her priority) a Contest Coordinator, and a Pokémon breeder.

Are you ready? Let's get started now!

THE HISTORY OF POKÉMON

Dates apply to US only.

1998 | September: *Pokémon: Indigo League*

1999 | September: *Pokémon: Indigo League/Pokémon: Adventures on the Orange Islands*

2000 | September: *Pokémon: The Johto Journeys*

2001 | September: *Pokémon: Johto League Champions*

2002 | September: *Pokémon: Master Quest*

2003 | September: *Pokémon: Advanced*

2004 | September: *Pokémon: Advanced Challenge*

2005 | September: *Pokémon: Advanced Battle*

2006 | September: *Pokémon: Battle Frontier*

2007 | June: *Pokémon: Diamond and Pearl*

2008 | April: *Pokémon: DP Battle Dimension*

2009 | May: *Pokémon: DP Galactic Battles*

WHAT ARE POKÉMON?

Pokémon: unique creatures of every shape and size, each species endowed with its own special powers and abilities.

Pokémon are able to communicate amongst themselves, but few Pokémon have been known to use human language. Nevertheless, Pokémon clearly demonstrate intelligence, feelings, and individual personalities.

For the most part, people and Pokémon coexist in relative peace. In the ancient past, some cultures revered Legendary Pokémon for their powers, and Pokémon have lived and worked alongside people as partners and friends since time immemorial. In the modern day, Pokémon are often seen paired with Pokémon Trainers, people who raise Pokémon to compete in friendly battles.

LIFE IN THE POKÉMON WORLD

There are various inhabited regions in the Pokémon world; some of the regions of the world explored so far include Kanto, Johto, Hoenn, Sinnoh, Unova, and Kalos. In addition, there are smaller groups of islands, such as the Orange Islands and Whirl Islands. All these regions are separated by water, but travel between them is not difficult, especially by ferry.

2010 | June: *Pokémon Sinnoh League Victors*

2011 | February: *Pokémon: Black & White*

2012 | February: *Pokémon: BW Rival Destinies*

2013 | February: *Pokémon: BW Adventures in Unova*

2014 | January: *Pokémon: XY*

2015 | February: *Pokémon: XY Kalos Quest!*

2016 | February: *Pokémon: XYZ*

2017 | May: *Pokémon: Sun and Moon*

2018 | March: *Pokémon: Sun and Moon Ultra Adventures*

2019 | March: *Pokémon: Sun and Moon Ultra Legends*

2020 | **MORE ADVENTURES TO COME!**

ASH

He is a Pokémon dreamer who wants to one day have it all—including becoming a Pokémon Master. Ash battles impossible odds while maintaining personal relationships with all his friends and Pokémon.

Almost every adventure brings on new surprises—and new outfits. Even though Ash has an outfit redesign with every new region he visits, he likes to maintain his overall ensemble: a baseball cap, short-sleeved shirt and jacket, fingerless gloves, jeans, sneakers, backpack, and the most important item of all, his region-specific Pokédex! In fact, the only things that stay the same are his Poké Balls!

BRASH ASH

Ash, like any ten-year-old boy, finds it hard to see the world in anything but black and white. His arrogance often ends up hurting him somehow, but he usually ends up learning from his mistakes. Don't let the boy-ego fool you; he is exceedingly compassionate and often sacrifices himself for his friends and Pokémon.

KANTO & JOHTO

Ash's first outfit is very straightforward. His original hat is a special Pokémon Expo hat that Ash got by mailing in cereal box tops.

HOENN

The most notable change in the second coming of Ash is the baseball cap, which does away with the swoop logo, and moves to a pattern that resembles half of a Poké Ball. This symbol can also be seen on Ash's shirt.

SINNOH

In Sinnoh, the changes to Ash's outfit are fairly subtle. The half Poké Ball pattern on his hat changes from green to blue, his pants gain some useful cargo pockets, and he now has a stylish stand-up collar.

WHAT'S A MOTHER TO DO?

Ash's mother is Delia Ketchum. She resides in Ash's hometown of Pallet Town with her own Pokémon, Mr. Mime. Often calling Ash to praise him after a victory or worry about him in a particularly dangerous adventure, like all mothers, she supports him in everything he does.

Badge Master

From Kanto, through the Orange Islands, to Johto, Hoenn, Sinnoh, Unova, and now Kalos, Ash has won quite a few Gym badges during his travels. He's also won 7 Frontier Symbols from The Battle Frontier, making him a Battle Frontier Champion. He's won all of his Sinnoh Gym badges, but lost to Tobias in the semi-finals. He has earned his share of Gym badges in Unova and Kalos as well.

UNOVA

Ash's Unova threads reflect a more mature approach to his Pokémon Master quest. A sporty and practical zipped hoodie with pockets, relaxed cargo pants, and high-top sneakers highlight his new outfit.

KALOS

Ash's clothing in Kalos has pops of bright primary colors to play off gray. From his hat, to his fingerless gloves, to his high tops, the classic red perfectly matches a Poké Ball. He also sports a short sleeve blue jacket. This ensemble is sleek and comfortable so nothing will get in his way as he battles for a place in the Kalos League Tournament.

ALOLA

In Alola, Ash wears a beach-style outfit, with capri pants and water shoes. The Pokéball styling is less obvious on his red cap, but picked up in the top stripe of his blue and white t-shirt. The sky-blue straps on his backpack brighten the look even more. On his wrist he has his black Z-Ring.

ASH'S POKÉMON

Ash and Pikachu are certainly well paired, but there's no way that Ash is going to make it through all of his Pokémon championships and Gym badges without a little more help… without a lot of help, actually. Ash has a number of Pokémon at his side helping with the hundreds of battles he's experienced. All are very important to Ash. But as a Trainer, Ash can only carry six Pokémon at a time. The six he carries determine the course of the battle.

PIKACHU

Although Ash's First Partner Pokémon and long time companion is Pikachu, they didn't get along at all in the beginning.

SLEEPING LATE

Pikachu was not Ash's first choice (he wanted Squirtle). After sleeping in and missing his chance to choose, he was given Pikachu. Pikachu was not very pleased with being paired with Ash and didn't listen very well, and thus one of the funniest partnerships ever was created. After many shocking developments the two, who once seemed destined for disaster, bonded in the face of mutual danger and the legend of Ash and Pikachu was born.

PIDOVE

Pidove is the first Pokémon Ash catches in Unova, and it battles to save Pikachu from Team Rocket. It evolves into Tranquill while helping herd the Venipede stampede in Castelia City. During an incredible battle with Mistralton City Gym leader Skyla, Tranquill evolves into Unfezant. It helps Ash earn the coveted Jet Badge. Together, they are a high-flying team!

TRANQUILL

UNFEZANT

SANDILE

Ash met Sandile when it was digging holes at a resort to warn people that the geysers were going to burst. Behind its cool shades was a strong fighter with one match on its mind: Pikachu! The battle was so heated that it evolved into Krokorok. Later, with Ash by its side, Krokorok again evolved into Krookodile during an epic battle in the Pokémon World Tournament Junior Cup with Iris and Dragonite.

KROKOROK

KROOKODILE

HAWLUCHA

Better known as The Forest Champion, Hawlucha was always there to fight the good fight for the local Pokémon. When Ash gave Hawlucha some advice on how to incorporate its trademark stance in Flying Press, it knew it could learn a lot from Ash. So, it asked to join him on his journey.

CHARMANDER

After rescuing Charmander from a rainstorm, Ash nurses the fiery Pokémon back to health. It evolves two more times. As Charmander, it comes back to reunite with its old pal from time to time. Ash and Charizard have a heated relationship at times—it can be very temperamental.

CHARIZARD

CHARMELEON

ROGGENROLA

Ash first met Roggenrola when it was looking for help. Team Rocket had captured all of its friends to form a Roggenrola-powered Flash Cannon. Ash saved the Rock-types and Roggenrola's been with Ash ever since. During a heated Gym battle with Clay, it seemed as though Excadrill would win the match. But Roggenrola found new strength and evolved into Boldore. Then, together they won the Quake Badge.

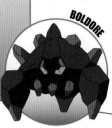

BOLDORE

PALPITOAD

When a practice battle with some wild Foongus leaves their Pokémon pals sick, Ash and Oshawott search for Remeyo Weed medicine at the bottom of the lake. But when Palpitoad sees them, it defends its turf. This coaxes Oshawott to raise the courage to open its eyes underwater. With the first burst of Aqua Jet it's able to control, it wins the battle. Then Ash catches his new pal, Palpitoad.

SNIVY

Ash met this ninja-like Grass-type when it snuck into the campsite to munch on Cilan's lunch. Impressed by Snivy's skill, Ash was determined to catch it, but it kept slipping through his fingers. Finally, clever Snivy saw how kind Ash was to his Pokémon and it was happy to join Ash's crew.

SCRAGGY

When Ash helps a school teacher named Karena with Trubbish trouble, she gifts him a Pokémon egg, and out pops Scraggy, a Pokémon born ready to battle! Pikachu accepts its challenge, and it is welcomed into the world with a match. Although Scraggy can't seem to win a round, that certainly never stops it from trying! In fact, its favorite way to greet someone isn't with a hello; it's with a battle challenge.

SEWADDLE

After Ash shares his food and sleeping bag, and saves it from being kidnapped, Sewaddle gladly travels with its new pal. While battling Burgh for the Insect Badge in its first Gym Battle, Sewaddle evolves into Swadloon. Later, when Ash and Swadloon are training for their Icirrus City Gym Battle, Swadloon evolves into Leavanny!

SWADLOON

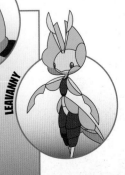

LEAVANNY

TEPIG

Don George first thinks this Pokémon covered in black soot and hiding out in his storage room is a mysterious Umbreon. But Ash discovers it's a Tepig abandoned by a mean Trainer named Shamus. At first, Tepig was afraid to accept Ash's help, but after a good meal, it falls asleep in Ash's arms and they become buddies for life. Later, Don George suggests they battle Shamus. Eventually, Tepig's friendship with Ash and Snivy gives it the courage to win the battle against its former Trainer. Plus, it evolves into a powerful Pignite in the process!

PIGNITE

KRABBY

In an effort to prove his capturing prowess to Misty, Ash caught Krabby. It immediately was sent to Professor Oak's as Ash already had six Pokémon with him. Krabby evolved into a Kingler when Ash battled Mandi in the first round of the Pokémon League.

KINGLER

MONFERNO

CHIMCHAR

Ash never lets a Pokémon in need suffer. Chimchar was abandoned by its original Trainer, Ash's rival, Paul. Ash offered Chimchar a spot on his team. Infernape still has rage issues, and it almost cost Ash a win in the semi-finals against Paul in Sinnoh. But Infernape keeps it together wielding the powerful Flare Blitz.

INFERNAPE

PRIMAPE

After watching energetic Mankey evolve, Ash knew he and the punchy Pokémon would be an unstoppable pair in battle!

GIBLE

To catch Gible, Ash not only had to battle the Pokémon, he also had to battle Barry. But when Gible saved Ash from falling off a cliff by holding onto Ash in its chompers, these two friends bonded forever in one bite.

MUK

The only thing more powerful than Muk's awesome attacks is its stench. But in battle, Ash and his pal Muk definitely do not stink!

CHIKORITA

Ash severely injured Chikorita in a battle, but after nursing it back to health, Chikorita becomes enamored with Ash. It even gets jealous when Pikachu is around! Chikorita evolved into Bayleef to protect Ash from Team Rocket.

BAYLEEF

PIDGEY

Ash mistakenly catches a Pidgey, which stayed with him until it evolved.

PIDGEOT

PIDGEOTTO

TOTODILE

Ash had to fight Misty for this one. They each threw a Poké Ball at it, but because they didn't know whose Ball caught it, they battled for it. Ash won the battle.

CYNDAQUIL

Caught almost by accident, Cyndaquil has proven a formidable partner, after overcoming early bouts of shyness. Ash leaves it with Professor Oak before setting out for Hoenn.

SQUIRTLE

After forming a bond with Ash, Squirtle becomes a vital member of his team, but decides to go back to its roots after the Squirtle Squad starts to fall apart.

QUILAVA

FROAKIE

Fearless Froakie had a bad reputation because it had been returned to Professor Sycamore by a few Trainers, but Ash was so excited when Froakie asked to join him on his journey after the brave Bubble Pokémon helped fend off Team Rocket with its Gummy Frubbles. Ash's pal has since evolved into Frogadier and then, Greninja.

FROGADIER

GRENINJA

NOIBAT

Hawlucha found an egg that Ash and his pals worked hard to keep warm until it hatched into Noibat! At first, it struggled with flying, so its pal Hawlucha gave it special lessons. Then, when an angry Zapdos attacked Hawlucha, Noibat quickly swooped in to help his pal and amazingly enough, it evolved into Noivern.

NOIVERN

HERACROSS

Heracross is the first Pokémon that Ash catches in Johto, and although this sweet-loving herbivore seems harmless, it is one of the more powerful Pokémon that Ash has known.

TAUROS

Ash's pal Tauros stood out from the pack when it spotted a stampede in the Kanto Region.

GOOMY

Who says good things don't just fall from the sky and land on your head? That's exactly how Ash met his Dragon-type pal. During different battles with the terrible Team Rocket, Goomy evolved into Sliggoo then Goodra to protect its pals.

SLIGGOO

GOODRA

OSHAWOTT

Brave and eager, just like Ash, Oshawott snuck out of Professor Juniper's lab to follow him on his Unova journey. Oshawott is always ready to battle. In fact, when it simply hears the word battle, it lets itself out of its Poké Ball. But if the opponent looks too tough, it'll gladly push Pikachu to take its place. However, Oshawott is training hard so its strength will match its enthusiasm.

FLETCHLING

It was such a strong fighter, it took Ash and Froakie a few tries to catch wild Fletchling. During Ash's first Sky Battle, Ash's Flying-type friend evolved into Fletchinder. Then, when the Legendary Pokémon Moltres mistook Ash and his pals for troublemaking Team Rocket, it evolved into Talonflame to protect its beloved Trainer.

FLETCHINDER

TALONFLAME

CATERPIE

Caterpie is the first Pokémon that Ash ever catches, but he catches it in a fashion that is not standard with Pokémon Trainers—he doesn't weaken it first!

BUTTERFREE

METAPOD

BUIZEL

Acquired in a trade with Dawn, Buizel wanted to battle instead of competing in Contests.

GLIGAR

The Gligar that Ash comes across is a slow one—slower than the rest of its flock. After Ash's rival, Paul, captures Gliscor, the leader of the flock, Gligar decides to go with Ash.

GLISCOR

BULBASAUR

Bulbasuar is a reluctant addition to Ash's arsenal. It agrees to go if Ash beats it in a battle, which he does.

TREECKO

Ash catches a Treecko after defending the Giant Tree. Treecko evolved into a Grovyle during its battle with a fellow Trainer's Loudred. It later evolved into a Sceptile to protect a Meganium it loved, although it forgot how to use its abilities after Meganium didn't return its affection.

GROVYLE

SCEPTILE

SNORUNT

Snorunt steals Ash's Badge Case and hat (Pokémon love Ash's hats), and then joins Ash. It evolves into a Glalie after some intensive training to help it use Ice Beam better.

TAILLOW

Taillow makes off with chocolate from Ash and his crew, and as Ash hunts down Taillow for this misdeed, it becomes the leader of a larger flock of Taillow and attacks him. A battle ensues, and Ash eventually captures it. During the final round of a flying tournament, it evolved into a Swellow to achieve victory.

SWELLOW

GLALIE

AIPOM

Aipom befriends Ash, but only after it steals his hat (the hat has got to be some kind of Pokémon-catching charm!). Ash captures Aipom in battle, but eventually trades it to Dawn for her Buizel.

SNORLAX

Ash captured Snorlax in the Orange Islands after he found out that it was consuming nearly all the island's plant life. Snorlax doesn't travel with Ash much, because he can't keep it fed.

GROTLE

TURTWIG

Turtwig is a mediator, helping other Pokémon with their squabbles, and facing down those that don't want to let things go. It befriended Ash, who later captured it in battle. Ash's Turtwig has come a long way and is a formidable teammate. It has mastered Rock Climb and uses its massive weight to its advantage.

TORTERRA

PHANPY

Ash's prize for winning a Pokémon Riding Contest is a Pokémon Egg that hatches into Phanpy. Phanpy evolved into a Donphan while attempting to take down a Team Rocket mecha. Don't let it fool you, Donphan packs quite a powerful punch in its trunk.

DONPHAN

CORPHISH

After doing a number on Dewford Town and its citizens, the jealous Corphish was captured and calmed down quite a bit. Although it joined Ash's team, it still flared with envy when another teammate evolved or received praise.

TORKOAL

Torkoal befriended Ash after he defended it. Although Torkoal fled, it followed Ash and eventually joined up with his team. Ash used Torkoal quite a bit, but decided to leave him with Professor Oak for a while.

STARLY

Ash's Aipom injured a wild Starly, which in turn attacked. Ash captured the Starly, evolving it into a Staravia during a battle with Team Rocket. Powerful Staravia mastered Brave Bird. Staraptor became Ash's go-to Pokémon in Sinnoh. It met the challenges of its battles with bravery. It also helped out in tight spots where Ash needed to stay off the battlefield.

STARAVIA

STARAPTOR

ROCKRUFF

Ash met Rockruff at the Pokémon school. At first Rockruff had issues with its temper and it seemed Rockruff's red-eye rage may have prevented it from being a useful ally, but it managed to become a formidable Lycanroc.

LYCANROC

LITTEN

This tough Pokémon hides a kind heart as Ash first met Litten while the Pokémon was looking after its old mentor, Stoutland. Litten evolved into Torracat and Incineroar and made a great wrestling partner.

TORRACAT

INCINEROAR

ROWLET

This Pokémon was Ash's first catch in Alola. Sleepy in the day, it stores up energy for attacks like leafage, a shower of sharp feathers. A Grass- and Flying-type, Rowlet later evolves into Dartrix and then Decidueye—a Grass- and Ghost-type.

DARTRIX

DECIDUEYE

NOCTOWL

Noctowl is a Pokémon with unusual coloring that Ash uses in the finals in Sinnoh. Noctowl is highly intelligent, and even fooled Ash, who eventually captured it.

ESSENTIAL GEAR

Pokémon Trainers do not take their mission lightly. In order to maintain the high standards of training, raising, and caring for Pokémon, there is an essential list of items that each Trainer should carry at all times.

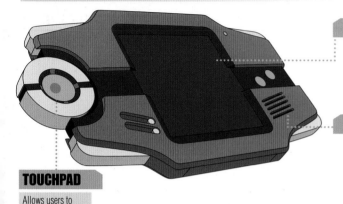

SCREEN

The screen shows the Pokémon being observed, and various stats about it.

VOICE MODULE

A speaker allows a Trainer to hear what the computer is saying about a Pokémon.

TOUCHPAD

Allows users to navigate the various menus in the Pokédex.

Kalos Pokédex

POKÉDEX

Everyone needs information, but for Pokémon Trainers, that information is a vital part of their training. The Pokédex acts as a miniature electronic encyclopedia of Pokémon facts and figures.

ROTOMDEX

Ash's Pokédex on Alola is Rotomdex, a dex that has been brought to life by a cheerful Rotom.

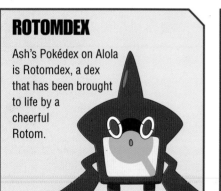

Z-RING

On Alola Ash wears a Z-Ring, given by Tapu Koko, to house the Z-Crystals needed to perform Z-Moves.

POKÉ BALLS

If you're gonna catch Pokémon, you're going to need something to catch them with. The Poké Ball is the most common capture system. It is thrown at a weakened Pokémon to ensnare it. Poké Balls come in many varieties, with some types more suited for catching specific types of Pokémon. The one shown here is the standard—and most common—type of Poké Ball.

Kanto Pokédex

Johto Pokédex

Hoenn Pokédex

Sinnoh Pokédex

Unova Pokédex

Voices Carry

The Kanto, Johto, and Unova Pokédex have a male voice. The Hoenn, Sinnoh, and Kalos Pokédex have a female voice. Ash's first Pokédex, from Professor Oak in Kanto, introduced itself as "Dexter." The name stuck through his Pokédex in Johto. Then, since the Hoenn and Sinnoh Pokedex have a female voice, Ash used the nickname "Dextette."

FOOD

Food is used by Trainers to sustain themselves during long journeys. Thankfully, while in Unova Ash teamed up with Cilan, a Pokémon Connoisseur whose passion for Pokémon was nearly matched by his passion for food.

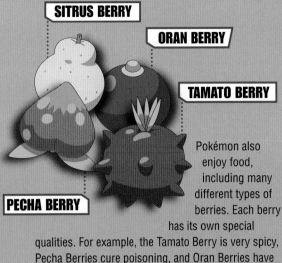

SITRUS BERRY

ORAN BERRY

TAMATO BERRY

PECHA BERRY

Pokémon also enjoy food, including many different types of berries. Each berry has its own special qualities. For example, the Tamato Berry is very spicy, Pecha Berries cure poisoning, and Oran Berries have healing properties.

TRAINER TECH

In addition to the Pokédex, Ash and his pals have used many other gadgets and gizmos during their travels. In Sinnoh, Ash helped Dawn get a Pokétch, which is a bit like a pocket watch with all sorts of amazing abilities. In Unova, Cilan had to find a Wonder Launcher as part of a scavenger hunt. Ash is always on his Xtransceiver making calls to Professor Juniper or issuing the occasional challenge to his Unova rival, Trip!

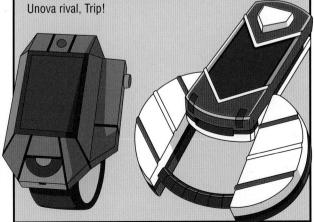

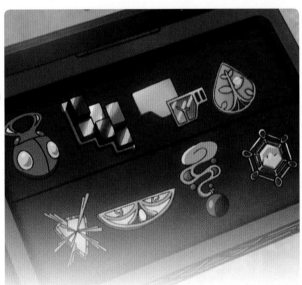

BADGE CASE

Most Trainers don't wear their Gym badges on their clothing, so you've got to put them somewhere. Ash has had his Gym badge case stolen on more than one occasion, which must have been greatly upsetting considering how hard he had to work to fill it with Gym badges. Gym badges are symbols of a Pokémon Trainer's prowess. They are given by Gym Leaders for victory and are necessary to enter League Championships.

POKÉMON TRAINERS

A Pokémon Trainer can be considered anyone who owns a Pokémon and works with it for a specific purpose—Pokémon Breeders, Pokémon Coordinators, and Pokémon Connoisseurs are also Trainers, in a sense. But for the most part, a Pokémon Trainer is thought of as someone who trains his or her Pokémon to battle, forging a bond that makes both partners stronger.

THE JOURNEY BEGINS

Each Trainer's journey can start as early as age 10, when a kid can become a Trainer and select one of three Pokémon to be his or her First Partner. The selection varies by region, but Trainers can always choose from a Fire-type, Grass-type, or Water-type Pokémon.

KANTO

BULBASAUR

SQUIRTLE

CHARMANDER

JOHTO

TOTODILE

CHIKORITA

CYNDAQUIL

HOENN

TORCHIC

TREECKO

MUDKIP

SINNOH

TURTWIG

PIPLUP

CHIMCHAR

TO EVOLVE OR NOT TO EVOLVE?

Sooner or later, most Trainers will have to figure out what to do about their Pokémon's Evolution. Evolving a Pokémon makes it stronger, which seems like a no-brainer decision for someone interested in battles. But raw power alone doesn't determine whether Evolution is the best choice for a Trainer; since Pokémon can excel in different things for each stage of Evolution, it might not make sense to evolve a Pokémon right away. To make it more complicated, some Pokémon are simply happy the way they are and have no interest in evolving.

Ash and Pikachu now know Pikachu is happy to stay a Pikachu, but Ash was excited when he thought his Bulbasaur would evolve. As it turned out, Bulbasaur didn't want to evolve at all—so Ash not only apologized to Bulbasaur for being inconsiderate, he made a speech about how a Pokémon should be able to freely choose when it wants to evolve.

TRUST YOUR POKÉMON

Trainers need to trust their Pokémon, but Pokémon are also intelligent enough to pick up on a Trainer's uncertainty. It's a two-way street; if a Trainer hesitates when giving orders or doesn't feel comfortable with a Pokémon, the Pokémon reacts accordingly.

Honesty is the best policy: Pokémon dislike being the butt of a joke as much as anyone else, so when Ash tries to spook his Corphish to teach it a lesson, Corphish is none too happy to discover it's been tricked. It doesn't take much for Corphish to turn on Ash when it thinks it's been played for a fool a second time, either!

KNOW YOUR POKÉMON

Good Trainers also need to be in synch with their Pokémon. Ideally, Trainer and Pokémon should work together as if each knows what the other is thinking. That doesn't mean teaching a Pokémon to blindly obey commands; instead, a Trainer needs to be aware of a Pokémon's own rhythms and preferences in order to work as an effective team in battle.

Starting Trainers also receives Poké Balls so they can start catching Pokémon. There's no limit to how many Pokémon Trainers can catch, but they can only bring up to six Pokémon with them at any time. If they want to use another Pokémon after they've reached their limit, they'll need to send at least one of their Pokémon back to a Pokémon professor or other person for holding.

> *I will journey to gain the wisdom of Pokémon training.*
>
> ~Ash Ketchum

UNOVA

OSHAWOTT

SNIVY

TEPIG

KALOS

FROAKIE

CHESPIN

FENNEKIN

ALOLA

POPPLIO

ROWLET

LITTEN

WHAT ARE THE QUALITIES OF A GOOD TRAINER?

There's no "right" way to train a Pokémon; every Pokémon's personality is unique, just as every Trainer's personality is unique. Ash may be an excellent Trainer, but not all good Trainers have to interact with their Pokémon just like he does. The one thing that all good Trainers do have in common, however, is a bond of trust and understanding with their Pokémon.

WHEN POKÉMON JUST WON'T OBEY

It takes more than a Gym badge to make a Trainer an expert, and even good Trainers may find themselves outmatched by a Pokémon. That in itself is no great shame, but a Trainer shouldn't use a Pokémon if he's not sure he can control it. A good example is Ash's Charizard: perfectly obedient as a Charmander, it became more and more unruly as it quickly evolved into Charmeleon and then Charizard. As Charizard, it was simply too powerful and willful for a novice Trainer like Ash to control.

Time, experience, and a few hard lessons helped Ash regain control over Charizard, but he simply wasn't ready to handle a Pokémon like that back in his Indigo League days.

Dawn and her Buizel had trouble battling at first, since Dawn was out of synch with Buizel's timing. After a helpful lesson from Lucian of the Elite Four, Dawn learned how to work with Buizel—although it remained more interested in battles than Pokémon Contests.

Why Become a Pokémon Trainer?

No one can deny it looks fun to travel the world with a best friend who rides on your shoulder and unleashes high voltage blasts on your opponents. But beyond making powerful new Pokémon friends, what's the real point of becoming a Pokémon Trainer?

Just as caring for a pet can teach children responsibility, training Pokémon is a growth experience. A Trainer has to work hard to help a Pokémon achieve its full potential—beyond simply putting in the time for training workouts, a Trainer also learns to understand another living creature's needs and desires.

A Pokémon journey itself is also a catalyst for growth. Most young Trainers still have a lot of hard lessons to learn about winning, losing, and how they relate to their Pokémon. The experience of leaving home and facing new situations helps both people and Pokémon develop maturity and confidence.

POKÉ BALL

You can travel the lands of Pokémon far and wide—and see hundreds of Pokémon—but you can't capture them if you don't have the right tool. The Poké Ball is the Trainer's capture system of choice, and the many varieties of Poké Balls ensure that you can match the Poké Ball to the situation, increasing your odds of a capture. These are only some of the Poké Balls available.

THE MECHANICS

When a wild Pokémon is weakened in battle, the opposing Trainer can throw a Poké Ball at the Pokémon target in an attempt to catch it. If successful, the Pokémon is trapped inside, and the Trainer becomes its owner. Poké Balls not only capture Pokémon, but they also update a Trainer's Pokédex with a captured Pokémon's information. Ash's Pokémon have been transferred from Professor Oak's lab to a nearby Pokémon Center for Ash to pick up.

DUSK BALL

Most effective at catching Pokémon at night or in dark places, such as caves.

HEAL BALL

Heals the caught Pokémon and helps it recover from Special Conditions.

TIMER BALL

The longer the battle lasts, the better this Poké Ball works.

When the Trainer needs a Pokémon, she has only to throw the ball and call the Pokémon to action. When retrieving her Pokémon, a Trainer will simply point the Poké Ball at the Pokémon in question and press the button on the front of the ball. The Poké Ball itself can be miniaturized so that several can fit at one time in the palm of the Trainer's hand, allowing for easier storage and transportation.

PREMIER BALL

The same as the basic Poké Ball.

LUXURY BALL

This special Poké Ball helps the Pokémon captured In It bond with you more quickly.

MASTER BALL

The ultimate Poké Ball. It enables you to capture any Pokémon. The elusive Master Ball has been seen by Ash only once.
These are often used to capture Legendary or one-of-a-kind Pokémon. Unique in every sense of the word, these balls have a letter "M" emblazoned upon the upper hemisphere of the Poké Ball.

QUICK BALL

A Poké Ball that is more effective when thrown at the very beginning of a battle.

GREAT BALL

The intermediate Poké Ball, it is slightly more effective than the basic Poké Ball.

NET BALL

A special Poké Ball, the Net Ball excels in the capture of Bug-type and Water-type Pokémon.

SAFARI BALL

A Poké Ball that can be used only in the Safari Zone.

REPEAT BALL

Awesome against Pokémon the Trainer has already captured.

ULTRA BALL

The advanced Poké Ball, it is slightly more effective than the Great Ball.

NEST BALL

This is the Poké Ball of choice when capturing weaker Pokémon.

DIVE BALL

The Dive Ball is highly effective against Pokémon encountered in or under the water.

POKÉMON CENTER

It's not just a hospital, it's not just a learning center, it's not just a rec room—it's a Pokémon Center. It is as vital to the healing and raising of a Pokémon as a Trainer is. But what does it really do and how does it do it?

THE NURSE IS IN!

Each Pokémon Center, though unique, has one thing in common—Nurse Joy. Like Officer Jenny, Nurse Joy is part of a family of nearly identical relatives (all named Nurse Joy) who take it upon themselves to care for wounded Pokémon.

TELL WIGGLYTUFF WHERE IT HURTS

Wonderful Wigglytuff are a cheerful staple at Pokémon Centers in Kalos. Like Chansey or Blissey in the Pokémon Centers of Kanto, Johto, Hoenn, and Sinnoh, or Audino in Unova, these terrific Wigglytuff help Nurse Joy take care of Pokémon in Kalos. Wigglytuff is particularly suited for this important role because it's very caring and has soothing, soft fur.

ONE-STOP SHOP

Pokémon Centers are central gathering areas for Trainers, Contest Coordinators, Tournament participants, and generally anyone who needs a break from the rigors of Pokémon competition.

Having video phones and the ability to retrieve Pokémon left with Pokémon professors, the Pokémon Center is a must stop for thriving Pokémon Trainers.

A CENTER OF ATTENTION

Pokémon Centers all vary in appearance, except for one distinguishable landmark—they all have a giant "P" on or near their building. Their architectural differences are due to the varying habitats and cultures.

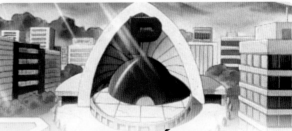

NOT JUST FOR POKÉMON

The Pokémon Center is a healing place not only for Pokémon, but for Trainers as well. Many a weary Trainer has come through the doors, and Nurse Joy has always been there to greet them.

The Pokémon Center can be a very supportive place—even more supportive than home for most Trainers! They can eat at a Pokémon Center without charge, and can even extend their stay until their Pokémon recover.

COMMUNICATION

Many Pokémon communicate using a variation of their name or the entire name spoken with inflection and emotion. Still others make sounds that aren't discernable, but they are still clearly communicating. But there are some that speak our language.

Very few Pokémon have language skills that can be interpreted by humans. Even Ash mostly guesses what his Pokémon are feeling, and never speaks directly to them. However, there are a few Pokémon that have bridged the communication gap and actually speak to humans.

They fall into two categories: telepathy and real language skills.

SPEAK YOUR MIND

At the Nacrene City Museum, Hawes, the museum's co-curator, is worried that ghosts are haunting the institution just before a big exhibition is scheduled to start. Ash, Cilan, and Iris spend the night to investigate. In a rare example of a Pokémon using more than the syllables of its name to communicate, a Yamask interacts with the group by using Cilan as a bridge to verbalize its intentions. It turns out that the Yamask got separated from its mask when it was locked into a display case as part of the upcoming exhibit. With the misunderstanding resolved, all returns to normal.

SPEAK UP!

The most talkative of all Pokémon is Meowth, the third wheel in the Team Rocket trio. To his credit, Meowth has been used by Ash and others to interpret for a hurt or scared Pokémon, and often shows compassion and a willingness to help other Pokémon in need. Meowth's ability to communicate is unprecedented among Pokémon.

POKÉMON EGGS

Where do Pokémon come from? The true origins of Pokémon have yet to be revealed, but all Trainers know that Pokémon normally hatch from Eggs.

Pokémon Eggs are usually the same size and shape, regardless of species—it's the patterns on the Eggs that hint at the species of the Pokémon within. Eggs are surprisingly hardy, capable of surviving some bounces and jolts. Gentle loving care is always preferable. An Egg is ready to hatch once it starts to glow.

WHAT DOES A POKÉMON EGG FEEL?

If a Pokémon Egg can survive a couple of misadventures and still hatch okay, then it's no harm done, right? To the contrary, Ash's experience with a troubled baby Larvitar shows that trauma to a Pokémon Egg can affect the baby Pokémon even after it hatches. Once the Larvitar hatched, it remained unresponsive and sick due to its experiences while still in the Egg.

Before Larvitar hatched, its Egg would glow but then fade. Once it hatched, the baby Larvitar was cold and unmoving, a sign that something was dreadfully wrong; it had to be kept warm so it could recover.

Even after it physically recovered, Larvitar refused to respond to stimuli. Ash figured out the problem after he fell asleep with the baby Larvitar in his lap and had a bad dream: he saw the Egg being stolen, knocked into a stream, kicked around, and almost run over. It might all have been part of Larvitar's own nightmares, but it suggests that Larvitar had some awareness of the outside world even while inside the Egg.

POKÉMON EGG RAISERS

Similar to the Pokémon Nesters, Pokémon Egg Raisers take care of both their own Pokémon Eggs and the Eggs they've received for safekeeping. In Hoenn, May and Ash visit an Egg Nursery that's as big as a veritable farm, housing five large barns filled with Pokémon Eggs.

DAY CARE

Bobby's Day Care, near Driftveil City in Unova.

There are facilities known as Day Cares that are devoted to the care of Pokémon Eggs and baby Pokémon. One place where Day Cares proliferate is the rural town of Eggseter, located in a lush area of Johto with ideal weather. The area has long been home to Nesters, the people who care for baby Pokémon and Pokémon Eggs, and visitors will see a variety of Day Care facilities as they travel through the area. But Day Cares can be found throughout most regions.

In addition to a high-tech room for monitoring Eggs that are about to hatch, there's no substitute for old-fashioned hands-on care. That includes gently polishing each Pokémon Egg with a cloth.

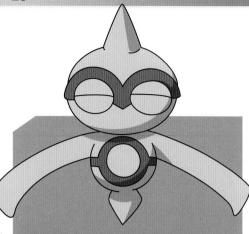

HIDDEN HISTORY

From long-forgotten civilizations to temples dedicated to Dialga and Palkia, to ancient shrines honoring Thundurus, there's abundant evidence that Pokémon have had a tremendous influence on the history of their world.

POKÉMOPOLIS

Stories speak of an ancient city where people believed Pokémon symbolized nature's power and even built temples to them. Although the city was supposedly destroyed in a storm and never seen since, its relics have since been uncovered not far from Pallet Town.

Contained within some of the artifacts of Pokémopolis are giant Pokémon, including a giant Alakazam and Gengar who immediately begin to battle each other when released. Fortunately, among the artifacts is a large bell that's awakened by the song of Jigglypuff. Contained within the bell is a giant Jigglypuff, which is the only thing that can put Alakazam and Gengar back to sleep and into their respective artifacts.

BALTOY CIVILIZATION

Not all ancient civilizations involve dangerous giant Pokémon and sinister spirits. Long ago, there was said to be a Baltoy civilization where Baltoy lived together with humans. Today, the remains of this civilization can be found within Kirikiri Mountain in Hoenn, and the legends say that the relics of this civilization include the most precious thing in the universe—time.

POKÉLANTIS

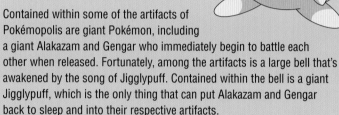

There are always people who unwisely wish to control the power of Legendary Pokémon, and the fate of ancient Pokélantis is an example to others. Under the rule of an arrogant king, this once-great empire attempted to use Ho-Oh's power to conquer the world. Pokélantis was completely destroyed, but the king escaped and supposedly got his revenge on Ho-Oh by sealing it underground in a stone orb.

Within the ruins lies the King's Chambers, where a stone orb was found on a throne at the base of the king's statue. But instead of Ho-Oh, the orb contained the King's malevolent spirit, eager to possess a body and use it to revive his plans of world domination.

RUINS

Archaeologists and researchers continue to come across undiscovered relics and secrets of long-forgotten civilizations, from the prehistoric Pokémon fossils in the ruins of Alph to the Solaceon Ruins in Sinnoh, where Dialga and Palkia were once revered.

In Johto, the ruins of Alph and its abundant fossils have made it an ideal place to set up a domed research center. But fossils aren't the only finds here: the Alph ruins have also yielded many ancient artifacts.

The Solaceon Ruins are just one of several places in Sinnoh where statues of Dialga and Palkia can be found. These Pokémon play a key role in the region's legends and origin stories.

POKÉMON BREEDERS

Every Pokémon Trainer should know how to raise their Pokémon to be healthy and strong, but Pokémon breeders take special pains to bring out the best qualities in their Pokémon. Despite the name, they're not necessarily concerned with breeding more Pokémon, just raising healthy Pokémon.

Pokémon breeders sometimes use their Pokémon for battle, and they even endorse battling as a good way for Trainers and Pokémon to bond with each other. However, breeders focus on a Pokémon's overall health and appearance, not just its battling strength. As such, breeders like Brock may not have many battle trophies to boast of, but they're often the best source of advice on how to keep a Pokémon in peak physical shape.

Two Types of Breeders: Suzie and Zane

Even among Pokémon breeders, opinions differ on what's most important for a Pokémon. Suzie, the breeder who lent Brock her Vulpix, believes that a Pokémon's inner beauty is what counts. She may have run a noted Pokémon salon, but she doesn't believe that Pokémon need to be cut and styled to look their best. Suzie's old friend and rival, Zane, believes it's outward beauty that matters the most, and he's a successful breeder too. There's no right answer to the question of whether outer looks or inner beauty counts the most—instead, both breeders pool their different talents and outlooks to open a Pokémon salon together.

STRUTTING THEIR STUFF

If Coordinators have Contests and Trainers have tournaments, what do breeders have? There's a World Pokémon breeders' Contest, but no formal competitive system exists for Pokémon breeders as it does for Trainers and Coordinators. Nevertheless, breeders do compete in special events to see whose Pokémon shines the brightest.

Breeders turn out in droves for Bonitaville's Pokémon beauty contest, where Pokémon accessories aren't required but definitely help. A similar trend exists in Sinnoh, where fans of the fashion magazine PokéChic dress up themselves and their Pokémon.

Outside of competitions, some breeders congregate around certain neighborhoods. Celadon City's Scissor Street, also known as "Breeder's Lane," is where Pokémon beauty parlors abound. Not all Pokémon breeders believe in decking out Pokémon with accessories and fancy cuts, but this is where their latest fashions are on display.

NUTRITION

Although anyone can keep a Pokémon well fed with just basic Pokémon chow, any breeders worth their salt develop their own recipes for Pokémon food formulas to suit an individual Pokémon's needs. This includes food designed for a particular Pokémon type or specially formulated for a picky eater.

GROOMING

Grooming is another must for Pokémon breeders, even though their Pokémon are already in good physical condition. During grooming sessions, a breeder can closely examine a Pokémon's health. It also gives breeders an opportunity to bond with their Pokémon.

EXERCISE

Just because a Pokémon can remain in a Poké Ball indefinitely, that doesn't make it a good idea to keep it there. Pokémon benefit from regular outings, even if it's just to play. A Pokémon's type should also be considered: Water-type Pokémon will benefit from getting regular opportunities to swim in a large body of water.

HEALTH CARE

For most Trainers, all a Pokémon needs after a battle is some healing at a Pokémon Center and plenty of rest. A Pokémon can thrive with that alone, but it's not enough for serious breeders! They're more likely to recommend additional post-battle treatment such as therapeutic massages.

My Pokémon Won't Listen to Me!

Problem: Autumn's new Miltank Ilta doesn't listen to a thing she says, and she's so frustrated she's ready to give it away. Once again, Brock comes to the rescue with a hands-on demonstration of how to repair the rift between Autumn and Ilta.

Solution: Giving up on a Pokémon is the wrong answer—instead, it's key to develop a friendship with a Pokémon through various activities. Stay calm, give lots of encouragement, interact with it as a friend and not just a boss, and groom it regularly—all these things may not come automatically, but they'll provide the foundation for a solid relationship.

It takes a few false starts, but before long, Autumn and Ilta are battling and acting just like a team should.

HEIGHT RULES

While Pokémon has always been about the size of Ash's and his Pokémon's hearts, height and weight cannot be ignored. From the huge Yveltal and Xerneas to the tiny Dedenne, Pokémon come in all shapes and sizes. Have you ever wanted to see Iris's Dragonite beside the spunky Pikachu? Here is your chance.

TALONFLAME
Height: 3' 11" (1.2 m)

XERNEAS
Height: 9' 10" (3.0 m)

NOIVERN
Height: 4' 11" (1.5 m)

BRAIXEN
Height: 3' 3" (1.0 m)

EEVEE
Height: 1' 0" 0.3 m)

BUNNELBY
Height: 1' 4" (0.4 m)

SERENA'S PANCHAM
Height: 2' 0" (0.6 m)

DEDENNE
Height: 0'8" (0.2 m)

PIKACHU
Height: 1' 4" (0.5 m)

YVELTAL
Height: 19' 0" (5.8 m)

ASH'S GRENINJA
Height: 4' 11" (1.5 m)

LUXRAY
Height: 4' 7" (1.4 m)

HAWLUCHA
Height: 2' 7" (0.8 m)

MEOWTH
Height: 1' 4" (0.4 m)

CHESPIN
Height: 1' 4" (0.4 m)

ZYGARDE CORE

8
7
6
5
4
3
2
1
0

HOW TO FIND AND CATCH POKÉMON

Every new Trainer can visit a Pokémon Professor to receive a First Partner Pokémon, but catching more Pokémon isn't as easy. Wild Pokémon are easy to find, at least if a Trainer isn't choosy; it's learning the art of capture that takes time.

In addition to a First Partner Pokémon, each Trainer normally receives several Poké Balls. There's more to catching Pokémon than just throwing a Poké Ball—unless injured, weak, or willing to be caught, a wild Pokémon is normally too strong to be caught without battling it first to tire it out.

A Trainer must remember to first click the button on the front of the Poké Ball to expand it to normal size. The Poké Ball is then thrown at the target Pokémon, but even if the Pokémon is absorbed inside the Poké Ball, it doesn't mean the capture is complete. The Poké Ball rocks back and forth and its button will glow red while the capture is in progress.

Once the Poké Ball chimes and the button returns to its normal white color, the capture is complete. If the capture fails, the Poké Ball reopens and the Pokémon is once again released. Odds are it won't be keen on sticking around to facilitate another capture attempt.

When a Pokémon Just Doesn't Want to Be Caught

Some Pokémon swat away any Poké Ball thrown in their direction, while others avoid any attempt to battle and catch them. It can take true persistence to convince a reluctant Pokémon to stick around. When Ash encounters a wild Snivy as he travels toward Nacrene City, he can't resist trying to catch it. But Snivy proves to be quick and clever, eluding Ash multiple times. Only after Ash proves his worth as a Trainer by displaying courage, selflessness, sheer obstinacy, and an unwavering spirit does Snivy allow itself to be captured.

WHERE TO FIND POKÉMON

Pokémon can be found just about anywhere, but most Trainers head to the wilderness to look for them. Some Pokémon are more common than others and thus easier to catch—they can be found hanging from trees, standing in the grass, or even just nosing across a forest path.

Pokémon aren't always so obliging as to hang around in the open waiting to be caught, so special lures or strategies are sometimes called for. A Trainer's Pokémon may know moves that can help, but putting out bait and waiting can work too.

Owned Pokémon
From time to time, a Trainer accidentally tries to catch a Pokémon that's already owned by another Trainer. If a Pokémon has already been captured, it can't be caught by using another Poké Ball on it.

FISHING

Not all Pokémon can be found on land. Large numbers of Pokémon prefer aquatic habitats, so a different approach is required: fishing! With a fishing rod and a lure, all that's needed is to find the nearest promising body of water, throw out a line, and wait for a bite.

Of course, as with any other capture, once you hook a Pokémon, you still have to subdue and catch it. Otherwise, it'll simply scurry around and then leap back into the water.

Fishing is enjoyed by all Pokémon enthusiasts, especially the food-minded Connoisseurs. Cilan brings his own fishing rod with him wherever he goes, as witnessed in "A Fishing Connoisseur in a Fishy Competition!"

FRIENDSHIP

Sometimes, wild Pokémon take an interest in people and are actually interested in accompanying a Trainer. Ash and his friends have caught plenty of Pokémon this way, but even if a Pokémon wants to accompany a Trainer, it typically wants to battle that Trainer first.

TRADING

Pokémon Trainers often trade Pokémon with each other, whether it's because they see a Pokémon they like or think a Pokémon will do better with someone else. Trade machines are found at special events and Pokémon Centers, and they all accomplish the same thing: swapping Pokémon between two different Poké Balls. Trainers insert the Poké Balls holding the Pokémon they want to trade in the machine, and it does the rest.

Ash's Turtwig wanted to tag along with him, and Ash observed proper Trainer protocol by first having a friendly battle with it.

In the Johto town of Palmpona, the annual festival is a great opportunity for people to show off and trade Pokémon.

When They Were Young

Even the best Trainers sometimes have a rocky start—it's not uncommon for a few mistakes to be made in the beginning.

Ash's First Catch

Caterpie was the first Pokémon Ash ever caught, and he did it just by using a Poké Ball. But before that, he tried to catch a Pidgey, a Pokémon that's normally easy for beginners to get, without having Pikachu battle it. After using a Poké Ball, then a shirt, and finally a rock, he learned his lesson when he brained a wild Spearow by mistake and incurred its wrath.

May's First Catch

Hoping to someday have a gorgeous Beautifly, May chases down a Wurmple and tries to catch it with Torchic's help. But one hit from Torchic isn't enough—Wurmple escapes from the Poké Ball and attacks Torchic. Fearing a repeat performance of her first attempt to catch an Azurill, in which she failed miserably, she has Torchic attack again with Ember. This time Wurmple is tired enough that May makes a successful catch on her second try.

Dawn's First Catch

Ash tried to coach Dawn through her first catch, but they got on each other's nerves and the Pokémon easily escaped. The next time around, Dawn tried to get a Buneary, but it easily overpowered her Piplup. On her second try, she was prepared for Buneary's attacks and managed to subdue it with Piplup so she could make the catch.

NURSE JOY

Every Pokémon Center needs a nurse, and every one has the same nurse—Nurse Joy! These nurses are actually identical members of the same family. Brock's goggle-eyed love of Nurse Joy doesn't stop them from their important duties: to help care for and protect Pokémon!

JOY TO THE WORLD

Nurse Joys have been known to act as assistants to the Pokémon professors from time to time, handing out Pokémon to able Trainers when there is no Pokémon professor available to do so. The Nurse Joy in Slateport City has handed out Treecko, Mudkip, and Torchic Pokémon to Trainers.

There is one group of Joys that is different from the others. These would be the Nurse Joys who reside in the Orange Islands. The Orange Island Nurse Joys are a little leaner, and a little more tanned (Island living does that). They aren't above traveling; there is a traveling clinic, going from small island to small island in the Orange Archipelago when resources are tight.

NOT YOUR TYPICAL NURSE

Nurse Joy can be a lot of things besides nurses. Ash has been rescued by an undercover Official Pokémon League Inspector, who also happened to be a Nurse Joy!

Ash and friends go on a rescue mission for a Nurse Joy that is actually kidnapped by a menacing Shiftry. After battling against gangs of Seedot, Nuzleaf, and Oddish, they face down the Shiftry and find that it is merely trying to help an injured Nuzleaf. Nurse Joy attends to the Pokémon, wiping down the chlorophyll from one of its appendages.

Ash, Misty, and Brock come across a deep-sea diving Nurse Joy in charge of the Lake Lucid Pokémon Center. She also happens to be a star among Trainers who love Water-type Pokémon. However, she turns out to be the least compassionate Nurse Joy you'll ever meet. She can't bear to be around Water-type Pokémon unless she's wearing her deep-sea suit.

On their way to Mistralton City, Ash, Cilan, Iris, and their Pokémon get separated into two groups by a stampeding herd of Bouffalant. Iris's group runs into Nurse Joy and Audino, who are wearing curly wigs! Nurse Joy warns them that they're trespassing on Bouffalant territory. Somehow, the curly wigs keep the Bouffalant from stampeding—when Iris's group puts on the wigs, sure enough, the Bouffalant back off! When Ash's and Cilan's group finds Nurse Joy, they also don the wigs. Meanwhile, Iris finds and treats an injured Bouffalant. Grateful for Iris's help, the recovering Bouffalant stops several angry herd members from charging. Soon enough, everyone reunites, saying goodbye to Nurse Joy and Audino!

Judge Not, Lest You Be Joy
Pokémon Contests are contests where Pokémon are judged by how strong or how beautiful they are. One of the judges in these contests is usually a Nurse Joy.

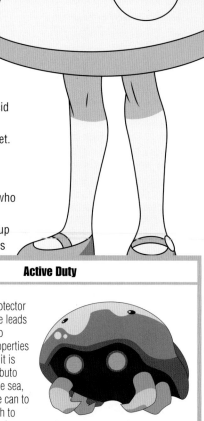

Active Duty

A Nurse Joy even has a memorable turn as a protector of Pokémon legend. She leads an expeditionary team to research the healing properties of Kabuto shells. When it is later learned that the Kabuto will rise and return to the sea, she does everything she can to protect them and get Ash to safety. That's some nurse!

OFFICER JENNY

Another loyal civil servant is Officer Jenny. Officer Jenny, like Nurse Joy, is not one entity but many who share the name. She shares other traits with Nurse Joy as well: they are all female, they exist to serve and protect Pokémon, and the only one who can tell them apart is the love-stricken Brock!

PARTNER PERFECT

Like Chansey, Blissey, or Audino for Nurse Joy, every Officer Jenny needs a helpful Pokémon sidekick. Loyal, obedient, and dedicated, that Pokémon helper is Herdier in Unova. Depending on the situation or the region, Officer Jenny has been known to work with other Pokémon as well, such as Growlithe for example.

Although Officer Jenny tries to uphold the law, she is hampered by understaffing. If she had more Jennys on her side, couldn't she easily stop Team Galactic, Team Aqua, Team Magma, and Team Rocket?

Officer Jenny's cap, much like Nurse Joy's, is one way to tell them apart. Different regions have different symbols.

JENNY TO THE RESCUE

Growlithe isn't the only Pokémon Officer Jenny uses. Depending upon the situation and the area she is from, she could have many types of Pokémon helpers.

While in Cattalia City, Ash and crew meet up with an Officer Jenny whose ancestor caught a thief using a loyal Spinarak. Since then, all Officer Jennys in Cattalia City use Spinarak as their main Pokémon. Likewise, in Wobbuffet Village on their way to Ecruteak City, the Officer Jenny has a Wobbuffet as her sidekick.

Sometimes Pokémon are used in very specific circumstances; Gastly's psychic powers are used by Officer Jenny to hunt down the person or persons responsible for turning Pokémon against their Trainers. Elsewhere, we are introduced to an Officer Jenny who enlists the aid of a Pidgeot to track down Team Rocket and Ash's Pikachu. Most recently, Officer Jenny in Eterna City in the Sinnoh region used a Stunky as her partner Pokémon to disable Team Rocket with Poison Gas.

There's even specialized Officer Jenny clones. Take for instance, the Officer Jenny in "Beheeyem, Duosion, and The Dream Thief!" She's Officer Jenny—Psychic Crimes division—and her partner, appropriately, is the Psychic-type Pokémon Duosion, the Mitosis Pokémon.

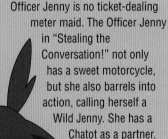

Officer Jenny is no ticket-dealing meter maid. The Officer Jenny in "Stealing the Conversation!" not only has a sweet motorcycle, but she also barrels into action, calling herself a Wild Jenny. She has a Chatot as a partner.

SQUIRTLE SQUAD

When the Squirtle Squad was first formed, it was nothing but a source of trouble, and Officer Jenny soon became involved. The Squirtle Squad then became a very effective fire-fighting crew under her tutelage.

SUPERNATURAL POKÉMON

Pokémon are behind many unexplained happenings and hauntings in the Pokémon world. But it's a world where anything can and often does happen; even people have been known to possess spooky psychic powers.

A HAUNTED NINETALES

Lost in a deep mist, Ash and his friends meet a girl named Lokoko and her faithful Ninetales. Lokoko invites them all to stay at her home, a palatial mansion otherwise devoid of residents. The mansion's owner left home long ago, and all the staff except for Lokoko have quit and gone away.

Brock is instantly at home, thanks to Ninetales' affection and Lokoko's lavish hospitality. When Lokoko asks him to stay for good, he's ready to accept! On the other hand, Ash and Misty are spooked by Lokoko's lack of a reflection—or even a corporeal body—and Brock's obliviousness to how his clothes have suddenly changed. The key to the mystery lies in an old-fashioned Poké Ball and a photo of a man who looks just like Brock, except that man was the mansion's owner from over 200 years ago.

The truth is revealed: for over a century and a half, Ninetales has waited for its master, during which time it gained the power to create the illusion of Lokoko. Although deeply lonely, it could never bear to leave and instead tried to bewitch Brock into staying. It's not until Brock breaks Ninetales' antique Poké Ball that it's finally free to leave the mansion.

THE GASTLY GHOST OF MAIDEN'S PEAK

Over 2000 years ago, a maiden fell in love with a young man who sailed off to war. She promised to await his return, but waited in vain until she finally turned into the stone known as Maiden's Rock. At least, so goes the legend in one of Kanto's seaside towns. Her portrait now hangs in a shrine near Maiden's Rock, and a local Gastly disguises itself as both a local crone and the Maiden's ghost to keep the stories alive to honor the real Maiden's spirit.

Brock and James are bewitched by an illusion of the Maiden, and soon they can think of nothing else but her. In its guise as an old woman, Gastly then sells Ash and his friends paper charms that are supposed to keep the Maiden's ghost at bay.

When Jessie decides to confront the Maiden's ghost, Gastly uses its powers to unleash a swarm of frightening apparitions. Fortunately, this Gastly is weak against sunlight, so the break of dawn drives it away…but only until next year's summer festival!

XATU FORETELLS THE FUTURE

It's said that Xatu can look backward and forward in time and their insight is vitally important to Calista, one in a long line of people who interpret Xatu prophecies. Even though Calista has access to a high-tech weather center, Calista's people rely on the Xatu to forecast the weather; the Xatu use their wings to speak in a form of semaphore, and Calista translates their gestures into predictions.

The Xatu long ago predicted that a flood would one day destroy everything in its path, ending Calista and the Xatu's duties. Just as they prophesied, a torrent of water sweeps through the canyon and amphitheater where people once gathered to witness the Xatu. But thanks to the Xatu's foretelling—and their ability to use Teleport—no one is injured by the disaster.

BEHEEYEM AND THE DREAM THIEF

When it comes to messing with your head, no one does it better than Darkrai—but don't overlook the Beheeyem that is under the Dream Thief's command! The illusions this small Pokémon throws at Ash and friends definitely make a dent in their dreams!

SCARE AT THE LITWICK MANSION

On the way to Nimbasa City Gym, Ash and friends take shelter in a spooky mansion in an out-of-the-way spot. When the furniture seems to attack with a mind of its own, our fearless friends aren't so fearless. They finally figure out that Litwick, the Candle Pokémon, is behind the shenanigans. They're not as cute as they seem—they have the ability to drain life energy from Pokémon and Trainers alike. They also draw Pokémon into the Ghost World, so our heroes need to find a way to defeat them before it's too late.

SECRET LIVES

Pokémon professors have only scratched the surface of the mysteries of Pokémon. Evolutions, migration patterns, communication, social structure—these are just some aspects of Pokémon life that still pose intriguing questions.

THE BLUE MOON RITUAL OF THE QUAGSIRE

Johto's Cherrygrove City prohibits the battling and capturing of Quagsire, since the presence of Quagsire indicates to humans where the cleanest water can be found. Once a year, during the full moon, masses of Quagsire swim down the river that runs from Blue Moon Falls into the city; they grab any round object they can find and return upstream. The locals tolerate this because all the missing items float back downstream the next day, and it's good luck if your item is returned. Whoever owns the last thing to float back downstream is considered the luckiest of all.

No one in Cherrygrove knows what the Quagsire want with all those round things, but Ash, May, and Brock have seen the Quagsire's secret with their own eyes. The Quagsire take the items back upstream, where they gather in large numbers and watch the moon until just the right moment. Acting on some unknown cue, the Quagsire then toss the round objects in the air and blow water jets to shoot the objects toward the moon. They seem to celebrate when a Quagsire shoots its item higher than the rest.

THE SECRET GARDEN OF THE BULBASAUR

Conventional Trainer wisdom says that Pokémon usually level up by battling. But for Pokémon, and especially wild Pokémon, Evolution is sometimes part of a natural cycle.

At a certain time of the year, Bulbasaur from all over the world gather in a secluded part of Kanto known as the Mysterious Garden. These Bulbasaur are all ready to evolve. During this time, the presence of the Bulbasaur causes plants in the area to bloom unnaturally quickly.

The Mysterious Garden seems to be nothing more than a field with a barren tree at its center, but soon the Pokémon cause the entire area to burst into fresh blossoms. Inside the tree lives a Venusaur who leads the Evolution ceremony.

The Venusaur who lives in the Garden leads the Evolution, beginning with a form of call and response between Venusaur and the gathered Bulbasaur. When the moment is right, the Bulbasaur all evolve—unless, like Ash's Bulbasaur, they defy the crowd and refuse to become Ivysaur.

ALIENS AMONG US

UFO sightings and Area 28? Sounds suspicious—and nobody is more skeptical than Cilan. After some investigating, Cilan and company come across the mysterious Professor Icarus. His work with UFOs and aliens is well-known to Cilan. They also spot an Elgyem, which they realize is a Pokémon and not an alien. Team Rocket decides they want the Elgyem for themselves, and they create a device that causes havoc at Icarus' lab. As our team of heroes tries to escape in a UFO found at the lab, they defeat Team Rocket once again and free Elgyem from their clutches.

SAWSBUCK SEASON

Ash and friends meet a young Pokémon Photographer named Robert who shows them a photo his grandfather took. Iris and Cilan are shocked to see a picture of four Sawsbuck together—from all four seasons of the year—at the same time! Robert wants to find the spot where the mysterious photo was taken, and our heroes want to go along.

On their way, they spot a Deerling, and Robert knows it might lead them to a Sawsbuck. However, a thick fog rolls in, and Ash and Robert are separated from the rest. They lose track of the Deerling and stop for the night. They are surprisingly awakened by the same Deerling, who wants them to follow it.

Sprayed by some poisonous Amoonguss, Robert falls ill. Ash vows to get him off the mountain, but as the fog rolls in again, the Deerling brings back a Sawsbuck. The two Pokémon lead Ash and Robert to the exact spot where Robert's grandfather's photo was taken, along with all four Sawsbuck from different seasons! The warming light from the same spring in Grandpa's picture heals Robert. He manages to take one picture of the four Sawsbuck from different seasons.

Ash and Robert then meet up with Iris and Cilan, but are surprised that what seemed like an overnight stay in the woods to Ash and Robert was only ten minutes to Iris and Cilan!

NEW POKÉMON DISCOVERIES

FAIRY TYPES

Through their tireless efforts, Pokémon scientists have discovered a new, 18th, type of Pokémon—Fairy-type! So far, it is known that Fairy-types are especially effective in battles against Dragon-types like Salamence and Haxorus. However, Fairy-types' power and abilities have yet to be fully understood.

Research has revealed new data that has some Pokémon being re-classified and also made some Pokémon Dual-type.

Some Pokémon can even change to Fairy-type temporarily during Mega Evolution.

While the reclassified and Dual-type Pokémon have not changed in appearance, they have shifted in battle strength. So a smart Trainer will take note and be sure to keep a Pokédex and this book close by for reference.

These Pokémon are Dual-types:

AZURILL - NORMAL/FAIRY-TYPE
IGGLYBUFF - NORMAL/FAIRY-TYPE
JIGGLYPUFF - NORMAL/FAIRY-TYPE
WIGGLYTUFF - NORMAL/FAIRY-TYPE
GARDEVOIR - PSYCHIC/FAIRY-TYPE
MIME JR. - PSYCHIC/FAIRY-TYPE
MR. MIME - PSYCHIC/FAIRY-TYPE
RALTS - PYSCHIC/FAIRY-TYPE
COTTONEE - GRASS/FAIRY-TYPE
WHIMSICOTT - GRASS/FAIRY-TYPE
TOGEKISS - FLYING/FAIRY-TYPE
TOGETIC - FLYING/FAIRY-TYPE
AZUMARILL - WATER/FAIRY-TYPE
MARILL - WATER/FAIRY-TYPE
KIRLIA - PSYCHIC/FAIRY-TYPE
MAWILE - STEEL/FAIRY-TYPE
MEGA GARDEVOIR - PSYCHIC/FAIRY-TYPE
MEGA ALTARIA - DRAGON/FAIRY-TYPE
MEGA AUDINO - NORMAL/FAIRY-TYPE
MEGA MAWILE - STEEL/FAIRY-TYPE

These Pokémon have been reclassified as Fairy-types:

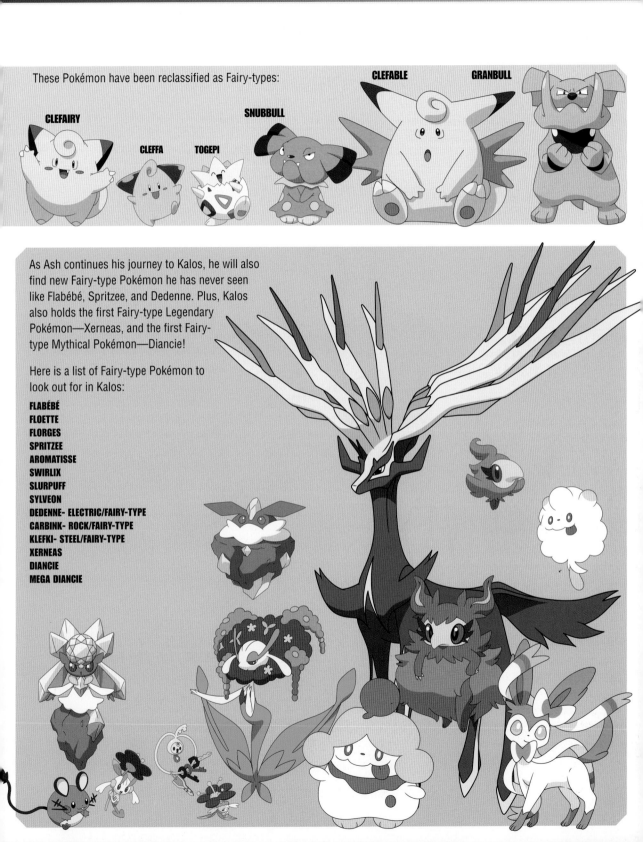

CLEFABLE

GRANBULL

CLEFAIRY

SNUBBULL

CLEFFA

TOGEPI

As Ash continues his journey to Kalos, he will also find new Fairy-type Pokémon he has never seen like Flabébé, Spritzee, and Dedenne. Plus, Kalos also holds the first Fairy-type Legendary Pokémon—Xerneas, and the first Fairy-type Mythical Pokémon—Diancie!

Here is a list of Fairy-type Pokémon to look out for in Kalos:

FLABÉBÉ
FLOETTE
FLORGES
SPRITZEE
AROMATISSE
SWIRLIX
SLURPUFF
SYLVEON
DEDENNE- ELECTRIC/FAIRY-TYPE
CARBINK- ROCK/FAIRY-TYPE
KLEFKI- STEEL/FAIRY-TYPE
XERNEAS
DIANCIE
MEGA DIANCIE

EEVEE AND ITS EVOLUTIONS

It's no wonder Eevee is called the Evolution Pokémon. Pokémon Researchers have discovered it has not one, not two, not three, but eight great Evolutions! How does it *rock* more magical transformations than a pop star? Pun intended. Eevee's genes are sensitive to the radiation in certain rocks, times of day, and even its Trainer's feelings. Depending on the special stone or its surroundings, Eevee will morph shape, size, and even type.

EEVEE: THE EVOLUTION POKÉMON

Height: 1'00" (0.3 m)
Weight: 14.3 lbs (14.3 kg)

NORMAL

VAPOREON: THE BUBBLE JET POKÉMON

Not only can Vaporeon control water, it can breathe underwater too thanks to the fins and gills it gained by its Evolution. Eevee evolves into Vaporeon near a Water Stone.

Height: 3'03" (1.0 m)
Weight: 63.9 lbs (29 kg)

WATER

FLAREON: THE FLAME POKÉMON

While a fur coat might keep some warm, Flareon's fluff helps it keep cool. The Flame Pokémon can run a temperature of up to 1650 degrees Fahrenheit and its mane helps it release the extra heat. Eevee evolves into Flareon by a Fire Stone.

Height: 2'11" (0.89 m)
Weight: 55.1 lbs (25 kg)

FIRE

Height: 2'07" (0.79 m)
Weight: 54 lbs (24.5 kg)

ELECTRIC

JOLTEON: THE LIGHTNING POKÉMON

Jolteon's prickly fur stands on end because of all the electric currents running through its body. From its charged cells to the static electricity that covers its coat, Jolteon is so amped up it can blast lightning bolts. Eevee evolves into Jolteon by a Thunder Stone.

ESPEON: THE SUN POKÉMON

When Eevee is bathed in sunshine, it can evolve into Espeon. The Sun Pokémon has a loyal nature. Once it finds a Trainer it trusts, it bonds so deeply that It can sense when that Trainer is in harm's way.

UMBREON: THE MOONLIGHT POKÉMON

When Eevee senses the moon's waves, it evolves into Umbreon. The Moonlight Pokémon is so in tune with the moon that it makes the rings on its body glow with an intense light.

Height: 3'03" (1.0 m)
Weight: 59.5 lbs (27 kg)

DARK

Height: 3'03" (1.0 m)
Weight: 56.2 lbs (25.5 kg)

GRASS

LEAFEON: THE VERDANT POKÉMON

Like a tree, Leafeon uses the process of photosynthesis to make fresh air. So, you'll often spot it soaking in some sunshine. Eevee can only evolve into Leafeon deep in the woods by a Moss Rock.

GLACEON: THE FRESH SNOW POKÉMON

Glaceon can make the temperature of its body drop so sharply that it can freeze the air around it and turn it into a fierce snowstorm. Eevee can evolve into Glaceon near an Ice Rock.

Height: 2'07" (0.79 m)
Weight: 57.1 lbs (25.9 kg)

ICE

Height: 2'11" (0.89 m)
Weight: 58.4 lbs (26.5 kg)

PSYCHIC

SYLVEON: THE INTERTWINING POKÉMON

This sensitive Pokémon is a lover, not a fighter. It can calm any anger or upset with the serene aura energy from its flowing feelers. The environmental factors that help Eevee evolve into Sylveon aren't found lying around or even in the sky, they are cultivated by the Trainer. To evolve Eevee into Sylveon a Trainer first needs to show Eevee lots of love. The Trainer also must successfully teach Eevee a Fairy-type move. Then, and only then, can Eevee evolve into Sylveon.

Height: 3'03" (1.0 m)
Weight: 51.8 lbs (26.0 kg)

FAIRY

STARSTRUCK

After Meowth saw a screening of *That Darn Meowth*, it was so entranced that it headed west in search of the wonderful food it saw in the film. But Meowth isn't the only one in the Pokémon world who's been affected by the media—there are plenty of stars and celebrities who have crossed paths with Ash and his friends.

DJ MARY

DJ Mary is Poké Radio's famous radio host, broadcasting live from Goldenrod City. She's a real pro who's good at easing her guests' stage fright. She also works together with Professor Oak on his own Poké Radio show. The two of them have done several live broadcasts from towns in the area.

ELESA

Elesa is an elegant and gorgeous supermodel that everyone's crazy about. She also happens to be the Gym Leader of the Nimbasa Gym. Elesa stays on the cutting edge of Unova trends, participating in fashion shows and shining as bright as the sun in Pokémon battles! After a tough battle, Ash earned his Bolt Badge from Elesa.

Pokétalk Radio's enthusiastic producer doesn't just stay in the studio, he'll even go out himself to grab interviewees. Everyone who wins a Plain Badge is interviewed on the show, so he goes to find Ash in person and ask him to come to the station.

Fiorello Cappucino

Fiorello's not just the movie star cohost of the Queen of the Princess Festival Contest, he's also the prize: in addition to a set of rare dolls, the winner receives a photo together with Fiorello. He's a perfect pick for the Princess Festival, since all the ladies just love him!

KLIEBAN SPIELBUNK

Winner of the Golden Growlithe for Best Director, Spielbunk is an artiste who's prone to melodrama. He takes a break from directing people to direct *Pokémon in Love*, a tragic Pokémon romance starring a prima donna Wigglytuff and Misty's Psyduck.

Spielbunk also directed *I Saw What You Ate Last Tuesday*, which was a big hit with Brock but a big flop at the box-office.

BRAD VAN DARN

Cooler than Articuno and hotter than Moltres: that's how the previews describe Brad van Darn, star of action films like Ultra Maximum. Behind the tough guy image is a man who dotes on his Smoochum, which upsets his manager. What would happen to Brad's image if his frenzied female fans saw him toting around a tiny Kiss Pokémon?

Ultimately, Brad decides he can't give up his precious "Smoochie-kins." Smoochum always supported him during his early days when he was washing dishes to earn meals and struggling through dance lessons. After Brad demonstrates some real-life heroics to save his Smoochum from Team Rocket during a live stage show, the fans go wild with delight. Now Brad and Smoochum act in films together and they're more popular than ever.

FUN AND GAMES

Sports and athletics are always popular in the Pokémon world, even when the athletics involve Pokémon instead of people! Most of the time Pokémon shouldn't be playing, but there are some exceptions.

BASEBALL

Baseball is a big sport with passionate fans, none more passionate than Ash's friend Casey.

Baseball teams include the Starmie, who play out of Cerulean City, and the questionably named Magikarp.

POKÉATHLON

There's even a Pokéathlon. This marathon event was first held in Johto and is comprised of ten events, three of which are randomly chosen when the event is held. Rules state that participating Trainers can only pick one Pokémon to participate in all the events. The first Pokéathlon held in Sinnoh included the disc catch, a halftime show instead of a normal second event, and a hurdle dash.

POKÉMON SUMO

What's Pokémon sumo? Like the actual sport of sumo, it's a 1-on-1 grappling match between Pokémon, using nothing more than sheer physical power. Pokémon sumo is the favored sport of a small village in Johto—the art was developed by local Trainers who were big fans of human sumo wrestling. Trainers in the village breed Pokémon just for sumo wrestling; Pokémon must weigh at least 80 kilograms in order to compete.

The town even has its own Pokémon Sumo Society and an annual Pokémon Sumo Conference, which has been held for over 35 years. The winner receives a King's Rock and a year's supply of Pokémon food.

SURFING

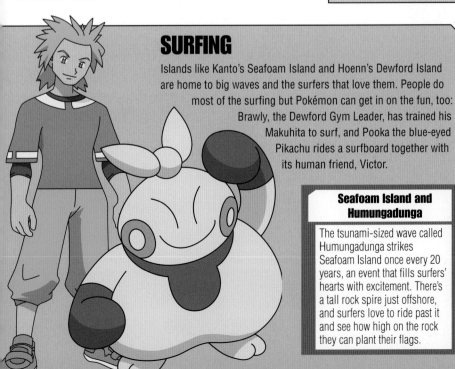

Islands like Kanto's Seafoam Island and Hoenn's Dewford Island are home to big waves and the surfers that love them. People do most of the surfing but Pokémon can get in on the fun, too: Brawly, the Dewford Gym Leader, has trained his Makuhita to surf, and Pooka the blue-eyed Pikachu rides a surfboard together with its human friend, Victor.

Seafoam Island and Humungadunga

The tsunami-sized wave called Humungadunga strikes Seafoam Island once every 20 years, an event that fills surfers' hearts with excitement. There's a tall rock spire just offshore, and surfers love to ride past it and see how high on the rock they can plant their flags.

EXTREME POKÉMON

Extreme Pokémon races are the most popular sport in Eggseter, a small Johto town. This type of racing involves a person riding a skateboard pulled by a harnessed Pokémon.

Eggseter holds an annual Extreme Pokémon race, with the golden Poké Ball trophy as the prize. The course leads out of town and out to the Shellby Ranch, where competitors pick up a dummy Pokémon Egg and then bring it back to the starting line using any route they wish.

KANTO

Kanto is Ash's home. Hailing from the small village of Pallet Town, which also happens to be the home of Professor Oak, Ash traveled across this region exploring everything from Mt. Moon in the north to the Indigo Plateau in the east.

From the island resort of Cinnabar Island in the south to Pewter City and Cerulean City in the north, Kanto offers many different walks of life. Kanto's Saffron City is the largest metropolis in the region, located in the center of Kanto, between Celadon City and Lavender Town.

Perhaps the most unique man-made feature is the oceanic bridge. Spanning the entire gulf area of Vermilion City, travelers can ride, walk, or bike across the great expanse.

PROFESSOR OAK

Professor Oak is an important figure in the Pokémon universe, and to Ash. He often serves as his mentor and friend. He is always there for Ash with timely advice or a piece of his world famous Pokémon poetry.

PROPS FOR THE PROFESSOR

Professor Oak is the first in a line of arborous professors we meet throughout the Pokémon universe. Professors are usually named after some type of tree or plant: Professor Birch, Professor Elm, Professor Ivy, Professor Juniper, and even Professor Rowan.

First and foremost, Professor Oak is a Pokémon researcher—a man who studies the behavior of Pokémon and their interaction with the human community. He's credited with a ton of material that's related to Pokémon, and all that data helped him to build his greatest invention ever—the Pokédex.

While he always shows a keen intellect and sage wisdom, Professor Oak actually knows a bit about battling as well. His Pokémon of choice is an extremely powerful Dragonite.

POETRY

Professor Oak is a skilled practitioner of Pokémon Poetry, expertly crafting haiku-like poems of 15 to 17 syllables. They not only describe different aspects and traits about Pokémon, but also serve as metaphors for important life lessons (whose deep meanings are often overlooked by the casual listener!). Some examples include, "Blastoise/ Fight or hide away/to fight again some other day." And "Sandslash/Rolls into a spiny ball/three meals a day and eats them all!

Wobbuffet

When life is a mystery, it's your answer.

HOME SWEET HOME

Professor Oak's vast lab (and it has to be vast since he holds hundreds of Pokémon) is in Pallet Town, Ash's home town. We get a few glimpses of the lab as Professor Oak reports to Ash or vice versa. It is the storage area for all Pokémon that Trainers wish to leave when their rosters get too full. He lives up the road from Delia Ketchum, Ash's mom. His most recent assistant is Tracey Sketchit, who shares similar interests in Pokémon and art. He has a cocky, brash grandson named Gary Oak.

The three Pokémon that Professor Oak offers to the young, new Trainers in the Kanto region from which they choose their First Partner Pokémon are the Grass-type Bulbasaur; the Fire-type Charmander; and the Water-type Squirtle. On Ash's first day he slept in, and by the time he made it to Professor Oak's lab all of the regular three choices for new Trainers were gone! So in a highly irregular move, Professor Oak was forced to offer Ash the only available Pokémon he had in his lab at that time: a Pikachu!

MISTY

She's a hothead, cranky, and very emotional. She also has a tender side that comes out when caring for Togepi. But what Misty has that few others possess is a determination to be the best, fueled by sibling rivalry.

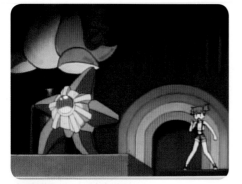

WATER, WATER, EVERYWHERE

Misty loves Water-type Pokémon, and she'd better—her sisters run the Cerulean Gym in Cerulean City. But her chance encounter with Ash sets off a series of events that turn her life upside down.

Misty and her three older sisters, Daisy, Violet, and Lily, run the Cerulean City Gym. In order to make a name for herself, Misty sets off on her own to become the greatest Water-type Pokémon Trainer ever. She eventually returns to the Gym out of a sense of duty, and makes a name for herself as a much better Gym Leader than her sisters.

THAT'S MY BIKE!

So how did Misty and Ash meet? Pikachu was fleeing a flock of Spearow, and Ash was in hot pursuit. After snagging Ash and Pikachu on her fishing pole, they beat a hasty retreat on Misty's "borrowed" bike.

Later, when Pikachu bravely faces down the flock, its ThunderShock fries everything to a crisp, including Misty's bike. Misty's bike was repaired and returned to her by the Viridian City Nurse Joy.

TRAUMA DRAMA

Misty fears a number of Pokémon, most notably Bug-type Pokémon. She won't even befriend Bug-types caught by Ash—she lists them as one of the three most disgusting things in the world: carrots, peppers, and Bug-types. She once had a fear of Gyarados—one tried to eat her when she was a baby. She got over it after calming and gaining the trust of an angry Gyarados at the Cerulean City Gym.

Misty's Pokémon

STARYU

Another original for Misty, this unassuming Pokémon has counted for quite a few victories.

STARMIE

This Pokémon was also one of Misty's original Pokémon, but was seldom seen in the show. She did use it against Ash in her Gym Battle for the Cascade Badge.

GOLDEEN

One of the Pokémon that Misty originally started out with. It can only be used in the water.

HORSEA

After Misty befriended this Horsea, it was later transferred back to the Cerulean City Gym for further strengthening.

PSYDUCK

Misty got Psyduck by accident. Misty trips, falls, loses a Poké Ball, and Psyduck hops in.

CORSOLA

Corsola was caught after Misty found it terrorizing other Corsola in the Whirl Islands. She used it in many battles, where it proved to be an admirable fighter.

TOGEPI

Togepi began as an Egg that became the center of a battle between everyone involved. Ash found the Egg. Brock took care of it. Meowth raised the Egg. But when it hatched, Togepi connected with Misty. It later evolved into Togetic.

TOGETIC

POLIWAG

Misty befriends Poliwag in the Orange Islands after a Vileplume uses its Stun Spore attack on Ash and Tracey. Although seldom used, it evolves into a powerful Poliwhirl, and then later into a Politoed.

POLIWHIRL

POLITOED

SENSATIONAL SIBLINGS

Misty's sisters perform a synchronized swimming act under the stage name The Three Sensational Sisters. Apparently, they don't count Misty as being that sensational, and refer to her as a "runt." But it was Misty, not her sisters, who battled Ash for the Cascade Badge when he fought at the Cerulean Gym.

AZURILL

Fellow Pokémon Trainer Tracey Sketchit gave Misty an Egg from his Marill, which later hatched into an Azurill.

CASERIN

Caserin is a Luvdisc that Misty acquired in Kanto. After trying unsuccessfully to foster a romantic relationship with another Luvdisc, it battles its way out of trouble and wins the affection of its target.

BROCK

Steady as the Rock-type Pokémon he once favored, Brock is a wise, talented Pokémon breeder with one big weakness: pretty girls. Most of the time, Brock takes care of his friends, dispensing sage advice and making sure everyone is fed. But when Brock goes ga-ga over a girl, it's his friends who have to rein him in.

Brock is a born caretaker, an ace hand at caring for his nine younger siblings as well as all types of Pokémon. His specialty is cooking delicious food for people and Pokémon, but he has a knack for just about anything domestic, from sewing to sweeping floors. What's more, he genuinely enjoys domestic work, but his household duties kept him chained to the Gym until his absent father Flint returned to take over the Gym.

Brock thought he'd found paradise in the Orange Islands helping out Professor Ivy, but he returned a broken man. For a time, he recuperated at Ash's house and fought with Mr. Mime for the privilege of doing chores and errands.

Brock has a book for everything—whenever he finds himself in a new situation, he takes diligent notes in his notebook. He also has a book to keep track of pretty girls and the instructions for all his chores are recorded in a notebook as well. It's not all cooking and laundry; polishing his Rock-type Pokémon with sand and a scrub brush is another one of Brock's regular chores. After Brock joined Ash and Misty, he eased up on the stern Gym Leader act. Not only did he start to show his goofy girl-crazy side, he's the gang's go-to man when it comes to region information, Battle strategy, and Pokémon - Trainer relationships.

Brock's Pokémon

GEODUDE

Like Brock's original Onix, Geodude was a mainstay of his Gym battling team at the Pewter Gym. Now it's back at the Gym under Forrest's care.

ONIX

Back when Steelix was an Onix, it was already so imposing that Pikachu tried to sneak out of their Gym battle. Brock left Onix with his brother Forrest, who raised it into a Steelix.

STEELIX

ZUBAT

Zubat took a very long time to evolve into a Golbat, finally evolving in a battle with Team Rocket. It reached its final stage, a sleek Crobat, in attempting to chase down Team Rocket in, of all things, a rocket.

CROBAT

GOLBAT

Brock the Gym Leader

Before Ash and Brock were pals, Ash was another challenger at the Pewter Gym. Brock was unimpressed with Ash's ability to raise his Pokémon and let him know as much; even then, he cared more about being a Pokémon breeder than battling.

ALL IN THE FAMILY

To understand Brock, it's essential to understand his family. Brock's parents, Flint and Lola, met in a Pokémon battle. They've kept the romance alive to this day, but Flint has difficulties adjusting to life as a family man: when things get tough, he runs off to the Pewter City outskirts and sits there in disguise. The first time, it was because he never became the Pokémon Trainer he wanted to be and couldn't face his family. The second time, he simply couldn't bear to stand up to his dear wife Lola.

Brock's mother Lola is loving but flighty, always busy with new hobbies. She likes to paint and decorate the house—and the Pewter Gym, unless she's stopped by Brock. Flint is hard in name only, and he had no choice but to let Lola turn the Pewter Gym into a Water-type Gym.

As for Brock's siblings, all nine of them (Forrest, Salvador, Yolanda, Tommy, Cindy, Suzy, Timmy, and the twins Tilly and Billy) look to him to keep the household functional.

The Many Loves of Brock

Brock professes his love to just about every pretty girl he sees, but fate has it that it never works out even when there's a girl who's attracted to him.

From time to time, Brock's unerring attraction for pretty girls does have its uses. For one thing, he's always able to tell Nurse Joys and Officer Jennys apart, based on their scent, or sometimes just a vibe. And even when the eyes may be fooled, Brock's heart isn't—just as a Pokédex correctly identifies Meowth even when it's in disguise, Brock feels nothing for Jessie disguised as Nurse Joy or Phantom Thief Brodie disguised as a lovely female researcher.

Temacu

She loves him, she loves him not… For once, Brock isn't interested when a girl falls in love with him, but he soon realizes he feels for Temacu after all. By then, it's already too late: fickle Temacu is completely over Brock and head over heels for the local doctor instead.

Pike Queen Lucy

The daring Pike Queen of the Battle Frontier is quiet, almost shy in person, but she blushes when Brock tries to charm her and seems to take a real interest in him.

MUDKIP

Marshtomp evolved from a responsible Mudkip that shared its caretaker instincts with Brock. It left its other Mudkip charges to join Brock's team and eventually evolved into a Marshtomp, but suffers from the same unluckiness in love as its Trainer.

MARSHTOMP

LOTAD

Brock's shy and earnest Lotad evolved into a Lombre after falling into a dry well. Lombre had a poor romantic track record; it lost the heart of another Trainer's Mawile when it evolved into a boisterous, outgoing Ludicolo after coming into contact with a Water Stone.

LOMBRE

LUDICOLO

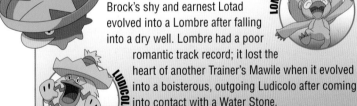

PINECO

While in Johto looking for apricorns, Brock saved a Pineco from Team Rocket. Pineco had a habit of self-destructing at the most inconvenient moments, but once it evolved into Forretress, it became a dependable member of Brock's team.

FORRETRESS

BONSLY

Brock lovingly cared for a baby Bonsly that he found haunting a ninja school. From that Bonsly, too young to even eat solid food, Brock eventually raised a loyal Sudowoodo that mimics anyone it's around.

SUDOWOODO

HAPPINY

Hatched from an Egg, Happiny was won when Brock entered Croagunk into a Pokémon dress-up contest. After rescuing Happiny from Team Rocket, Brock was able to bond with it. Then, while helping Brock nurse an ailing Pichu, it evolved into Chansey so it was able to use Soft-Boiled to heal it.

CHANSEY

CROAGUNK

Brock and Croagunk share a bond that can only be described as "special." Croagunk acts taciturn yet always looks out for Brock in its own way, usually by hitting him with Poison Jab whenever he tries to woo a beautiful lady.

TODD SNAP

Team Rocket once hired Todd Snap to capture Pikachu. What they didn't realize is that Todd only knows how to capture Pokémon one way, and that's with a camera—he doesn't call himself a number one photomaster for nothing!

Todd lives and breathes Pokémon photography—he has no Pokémon of his own, but he's captured countless on film and claims to have the world's best collection of candid Grass-type Pokémon photos. He first met Ash in Kanto and the two of them didn't hit it off immediately, even though they share a unique connection: Todd took a famous photo of the Aerodactyl that was carrying Ash away.

His obsession with photographing an Articuno finally paid off, and a print of his photo now hangs in the Snow Top Peak Pokémon Center in Johto. He decided to stay there for a while and continue photographing Pokémon that live in the mountains.

Todd and Ash soon bonded over their shared love of Pokémon, and he's even done some traveling with the gang in Kanto and Johto. Todd has smoothed out his early flashes of ego, but he's still obsessed with photography and will risk life and limb just to get the perfect shot.

RICHIE

Picture Ash, only mature for his age and adept at everything from solving problems to jump-starting a defunct elevator. That's Richie: he even has a Pikachu that likes to ride on his shoulder!

Richie and Ash first met at the Indigo League, where they teamed up to stop a Team Rocket Pokémon heist. Richie was taken aback by Ash's reckless antics, but they became great friends once they discovered just how similar they are. To their shock, they faced each other in the fifth round of the Indigo League; even though Ash was almost a no-show thanks to Team Rocket, Richie believed in his new friend and refused to let the referee call the match until Ash arrived.

Richie can go a little crazy over Pokémon, just like Ash, but he's usually the more level-headed of the two. Even when he loses in the Indigo League, he doesn't indulge in self-pity. He simply decides he'll do better next time, a maturity that makes an impression on Ash.

Richie's Pokémon

"SPARKY" (PIKACHU)

"ROSE" (TAILLOW)

"HAPPY" (BUTTERFREE)

"CRUISE" (PUPITAR)

"ZIPPO" (CHARMELEON)

PALLET TOWN

Throughout all of Ash's journeys, Pallet Town remains stable, the center of his adventures. There may not be much excitement in this little town, but there's everything a Trainer needs to welcome him home: a warm bed, a home-cooked meal, and the friendly faces of family and friends.

Pallet Town is a quiet town surrounded by rolling hills and fields, not far from a river, mountains, and even a rocky valley.

Much of Pallet Town is rural, and even the center of town is small and sleepy.

Delia Ketchum loves her garden, and she's taken Ash on many visits to nearby Xanadu Nursery for supplies. Filled with plants from top to bottom, Xanadu looks more like a botanical garden than a nursery. As lovely as it is, visitors must be careful since some of the plants have toxic defenses.

PROFESSOR OAK'S LABORATORY

Professor Oak and his assistant Tracey live and work in a complex on top of a hill, just across a small river. Behind his home and laboratory is a sprawling ranch that has ample room for lots of Pokémon to run free.

Trainers come to Professor Oak to receive their First Partner Pokémon or consult his expertise, while researchers contact him with their own scientific issues.

In addition to computers and scientific equipment, the lab has a storage area full of Poké Balls being held for traveling Trainers.

ASH'S HOUSE

Located on an unpaved road in a quiet neighborhood, Ash's house is as peaceful as can be. In the absence of her son, Ash's mother Delia keeps busy with her garden and social visits to Professor Oak; her Mr. Mime helps her out with the chores.

The upper level of the house has a workspace where Delia sews Ash's clothes.

GARY OAK

Every hero has a rival—someone who brings out the best in him. Rivals from day one, Gary and Ash seemed destined to get on each other's nerves. But their passion to always do better drives each to excel.

Their epic rivalry started very early. While fishing one day, Ash and Gary snag the same Pokémon. After some heated words, they both yank from opposite sides of a river at their prize. It turns out to be a Poké Ball. When the Poké Ball snaps in half, each youngster claims it as their own. To this day each keeps his half as symbol of their competition.

Cheerleaders

Gary is so overconfident that he has his own team of cheerleaders. Unfortunately, the cheerleaders have a bad effect on Brock, who becomes so infatuated with them in the finals that he can't seem to stay focused on his friend Ash's battles.

A REPUTATION TO UPHOLD

Gary Oak needs to be Gary Oak—that is, he needs to uphold the Oak family name. His grandfather is, after all, the famous and world-renowned Professor Samuel Oak, and those are some mighty big shoes to fill. Unfortunately, he doesn't get a lot of favoritism shown to him, and his brash and arrogant manner could be part of the problem. His overconfidence and attitude begin to change as he experiences more of the world.

In a furious 6-on-6 battle for the Silver Conference Finals, Ash beats Gary. Cocky at the beginning, Gary finally admits to Ash that they would have been better friends than rivals. Soon after he decides he wants to become a Pokémon researcher—just like his grandfather.

Gary's Pokémon

BLASTOISE

Squirtle was Gary's first choice and it also would have been Ash's first choice as well. It later evolves into Wartortle and then into Blastoise.

NIDOKING

In an early epic battle with Giovanni, Gary Oak goes for the Earth Badge at the Viridian City Gym. Giovanni plays the battle hard and fast… (continues at Arcanine)

NIDOQUEEN

When Oak's lab comes under attack by Team Rocket, a mysterious stranger, who turns out to be Gary, saves the day with his Nidoqueen.

SCIZOR

After some back and forth between Ash and Gary in the Johto League Silver Conference, the battle comes down to Snorlax and Scizor. Scizor defeats Snorlax.

"At least you get the chance to meet me... Mr. Gary to you. Show some respect."

ARCANINE

(continued from Nidoking) ...bringing a Mewtwo in that wipes out almost everything thrown at it, including two of Gary's Pokémon, Nidoking and Arcanine.

DODUO

Although making only a brief cameo as Gary returns to Professor Oak's lab, this Pokémon does end up evolving into Dodrio and playing a more major role later on.

DODRIO

EEVEE

Eevee is one of those rare Pokémon that can evolve a number of different ways: the time of day, the opponent, and it's feeling for the Trainer all are factors. So it's no wonder that Gary's Eevee evolved into Umbreon, but not before defeating Ash and Pikachu.

UMBREON

MAGMAR

Magmar is Gary's second Pokémon used against Ash in the finals. Magmar is sent packing by Ash's Heracross.

GOLEM

Golem comes in to battle Charizard, which seems like it would be a bad match-up for Charizard, but of course, Ash thinks outside the box and comes up with a unique way to defeat it!

ELECTIVIRE

Larger than Pikachu, Electivire has won the only time it has faced off with Pikachu.

JESSIE

Listen, is that a voice I hear?
It's speaking to me loud and clear.
On the wind.
Past the stars.
In your ear!
Bringing chaos at a breakneck pace.
Dashing hope, bringing fear in its place.
A rose by any other name is just as sweet.
When everything's worse, our work is complete.
Jessie!
James!
And Meowth, now dat's a name!
Putting the do-gooders in their place...
...we're Team Rocket...
...in your face!
Wobbuffet!

How could a trio of ineffective criminals possibly make it through dozens of lands, hundreds of adventures, and thousands of misfires into the annals of Pokémon lore? You'd have to be so spectacularly bad at your job that people would notice. And on that note, we introduce you to Team Rocket.

HUMBLE BEGINNINGS

Both Jessie and James have very intricate backstories that actually have you feeling sorry for them. Jessie had a troubled childhood. She was incredibly poor, having to eat snow to survive. Jessie tried nursing school for a while, but flunked out and eventually met James.

WURMPLE

Team Rocket later got Wurmple in the Hoenn region. Completely convinced that her Wurmple, which had evolved into a Cascoon, was going to evolve into a Beautifly, Jessie is disappointed at first when it finally evolves after a battle with May. She quickly comes to adore Dustox and only releases it so it can mate.

CASCOON

DUSTOX

WOOBAT

The Bat Pokémon is typically found in caves. Using its nose, it can pick up ultrasonic waves to sense its surroundings in pitch-black darkness. As Jessie's Pokémon buddy, it sees more time in combat than spelunking. This Woobat's Gust is so strong, it knocked Ash's Pokémon friend right out of the sky.

EKANS

Ekans was an obedient Pokémon that Jessie used often. It evolved into Arbok and became her go-to Pokémon. She eventually released it so that it could help a group of Ekans being threatened by poachers.

ARBOK

PUMPKABOO

While at a Gourgeist Festival, Jessie tries to trick a local prince into a trade—get her Ash's pal Pikachu and she'd hand over Pumpkaboo as payment. The deal goes awry when Pumpkaboo evolves into Gourgeist and the Prince loses interest.

GOURGEIST

YANMA

Team Rocket later got Yanmega in the Sinnoh region. Caught as a Yanma, Jessie's Yanmega evolved very quickly.

YANMEGA

WOBBUFFET

Team Rocket later got Wobbuffet in the Johto region. Wobbuffet was obtained mistakenly when Jessie accidently dropped her Ball into a Trading Machine. She was unaware that her Lickitung had been traded until later in a battle with "the Twerps."

SEVIPER

Team Rocket later got Seviper in the Hoenn region. A sturdy battler on Jessie's team, Seviper has a long running feud with Zangoose. It obeys Jessie, but will never back down from a fight with Zangoose. This has been Jessie's Pokémon of choice for some time.

FRILLISH

Beware this Pokémon's grip, because it can paralyze a Pokémon with poison. Although this Water- and Ghost-type can typically be found five miles deep in the ocean, Jessie asks her friend to fly above the White Ruins to fend of Ash and company with a Shadow Ball blast.

JAMES

James was born to a wealthy family, and has always enjoyed his status and wealth. So why would he give it all up for a life of crime? After attending Pokémon Tech (a school for Pokémon education), James grew bored of his lifestyle and ran away leaving Growlie at home. After a short stint in the Bridge Bike Gang, James set his sights somewhat higher and decided to join the Team Rocket syndicate.

GROWLITHE

Growlithe, or "Growlie" as James calls him, was one of his first Pokémon. His pet was beloved, but when James ran away from home, he left Growlie behind. When James does meet up with him again, he leaves Growlie as guardian over his scheming parents.

VICTREEBEL

Although Weepinbell was one of James's first Pokémon, he leaves it at a daycare center to evolve into Victreebel. He loses Victreebel in a Pokémon swap.

WEEPINBELL

MIME JR.

Team Rocket later got Mime Jr. in the Sinnoh region. James' Nanny and Pop-Pop are helping to heal his sick Chimecho. Mime Jr. jumps into an empty Poké Ball that falls to the ground, voluntarily becoming his newest Pokémon.

INKAY

The expression set a thief to catch a thief proved to work for James in Kalos. He met wild Inkay when it stole his breakfast and lunch. Impressed with its power to pilfer, he decided to catch the kindred spirit.

CHIMECHO

Team Rocket later got Chimecho in the Hoenn region. James calls Chimecho his first love. But after almost being duped into buying a Hoppip, a real Chimecho agrees to become one of his Pokémon. After it comes down with a fever, James leaves it with his Nanny and Pop-Pop, but vows to return for it after it heals.

KOFFING

Koffing is seen when we first meet Team Rocket, and has proven itself to be a formidable battler. It eventually evolves into a Weezing along with Jessie's Ekans. It was released along with Jessie's Arbok.

WEEZING

CARNIVINE

Early in Sinnoh, Team Rocket is trudging along after another defeat. They come across the old mansion where James spent his summers, and inside the playroom, James finds a beloved, albeit forgotten, childhood Pokémon of his—Carnivine.

YAMASK

This Ghost-type Pokémon embodies the spirit of a human ancestor and can still remember things about its past life. When Team Rocket first spotted this wild Spirit Pokémon in a warehouse, Jessie wanted to use Woobat to catch it. But James knew the way to this Pokémon's heart was through its stomach! After offering it food, James offered it his friendship and the two have been together ever since.

FOONGUS

The Mushroom Pokémon is known for waving its caps in a tantalizing dance to put its foes in a daze. James' Amoonguss also has a Body Slam so strong, it stopped Ash's pal Pikachu in its tracks.

AMOONGUSS

MEOWTH

Meowth is heartbreaking but his desire remains constant. He wants to supplant Giovanni's favorite pet Pokémon, Persian. All of Meowth's schemes almost work, but he always ends up paying for the bungling antics of Jessie and James.

CERULEAN CITY

Kanto's Cerulean City is Misty's hometown, a modern city located on the ocean. In keeping with its location, one of its featured attractions is the Water-type Cerulean Gym, but the city is home to other attractions with an oceanic theme. Cerulean City's own lighthouse is a scenic rendezvous spot in an area surrounded by trees.

CERULEAN CITY GYM

One look at the Cerulean Gym and it's clear what type of Gym it is. But it's more than just a Gym; Misty's sisters love to stage water ballet shows with the Gym's central tank as their stage.

For battles, the tank is usually recessed into the ground, just like a normal pool...

but the tank can be elevated aboveground for special events and shows.

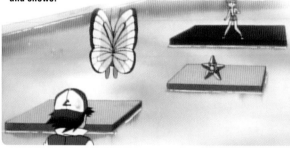

Although Misty's sister Daisy can't wait to get Misty and Tracey into some water ballet outfits and into the pool, Misty is happy to hand over the spotlight to Lily and Violet, the scriptwriting sister. Misty was already drafted to play a mermaid in one underwater show, and she's not keen on a repeat performance. Her Pokémon, including Goldeen, Starmie, Corsola, Horsea, and Staryu, continue to appear in water shows, while Kasurin and Loverin, two Luvdisc recently acquired by the Gym, can also help provide special effects.

The ceiling above the pool features lots of windows to let in light, and those windows can also swing open or shut. In the Gym's basement is an aquarium room filled with additional tanks for the Gym's Water-type Pokémon.

Making the Cascade Badge

The Cerulean Gym's Cascade Badges aren't just for show, they're handcrafted works of art. When supplies run out, Misty, Sakura, and Tracey pay a visit to the artist, Mr. Kinzo, who lives in Rafore Village. There they learn through hands-on experience that making a Gym badge is a grueling process that involves smithing, filing, welding, and a light hand with a brush!

Earning the Cascade Badge

But for all that work, Misty's sisters tend to be lax about the requirements for earning a Cascade Badge whenever Misty isn't around—it's not unusual for them to practically give the Gym badges away. One Trainer, Jimmy, "earned" his Cascade Badge for helping Daisy clean the pool—although Tracey has also done the same thing and has yet to receive a Gym badge for his troubles.

INDIGO CONFERENCE

The Kanto region's Indigo Conference is Ash's first big tournament and the culmination of everything he's worked for so far—not the least of which is the fact that his rival Gary will be there. Eight Kanto Gym badges earn entry into the tournament, after which it's down to a series of elimination rounds.

The Indigo Conference takes place on the Indigo Plateau. Located near a sparkling lake, Indigo Stadium is where the tournament's main events take place, but the first four rounds are held in other outlying stadiums.

Competitors can look forward to comfortable accommodations in the Pokémon League Village and free meals at area restaurants; parades and other special events add to the festive atmosphere for Trainers and spectators alike.

President Goodshow, a Pokémon League Torch Committee official, presides over the opening ceremonies. There's a ceremonial release of a flock of Pidgey and a parade of all the competing Trainers, followed by the lighting of the stadium's central torch.

TOURNAMENT STRUCTURE

The first four rounds are 3-on-3 battles in separate stadiums, each with one of four different battlefields: Rock, Grass, Water, and Ice. Each competitor must win matches on all four types, and competitors are assigned to fields at random.

Once a competitor advances past the first four rounds and into the top 16, they battle on a standard field in Indigo Stadium. Starting at the quarterfinal stage, battles are 6-on-6 instead of 3-on-3. For the top 16, brackets are determined by having each Trainer fish for a numbered Magikarp. Ash must battle Richie.

RICHIE DEFEATS ASH

Several of Ash's Pokémon are exhausted after a running struggle to escape Team Rocket and get to the stadium on time, so Ash's options are limited. Charizard is his last Pokémon, but when it refuses to battle, Ash loses the round and his final 16 match by default.

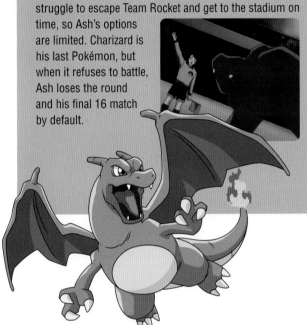

ASSUNTA DEFEATS RICHIE

Richie's own run ends here. His match comes down to a battle between Sparky and Assunta's Ivysaur. Sparky is knocked out.

CLOSING CEREMONIES

Everyone wins *something* in the Indigo League, so to speak. At the closing ceremonies, the winner receives a trophy, the rest of the competitors parade into Indigo Stadium and receive a commemorative badge, then bask in the light of a spectacular fireworks display.

KANTO GYM BATTLES!

On his way to becoming a Pokémon Master, Ash must first find and defeat the Gym Leaders for each region. He starts in Kanto, where the Gyms are spaced pretty far apart, leaving open the possibilities of endless adventures!

PEWTER CITY GYM

GYM LEADER: BROCK

BROCK **VS.** **ASH**

Gust works like a charm—a really, really bad charm. Flying attacks are weak against Rock-type Pokémon.

BROCK **VS.** **ASH**

Gedodude is no match for the strengthened Pikachu. Brock recalls Geodude.

BROCK **VS.** **ASH**

Pikachu fares better against Onix, but in the end, Brock stops the fight when it appears that it may hurt Pikachu. Luck is on their side, though, when a a small fire sets off the sprinkler system, and weakens Brock's Rock-type Pokémon.

Ash meets his first Gym Leader, Brock, while in Pewter City. Brock runs the Pewter City Gym, but also acts as a father to his abandoned siblings. Ash is reluctant to defeat Brock in front of his brothers and sisters, but his chivalry is rewarded when Brock joins his team, and grants him the Boulder Badge.

VERMILLION CITY GYM

GYM LEADER: LT. SURGE

Lt. Surge, a fierce Gym Leader, uses Pikachu's evolved form, Raichu. Raichu is more powerful and knows more Moves than Pikachu, so their first meeting is disastrous. While Pikachu is recuperating at the Pokémon Center, Nurse Joy offers Ash a Thunder Stone, which would evolve Pikachu into Raichu, but Pikachu refuses, instead opting to face Surge and his Pokémon on its own terms. Pikachu uses its agility to its advantage, winning the match, and winning Ash the Thunder Badge!

LT. SURGE **VS.** **ASH**

The first outing ended fairly quickly, as Lt. Surge predicted. Pikachu tried to use ThunderShock, but Raichu easily absorbed it, using a ThunderShock that was much more powerful. By the time Raichu got around to using Mega Punch, the match was over.

LT. SURGE **VS.** **ASH**

Pikachu was emboldened by its promise to protect its honor and not level up using the Thunder Stone. Raichu was ready with Body Slam, but Pikachu's Agility outmaneuvered it.

CERULEAN CITY GYM

GYM LEADER: MISTY

MISTY **VS.** **ASH**

Ash is a little overconfident going against Misty, and the battle volleys until Butterfree's Stun Spore does a number on Staryu. Staryu delivers a hard blow, and Ash recalls it.

MISTY **VS.** **ASH**

Realizing Staryu probably couldn't take much more, Misty recalls it and sends out Starmie. Wing Attack and Gust give Pidgeotto the edge, but before anyone can finish the match, Team Rocket arrives and rains on the parade.

The Sensational Sisters (Misty's sisters) are about to give the Cascade Badge to Ash when Misty intervenes. She wants to battle Ash for the badge, and does an admirable job. Unfortunately for Ash, Pikachu doesn't want to battle his new friend, Misty. When Team Rocket stops the pitched battle, Pikachu comes forward and blasts them off. The Sensational Sisters award the badge to Ash for saving the Gym.

SAFFRON CITY GYM

GYM LEADER: SABRINA

SABRINA **VS.** **ASH**

Pikachu is confused by Abra's indifference—which actually is a form of telekinesis. Abra evolves into the much stronger Kadabra, then proceeds to wipe the floor with Pikachu using Psychic attack and Confusion.

SABRINA **VS.** **ASH**

Using Psybeam, Kadabra expects to win easily, but then Haunter shows up and makes Sabrina laugh. This immobilizes her Kadabra and wins Ash the Marsh Badge.

CELADON CITY GYM
GYM LEADER: ERIKA

On their arrival in the sweet-scented Celadon City, Misty and Brock are taken by the town's perfume shop – but Ash is rude and dismissive, which angers the shop's owner and the town's Gym Leader, Erika. Ash now must find some other way into the Gym, and he enlists the help of Team Rocket to sneak in "Ashley." Pikachu uncovers his act, and Erika angrily takes him on in a battle for the Rainbow Badge.

ERIKA VS. **ASH**

Bulbasaur tries Vine Whip to attack Tangela from a distance, but Tangela counters with Constrict. After Tangela uses Stun Spore effectively against Bulbasaur, Ash withdraws his Grass-type Pokémon.

ERIKA VS. **ASH**

Weepinbell uses Razor Leaf, but Charmander's Flamethrower easily burns the Grass-type Weepinbell. Ash finishes with Skull Bash, and Erika removes Weepinbell from battle.

ERIKA VS. **ASH**

Erika calls out Gloom against Charmander, and because she has such a tight bond with her Pokémon, it lays the smack down on Charmander pretty easily.

Team Rocket shows up during the fracas to steal the secret formula for the Gym's world-renowned perfume, and sets the Gym on fire. Ash puts aside his battle to save the Pokémon, and in particular, Erika's Gloom, for which she rewards him with the Rainbow Badge.

CINNABAR ISLAND GYM
GYM LEADER: BLAINE

BLAINE VS. **ASH**

Squirtle seemed like an obvious choice for a lava gym, but Ninetales uses Fire Spin, the most powerful attack in its repertoire, and Squirtle is knocked out of the match.

BLAINE VS. **ASH**

Pikachu has to pick up for Charizard, and its use of Rhydon's horn as a lightning rod leads to an easy victory for Ash.

BLAINE VS. **ASH**

Charizard actually sleeps throughout the whole match, and forfeits the battle. It embarrasses Ash and disobediently leaves the arena.

BLAINE VS. **ASH**

No match. Pikachu is so outmatched that Ash forfeits the battle to save Pikachu.

BLAINE VS. **ASH**

The volcanic conclusion to the battle with Blaine is epic. A battle of Flamethrower attacks is useless, so Magmar uses Fire Blast, the most powerful move it knows. Charizard deflects it, and finally wins the match with its Seismic Toss, winning Ash the Volcano Badge.

FUCHSIA CITY GYM
GYM LEADER: KOGA

After surviving the strange booby traps, invisible walls, and an explosive Voltorb, Ash and his friends can finally challenge Koga for the Soul Badge.

KOGA VS. **ASH**

Bulbasaur and Venonat parry with limited results, until Bulbasaur's Leech Seed takes Venonat down.

KOGA VS. **ASH**

Charmander takes over for the fainted Pidgeotto, and gains the advantage with Flamethrower. Their battle, however, is interrupted by Team Rocket.

KOGA VS. **ASH**

Venonat evolves almost immediately into Venomoth, which uses Stun Spore and Sleep Powder with devastating results.

KOGA VS. **ASH**

Continuing their earlier battle, Charmander faces Golbat, and uses Ember attack to great effect. Golbat counters with Screech, but Charmander's Fire Spin does it in.

VIRIDIAN CITY GYM
GYM LEADER: GIOVANNI

Giovanni, the Gym Leader of Viridian City, is also the head of Team Rocket. He has a super-powerful Pokémon at his side, a Pokémon that wiped out all of Gary's Pokémon—Mewtwo. Giovanni is absent when Ash arrives, and he has to battle Jessie and James.

GIOVANNI VS. **ASH**

Machamp treats Squirtle like the squirt it is, and ends up hurting Ash in the process.

GIOVANNI VS. **ASH**

A combination of Quick Attack and Double-Edge attack puts things right for Ash.

GIOVANNI VS. **ASH**

Bulbasaur's Vine Whip has no effect when Kingler uses its Harden. When it hits Bulbasaur with Bubble attack, it seems as if Ash is destined to lose.

GIOVANNI VS. **ASH**

Pikachu evens everything out with a powerful Thunderbolt that wipes out the competition.

Team Rocket has rigged the battlefield so that Trainers feel the pain of their Pokémon. In true Team Rocket fashion, they rigged both sides of the field. When Ash uses Pikachu's Thunderbolt, and Team Rocket blasts off, he wins the eighth and final badge—the Earth Badge.

BELIEVE IT OR NOT!

A planet full of Pokémon is a fantastic place to begin, but the Pokémon world is full of other unusual sights. Magic? Mystical kingdoms? Giant Pokémon? Ash and his friends encounter all this and more…

Giant Claydol Spotted On Izabe Island!

IS THE GIANT CLAYDOL EVEN A REAL POKÉMON?

According to legend, a maiden crafted it from the mud of Lake Izabe, and the Claydol searched for her after it was released. That's how Ash and Team Rocket lure the Claydol toward the stone Poké Ball on the cliff—Wobbuffet bears a certain resemblance to the original maiden.

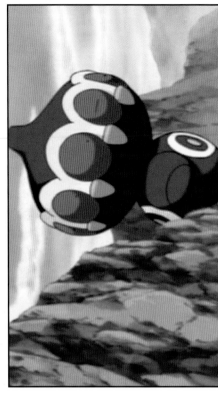

On Hoenn's Izabe Island lies the Valley of Destruction, where a giant stone Poké Ball was once perched high on a cliff. The valley acquired its ominous name in the Time of the Destruction, when the "Great Destroyer" was released from the stone Poké Ball. This Great Destroyer was a huge Claydol, 20 times the normal size—and a normal Claydol is already 4'11" tall! Claydol rampaged across the island for seven days and nights until a White Sage conjured up a giant Poké Ball and used it to seal Claydol in Lake Izabe.

The Claydol remained in the lake for a thousand years until Team Rocket let it out, and the stone Poké Ball in the lake was lost in the process.

Fortunately, Claydol's original Poké Ball was still perched on the valley cliff. After Claydol was sealed in the Poké Ball, the Poké Ball rolled into the lake, restoring the balance.

Out of This World?

Aliens are among us! Or are they? Weird looking Pokémon get mistaken for a lot of things, but aliens? In "A UFO for Elgyem!", Ash and company think they've spotted a real live alien, but what they've really discovered is a unique Pokémon known as Elgyem.

Lombre the Water Lord?

THE LOCALS HAVE A SHRINE TO LOMBRE

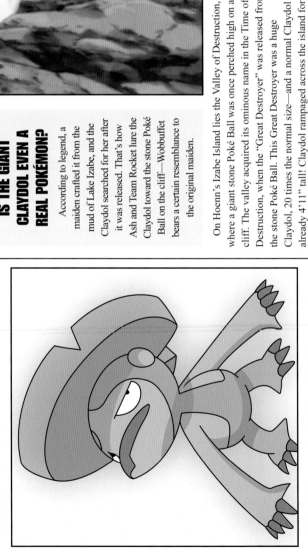

Mighty Pokémon such as Dialga and Palkia have long been revered for their power, but Lombre? There is indeed a town in Hoenn where the locals have a shrine to Lombre, their Water Lord, who is said to live in a spring upstream from their village. The Water Lord is honored with music and dancing in the hopes that it keeps the village supplied with water. But after a fateful encounter with Ash, Brock's Lombre, and a Solrock, the villagers now venerate Solrock instead.

I Scream, You Scream

Haunted suits of armor, a ghostly sarcophagus, and ancient artifacts—these are all elements that would make even the stoutest Trainer quiver like a Gastrodon on a salt lick. In "A Night in the Nacrene City Museum!", Ash and his friends find all this and more, including the Pokémon Yamask and Cofagrigus.

Pokémon Magic Turns a Boy Into a Pikachu!

It's science as much as sorcery: the vanishing art of Pokémon magic draws its power from aspects of Pokémon, and many of its secrets can be found in an ancient book carried by Lily the Pokémon Magician. Passed down across generations of her family, the book is written in an obscure script and describes how to work Pokémon magic—but bear in mind that this "magic" doesn't always work the way one would expect. A spell to make a girl's skin smooth and soft might involve summoning Spinarak to show up and cocoon the spell's target in silk. And a spell that lets a person read the thoughts of Pokémon—well, the full text of the spell is smudged, so it temporarily turns Ash into a talking Pikachu. Caster beware!

The pages of Lily's book describe the components for the Pokémon communication spell: Shuckle's secret cure, powdered Stantler horns, yogurt made from Miltank milk, a flower petal marked with a Jynx's kiss. That's not all—it calls for Aipom's tears and Parasect's Stun Spore, too. There's one more ingredient to go before it's time to use Pikachu's

Thunderbolt to activate the spell. Dirt from a Meowth's claw is another ingredient, and Lily the Pokémon Magician isn't shy about marching right up to Team Rocket to get it.

Giant Flying Pokémon!

Could a little candy make a Pokémon huge? Dr. Gordon's Mystery Candy Complete was invented by accident, but it's no dud. Just one of these blue candies makes Caterpie grow to the height of a ceiling and then beyond. Soon it's big enough to knock over the top of a metal tower, and when it evolves into Metapod and then Butterfree, it can easily carry people on its back.

Team Rocket uses some stolen candy to make their own giant Pokémon out of Cacnea and Dustox, setting up a giant aerial clash with Butterfree. Fortunately, the effects of the Candy are only temporary.

Downtown Rocked by a Battle of Giant Pokémon!

Professor Jacuzzi is a Gulpin expert who has a plan to save a town from its annual Gulpin infestation. One of his inventions is the Mach 3 Particle Cannon, which absorbs Gulpin using a subatomic particle beam and then uses power from the Gulpin's own attacks to launch them out of the city at Mach 3. But when the Particle Cannon is damaged, it causes a Gulpin and Ash's Treecko to grow to humongous size!

As the two battle in the middle the town, the exertion causes Treecko to return to normal size—but Gulpin remains a giant. Professor Jacuzzi captures Gulpin with a Heavy Ball and he's determined to return it to normal size, sooner or later…

Red Gyarados Scares Locals!

Especially viscious, the Red Gyarados is rumored to be much more aggressive and territorial than the average Gyarados. Often found in secluded underwater caves or in hidden underground lakes, the Red Gyarados is slightly larger but otherwise identical Although clearly believed to be a myth by many, Team Rocket has seen, and been blasted off by a Red Gyarados.

Togepi From Another World!

Hoenn residents aren't likely to find the Mirage Kingdom listed in any guidebook. To reach it, visitors must use an airship to cross a desert and the

ring of rocky peaks that hides the Kingdom from outside eyes. That alone is remarkable, but what makes the Mirage Kindgom truly unusual is a centuries-old connection with Togepi, its guardian of peace and freedom.

The palace and nearby temple both incorporate design elements reminiscent of Togepi, as do the fashions of the royal family.

Because Togepi are sensitive to the goodness—or lack thereof—that dwells in human hearts, conditions in the Togepi Paradise are closely linked to conditions in the Mirage Kingdom. That's why Princess Sarah, who (after a little help from Misty and her friends) now rules the Mirage Kingdom, has sworn to protect the Togepi Paradise. Misty's Togepi, now evolved into Togetic, is a stalwart guardian of the Paradise as well.

KANTO LEGENDARY POKÉMON

ARTICUNO • (ART-tick-COO-no)

Height	5'07" (1.7 m)	Category	Freeze
Weight	122.1 lbs (55.4 kg)	Type	Ice-Flying

A brilliant blue and white Pokémon, the beat of Articuno's wings chills the air, causing snow to fall wherever it flies. Articuno represents the element of ice.

Extremely agile, Articuno's most unique feature is its long, flowing tail. Like a dancer's ribbon, the tail rolls and whips behind Articuno as it flies, accentuating the majestic bird's path through the air.

MEWTWO • (MYU-too)

Height	6'07" (2.0 m)	Category	Genetic
Weight	269.0 lbs (122.0 kg)	Type	Psychic

Mewtwo is unique in the entire world. Mewtwo is not a natural Pokémon—it was created by human scientists using genetic manipulation. They crafted it with breathtaking power, but failed to endow it with a compassionate heart.

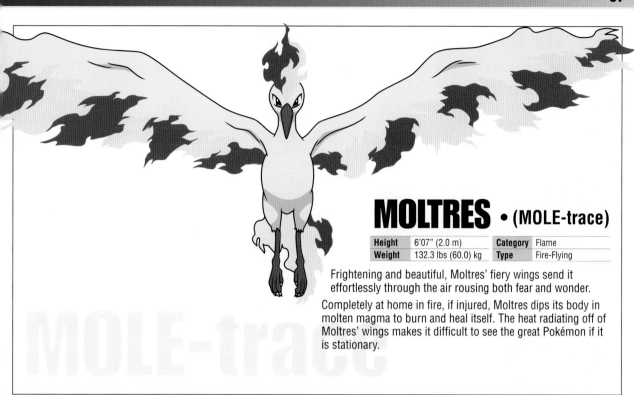

MOLTRES • (MOLE-trace)

Height	6'07" (2.0 m)	Category	Flame
Weight	132.3 lbs (60.0) kg	Type	Fire-Flying

Frightening and beautiful, Moltres' fiery wings send it effortlessly through the air rousing both fear and wonder.

Completely at home in fire, if injured, Moltres dips its body in molten magma to burn and heal itself. The heat radiating off of Moltres' wings makes it difficult to see the great Pokémon if it is stationary.

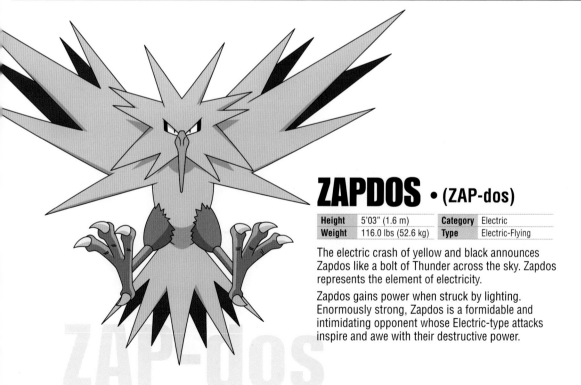

ZAPDOS • (ZAP-dos)

Height	5'03" (1.6 m)	Category	Electric
Weight	116.0 lbs (52.6 kg)	Type	Electric-Flying

The electric crash of yellow and black announces Zapdos like a bolt of Thunder across the sky. Zapdos represents the element of electricity.

Zapdos gains power when struck by lighting. Enormously strong, Zapdos is a formidable and intimidating opponent whose Electric-type attacks inspire and awe with their destructive power.

KANTO MYTHICAL POKÉMON

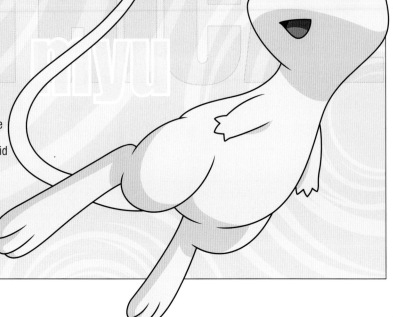

MEW • (myu)

Height	1'04" (0.4 m)	Category	New Species
Weight	8.8 lbs (4.0 kg)	Type	Psychic

Fun loving and innocent, Mew seems to inspire the best in people and Pokémon. Able to transform into any Pokémon at will, Mew is said to possess the genetic composition of all Pokémon.

Mew seems to be connected to the world of Pokémon unlike any other Pokémon. Severely affected when the environment is unbalanced, Mew's life has been in jeopardy on more than one occasion.

KANTO POKÉMON

This is the region that started it all—the home of Ash (Pallet Town), and the beginning of great adventures! You'll meet all sorts of Pokémon in Kanto, including everyone's favorite, Pikachu! It's also the home of Articuno, Zapdos, Moltres, Mew, and Mewtwo!

ABRA

Height: 2'11" (0.9 m)
Weight: 43.0 lbs. (19.5 kg)

PSYCHIC

AERODACTYL

Height: 5'11" (1.8 m)
Weight: 130.1 lbs. (59.0 kg)

ROCK | FLYING

ALAKAZAM

Height: 4'11" (1.5 m)
Weight: 105.8 lbs. (48.0 kg)

PSYCHIC

ARBOK

Height: 11'06" (3.5 m)
Weight: 143.3 lbs. (65.0 kg)

POISON

ARCANINE

Height: 6'03" (1.9 m)
Weight: 341.7 lbs. 155.0 kg)

FIRE

ARTICUNO

Height: 5'07" (1.7 m)
Weight: 122.1 lbs. (55.4 kg)

ICE | FLYING

BEEDRILL

Height: 3'03" (1.0 m)
Weight: 65.0 lbs. (29.5 kg)

BUG | POISON

BELLSPROUT

Height: 2'04" (0.7 m)
Weight: 8.8 lbs. (4.0 kg)

GRASS | POISON

BLASTOISE

Height: 5'03" (1.6 m)
Weight: 188.5 lbs. (85.5 kg)

WATER

BULBASAUR

Height: 2'04" (0.7 m)
Weight: 15.2 lbs. (6.9 kg)

GRASS | POISON

BUTTERFREE

Height: 3'07" (1.1 m)
Weight: 70.5 lbs. (32.0 kg)

BUG | FLYING

CATERPIE

Height: 1'00" (0.3 m)
Weight: 6.4 lbs. (2.9 kg)

BUG

CHANSEY

Height: 3'07" (1.1 m)
Weight: 76.3 lbs. (34.6 kg)

NORMAL

CHARIZARD

Height: 5'07" (1.7 m)
Weight: 199.5 lbs. (90.5 kg)

FIRE | FLYING

CHARMANDER

Height: 2'00" (0.6 m)
Weight: 18.7 lbs. (8.5 kg)

FIRE

CHARMELEON

Height: 3'07" (1.1 m)
Weight: 41.9 lbs. (19.0 kg)

FIRE

CLEFABLE

Height: 4'03" (1.3 m)
Weight: 88.2 lbs. (40.0 kg)

FAIRY

CLEFAIRY

Height: 2'00" (0.6 m)
Weight: 16.5 lbs. (7.5 kg)

FAIRY

CLOYSTER

Height: 4'11" (1.5 m)
Weight: 292.1 lbs. (132.5 kg)

WATER | ICE

CUBONE

Height: 1'04" (0.4 m)
Weight: 14.3 lbs. (6.5 kg)

GROUND

DEWGONG

Height: 5'07" (1.7 m)
Weight: 264.6 lbs. (120.0 kg)

WATER | ICE

DIGLETT

Height: 0'08" (0.2 m)
Weight: 1.8 lbs. (0.8 kg)

GROUND

DITTO

Height: 1'00" (0.3 m)
Weight: 8.8 lbs. (4.0 kg)

NORMAL

DODRIO

Height: 5'11" (1.8 m)
Weight: 187.8 lbs. (85.2 kg)

NORMAL | FLYING

DODUO

Height: 4'07" (1.4 m)
Weight: 86.4 lbs. (39.2 kg)

NORMAL | FLYING

DRAGONAIR

Height: 13'01" (4.0 m)
Weight: 36.4 lbs. (16.5 kg)

DRAGON

DRAGONITE

HEIGHT: 7'03" (2.2 M)
Weight: 463.0 lbs. (210.0 kg)

DRAGON | FLYING

DRATINI

Height: 5'11" (1.8 m)
Weight: 7.3 lbs. (3.3 kg)

DRAGON

DROWZEE

Height: 3'03" (1.0 m)
Weight: 71.4 lbs. (32.4 kg)

PSYCHIC

DUGTRIO

Height: 2'04" (0.7 m)
Weight: 73.4 lbs. (33.3 kg)

GROUND

EEVEE

Height: 1'00" (0.3 m)
Weight: 14.3 lbs. (6.5 kg)

NORMAL

EKANS

Height: 6'07" (2.0 m)
Weight: 15.2 lbs. (6.9 kg)

POISON

ELECTABUZZ

Height: 3'07" (1.1 m)
Weight: 66.1 lbs. (30.0 kg)

ELECTRIC

ELECTRODE

Height: 3'11" (1.2 m)
Weight: 146.8 lbs. (66.6 kg)

ELECTRIC

EXEGGCUTE

Height: 1'04" (0.4 m)
Weight: 5.5 lbs. (2.5 kg)

GRASS PSYCHIC

EXEGGUTOR

Height: 6'07" (2.0 m)
Weight: 264.6 lbs. (120.0 kg)

GRASS PSYCHIC

FARFETCH'D

Height: 2'07" (0.8 m)
Weight: 33.1 lbs. (15.0 kg)

NORMAL FLYING

FEAROW

Height: 3'11" (1.2 m)
Weight: 83.8 lbs. (38.0 kg)

NORMAL FLYING

FLAREON

Height: 2'11" (0.9 m)
Weight: 55.1 lbs. (25.0 kg)

FIRE

GASTLY

Height: 4'03" (1.3 m)
Weight: 0.2 lbs. (0.1 kg)

GHOST POISON

GENGAR

Height: 4'11" (1.5 m)
Weight: 89.3 lbs. (40.5 kg)

GHOST POISON

GEODUDE

Height: 1'04" (0.4 m)
Weight: 44.1 lbs. (20.0 kg)

ROCK GROUND

GLOOM

Height: 2'07" (0.8 m)
Weight: 19.0 lbs. (8.6 kg)

GRASS POISON

GOLBAT

Height: 5'03" (1.6 m)
Weight: 121.3 lbs. (55.0 kg)

POISON FLYING

GOLDEEN

Height: 2'00" (0.6 m)
Weight: 33.1 lbs. (15.0 kg)

WATER

GOLDUCK

Height: 5'07" (1.7 m)
Weight: 168.9 lbs. (76.6 kg)

WATER

GOLEM

Height: 4'07" (1.4 m)
Weight: 661.4 lbs. (300.0 kg)

ROCK GROUND

GRAVELER

Height: 3'03" (1.0 m)
Weight: 231.5 lbs. (105.0 kg)

ROCK GROUND

GRIMER

Height: 2'11" (0.9 m)
Weight: 66.1 lbs. (30.0 kg)

POISON

GROWLITHE

Height: 2'04" (0.7 m)
Weight: 41.9 lbs. (19.0 kg)

FIRE

GYARADOS

Height: 21'04" (6.5 m)
Weight: 518.1 lbs. (235.0 kg)

WATER FLYING

HAUNTER

HEIGHT: 5'03" (1.6 M)
Weight: 0.2 lbs. (0.1 kg)

GHOST POISON

HITMONCHAN

Height: 4'07" (1.4 m)
Weight: 110.7 lbs. (50.2 kg)

FIGHTING

HITMONLEE

Height: 4'11" (1.5 m)
Weight: 109.8 lbs. (49.8 kg)

FIGHTING

HORSEA

Height: 1'04" (0.4 m)
Weight: 17.6 lbs. (8.0 kg)

WATER

HYPNO

Height: 5'03" (1.6 m)
Weight: 166.7 lbs. (75.6 kg)

PSYCHIC

IVYSAUR

Height: 3'03" (1.0 m)
Weight: 28.7 lbs. (13.0 kg)

GRASS   POISON

JIGGLYPUFF

Height: 1'08" (0.5 m)
Weight: 12.1 lbs. (5.5 kg)

NORMAL   FAIRY

JOLTEON

Height: 2'07" (0.8 m)
Weight: 54.0 lbs. (24.5 kg)

ELECTRIC

JYNX

Height: 4'07" (1.4 m)
Weight: 89.5 lbs. (40.6 kg)

ICE   PSYCHIC

KABUTO

Height: 1'08" (0.5 m)
Weight: 25.4 lbs. (11.5 kg)

ROCK   WATER

KABUTOPS

Height: 4'03" (1.3 m)
Weight: 89.3 lbs. (40.5 kg)

ROCK   WATER

KADABRA

Height: 4'03" (1.3 m)
Weight: 124.6 lbs. (56.5 kg)

PSYCHIC

KAKUNA

Height: 2'00" (0.6 m)
Weight: 22.0 lbs. (10.0 kg)

BUG   POISON

KANGASKHAN

Height: 7'03" (2.2 m)
Weight: 176.4 lbs. (80.0 kg)

NORMAL

KINGLER

Height: 4'03" (1.3 m)
Weight: 132.3 lbs. (60.0 kg)

WATER

KOFFING

Height: 2'00" (0.6 m)
Weight: 2.2 lbs. (1.0 kg)

POISON

KRABBY

Height: 1'04" (0.4 m)
Weight: 14.3 lbs. (6.5 kg)

WATER

LAPRAS

Height: 8'02" (2.5 m)
Weight: 485.0 lbs. (220.0 kg)

WATER   ICE

LICKITUNG

Height: 3'11" (1.2 m)
Weight: 144.4 lbs. (65.5 kg)

NORMAL

MACHAMP

Height: 5'03" (1.6 m)
Weight: 286.6 lbs. (130.0 kg)

FIGHTING

MACHOKE

Height: 4'11" (1.5 m)
Weight: 155.4 lbs. (70.5 kg)

FIGHTING

MACHOP

Height: 2'07" (0.8 m)
Weight: 43.0 lbs. (19.5 kg)

FIGHTING

MAGIKARP

Height: 2'11" (0.9 m)
Weight: 22.0 lbs. (10.0 kg)

WATER

MAGMAR

Height: 4'03" (1.3 m)
Weight: 98.1 lbs. (44.5 kg)

FIRE

MAGNEMITE

Height: 1'00" (0.3 m)
Weight: 13.2 lbs. (6.0 kg)

ELECTRIC   STEEL

MAGNETON

Height: 3'03" (1.0 m)
Weight: 132.3 lbs. (60.0 kg)

ELECTRIC   STEEL

MANKEY

Height: 1'08" (0.5 m)
Weight: 61.7 lbs. (28.0 kg)

FIGHTING

MAROWAK

Height: 3'03" (1.0 m)
Weight: 99.2 lbs. (45.0 kg)

GROUND

MEOWTH

Height: 1'04" (0.4 m)
Weight: 9.3 lbs. (4.2 kg)

NORMAL

METAPOD

Height: 2'04" (0.7 m)
Weight: 21.8 lbs. (9.9 kg)

BUG

MEW

Height: 1'04" (0.4 m)
Weight: 8.8 lbs. (4.0 kg)

PSYCHIC

MEWTWO
Height: 6'07" (2.0 m)
Weight: 269.0 lbs. (122.0 kg)

PSYCHIC

MOLTRES

Height: 6'07" (2.0 m)
Weight: 132.3 lbs. (60.0 kg)

FIRE FLYING

MR. MIME
Height: 4'03" (1.3 m)
Weight: 120.1 lbs. (54.5 kg)

PSYCHIC FAIRY

MUK

Height: 3'11" (1.2 m)
Weight: 66.1 lbs. (30.0 kg)

POISON

NIDOKING

Height: 4'07" (1.4 m)
Weight: 136.7 lbs. (62.0 kg)

POISON GROUND

NIDOQUEEN

Height: 4'03" (1.3 m)
Weight: 132.3 lbs. (60.0 kg)

POISON GROUND

NIDORAN ♀
Height: 1'04" (0.4 m)
Weight: 15.4 lbs. (7.0 kg)

POISON

NIDORAN ♂

Height: 1'08" (0.5 m)
Weight: 19.8 lbs. (9.0 kg)

POISON

NIDORINA
Height: 2'07" (0.8 m)
Weight: 44.1 lbs. (20.0 kg)

POISON

NIDORINO

Height: 2'11" (0.9 m)
Weight: 43.0 lbs. (19.5 kg)

POISON

NINETALES

Height: 3'07" (1.1 m)
Weight: 43.9 lbs. (19.9 kg)

FIRE

ODDISH
Height: 1'08" (0.5 m)
Weight: 11.9 lbs. (5.4 kg)

GRASS POISON

OMANYTE

Height: 1'04" (0.4 m)
Weight: 16.5 lbs. (7.5 kg)

ROCK WATER

OMASTAR

Height: 3'03" (1.0 m)
Weight: 77.2 lbs. (35.0 kg)

ROCK WATER

ONIX
Height: 28'10" (8.8 m)
Weight: 463.0 lbs. (210.0 kg)

ROCK GROUND

PARAS
Height: 1'00" (0.3 m)
Weight: 11.9 lbs. (5.4 kg)

BUG GRASS

PARASECT

Height: 3'03" (1.0 m)
Weight: 65.0 lbs. (29.5 kg)

BUG GRASS

PERSIAN

Height: 3'03" (1.0 m)
Weight: 70.5 lbs. (32.0 kg)

NORMAL

PIDGEOT

Height: 4'11" (1.5 m)
Weight: 87.1 lbs. (39.5 kg)

NORMAL FLYING

PIDGEOTTO

Height: 3'07" (1.1 m)
Weight: 66.1 lbs. (30.0 kg)

NORMAL FLYING

PIDGEY

Height: 1'00" (0.3 m)
Weight: 4.0 lbs. (1.8 kg)

NORMAL FLYING

PIKACHU

Height: 1'04" (0.4 m)
Weight: 13.2 lbs. (6.0 kg)

ELECTRIC

PIKACHU BELLE

Height: 1'04" (0.4 m)
Weight: 13.2 lbs. (6.0 kg)

ELECTRIC

PIKACHU LIBRE

Height: 1'04" (0.4 m)
Weight: 13.2 lbs. (6.0 kg)

ELECTRIC

PIKACHU PHD

Height: 1'04" (0.4 m)
Weight: 13.2 lbs. (6.0 kg)

ELECTRIC

PIKACHU POP STAR

Height: 1'04" (0.4 m)
Weight: 13.2 lbs. (6.0 kg)

ELECTRIC

PIKACHU ROCK STAR
Height: 1'04" (0.4 m)
Weight: 13.2 lbs. (6.0 kg)

ELECTRIC

PINSIR

Height: 4'11" (1.5 m)
Weight: 121.3 lbs. (55.0 kg)

BUG

POLIWAG
Height: 2'00" (0.6 m)
Weight: 27.3 lbs. (12.4 kg)

WATER

POLIWHIRL

Height: 3'03" (1.0 m)
Weight: 44.1 lbs. (20.0 kg)

WATER

POLIWRATH

Height: 4'03" (1.3 m)
Weight: 119.0 lbs. (54.0 kg)

WATER | FIGHTING

PONYTA

Height: 3'03" (1.0 m)
Weight: 66.1 lbs. (30.0 kg)

FIRE

PORYGON

Height: 2'07" (0.8 m)
Weight: 80.5 lbs. (36.5 kg)

NORMAL

PRIMEAPE

Height: 3'03" (1.0 m)
Weight: 70.5 lbs. (32.0 kg)

FIGHTING

PSYDUCK
Height: 2'07" (0.8 m)
Weight: 43.2 lbs. (19.6 kg)

WATER

RAICHU

Height: 2'07" (0.8 m)
Weight: 66.1 lbs. (30.0 kg)

ELECTRIC

RAPIDASH

Height: 5'07" (1.7 m)
Weight: 209.4 lbs. (95.0 kg)

FIRE

RATICATE

Height: 2'04" (0.7 m)
Weight: 40.8 lbs. (18.5 kg)

NORMAL

RATTATA
Height: 1'00" (0.3 m)
Weight: 7.7 lbs. (3.5 kg)

NORMAL

RHYDON

Height: 6'03" (1.9 m)
Weight: 264.6 lbs. (120.0 kg)

GROUND | ROCK

RHYHORN
Height: 3'03" (1.0 m)
Weight: 253.5 lbs. (115.0 kg)

GROUND | ROCK

SANDSHREW

Height: 2'00" (0.6 m)
Weight: 26.5 lbs. (12.0 kg)

GROUND

SANDSLASH

Height: 3'03" (1.0 m)
Weight: 65.0 lbs. (29.5 kg)

GROUND

SCYTHER

Height: 4'11" (1.5 m)
Weight: 123.5 lbs. (56.0 kg)

BUG | FLYING

SEADRA

Height: 3'11" (1.2 m)
Weight: 55.1 lbs. (25.0 kg)

WATER

SEAKING
Height: 4'03" (1.3 m)
Weight: 86.0 lbs. (39.0 kg)

WATER

SEEL

Height: 3'07" (1.1 m)
Weight: 198.4 lbs. (90.0 kg)

WATER

SHELLDER

Height: 1'00" (0.3 m)
Weight: 8.8 lbs. (4.0 kg)

WATER

SLOWBRO

Height: 5'03" (1.6 m)
Weight: 173.1 lbs. (78.5 kg)

WATER | PSYCHIC

SLOWPOKE

Height: 3'11" (1.2 m)
Weight: 79.4 lbs. (36.0 kg)

WATER PSYCHIC

SNORLAX

Height: 6'11" (2.1 m)
Weight: 1014.1 lbs. (460.0 kg)

NORMAL

SPEAROW

Height: 1'00" (0.3 m)
Weight: 4.4 lbs. (2.0 kg)

NORMAL FLYING

SQUIRTLE

Height: 1'08" (0.5 m)
Weight: 19.8 lbs. (9.0 kg)

WATER

STARMIE

Height: 3'07" (1.1 m)
Weight: 176.4 lbs. (80.0 kg)

WATER PSYCHIC

STARYU

Height: 2'07" (0.8 m)
Weight: 76.1 lbs. (34.5 kg)

WATER

TANGELA

Height: 3'03" (1.0 m)
Weight: 77.2 lbs. (35.0 kg)

GRASS

TAUROS

Height: 4'07" (1.4 m)
Weight: 194.9 lbs. (88.4 kg)

NORMAL

TENTACOOL

Height: 2'11" (0.9 m)
Weight: 100.3 lbs. (45.5 kg)

WATER POISON

TENTACRUEL

Height: 5'03" (1.6 m)
Weight: 121.3 lbs. (55.0 kg)

WATER POISON

VAPOREON

Height: 3'03" (1.0 m)
Weight: 63.9 lbs. (29.0 kg)

WATER

VENOMOTH

Height: 4'11" (1.5 m)
Weight: 27.6 lbs. (12.5 kg)

BUG POISON

VENONAT

Height: 3'03" (1.0 m)
Weight: 66.1 lbs. (30.0 kg)

BUG POISON

VENUSAUR

Height: 6'07" (2.0 m)
Weight: 220.5 lbs. (100.0 kg)

GRASS POISON

VICTREEBEL

Height: 5'07" (1.7 m)
Weight: 34.2 lbs. (15.5 kg)

GRASS POISON

VILEPLUME

Height: 3'11" (1.2 m)
Weight: 41.0 lbs. (18.6 kg)

GRASS POISON

VOLTORB

Height: 1'08" (0.5 m)
Weight: 22.9 lbs. (10.4 kg)

ELECTRIC

VULPIX

Height: 2'00" (0.6 m)
Weight: 21.8 lbs. (9.9 kg)

FIRE

WARTORTLE

Height: 3'03" (1.0 m)
Weight: 49.6 lbs. (22.5 kg)

WATER

WEEDLE

Height: 1'00" (0.3 m)
Weight: 7.1 lbs. (3.2 kg)

BUG POISON

WEEPINBELL

Height: 3'03" (1.0 m)
Weight: 14.1 lbs. (6.4 kg)

GRASS POISON

WEEZING

Height: 3'11" (1.2 m)
Weight: 20.9 lbs. (9.5 kg)

POISON

WIGGLYTUFF

Height: 3'03" (1.0 m)
Weight: 26.5 lbs. (12.0 kg)

NORMAL FAIRY

ZAPDOS

Height: 5'03" (1.6 m)
Weight: 116.0 lbs. (52.6 kg)

ELECTRIC FLYING

ZUBAT

Height: 2'07" (0.8 m)
Weight: 16.5 lbs. (7.5 kg)

POISON FLYING

ORANGE ISLANDS

Everything is slightly different in the Orange Islands. From the Gym battles to the civil servants, Nurse Joy and Officer Jenny, the Orange Islands are a world away from the normalcy of the mainland. They are a large group of tropical islands (about 24 islands). Professor Ivy works in and around the Orange Islands.

There are many islands of interest. Kumquat Island is perhaps the most luxurious resort of the islands. Fantastic hotels, natural hot springs, and the pristine beaches make this island the top destination for anyone wanting rest and relaxation. The seven small islands in the Grapefruit Archipelago supply nearly all the grapefruit for the world regions. Sunburst Island is world famous for its glassblown works of art. The strange Meowth of Bounty worshippers of Golden Island mistake Team Rocket's Meowth for the one in prophecy. The largest island is Mandarin Island South; its largest principality is Trovitopolis—a large port on the western end of the island.

PROFESSOR IVY

Professor Ivy certainly doesn't resemble the other Pokémon Professors. She's young and very stylish. She also makes the briefest appearance of the other Professors. So what's Ivy's deal?

IVY LEAGUE

Professor Felina Ivy is the resident Professor of the Orange Islands. Since the island chain is so scattered, her research takes her to many of the distant land masses. She specializes in the physiological differences among Pokémon in the various regions. For example, she tries to determine why a Vileplume may look different on one island as opposed to another island.

BROCK'S MATCH

Brock decides that he wants to stay with Professor Ivy during the Orange Island journeys, but he appears back in Pallet Town during the reunion celebration. So what happened to his internship with Ivy? No one knows, but Brock responds with quaking, shaking fear every time her name is mentioned. "Don't mention that name!" is his only response.

Professor Ivy's swimsuit-clad figure and introduction to Ash and friends is certainly unique and most unProfessorlike. But like other Professors, she is very smart and an accomplished author: "Pokémon Adaptive Variations as a Function of Regional Distribution"

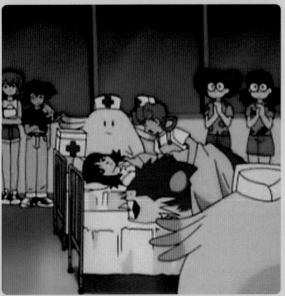

Professor Ivy's Researched Pokémon

GYARADOS

Ivy rides to shore on a Gyarados, which she seems to be very close to.

POLIWHIRL

When Professor Ivy is first introduced, Poliwhirl is in the lagoon.

VILEPLUME

The Vileplume on Valencia Island are somewhat different than the Vileplume in Ash's Pokédex. This is Ivy's field of study: the physical differences in Pokémon from different regions.

RATICATE

Ivy tries to save a Raticate that gets caught in Vileplume's spore-spreading defensive maneuvers. Unfortunately, Ivy pays the price and is hospitalized but they both recover.

MAGIKARP

What exactly is Ivy doing with the Magikarp in her lab? The hapless Magikarp has wires attached to it in several places.

BUTTERFREE

Butterfree is not eating well, which worries Professor Ivy. This is Brock's chance to shine, as he concocts a berry-enhanced bowl of food for the Butterfree to impress Professor Ivy.

TRACEY SKETCHIT

Tracey is fascinated by Pokémon but, unlike many Trainers, his goal isn't to win battles or catch lots of Pokémon. In contrast, he's a Pokémon watcher, one dedicated to the study and observation of Pokémon, plus he's a talented sketch artist to boot!

After Ash and Misty left Brock behind on Valencia Island with Professor Ivy, they ended up finding a new friend in Tracey Sketchit. Like Brock, Tracey plays the role of Pokémon expert and middle man during Ash and Misty's squabbles, but Tracey is notable for being easygoing—almost to a fault. His single-minded interest in Pokémon often renders him oblivious to everything else around him. Tracey walked straight into a battle between Ash and several nasty Trainers, unaware of the danger, in order to study and sketch their Pokémon.

Tracey is a typical Pokémon watcher, one of many people with a special interest in the study and observation of Pokémon. Because they spend so much time observing, good Pokémon watchers can judge a Pokémon's health and strength with just a visual inspection.

Tracey's no Brock, but he does take an interest in girls. He's just more likely to sketch an attractive girl like Cissy, the Mikan Island Gym Leader, than he is to actually approach one.

Tracey's Pokémon

VENONAT

Tracey's Venonat is more useful to him as a tracker than as a battler—he often uses its Radar Eye to locate things.

MARILL

Together with Venonat, Marill is great at helping Tracey track down whatever he's searching for. Its supersensitive hearing can track Pokémon and other targets.

SCYTHER

Scyther was the head of its swarm until it was deposed in a battle for leadership. Tracey found the old Scyther injured and alone, but Scyther didn't appreciate Tracey catching it so he could get it to a Pokémon Center. Now it gets along very well with Tracey, but Scyther is still touchy about its pride.

PROFESSOR OAK'S ASSISTANT

Tracey outright idolizes Professor Oak; as soon as he learned that Ash knew Professor Oak, he cheerfully declared himself to be Ash and Misty's new traveling companion.

After meeting the Professor in person, Tracey was nervous about the Professor's opinion of his work and too petrified to admit he wanted to be Professor Oak's assistant. Eventually, inspired by Ash's own determination, Tracey worked up enough courage to request a position as the Professor's assistant.

Now Tracey is anything but shy around Professor Oak. Not only does Tracey assist with research and care for the Pokémon on Professor Oak's ranch, he also keeps an eye on the Professor, prodding him to follow his own advice and eat regular meals.

ORANGE ISLAND LEAGUE

The Orange Islands were not meant to be so involved. Professor Oak asked Ash and friends to find out about the mysterious GS Ball, but they found a tropical paradise complete with new Pokémon, new friends, and new battles!

The Orange Island Gyms are centered more around contests of skill, not battles. The philosophy of the Orange League is that Pokémon Trainers must know all aspects of their Pokémon, not just their prowess on the battlefield.

MIKAN ISLAND GYM

GYM LEADER: SISSY

WATER GUN CHALLENGE
Seadra uses Water Gun and knocks out the cans with ease, as does Ash's Squirtle. When they move on to moving targets, both Pokémon excel. The match ends in a draw.

POKÉMON WAVE RIDE
With Sissy using Blastoise and Ash using Lapras, this relay turns into a hotly contested race for the finish line. Ash gets creative when he has Lapras use an Ice Beam and skids into first place, earning his Coral-Eye Badge.

NAVEL ISLAND GYM

GYM LEADER: DANNY

Geyser Freezing: Danny sends out Nidoqueen to compete against Ash's Lapras, but the Ice Beam attack Ash uses hits Nidoqueen.

Ice Sculpting: Ash calls out Pikachu, Bulbasaur, and Charizard to carve out an ice sculpture. Charizard starts to snooze again, but rouses itself and with Flamethrower, sculpts an awesome ice-luge, winning the round.

Race: Ash and Danny now have to race to the goal line from the icy mountaintop to the beach, with their Pokémon as passengers. It looks like Danny is about to win, when suddenly Ash and his team charge from the bushes and take the lead. Ash earns the Sea Ruby Badge.

TROVITA ISLAND GYM

GYM LEADER: RUDY

RUDY VS. **ASH**
The two Electric-types go at it, but Electabuzz handily defeats Pikachu's electric attacks, absorbing their power. Electabuzz uses Quick Attack and ThunderPunch with devastating results.

 RUDY VS. **ASH**
The battle of the Grass-types starts with Bulbasaur using Razor Leaf, but the dancing, prancing Exeggutor deftly avoids it. When Exeggutor uses Egg Bomb, Bulbasaur counters with Sleep Powder and the match goes to Ash.

 RUDY VS. **ASH**
Starmie has an Electric-type attack up its sleeve, but luckily, Squirtle learns Hydro Pump and takes Starmie out. Ash wins the Spike Shell Badge.

KUMQUAT ISLAND GYM

GYM LEADER: LUANA

LUANA   VS. **ASH**

You know things don't look good when the two teammates start frying and electrocuting each other before the battle starts. At the beginning, Pikachu refuses to help its teammate out. However, Pikachu comes around and saves Charizard from utter defeat. Marowak tries to deliver a Body Slam to Pikachu, but Charizard catches it, saving Pikachu. Suddenly working like a well-oiled machine, Pikachu and Charizard combine Thunderbolt and Flamethrower to defeat Luana's team, scoring the Jade Star Badge.

ORANGE LEAGUE FINALS

GYM LEADER: DRAKE

DRAKE VS. **ASH**
Ditto is an interesting choice for Drake. It simply transforms its opponent's strengths into its own. In the end, Pikachu uses Quick Attack against Ditto, and when Ditto falls, Pikachu shocks it into submission.

DRAKE VS. **ASH**
Rock-types are strong against electrical attacks, so Ash recalls Pikachu and sends out Squirtle. Drake is no slouch—when Squirtle uses Water Gun, Onix digs underground. Squirtle uses its newly learned Hydro Pump attack and knocks Onix out.

DRAKE VS. **ASH**
When Gengar Confuses Tauros, Ash uses Lapras. Lapras avoids Gengar's Hypnosis, then uses its Water Gun attack. The match ends in a dramatic draw with both Pokémon knocked out.

DRAKE VS. **ASH**
Ash sends out Tauros once again, and this time Drake sends out Venusaur. The field changes, and the Trainers are now on sandy ground. Tauros' first attack, Fissure, misfires, and Venusaur counters with SolarBeam, but Tauros uses Take Down to knock Venusaur out.

DRAKE VS. **ASH**
A Thundershock does little, but Electabuzz follows it up with ThunderPunch and Bulbasaur goes flying. Electabuzz easily defeats Bulbasaur.

DRAKE VS. **ASH**
Electabuzz tries to devastate Charizard with its ThunderPunch, followed by Thunder. Charizard uses Ember, and when Electabuzz tries to use Thunderbolt, Charizard takes it out with Seismic Toss.

DRAKE   VS. **ASH**
The mighty Dragonite seems like a formidable opponent, and when Charizard uses Flamethrower, Dragonite counters with Water Gun, which is super-effective. As both Pokémon fly, it is obvious that Dragonite possesses superior aerial skills, and takes Charizard out.

The Final Battle

Ash uses two of his last three Pokémon to tire Dragonite out. When Squirtle bravely tries and fails to take Dragonite out, Tauros comes in and weakens Dragonite further. When Tauros goes down, it's up to little Pikachu to finish Dragonite out, and it does, with a well-placed Thunderbolt to the head. Dragonite goes down. Ash is the new champion of the Orange League!

JOHTO

Johto is a very large area. Home of Professor Elm, Johto seems more eco-friendly than other regions; a region of wide forest dominates the landscape of Johto.

Johto is connected to Kanto in a couple ways: there is a ship that runs from Olivine City to Vermilion City, and a speed train runs from Saffron City to the mammoth Goldenrod City. Goldenrod City is a monstrous sprawling city: one of the largest cities in the world. Ash, Brock, and Misty get lost inside the urban sprawl; they find that even residents of Goldenrod City have trouble getting around, because many of the streets are dead ends.

Johto has other attractions: the Whirl Islands' Whirl Cup, Mahogany Town's ninja, and Ecruteak City's ancient history.In ancient times, Ho-Oh lived in a tower in Ecruteak City, but war came and the tower was burned down. During its destruction Entei, Raikou, and Suicune were created.

PROFESSOR ELM

Professor Elm is a nerdy, timid person who loves the sound of his own voice. He is still respected by others and his contributions to the Johto region are welcomed by all the Trainers.

He is also an author of the book *A Brilliant Analysis of the Hypersized Communicative Faculties of Pokémon.*

Professor Elm was at the top of his class and a favorite of Professor Oak's. He often argues with the Professor over research, but he still respects and admires Professor Oak greatly.

Professor Elm's lab is located in New Bark Town. The lab is spotless (unlike Professor Ivy's), but Elm spends so much time there you have to wonder what his living quarters look like. It's also one of the bigger labs used by the various Professors.

AS THE WHIRL TURNS

Professor Elm catches up with Ash and his friend and reveals some background information about the Whirl Islands. He also tells them about the Whirl Cup, a Water-type Pokémon competition, and provides a researcher's-eye view of Corsola.

ELM'S EGG-SCITING HOBBIES

Professor Elm is the head of the Pokémon Preservation Council and, as one of his duties, he asks Ash and his friends to bring back an Egg from the Pokémon Marine Conservatory. This Egg eventually hatches into a Larvitar.

Professor Elm's Pokémon

CORSOLA

Although it only appears briefly in the Whirl Islands. Misty sees it and wants one, too!

TOTODILE

Professor Elm hands out the First Partner Pokémon in Johto. Plus, we learn that he gave a Totodile to Marina, a young Trainer.

CHIKORITA

Professor Elm bestows a Chikorita to Vincent, another young Trainer. This is also the First Partner Pokémon he gives to Casey.

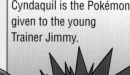

CYNDAQUIL

Cyndaquil is the Pokémon given to the young Trainer Jimmy.

CASEY

When Ash and Casey first met, Casey was a novice Trainer who challenged Ash to a battle after an argument over baseball. Ash smugly used Charizard to crush her, a defeat that brought her to tears—but the Electabuzz Baseball Team never gives up, and neither does their number one fan.

Casey is a Pokémon Trainer, but she thinks of herself first and foremost as a third-generation Electabuzz fan. She holds and throws a Poké Ball like a baseball, she swings a mean bat, and she talks in nonstop baseball references even when there's no one around to hear her or her enthusiastic rendition of the Electabuzz fight song.

She takes defeat hard but even when she's down, she's not out; her fighting Electabuzz spirit usually has her back up and swinging in no time. Casey's competitive streak can get the better of her, although she learned a valuable lesson when she pushed Chikorita too hard while trying to beat Ash in a Pokémon Bug Catching contest.

Her Dream Team is Beedrill, Elekid, Electabuzz, and Pikachu: four yellow Pokémon with stripes, an homage to the Electabuzz team colors.

Casey's Pokémon

BEEDRILL

MEGANIUM

PIDGEY

ELEKID

RATTATA

SAKURA

Sakura longed to go on a Pokémon journey, but her four older sisters were reluctant to grant permission.

When Ash and his friends met Sakura in Ecrutreak City, she was a sweet but meek young girl. That was hardly surprising, since she lived in the shadow of four older sisters—Satsuki, Sumomo, Tamao, and Koume, the Four Beautiful Tea Ceremony Sisters. They told Sakura she's not included in that count because she's not beautiful.

Sakura and Misty are particularly good friends; both know all too well how it feels to be invisible while their older sisters get all the attention.

Despite their teasing, Sakura's sisters love her and don't want her to leave home until she's ready. She almost decided to travel with Misty and the gang, but decided to stay home until she was strong enough to travel on her own. The second time Misty sees her in Ecruteak City, Sakura's Eevee is an Espeon and Sakura is tough enough to take on Team Rocket. It's clear to everyone how much Sakura has grown, and she finally gets to depart on her own solo journey.

Sakura's Pokémon

ESPEON

BEAUTIFLY

TEAM ROCKET'S MACHINES

Villains can be lonely people; sometimes they need a helping hand when pulling off their dastardly schemes. Unfortunately, Jessie and James used to be bumbling, ineffectual knuckleheads who couldn't pour water out of a shoe if the directions were on the heel. Somehow, though, they managed to create the most elaborate, nefarious contraptions in their spare time. Thankfully, they seem to have become more competent. These are just a few of their crazy inventions.

THE MEOWTH BALLOON

Incredibly unsafe and easily destroyed, this is Team Rocket's most identifiable mode of transportation. It often is modified with some sort of resistance, but never enough to keep them from blasting off. The balloon usually has the ability to capture Pikachu or other unsuspecting Pokémon through the use of an extendable clamping hand, or an electric-proof net. Though they are never able to fully trick-out the Meowth balloon, it is a sturdy, eco-friendly reminder of just how persistent Jessie and James are.

ROBOT BUILDING

Upset from getting ripped off in another Team Rocket get-rich-quick scheme, a large mob surrounds the building in which they're located. With just a single button press, though, the building sprouts legs and arms and walks away. When they use the building in an attempt to capture Pokémon, however, some accurate attacks by Harrison and Ash destroy the building.

ARBO TANK

In their never-ending quest to show Giovanni how intelligent they are, Team Rocket has a bright idea: use a multi-ton tank as a getaway car! Still, not even Jessie and James could foresee Togepi and Sentret's takeover and subsequent joy ride inside their tank.

MAGIKARP SUBMARINE

This submarine is the primary mode of underwater transportation for Team Rocket. Pedal-powered, James and Meowth often pick up the slack for a plotting Jessie.

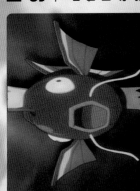

POKÉMON MECHAS

A number of mechas have been created and used by Team Rocket over the years. For example, as the crew discovers a wild Buneary, Team Rocket also finds it. They soon construct a wild and partially effective mech to battle our friends. The machine is resistant to electricity (sorry, Pikachu!) and has extendable claws that it uses to catch Pokémon, along with containers to store them. What it doesn't have is a warranty and, eventually, it needs one.

JOHTO GYM BATTLES!

The Johto region proved to be an extensive trek for Ash and his friends. Numerous side adventures didn't deter Ash from getting his required eight badges to compete in the Johto League Championships. Fresh from his Orange Islands triumph, Ash proves once again that he is on the road to becoming a Pokémon Master.

VIOLET CITY GYM

GYM LEADER: FAULKNER

FAULKNER VS. ASH

Chikorita is definitely at a disadvantage against the Flying-type, Hoothoot, but it holds its own fairly well. In the end Hoothoot goes into a top-speed Tackle attack combo, and it's game over for Chikorita.

FAULKNER VS. ASH

Faulkner calls out Dodrio. Dodrio's Drill Peck followed by its Tri-Attack almost does Pikachu in, but Pikachu's Thunder attack ends the round with a win for Ash.

FAULKNER VS. ASH

The battle against Hoothoot is short and sweet, ending after one Thunderbolt. Hoothoot never even had a chance.

FAULKNER VS. ASH

Faulkner takes out his last Pokémon, but Pikachu needs a break. It gamely tries to use Thunderbolt, but Pikachu is discharged and Pidgeot's Whirlwind attack takes it out.

FAULKNER VS. ASH

The match begins with both Pokémon taking to the air. Charizard uses Flamethrower, but Pidgeot uses Whirlwind to send the flames back. Charizard is injured and the match looks over, but Charizard comes through in the end and defeats Pigeot. Ash earns the Zephyr Badge.

GOLDENROD CITY GYM

GYM LEADER: WHITNEY

WHITNEY VS. ASH

Cyndaquil uses Tackle, but gets smashed repeatedly. It looks like Ash is going for a repeat of his earlier loss to Whitney.

WHITNEY VS. ASH

Totodile digs huge trenches in the ground using its Water Gun attack. Miltank is befuddled and just as Totodile is about to deliver the final blow, Ash recalls it.

WHITNEY VS. ASH

Pikachu hides in the trenches created by Totodile, and when Miltank gets stuck Pikachu slams it into the air. A full power Thunderbolt knocks Miltank out, earning Ash the Plain Badge.

ECRUTEAK CITY GYM

GYM LEADER: MORTY

MORTY VS. ASH

Noctowl uses its Foresight, and follows up with Tackle. Gastly hits Noctowl with Lick, but Ash recalls Noctowl now that Gastly has been revealed.

MORTY VS. ASH

Haunter is faster than Gastly, and uses Mean Look, which forces Ash to stay with Cyndaquil until the end of the match. Cyndaquil uses Swift, then SmokeScreen to counter the Hypnosis but Hanuter grabs it out of the smoke and ends the round with Lick.

MORTY VS. ASH

Using Quick Attack, Pikachu gains a slight advantage, but after Gastly dodges its Thunderbolt, it counters with Night Shade and knocks Pikachu out.

MORTY VS. ASH

Noctowl uses Hypnosis, but is hit with Haunter's Confuse Ray. It decides to battle on, and takes Haunter down with a well-placed Tackle attack. It also learns Confusion.

MORTY VS. ASH

The weakened Gastly tries Night Shade again, but Cyndaquil dodges it, and uses Tackle to defeat it.

MORTY VS. ASH

Gengar is twice as fast as Haunter. Noctowl uses its newly learned Confusion, while Gengar uses Night Shade. Ash has Noctowl use Confusion through the whole Gym in order to pinpoint Gengar, then uses Tackle to win the round. Ash earns the Fog Badge.

AZALEA TOWN GYM

GYM LEADER: BUGSY

BUGSY VS. ASH

The Fire-type Cyndaquil should be a no-brainer, but Cyndaquil is cold and its fire fails to ignite. Ash is forced to reevaluate the fight, and he recalls it.

BUGSY VS. ASH

Pikachu comes out swinging; Metapod tries Tackle, but Pikachu's speed and agility are too much. A well-placed Thunderbolt wins the round for Ash.

BUGSY VS. ASH

Chikorita then uses Sweet Smell in conjunction with Tackle and takes Spinarak down.

BUGSY VS. ASH

Scyther is a formidable opponent. Pikachu's Agility is no match for Scyther's speed. Scyther's Fury Cutter does Pikachu in.

BUGSY VS. ASH

Cyndaquil is Ash's last hope. Scyther tries to end the match with Fury Cutter, but Cyndaquil dodges and its fire comes back. Scyther uses Swords Dance, but Ash is able to get Cyndaquil above Scyther, blasting it through the open space above. Ash earns the Hive Badge.

CIANWOOD CITY GYM

GYM LEADER: CHUCK

CHUCK VS. **ASH**

Ash's assessment of the battle is partially right: Poliwrath is somewhat susceptible to Electric-type attacks. But the round goes sour when Poliwrath is relentless in its attacks.

CHUCK VS. **ASH**

Poliwrath uses Water Gun, which misses. Bayleef comes back with Razor Leaf, ending the round with a constricting Vine Whip and a Body Slam.

CHUCK VS. **ASH**

Machoke smacks Bayleef around, using Cross Chop against Bayleef's Vine Whip. During the tug-of-war with the Vine Whip, Ash decides to go toe-to-toe with Chuck's Pokémon, and Ash's confidence in Bayleef provides inspiration. It stays focused and tosses Machoke, ending the match with a Body Slam and Razor Leaf attack. Ash earns his Storm Badge.

MAHOGANY TOWN GYM

GYM LEADER: PRYCE

PRYCE VS. **ASH**

Dewgong tries to freeze Cyndaquil with an Ice Beam, but the flame on Cyndaquil's back melts the ice! Pryce sends Dewgong underwater. Cyndaquil follows with Swift, then Flamethrower, knocking Dewgong out.

PRYCE VS. **ASH**

Cyndaquil tries Flamethrower, but Piloswine uses Blizzard to freeze the pool of ice, and finishes Cyndaquil with a Take Down.

PRYCE VS. **ASH**

Pikachu comes out next, but the slippery surface proves tough for Pikachu. Ash realizes that the ice is a problem, so he changes his strategy. Pikachu eventually slides under Piloswine and uses Thunder to weaken it. Pryce is afraid of hurting Piloswine, and throws in the towel, giving the Glacier Badge to Ash.

OLIVINE CITY GYM

GYM LEADER: JASMINE

JASMINE VS. **ASH**

Pikachu starts the party with Thunderbolt, which Magnemite easily avoids. Pikachu finally lets Magnemite hit it with Thunder Wave, and after absorbing the hit, uses Quick Attack to knock Magnemite out.

JASMINE VS. **ASH**

Pikachu is ineffective against Steelix. Pikachu's speed is a problem for Steelix, but after a short time a very tired Pikachu is knocked out with Iron Tail.

JASMINE VS. **ASH**

Cyndaquil uses Flamethrower right from the get-go, but Steelix uses Sandstorm and digs itself underground. After nearly getting knocked out, Cyndaquil superheats Steelix's Sandstorm and melts Steelix into a defeat. Ash earns the Mineral Badge.

BLACKTHORN CITY GYM

GYM LEADER: CLAIR

CLAIR VS. **ASH**

Snorlax starts with Hyper Beam, which Kingdra dodges. Snorlax wears Kingdra out, and ends the round with an Ice Punch.

CLAIR VS. **ASH**

Clair sends out Gyarados next, and the two exchange Hydro Pump and Hyper Beams. But Gyarados paralyzes Snorlax with its DragonBreath, and before Snorlax has a chance to snap out of it, Gyarados' Hyper Beam takes Snorlax out.

CLAIR VS. **ASH**

Gyarados leaves the water and attempts to use Bite on Pikachu, but Pikachu's Agility allows it to ride Gyardos' incoming Hydro Pump! The water intensifies Pikachu's Thunderbolt, leaving Gyarados unable to continue the battle.

CLAIR VS. **ASH**

Clair goes with Dragonair as her third and final Pokémon. All it takes is one Hyper Beam to knock Pikachu out.

CLAIR VS. **ASH**

Charizard is Ash's last hope. The playing field changes to an earth, wind, and fire environment. Charizard uses Flamethrower, while Dragonair ducks underwater and uses Hyper Beam. Fire Spin evaporates all the water in the arena, leaving the earth and sky as Dragonair's only refuge. Charizard uses a Seismic Toss/Fire Spin combo to knock out Dragonair, giving Ash the victory and the Rising Badge.

WHIRL CUP COMPETITION

There are other tournaments that specialize in a single type of Pokémon, but the Whirl Cup's history makes it something special. Held only once every three years, this Water-type Pokémon tournament is infused with the Whirl Islands' age-old traditions.

The Whirl Cup is six days of intense competition that will crown one Trainer as the Water Pokémon Alpha Omega, a title that legend says was once held by expert Water-type Pokémon Trainers who lived underwater. The winner also receives a Mystic Water Pendant, which can power up Water-type Pokémon attacks.

Water-type Pokémon have always been a vital part of life in the Whirl Islands. At the start of the Whirl Cup, Maya, the Sea Priestess who presides over the event, uses the Sea Spirit orb on the end of her staff to call forth the energy of all Water-type Pokémon. She also closes the Whirl Cup by using the Sea Spirit to invoke the harmony between people and Water-type Pokémon.

The Whirl Islands

The Whirl Islands are a chain of islands located in the sea between Johto's Cianwood City and Olivine City. From north to south, its four main islands are Silver Rock Isle, Red Rock Isle, Yellow Rock Isle, and the largest, Blue Point Isle.

Registration for the preliminaries takes place in Scarlet City's Pokémon Center, located on a cliff outside the city. Competitors can also bunk at the Pokémon Center during the competition.

Preliminary matches take place at different stadiums—although "stadiums" may be a grand word to describe these bare-bones match facilities.

The coliseum for the finals is just up the coast from the Pokémon Center. Open to the sea on one side and adjacent to classical-looking ruins, it's a setting that captures the Whirl Islands' history and ties to the sea. The first round of the finals is all 1-on-1 battles, while later rounds are 2-on-2.

WHIRL CUP RESULTS

FIRST ROUND (1-ON-1 BATTLES)

Ash and Totodile defeat Christopher and Kingdra.

Christopher

Christopher, a natural showman, likes to make an entrance by using a fishing rod to cast his Lure Ball into the water and release his Kingdra.

THIRD ROUND (2-ON-2 BATTLES)

Trinity uses Gyarados and Chinchou to defeat Misty's Poliwhirl and Corsola.

Trinity

Elegantly composed and always sportsmanlike, Trinity's poise and experience wins Misty's admiration as well as their match.

Poliwhirl's quick defeat leaves Corsola with two opponents to battle. It beats Gyarados, but can't evade the attacks of Trinity's Chinchou.

FIRST ROUND (1-ON-1 BATTLES)

Misty and Corsola defeat Harrison and Qwilfish.

Harrison

Harrison is a knowledgable Trainer, but he doesn't know what to do when his Qwilfish gets stuck in Corsola's horns during the match.

FINALS

Semifinal Match: Trinity and Golduck defeat an unknown opponent.

Final Match: A male Trainer and his Feraligatr defeat Trinity's Golduck and win the Whirl Cup.

SECOND ROUND (2-ON-2 BATTLES)

Misty uses Poliwhirl and Psyduck to defeat Ash's Totodile and Kingler.

Misty plans to use Corsola as her second Pokémon, but Psyduck lets itself out instead. Things look grim until Kingler uses ViceGrip on Psyduck's head, which triggers Psyduck's Confusion attack.

THINK GREEN

A major Pokémon theme is the importance of nature and, just as importantly, balance. Preservation of the environment is portrayed as a good thing, but without condemnation of humanity, people can live in cities, manufacture goods, and mine coal as long as they're also considerate of the natural world around them. This underlying message is presented in several different ways, some explicit, some implicit.

NATURE WILL DEFEND ITS OWN

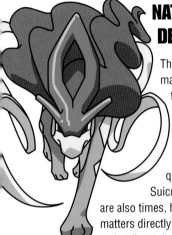

The Pokémon world has one major safeguard to fall back on: the Pokémon themselves. Some Pokémon can use their powers to protect or repair the environment; Celebi can use vines to quench a forest fire, while Suicune can purify water. There are also times, however, when Pokémon take matters directly into their own appendages and strike at threats to their natural habitat.

GETTING EVERYONE TO PITCH IN

No matter how bad things get, Pokémon has a message of hope: through hard work and dedication to the environment, things can be turned around. This message conveys an emphasis on direct personal action, because in the Pokémon world environmental protection is a task that often falls upon the individual, rather than the largely unseen government or any expectation that future technology will fix humanity's errors.

PORTRAYING THE WONDER OF NATURE

An ecological message can be more than just a reminder to preserve the environment—it's also important for people to understand why nature should be preserved. It should come as no surprise, then, that Pokémon depicts the nature world and its marvels as worthy of sincere appreciation.

When Ash first met his Pokémon pal Treecko, it was struggling to save the tree where it lived. Ash and Pikachu immediately chipped in to help, but the tree was beyond saving. Although the tree died, it left behind a seed for the future and a vision for Ash and Treecko, an eloquent sequence that shows the cycles of nature and reminds the viewer that even a tree's life has importance.

CASE STUDY: LAKE LUCID

These days, Johto's Lake Lucid, a body of crystal-clear water surrounded by trees, is a haven for Water-type Pokémon. Lake Lucid wasn't always this way; pollution devastated the lake and it took decades of dedicated effort to restore the environment to good health.

Lake Lucid then: About 50 years ago, the lake was a toxic wonderland filled with pollution from factories and nearby towns. When Nurse Joy studied the lake, she didn't wear a gas mask and overalls just for looks—it was so dirty that even Muk wouldn't live there!

Lake Lucid now: With water so clean and clear that it's a haven for recuperating Water-type Pokémon, Lake Lucid is unrecognizable as the wasteland it was some 50 years ago. Even now, the lake is still protected by a watchful Nurse Joy—the granddaughter of the first Nurse Joy who worked to save the lake.

JOHTO SILVER CONFERENCE

This is what every Trainer in Johto dreams of: the Johto Silver Conference in Silver Town. To get here, a Trainer must earn eight Johto Gym Badges, but even that doesn't guarantee a spot in the Silver Conference tournament.

Silver Stadium lies at the heart of Silver Town, which is—unsurprisingly—not far from Mt. Silver.

Competitors stay in the well-appointed Athlete's Village, where rooms feature lake views and computer terminals with information on all the participating Trainers.

JOHTO SILVER CONFERENCE RULES

- FOR EVERY BATTLE, A COMPUTER RANDOMLY DETERMINES WHICH TRAINER WILL SEND OUT HIS OR HER POKÉMON FIRST.
- ALTHOUGH SPARRING IS PERMITTED, YOU MAY LOSE POINTS OR BE DISQUALIFIED IF YOUR POKÉMON ARE CAUGHT FIGHTING WHILE THE TOURNAMENT IS BEING HELD.
- THE SILVER CONFERENCE CONSISTS OF THE FOLLOWING THREE STAGES:
- THE ATHLETE SCREENING ROUND (1-ON-1 BATTLES)
- ROUND-ROBIN ROUND (3-ON-3 BATTLES)
- VICTORY TOURNAMENT (6-ON-6 BATTLES)

SILVER CONFERENCE STAGES

ATHLETE SCREENING ROUNDS

Before any Trainer can step foot in an actual stadium, he or she must make it past the athlete screening battles. These are held in small, barebones courts where Trainers compete in three 1-on-1 battles. A single loss doesn't automatically disqualify a Trainer from moving on to the next round, but the competition is tough—this stage reduces the number of Trainers from over 200 to just 48.

OPENING CEREMONIES

After the athlete screening round, the remaining 48 Trainers enter Silver Stadium for the opening ceremonies, which also marks the end of the torch run bringing Ho-Oh's Sacred Flame from the Ho-Oh Shrine to Silver Town.

The torch bearer is injured by a collision with Team Rocket just as he enters Silver Stadium and Ash carries the torch in his place. The flame is the symbol of the Silver Conference and nothing can get underway until the Stadium's main torch is lit!

ROUND ROBIN SEMIFINAL

The 48 Trainers who pass the initial screening are then sorted into groups of three for a series of 3-on-3 battles. Each Trainer fights the other Trainers in their group once and only the Trainer with the most points will advance. A win earns 3 points, a draw is 1 point, and a loss is 0 points. After completion of the semifinals, there's a vacation day to allow Trainers to prepare for the Victory Tournament.

VICTORY TOURNAMENT

The Victory Tournament is what it all comes down to: 16 Trainers and full-on, 6-on-6 battles in front of a packed stadium. The battlefield can rotate between four different types (Grass, Rock, Water, and Ice) and a computer randomly selects the type at the beginning of each match.

VICTORY TOURNAMENT, FINAL 16

Ash defeats Gary on the Rock Field.

The battle between Ash and Gary comes down to Charizard versus Blastoise. Blastoise uses Rapid Spin to deflect Charizard's Flamethrower attack. In the end, Charizard edges out Blastoise through physical might.

ASH'S POKÉMON	GARY'S POKÉMON
Tauros	Nidoqueen
Heracross	Magmar
Muk	Blastoise
Bayleef	Arcanine
Snorlax	Scizor
Charizard	Golem

VICTORY TOURNAMENT, FINAL 8

Harrison defeats Ash on the Grass Field.

Ash's powerhouse, Charizard, takes on Harrison's equally tough Blaziken, a novel Pokémon in this competition. Blaziken manages to endure just a bit more than Charizard, securing Harrison the win.

ASH'S POKÉMON	HARRISON'S POKÉMON
Pikachu	Kecleon
Totodile	Sneasel
Snorlax	Hypno
Noctowl	Steelix
Bayleef	Houndoom
Charizard	Blaziken

Harrison

Harrison, from Hoenn's Littleroot Town, is a good-natured Trainer who is one of Ash's friendlier rivals. He even helped cover for Ash after Ash's Squirtle and Bulbasaur were caught fighting outside of a tournament match, a big Silver Conference no-no. The two Trainers first met at the Ho-Oh Shrine, where Harrison caught a Sneasel that was blocking access to Ho-Oh's Sacred Flame. After his Silver Conference run ended, Harrison told Ash about Hoenn and the inspirational Professor Birch, setting the stage for Ash's next big Pokémon journey.

VICTORY TOURNAMENT, FINAL MATCH

Jon Dickson of Sento Cherry Town defeats Harrison and wins the Silver Conference.

Jon Dickson ends Harrison's winning streak, but Jon may have had an advantage since Harrison chose not to use his Blaziken. Harrison probably decided to give Blaziken a rest after its grueling fight with Ash's Charizard.

JOHTO LEGENDARY POKÉMON

ENTEI • (EN-tay)

Height	6'11" (2.1 m)
Weight	436.5 lbs (198.0 kg)
Category	Volcano
Type	Fire

Entei embodies the passion of magma, and is thought to have been born in the eruption of a volcano. One of the three Legendary Trio, Entei has an intimidating and powerful presence.

Entei is physically powerful; its fiery red frame constantly smokes, adding another layer to its amazing mane. Its Fire-type attacks are to be respected and feared; its flames are hotter than a volcano's magma.

HO-OH • (HOE-oh)

Height	12'06" (3.8 m)
Weight	438.7 lbs (199.0 kg)
Category	Rainbow
Type	Fire-Flying

A mysterious, magnificent bird, its feathers, which bring happiness, are a breathtaking array of seven different colors, which vary depending on the angle from which they are struck by light. This unique feather has a secondary effect: a rainbow follows Ho-Oh whenever it flies.

One of the most rare Legendary Pokémon, it could be that Ho-Oh is a singular Pokémon that has existed for generations. Considered to be the guardian of the sky, Ho-Oh has vast ancient powers.

LUGIA
• (LOO-gee-uh)

Height	17'01" (5.2 m)
Weight	476.2 lbs (216.0 kg)
Category	Diving
Type	Psychic-Flying

The great guardian of the sea, Lugia's presence brings balance to the weather. Tied to the Titan Trio in mysterious ways, it can create and calm storms at will. Lugia's wings pack devastating power—a light fluttering of its wings can blow apart regular houses.

Capable of telepathic communication, Lugia is both kind and intelligent. It remains secluded from humanity, not because it fears them but because it fears harming them. This fear is well founded, as Lugia possess such incredible power over the winds and weather, it could easily ravage human civilization. Unlike most Legendary Pokémon, Lugia has been seen with its offspring.

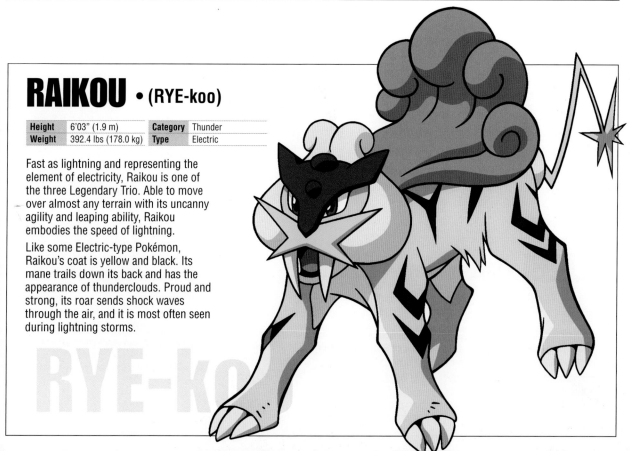

RAIKOU • (RYE-koo)

Height	6'03" (1.9 m)	Category	Thunder
Weight	392.4 lbs (178.0 kg)	Type	Electric

Fast as lightning and representing the element of electricity, Raikou is one of the three Legendary Trio. Able to move over almost any terrain with its uncanny agility and leaping ability, Raikou embodies the speed of lightning.

Like some Electric-type Pokémon, Raikou's coat is yellow and black. Its mane trails down its back and has the appearance of thunderclouds. Proud and strong, its roar sends shock waves through the air, and it is most often seen during lightning storms.

SUICUNE • (SWEE-koon)

Height	6'07" (2.0 m)
Weight	412.3 lbs (187.0 kg)
Category	Aurora
Type	Water

The first of the Legendary Trio, Suicune represents the element of Ice. It also has unparalleled restorative powers; tears from a Suicune are said to have the ability to purify any water.

Like all the Legendary Trio, Suicune lives a secluded existence. It embodies the compassion of a pure spring, often helping those in dire need. Accompanied by the north wind, Suicune's most unique features are the two streamer-like appendages that run up the length of its body.

JOHTO MYTHICAL POKÉMON

CELEBI • (SEL-ih-bee)

Height	2'00" (0.6 m)	**Category**	Time Travel
Weight	11.0 lbs (5.0 kg)	**Type**	Psychic-Grass

Celebi is the spirit of the forest. A protector of nature and the environment, Celebi came from the future by crossing over time. As long as it appears, a bright and shining future awaits us.

Highly sought after by poachers because of its ability to manipulate time, Celebi's handling of time is at the heart of the strange relationship between Professor Oak and Ash Ketchum.

JOHTO POKÉMON

This region is full of surprising new characters—and especially fierce ones, like Tyranitar, Ursaring, and Lugia!

AIPOM

Height: 2'07" (0.8 m)
Weight: 25.4 lbs. (11.5 kg)

NORMAL

AMPHAROS

Height: 4'07" (1.4 m)
Weight: 135.6 lbs. (61.5 kg)

ELECTRIC

ARIADOS

Height: 3'07" (1.1 m)
Weight: 73.9 lbs. (33.5 kg)

BUG | POISON

AZUMARILL

Height: 2'07" (0.8 m)
Weight: 62.8 lbs. (28.5 kg)

WATER | FAIRY

BAYLEEF

Height: 3'11" (1.2 m)
Weight: 34.8 lbs. (15.8 kg)

GRASS

BELLOSSOM

HEIGHT: 1'04" (0.4 M)
Weight: 12.8 lbs. (5.8 kg)

GRASS

BLISSEY

Height: 4'11" (1.5 m)
Weight: 103.2 lbs. (46.8 kg)

NORMAL

CELEBI

Height: 2'00" (0.6 m)
Weight: 11.0 lbs. (5.0 kg)

PSYCHIC | GRASS

CHIKORITA

Height: 2'11" (0.9 m)
Weight: 14.1 lbs. (6.4 kg)

GRASS

CHINCHOU

Height: 1'08" (0.5 m)
Weight: 26.5 lbs. (12.0 kg)

WATER | ELECTRIC

CLEFFA

Height: 1'00" (0.3 m)
Weight: 6.6 lbs. (3.0 kg)

FAIRY

CORSOLA

Height: 2'00" (0.6 m)
Weight: 11.0 lbs. (5.0 kg)

WATER | ROCK

CROBAT

Height: 5'11" (1.8 m)
Weight: 165.3 lbs. (75.0 kg)

POISON | FLYING

CROCONAW

Height: 3'07" (1.1 m)
Weight: 55.1 lbs. (25.0 kg)

WATER

CYNDAQUIL

Height: 1'08" (0.5 m)
Weight: 17.4 lbs. (7.9 kg)

FIRE

DELIBIRD

Height: 2'11" (0.9 m)
Weight: 35.3 lbs. (16.0 kg)

ICE | FLYING

DONPHAN

Height: 3'07" (1.1 m)
Weight: 264.6 lbs. (120.0 kg)

GROUND

DUNSPARCE

Height: 4'11" (1.5 m)
Weight: 30.9 lbs. (14.0 kg)

NORMAL

ELEKID

Height: 2'00" (0.6 m)
Weight: 51.8 lbs. (23.5 kg)

ELECTRIC

ENTEI

Height: 6'11" (2.1 m)
Weight: 436.5 lbs (198.0 kg)

FIRE

ESPEON

Height: 2'11" (0.9 m)
Weight: 58.4 lbs. (26.5 kg)

PSYCHIC

FERALIGATR

Height: 7'07" (2.3 m)
Weight: 195.8 lbs. (88.8 kg)

WATER

FLAAFFY

Height: 2'07" (0.8 m)
Weight: 29.3 lbs. (13.3 kg)

ELECTRIC

FORRETRESS

Height: 3'11" (1.2 m)
Weight: 277.3 lbs. (125.8 kg)

BUG | STEEL

FURRET

Height: 5'11" (1.8 m)
Weight: 71.6 lbs. (32.5 kg)

NORMAL

GIRAFARIG

Height: 4'11" (1.5 m)
Weight: 91.5 lbs. (41.5 kg)

NORMAL | PSYCHIC

GLIGAR

Height: 3'07" (1.1 m)
Weight: 142.9 lbs. (64.8 kg)

GROUND | FLYING

GRANBULL

Height: 4'07" (1.4 m)
Weight: 107.4 lbs. (48.7 kg)

FAIRY

HERACROSS

Height: 4'11" (1.5 m)
Weight: 119.0 lbs. (54.0 kg)

BUG | FIGHTING

HITMONTOP

Height: 4'07" (1.4 m)
Weight: 105.8 lbs. (48.0 kg)

FIGHTING

HO-OH

Height: 12'06" (3.8 m)
Weight: 438.7 lbs. (199.0 kg)

FIRE | FLYING

HOOTHOOT

Height: 2'04" (0.7 m)
Weight: 46.7 lbs. (21.2 kg)

NORMAL | FLYING

HOPPIP

Height: 1'04" (0.4 m)
Weight: 1.1 lbs. (0.5 kg)

GRASS | FLYING

HOUNDOOM

Height: 4'07" (1.4 m)
Weight: 77.2 lbs. (35.0 kg)

DARK | FIRE

HOUNDOUR

Height: 2'00" (0.6 m)
Weight: 23.8 lbs. (10.8 kg)

DARK | FIRE

IGGLYBUFF

Height: 1'00" (0.3 m)
Weight: 2.2 lbs. (1.0 kg)

NORMAL | FAIRY

JUMPLUFF

Height: 2'07" (0.8 m)
Weight: 6.6 lbs. (3.0 kg)

GRASS | FLYING

KINGDRA

Height: 5'11" (1.8 m)
Weight: 335.1 lbs. (152.0 kg)

| WATER | DRAGON |

LANTURN

Height: 3'11" (1.2 m)
Weight: 49.6 lbs. (22.5 kg)

| WATER | ELECTRIC |

LARVITAR

Height: 2'00" (0.6 m)
Weight: 158.7 lbs. (72.0 kg)

| ROCK | GROUND |

LEDIAN

Height: 4'07" (1.4 m)
Weight: 78.5 lbs. (35.6 kg)

| BUG | FLYING |

LEDYBA

Height: 3'03" (1.0 m)
Weight: 23.8 lbs. (10.8 kg)

| BUG | FLYING |

LUGIA

Height: 17'01" (5.2 m)
Weight: 476.2 lbs. (216.0 kg)

| PSYCHIC | FLYING |

MAGBY

Height: 2'04" (0.7 m)
Weight: 47.2 lbs. (21.4 kg)

| FIRE |

MAGCARGO

Height: 2'07" (0.8 m)
Weight: 121.3 lbs. (55.0 kg)

| FIRE | ROCK |

MANTINE

Height: 6'11" (2.1 m)
Weight: 485.0 lbs. (220.0 kg)

| WATER | FLYING |

MAREEP

Height: 2'00" (0.6 m)
Weight: 17.2 lbs. (7.8 kg)

| ELECTRIC |

MARILL

Height: 1'04" (0.4 m)
Weight: 18.7 lbs. (8.5 kg)

| WATER | FAIRY |

MEGANIUM

Height: 5'11" (1.8 m)
Weight: 221.6 lbs. (100.5 kg)

| GRASS |

MILTANK

Height: 3'11" (1.2 m)
Weight: 166.4 lbs. (75.5 kg)

| NORMAL |

MISDREAVUS

Height: 2'04" (0.7 m)
Weight: 2.2 lbs. (1.0 kg)

| GHOST |

MURKROW

Height: 1'08" (0.5 m)
Weight: 4.6 lbs. (2.1 kg)

| DARK | FLYING |

NATU

Height: 0'08" (0.2 m)
Weight: 4.4 lbs. (2.0 kg)

| PSYCHIC | FLYING |

NOCTOWL

Height: 5'03" (1.6 m)
Weight: 89.9 lbs. (40.8 kg)

| NORMAL | FLYING |

OCTILLERY

Height: 2'11" (0.9 m)
Weight: 62.8 lbs. (28.5 kg)

| WATER |

PHANPY

Height: 1'08" (0.5 m)
Weight: 73.9 lbs. (33.5 kg)

| GROUND |

PICHU

Height: 1'00" (0.3 m)
Weight: 4.4 lbs. (2.0 kg)

| ELECTRIC |

PILOSWINE

Height: 3'07" (1.1 m)
Weight: 123.0 lbs. (55.8 kg)

| ICE | GROUND |

PINECO

Height: 2'00" (0.6 m)
Weight: 15.9 lbs. (7.2 kg)

| BUG |

POLITOED

Height: 3'07" (1.1 m)
Weight: 74.7 lbs. (33.9 kg)

| WATER |

PORYGON2

Height: 2'00" (0.6 m)
Weight: 71.6 lbs. (32.5 kg)

| NORMAL |

PUPITAR

Height: 3'11" (1.2 m)
Weight: 335.1 lbs. (152.0 kg)

| ROCK | GROUND |

QUAGSIRE

Height: 4'07" (1.4 m)
Weight: 165.3 lbs. (75.0 kg)

| WATER | GROUND |

QUILAVA

Height: 2'11" (0.9 m)
Weight: 41.9 lbs. (19.0 kg)

| FIRE |

QWILFISH

Height: 1'08" (0.5 m)
Weight: 8.6 lbs. (3.9 kg)

| WATER | POISON |

RAIKOU

Height: 6'03" (1.9 m)
Weight: 392.4 lbs. (178.0 kg)

| ELECTRIC |

REMORAID

Height: 2'00" (0.6 m)
Weight: 26.5 lbs. (12.0 kg)

| WATER |

SCIZOR

Height: 5'11" (1.8 m)
Weight: 260.1 lbs. (118.0 kg)

| BUG | STEEL |

SENTRET

Height: 2'07" (0.8 m)
Weight: 13.2 lbs. (6.0 kg)

| NORMAL |

SHUCKLE

Height: 2'00" (0.6 m)
Weight: 45.2 lbs. (20.5 kg)

| BUG | ROCK |

SKARMORY

Height: 5'07" (1.7 m)
Weight: 111.3 lbs. (50.5 kg)

| STEEL | FLYING |

SKIPLOOM

Height: 2'00" (0.6 m)
Weight: 2.2 lbs. (1.0 kg)

| GRASS | FLYING |

SLOWKING

Height: 6'07" (2.0 m)
Weight: 175.3 lbs. (79.5 kg)

| WATER | PSYCHIC |

SLUGMA

Height: 2'04" (0.7 m)
Weight: 77.2 lbs. (35.0 kg)

| FIRE |

SMEARGLE

Height: 3'11" (1.2 m)
Weight: 127.9 lbs. (58.0 kg)

| NORMAL |

SMOOCHUM

Height: 1'04" (0.4 m)
Weight: 13.2 lbs. (6.0 kg)

| ICE | PSYCHIC |

SNEASEL

Height: 2'11" (0.9 m)
Weight: 61.7 lbs. (28.0 kg)

| DARK | ICE |

SNUBBULL

Height: 2'00" (0.6 m)
Weight: 17.2 lbs. (7.8 kg)

| FAIRY |

SPINARAK

Height: 1'08" (0.5 m)
Weight: 18.7 lbs. (8.5 kg)

| BUG | POISON |

STANTLER

Height: 4'07" (1.4 m)
Weight: 157.0 lbs. (71.2 kg)

| NORMAL |

STEELIX

Height: 30'02" (9.2 m)
Weight: 881.8 lbs. (400.0 kg)

| STEEL | GROUND |

SUDOWOODO

Height: 3'11" (1.2 m)
Weight: 83.8 lbs. (38.0 kg)
ROCK

SUICUNE

Height: 6'07" (2.0 m)
Weight: 412.3 lbs. (187.0 kg)
WATER

SUNFLORA

Height: 2'07" (0.8 m)
Weight: 18.7 lbs. (8.5 kg)
GRASS

SUNKERN

Height: 1'00" (0.3 m)
Weight: 4.0 lbs. (1.8 kg)
GRASS

SWINUB

Height: 1'04" (0.4 m)
Weight: 14.3 lbs. (6.5 kg)
ICE   GROUND

TEDDIURSA

Height: 2'00" (0.6 m)
Weight: 19.4 lbs. (8.8 kg)
NORMAL

TOGEPI

Height: 1'00" (0.3 m)
Weight: 3.3 lbs. (1.5 kg)
FAIRY

TOGETIC

Height: 2'00" (0.6 m)
Weight: 7.1 lbs. (3.2 kg)
FLYING   FAIRY

TOTODILE

Height: 2'00" (0.6 m)
Weight: 20.9 lbs. (9.5 kg)
WATER

TYPHLOSION

Height: 5'07" (1.7 m)
Weight: 175.3 lbs. (79.5 kg)
FIRE

TYRANITAR

Height: 6'07" (2.0 m)
Weight: 445.3 lbs. (202.0 kg)
ROCK   DARK

TYROGUE

Height: 2'04" (0.7 m)
Weight: 46.3 lbs. (21.0 kg)
FIGHTING

UMBREON

Height: 3'03" (1.0 m)
Weight: 59.5 lbs. (27.0 kg)
DARK

UNOWN

Height: 1'08" (0.5 m)
Weight: 11.0 lbs. (5.0 kg)
PSYCHIC

URSARING

Height: 5'11" (1.8 m)
Weight: 277.3 lbs. (125.8 kg)
NORMAL

WOBBUFFET

Height: 4'03" (1.3 m)
Weight: 62.8 lbs. (28.5 kg)
PSYCHIC

WOOPER

Height: 1'04" (0.4 m)
Weight: 18.7 lbs. (8.5 kg)
WATER   GROUND

XATU

Height: 4'11" (1.5 m)
Weight: 33.1 lbs. (15.0 kg)
PSYCHIC   FLYING

YANMA

Height: 3'11" (1.2 m)
Weight: 83.8 lbs. (38.0 kg)
BUG   FLYING

HOENN

Home of Professor Birch of Littleroot Town, Hoenn offers visitors spectacularly different environments all in one place. From sunny coastlines to bursting-with-life forests, Hoenn is in many ways an encapsulation of every experience of the mainland regions.

Hoenn is also home to Ash's friends May and Max. Their dad, the Gym Leader Norman, lives in Petalburg City. Slateport City is a very busy port town in the south of Hoenn. Two unique features dominate the landscape of Hoenn.

First, the active volcano, Mt. Chimney, is home to many hot springs. Rising from the middle of Hoenn, Mt. Chimney is always smoking, on the verge of eruption. Second, the crater island city, Sootopolis City, rests inside a dormant underwater volcano. Only reachable by a ferry, Sootopolis City is an amazing tiered city marked by terraced dwellings reachable by stairs.

May's Pokémon

MAY

TORCHIC

May's First Partner Pokémon, Torchic, was friendly, but ended up getting itself into trouble with other Pokémon often. As it evolved from Torchic into Combusken and from Combusken into Blaziken, it shed some of its temper but remains a tough, experienced fighter.

WURMPLE

Wurmple has had an interesting life; after evolving into a Silcoon, it was accidentally swapped with Jessie's Casoon. Finally, after a great deal of arguing, Silcoon was returned to May and evolved into a Beautifly.

BULBASAUR

Caught in the Forbidden Forest of Hoenn, May first discovered Bulbasaur while it was trying to pick flowers. Since then she has evolved it into an Ivysaur, then into a mighty Venusaur.

Although May is the daughter of Norman, Petalburg City's famous Gym Leader, she never intended to be a Pokémon Trainer or a Coordinator—what she really wanted was to see the world. During her travels, she developed an interest in Pokémon Contests and realized she had the makings of a great Coordinator.

May became a Pokémon Trainer when she was 10, but she wasn't even interested in Pokémon; food and travel have always been two of her biggest passions. Knowing little about Pokémon, she only chose Torchic as her First Partner Pokémon because it seemed friendly. Things changed once she joined Ash on his travels and met Janet, a Pokémon Coordinator; intrigued by Pokémon Contests, May decided to become a Coordinator herself.

May wouldn't be a talented Coordinator if she didn't have some competitive mettle, but she's also a soft-hearted girl who's sometimes too easily swayed for her own good. After all, she became a Coordinator partly by chance instead of choice, and even as she grows in experience, she struggles to develop confidence in her own skills. But once she realizes she could be a top Coordinator if she just works hard, there's no looking back for the girl who will one day be known as the Princess of Hoenn.

There was a time when May would fall for everything from Harley's glib advice to the promises of Team Rocket's fake PokéBlock, but she's learned her lessons by now with help from her true friends and her rival, Drew.

THE WORLD IS HER OYSTER, MELON BREAD, AND CHICKEN NOODLE SOUP

May loves travel and adventure, but she's definitely a big-city girl. For one thing, she likes to shop—but more importantly, she loves to eat! Wherever she goes, she's sure to have guidebook tips on the best places to eat, even when the local specialties sound strange instead of savory.

SQUIRTLE

While at Professor Oak's, a Squirtle become enamored with May. Though intended to be a First Partner Pokémon, Squirtle was given to May, and has since become very confident in Contests. It has evolved into a Wartortle.

MUNCHLAX

Munchlax was an unusual capture: it was caught from the inside after it gulped down May's Poké Ball. When Contest time rolls around, Munchlax isn't above putting a little extra swagger in its step.

SKITTY

Skitty is affectionate but hyperactive, and May has managed to put its energy to good use in her Contests. Skitty's Assist move in particular has saved her from more than one Contest battle crisis.

EEVEE

May received an Egg during her adventures in Kanto. It hatched into an Eevee which she soon introduced to Contests; just before the Wallace Cup, she made a special trip to Snowpoint City to evolve it into Glaceon.

Faced with a choice between finding her lost brother and boarding the last ferry to the last Contest before the Grand Festival, May decides to turn around and go find Max. Even though Ash offers to find him while May goes ahead, May knows she has to do the right thing, even if it costs her dream: there's always another Grand Festival, but she only has one brother.

MAY AND MAX HIT THE ROAD

Before she left home, May promised her mother and her father, Norman, that she'd look after her little brother Max. Max fancies himself the smarter of the two, and that's at least true when it comes to Pokémon trivia. He hates it when May treats him like a kid, but a big sister's responsibility never ends. Yet for all their squabbles, the genuine bond between them is never in question. After their Hoenn and Kanto journeys end, May goes on to Johto, while Max helps out his father in the Gym.

NORMAN

FLYING SOLO

After the Kanto Grand Festival, May decides to head for Johto on her own. That means no more looking after Max, but it also means she'll have to rely on herself without Ash and Brock to help out. It's the next step in her growth as a Coordinator and a person; when she revisits her old friends in Sinnoh at the Wallace Cup, she reports having a rough time trying to beat Harley and Drew—but she's won three Ribbons already, and she's strong enough to keep going even when times are tough

MAX

Nerdy, know-it-all. That is Max in a nutshell. If you look beyond the oversized glasses and screechy voice you will find all the desire, commitment, and dedication that makes a Pokémon Trainer stand above all others. It is more important to know that one day Max will be a Trainer, and a formidable one.

FAMILY MATTERS

Although Max and May are brother and sister, it doesn't mean that he has the warmest feelings for her. After all, what kind of little brother would he be if he didn't tease her or complain about her once in a while? He certainly let loose on her with an embarrassing story about how she was mistaken for a Tentacruel in her fifth Ribbon Contest battle against Harley!

Max had a heartbreaking moment where he saw his own father lose to Ash in a hotly contested Gym Battle. After running away with the Balance Badge, Max goes on a tirade about Norman's loss to Ash. It is a coming-of-age realization for Max, whose father explains that losing is an important part of being a Gym Leader.

Max's parents, Caroline and Norman, want Max to travel with Ash, May, and Brock to learn more about Pokémon through observation. They are worried that Max is too entrenched in the books about Pokémon, and not involved enough in field training. Maybe Max is shooting for a professorial position?

GOODBYE AND GOOD LUCK

At the end of their Kanto journey, May decides that she wants to travel through Johto alone, but agrees to escort Max back to the Petalburg Gym. Max is furious, not just at the thought of being abandoned, but also because he has become somewhat jealous of his sister's success. But when Ash agrees to battle him when he becomes a Trainer, Max calms down. He then goes back to Petalburg Gym to help his father train and to care for the Petalburg Gym Pokémon.

Max's Pokémon

What are Max's Pokémon? This is kind of a trick question, since Max is not allowed Pokémon because of his age. That doesn't mean that Max hasn't formed some significant bonds with certain Pokémon, including some Legendary Pokémon.

POOCHYENA

Max comes across a Poochyena that does not evolve, even though the rest of the pack has. He trains it to level it up, but Team Rocket steps in. During the battle, it finally evolves into Mightyena.

RALTS

Max finds a sick Ralts in the Izabe Forest, so Ash and his crew take it to the nearest Pokémon Center. Team Rocket intervenes, and in the ensuing getaway, a Gardevoir and Kirlia battle Max for the sick Ralts. Max does everything in his power to protect the Ralts, and finally makes it to the Pokémon Center. Max promises to return once he's a Trainer.

DEOXYS

When everything mechanical starts to malfunction, Pokémon Ranger Solana explains that it is an electromagnetic disturbance, caused by…Deoxys! Deoxys is scared and alone during its flight through space, and kidnaps Max and Meowth. Befriending Deoxys, Max is able to calm it, giving it hope that it will never truly be alone again.

PROFESSOR BIRCH

As Ash and his friends move from region to region in search of more badges, contests and battles, they encounter the resident Pokémon professor for each area. At the start of their adventures in Hoenn, Ash meets one of the most gregarious Pokémon professors, Professor Birch.

HOENN

Birch is responsible for delivering the First Partner Pokémon to Trainers who come by his lab. He has Torchic, Treecko, and Mudkip under his care.

He also keeps a Poochyena on hand to help out with any problems that may arise.

He Knows His Stuff, Part I

Whether rolling around on the ground with a group of Seedot or trying to help Trainers identify Pokémon, Birch is more of a hands-on Pokémon professor compared to the others. He desperately tries to tell Jessie that her Silcoon is actually a Cascoon, but before she can learn from his wisdom it evolves into Dustox.

Professor Birch makes it well known that he "doesn't want to stay cooped up in his lab." This leads him outdoors with an opportunity to frequently cross paths with Ash and his friends.

His specialty in Pokémon research revolves around the habits of wild Pokémon, which means he must get closer to Pokémon than Professor Oak. To that end, he drives a jeep all around Hoenn, but not very carefully. He is also good friends with Norman, the Gym Leader of Petalburg City—May and Max's father.

SCALING NEW HEIGHTS

Professor Birch is no slouch when it come to field work. As a matter of fact, our friends catch him scaling the cliffs in Dewford Town looking for a Wingull nest. In addition, he uncovers lots of mysteries while working, like when he discovers Team Aqua for the first time while investigating Keanu's secret base!

He Knows His Stuff, Part II

Birch is one of the Pokémon professors Ash sees the most, usually explaining strange Evolutions. For example, he explains that a DeepSeaTooth is needed for Clamperl to evolve into Huntail, while a DeepSeaScale evolves Clamperl into Gorebyss.

FIELD RESEARCH

Unlike the other Pokémon professors, Birch is most comfortable when out in the field. He combs the various forests, mountains, and towns of Hoenn researching Pokémon in the wild. However, his base and research lab is in Littleroot Town, which is located between Dewford Town and Slateport City.

TEAM MAGMA

Land-loving Team Magma is always trying to gain ground, literally. As their name suggests, they pay particular attention to volcanoes; they know, when hot lava cools, it can turn into livable land. Their ultimate goal is to take over the world and create more territory. However, they must first capture the Legendary Pokémon of magma, Groudon, and the Blue Orb that controls its will. To complete their mission, Team Magma has created an arsenal of sophisticated technology, from their meteorite-powered laser, to their massive boat hideout, to their submarine, to their machine that can burrow straight through solid mountain rock. Team Magma is like a force of nature, and their enemies, Team Aqua, are just as devoted to controlling the planet through another natural element.

MAXIE

With slicked-back red hair and a powerful presence, the head of Team Magma has one thing on his mind: making more land for him to rule. Maxie leads his crew to capture the Legendary Pokémon Kyogre and the Blue Orb. But when he tries to broker a deal with his sworn enemies, Team Aqua, he nearly loses his entire team in their trickery. Foolish enough to trust his foes, Maxie is his own worst enemy. Eventually, as the world brushes with destruction during a Legendary Pokémon power grab that he orchestrates and loses, he finally sees the errors of his evil ways. He is never heard from again in Hoenn.

TABITHA

Maxie's right-hand man, Commander Tabitha is always in the field to steal what Team Magma needs. He also fends off their enemies, Team Aqua. Tabitha leads his crew though difficult missions and is always there to do Maxie's dirty work. Even if his aim is bad, his intentions are good. Dependable Tabitha is a true leader. When the going gets tough, Tabitha always thinks of his team's safety first.

Members of Team Magma always have Mightyena and Golbat on hand.

THE FOUR FACE-OFFS: MAGMA VS. AQUA

DIG SOME DIRT UP
Tabitha, along with his Team Magma crew, planned to tunnel their way through a mountain, past a secret Pokémon training hideout, to the Cave of Origin. A group of Team Aqua associates, led by Shelly, had their eye on the same prize, but they swam their way through the deep sea and up to the sacred spot. Although they both found the hidden shrine, there was one problem with both their plans: they were in the wrong place. The orb they sought wasn't there because they did not accurately locate the Cave of Origin. Both teams came up empty handed. But, since both teams were faced with their rivals, they decided they might as well have a mini battle. Ash and his friends consider themselves warned: wherever Team Aqua and Team Magma are, there's trouble.

MENACING AT MT. CHIMNEY
Professor Cosmo, a space researcher, located a meteorite on top of Mt. Chimney. It wasn't in his capable hands long when Team Magma and Team Aqua waged a fight to steal it. While Magma and Aqua battled it out, Ash tried his best to help Professor Cosmo thwart their evil plans. The meteorite ended up in the wrong hands, or rather the wrong laser—it was the missing power source for Team Magma's volcano-blasting laser. Professor Cosmo saved the day by pushing the whole machine deep into the volcano, where the meteorite's power couldn't be exploited.

FOR YOUR INFORMATION
Ash, Max, Brock, and May stepped in to save the Weather Institute from Shelly and her gang of Team Aqua goons. But they accidentally teamed up with a researcher at the lab: Team Magma operative Brodie in disguise. Although they stopped Shelly and Team Rocket, Brodie slipped through their fingers with the lab's data on the Legendary Pokémon.

LEGENDARY SHOWDOWN
It was all going according to Team Magma's evil plan. They had captured the Legendary Pokémon Kyogre and the mythical Blue Orb that controls Groudon, as well as Ash, Max, May, and Brock! Maxie informed the kids that he was about to trade with his archenemies, Team Aqua. He would give them the Blue Orb in exchange for the Red Orb that controls Kyogre. The two teams would meet at Monsu Island. Both had tricks up their sleeves. Little did Maxie know, Team Aqua had already captured Groudon. When the power of the orbs that control the Legendary Pokémon overtook Pikachu and Archie, an explosive battle between Kyogre and Groudon almost wrecked the whole island. Luckily, Ash and his friends had some help from Elite Four member Lance, and even some accidental help from Team Rocket. Peace was restored. Plus, all the lava that cooled off in the battle flooding formed a new world. Lance pointed out that, much like the ancient text about Groudon and Kyogre promised, the two Legendary Pokémon embody Mother Nature. Nothing can destroy their order, no matter how much greedy meddling Team Aqua and Team Magma try to pull off.

TEAM AQUA

Water-wielding Team Aqua has dreams of world domination, just like Team Magma. As you might guess by their name, they're all about the ocean. Team Aqua plots to gain enough power to see the sea dominate the world. First, they must nab the Legendary Pokémon Kyogre and the Red Orb that can force it to do their bidding. Ash and his friends encounter a Team Aqua member during a visit to the Devon Corporation's lab. This sneak infiltrates the research room to steal creation capsules right out of the Pokémon Producing Machine. While Team Aqua sneakily travels by submarine and jetpack around Hoenn to gather all the elements, their wicked and ill-conceived plans typically land them in hot water. As long as Ash and his crew—as well as Team Magma—are around, they can run, but they certainly can't hide.

ARCHIE

Archie, Team Aqua's leader, has a finely sculpted facial hair and plans that are just as artfully crafted. His word means nothing when power is at stake. He will lie to someone's face, even members of his own crew, if the web he weaves can make him stronger. When he finally gets to use the Red Orb to control Kyogre, he doesn't care if its attacks wipe out his own loyal gang. And once he's in control, he expects his team to be all for one, but he's only out for himself. Although Archie seems to snap out of his super-evil stance once Groudon calms Kyogre, it doesn't seem wise to trust the wishy-washy leader of Team Aqua.

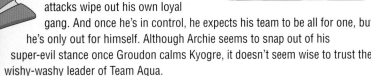

Members of Team Aqua always choose Walrein and Crawdaunt.

SHELLY

This Team Aqua commander can make messes as big as her curly red-hair. Although she usually commands a crew of her teammates, she's sneaky enough to infiltrate Team Magma alone and release the captured Kyogre. Smart and stealthy, Shelly doesn't back down; she always stands her ground. She doesn't just blindly follow Archie. When the Red Orb makes him a super villain, she realizes he must be stopped. But she's still compassionate enough to catch his fall when the Legendary Pokémon seize control again.

BRODIE

Shape-shifting Brodie is as slippery as his Pokémon pal Ditto. One incredible actor, he tricks the manager of The Weather Institute, Bart, into thinking he's their new hire—a woman named Millie. He even pulls a fast one on Ash and the crew, who also believe his act and accidentally help him complete his mission! This guy is a fantastic faker. He

steals all the data on the Legendary Pokémon from the institute before anyone even suspects he's not really a researcher. Then he's gone in a flash, having the last laugh.

THREE-RING CIRCUS

Where there's trouble, make that double... er, triple in this case. There's a third team that wants in on all the action: Team Rocket! Or rather, they wait on the sidelines to swoop in and steal whatever Team Aqua and Team Magma are battling over because they figure if it's worth fighting for, their boss will be impressed when they steal it. Well, that is if they could ever snag something before they get blasted off.

DREW

Sometimes May's friend and sometimes her rival, Drew has grown to see May as genuine competition instead of just a rank novice. He was once a novice Coordinator just like everyone else, on the verge of tears after being beaten by Soledad in his Contest debut, but now he's a Coordinator from LaRousse City and a well-known figure on the Contest circuit.

Although Drew's criticisms of May are usually helpful in their own way, he's snapped at her on a few occasions. At first, he was frustrated with the way May's lack of confidence led her to believe Harley's constant lies. But at the Grand Festival in Kanto, Drew lashes out at both May and his Absol because May's up-and-coming presence puts him under pressure to stay one step ahead. Drew isn't big on coming in second; even after the Grand Festival in Hoenn, he skipped the afterparty to keep training.

He has a habit of handing out roses that add to his cool, aloof image—but he does become flustered in the face of his adoring public. And though Drew is a perfectionist, he doesn't bother to dress up for Contests because he wants the sole focus to be his Pokémon, not him.

May once described Drew as a guy who liked to make fun of her, not a friend, but their relationship has more than thawed; they even saved each other when they were both stranded on Mirage Island.

Drew's Pokémon

BUTTERFREE

MASQUERAIN

FLYGON

ROSERADE

ABSOL

HARLEY

Harley's demeanor is all sweetness and light, but cross this Slateport City Coordinator in any fashion and his true nature becomes all too apparent.

Harley's Pokémon

CACTURNE

BANETTE

OCTILLERY

ARIADOS

Some Coordinators try to wow a crowd with beauty, but Harley prefers to send a shiver down the audience's spine. Of course, he thinks his intimidating Pokémon are absolutely darling.

May made the unwitting mistake of not recognizing his Cacturne and saying his cookies "aren't half-bad," which infuriated Harley so much he took an instant photo of her for his little book of vengeance. Since then, he's been determined to beat her by any means, whether fair or foul. Time and time again, Harley played dirty tricks on May and then made a show of apologies so he could trick her again.

HOENN GRAND FESTIVAL

Slateport City hosts the Grand Festival, Hoenn's annual top-tier Pokémon Contest, where Coordinators and Pokémon put on shows of beauty and power to see who is truly worthy of the Ribbon Cup.

To enter the Grand Festival, Coordinators must supply their Hoenn Contest pass and their five prize ribbons. Once the ribbons are scanned in and registration is complete, each contestant receives a guide book with Grand Festival rules, stadium maps, and even restaurant locations. Contestants also get to stay in comfortable rooms with an ocean view.

PRELIMINARY ROUND

Held on outdoor contest stages, the preliminary appeals are scored on a scale of 1-100 and only the top 64 Coordinators advance to the main competition. Those are tough odds considering there are 247 preliminary round entries in the year May competes. These rounds are judged by auxiliary judges instead of the usual combination of Mr. Contesta, Mr. Sukizo, and Nurse Joy.

MAIN COMPETITION

Contestants take the stage for main competition appeals in the reverse order of their preliminary round standings. Three minutes are allotted for each appeal and each judge scores on a 1-20 point scale. The judges' individual scores are added up and the top 32 contestants advance to the next round. For the next day's five-minute double battle rounds, the top 32 are paired off based on their scores in the main competition appeals.

MAY DEFEATS HARLEY

Harley makes the first move, but May comes up with quick combinations like Vine Whip and Silver Wind to turn the game around and earn a clear victory.

DREW DEFEATS MAY

Drew unveils a Flygon he raised just for this tournament and, despite May's creative strategies, the power of Flygon's Steel Wing together with Roselia's Stun Spore is just too much for Combusken and Skitty.

MAY DEFEATS ANTHONY

Although Anthony's Pokémon hold their own against Bulbasaur and Combusken, when time runs out with both sides still standing, May takes the win due to her slight edge in the points.

Anthony

A shy but hard-working Coordinator, Anthony was lucky to make it to the main competition after Team Rocket stole his ribbons and Contest pass. Without his ribbons, he didn't have the heart to compete, but Ash and Officer Jenny helped apprehend Team Rocket and Anthony took the stage after all. He made a good showing with his Swalot, which he'd raised ever since it was a Gulpin.

ROBERT DEFEATS DREW

Robert

Robert and his Milotic have made several other appearances throughout the Hoenn Contest season; he's a classy Coordinator. Team Rocket tries to steal his identity as well—by conducting an actual kidnapping—but the attempt is cut short by Ash and his Snorunt. Even though Robert wins the Grand Festival, he doesn't even stick around for the closing ceremony party— he's already off to practice for his next competition.

POKÉMON CONTESTS & COORDINATORS

In Hoenn, Contests were introduced as a new form of battling. Contestants, known as Contest Coordinators instead of Trainers, showcased their Pokémon's skills in beauty and grace competitions. Instead of competing for badges, Coordinators competed for ribbons.

MAIN COORDINATORS

Piplup, Buneary, Pachirisu, Ambipom, Swinub	SINNOH	DAWN

Dawn, like May, wants to compete and win ribbons so that she can be the best Contest Coordinator ever. However, there are differences between the two: Dawn is more aggressive and more confident than May. She doesn't "wonder" what she should do, nor does she rely on luck or fate. Instead, she trains and enters each battle with knowledge and foresight.

Glameow, Misdreavus, Shellos, Finneon	SINNOH	ZOEY

Zoey is Dawn's rival, much like Drew is to May. She is a little more outgoing than others in Sinnoh and a lot more helpful. She suggested and facilitated the trade of Aipom and Buizel between Ash and Dawn when she observed that Buizel was more attuned to battling. She also has expressed her distaste for people who seek out Gym Badges and Coordinator ribbons at the same time.

Roselia, Sunflora, Kricketune	SINNOH	NANDO

Nando is a wandering minstrel of sorts, playing a Mew-shaped harp wherever he goes. Keeping with his lifestyle, Nando has trouble making up his mind. Ultimately, he decides to becomes a Trainer and a Coordinator.

KENNY	SINNOH	Prinplup, Alakazam, Breloom

Kenny is a Coordinator who has a previous history with Dawn. The two were childhood friends and he even refers to her affectionately as "Dee-Dee." He also chose Piplup as his First Partner Pokémon, although he had begun his quest for ribbons before her. When Kenny faced Dawn in Floaroma, he lost to her in a very tight battle.

DREW	HOENN	Roserade, Masquerain, Flygon, Absol, Butterfree

Drew is to May what Gary Oak is to Ash—a competitor, a friend, and a rival to the end. And like Gary Oak, Drew continues to inspire and assist May although his competitive nature flares from time to time. Drew has his own rival and longtime friend in Solidad, another Coordinator.

JESSIE	SINNOH AND HOENN	Dustox, Aipom (borrowed), Wobbuffet, Seviper, Yanmega

Jessie has a deep desire to win the coordinator contests, but she rarely does so in honest ways and usually competes masked. More effort goes into her disguises (Jessabelle, Jessalina, The Jester) than into her training. She has won two ribbons, one in an unofficial showdown using Ash's Aipom and another legitimate win in Solaceon Town using her Dustox.

MAY | HOENN | Blaziken, Beautifly, Wartortle, Glaceon, Venusaur, Munchlax, Skitty

May announced early on in Hoenn that she had no desire to become a Trainer. After watching a Pokémon Contest, however, she realized her true calling. Although outmatched in almost every event, she trained diligently and won all five of her ribbons with style.

SOLIDAD | HOENN | Slowbro, Lapras, Pidgeot, Butterfree

Solidad is a Pokémon Coordinator from Pewter City (and an apparent acquaintance of Brock's) who competed against May in the Kanto Grand Festival, which she won. She is also old friends with Drew and Harley. She is always willing to help or offer advice.

HARLEY | HOENN | Cacturne, Banette, Ariados, Octillery, Wigglytuff

Harley is a snobby, easily-offended coordinator whose issues with May stem from the fact that she didn't over-praise the cookies that Harley made for her on their first meeting. Plus, she didn't even know what a Cacturne was! Since then, Harley has made it his life mission to antagonize, embarrass, and demean May in any way possible.

Introducing the Judges

RAOUL CONTESTA

Not much is known about Mr. Contesta, but he is the Pokémon Contest Director and head of the judging committee.

MR. SUKIZO

Another judge in the contest is Mr. Sukizo, the president of the Pokémon Fan Club. He joins Mr. Contesta and Nurse Joy on the panel, but says very little. His catch phrase is "Remarkable."

NURSE JOY

A Nurse Joy from the town in which the contest is being held is usually asked to serve as a contest judge as well.

CONTEST RULES

- EACH CONTESTANT WILL USE ONE POKÉMON PER ROUND, UNLESS IT IS A DOUBLE PERFORMANCE. A COORDINATOR CAN CHANGE POKÉMON BETWEEN ROUNDS.
- POKÉMON WILL PERFORM IN A QUALIFYING ROUND.
- HIGH SCORES IN THE QUALIFYING ROUND DETERMINE PLACEMENT IN THE SEMI-FINALS.
- DURING A MATCH, POKÉMON ARE JUDGED ON SKILL, GRACE, AND PERFORMANCE.
- POKÉMON CAN USE SINGLE, DOUBLE, OR TRIPLE COMBINATION ATTACKS TO LOWER AN OPPONENT'S TALLY.
- THERE IS A FIVE-MINUTE TIME LIMIT.
- AFTER FIVE MINUTES, THE COORDINATOR WITH THE HIGHER POINT TALLY IS DECLARED THE WINNER.

HOENN GYM BATTLES!

When Ash heads into Hoenn, he doesn't know what to expect. The Gyms in Hoenn are staffed by expert warriors, specializing in Electric-types, Fighting-types, and Fire-types.

RUSTBORO CITY GYM

GYM LEADER: ROXANNE

 ROXANNE VS. **ASH**

ROXANNE VS. **ASH**

Geodude uses Rollout followed by Mega Punch, which takes Treecko out.

Roxanne questions using an Electric-type Pokémon in a Rock Gym, but Pikachu has a trick up its sleeve. A massive Thunder attack changes the terrain of the Gym, and because the terrain has been altered, Geodude cannot perform his moves and Pikachu takes the match.

ROXANNE VS. **ASH**

Nosepass uses Zap Cannon, but the electricity charges Pikachu, and it uses it against Nosepass (and a well-placed Iron Tail attack) for the win. Ash earns the Stone Badge.

DEWFORD ISLAND GYM

GYM LEADER: BRAWLY

BRAWLY VS. **ASH**

BRAWLY VS. **ASH**

Machop starts with Karate Chop, but Treecko dodges it. Treecko uses the formation of the Gym as Ash defends against another two Karate Chops. Worrying about the geysers in the Gym, Ash recalls Treecko just in time.

Corphish succumbs to Hariyama's onslaught, as it's blown out of the water, then finished with a Seismic Toss.

BRAWLY VS. **ASH**

BRAWLY VS. **ASH**

Corphish comes out swinging, using Bubblebeam, then Crabhammer. Machop tries to block with Karate Chop, but a subsequent Crabhammer makes short work of Machop.

Hariyama starts with Arm Thrust, which Treecko deftly dodges. Treecko uses Pound attacks on Hariyama's legs, which weaken Hariyama. Eventually, Treecko wins, earning Ash the Knuckle Badge.

MAUVILLE CITY GYM

GYM LEADER: WATTSON

WATTSON VS. **ASH**

WATTSON VS. **ASH**

Jovial Wattson starts with Magnemite, which tries Swift on for size. Pikachu uses Dodge, then Thunderbolt, which surprisingly takes Magnemite down.

Voltorb is next, and uses Screech, before Pikachu uses one Thunderbolt and takes the victory.

WATTSON VS. **ASH**

Finally, Magneton uses Shock Cannon to take Pikachu out, but Pikachu takes down Magneton with a Thunder attack, giving Ash the Dynamo Badge!

Electric-type vs. Electric-type

Wattson is the fun-loving Gym Leader of Mauville City. He accepts Ash's challenge, and after a few tense battles, Ash beats him. However, the battles are one-sided—Pikachu easily wipes the floor with Wattson's Pokémon. After the match, however, Pikachu falls ill, and a trip to the local Pokémon Center reveals that Pikachu is suffering from overcharge again, making all its attacks super-powerful. Wattson, however, is so depressed after his defeat that he gives up the Mauville City Gym.

Ash tries to return the badge to Wattson, who won't hear of it. Ash is rewarded the badge for helping the Electric-type Pokémon.

LAVARIDGE TOWN GYM

GYM LEADER: FLANNERY

FLANNERY VS. **ASH**

FLANNERY VS. **ASH**

The inexperienced Flannery seems like an easy target for Ash, but the ease turns to unease once Flannery settles in and uses Reflect to reduce Corphish's ViceGrip by half. Corphish's Crabhammer takes Magcargo out for good.

When Slugma tries using Smog again, Pikachu uses Thunderbolt, charging the cloud, then counters Yawn with Quick Attack, before applying Thunder for the win.

FLANNERY VS. **ASH**

FLANNERY VS. **ASH**

Surprisingly, Ash sends out the Grass-type Treecko against a Fire-type, which is a type disadvantage. The battle goes back and forth, but when Slugma burns Treecko, Ash calls it back.

Down to her last Pokémon, Flannery chooses Torkoal, and manages to take out Pikachu with a combination of Iron Defense and Flamethrower.

FLANNERY VS.  **ASH**

FLANNERY VS. **ASH**

As Corphish charges Slugma with ViceGrip, it gets hit with a Yawn attack, putting it to sleep! Ash is forced to pick another Pokémon.

Ash takes out Treecko next, which gets eliminated by Overheat the minute it leaves the Poké Ball.

FLANNERY VS. **ASH**

Ash's only Pokémon left is the napping Corphish. Torkoal starts with Overheat, then follows up with Flamethrower. This time Corphish gets around Iron Defense by spinning Torkoal to its feet with ViceGrip, then BubbleBeam. The battle goes in favor of Ash netting him the Heat Badge!

PETALBURG CITY GYM

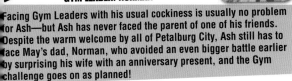

GYM LEADER: NORMAN

Facing Gym Leaders with his usual cockiness is usually no problem for Ash—but Ash has never faced the parent of one of his friends. Despite the warm welcome by all of Petalburg City, Ash still has to face May's dad, Norman, who avoided an even bigger battle earlier by surprising his wife with an anniversary present, and the Gym challenge goes on as planned!

NORMAN VS. **ASH**

Pikachu can't get in one attack, as Slakoth dodges everything. Pikachu faces even more problems when Blizzard is used. Ash calls Pikachu back.

NORMAN VS. **ASH**

Ash has Torkoal start out with Overheat, but Vigoroth uses Scratch attack. Its speed and power knock out Torkoal with one attack.

NORMAN VS. **ASH**

Ash has Torkoal use Flamethrower, against another Blizzard from Slakoth. Torkoal knocks out Slakoth.

NORMAN VS. **ASH**

Ash goes back to Pikachu. After a back-and-forth battle, a static electricity charge paralyzes Vigoroth, and Pikachu ends the battle with Iron Tail. Unfortunately, Pikachu also succumbs, ending in a draw.

NORMAN VS. **ASH**

Grovyle uses Bullet Seed and Slaking counters with Hyper Beam, but the toughened Grovyle fights back and uses Overgrow, an ability that magnifies Grass-type attacks, and takes down Slaking with a Leaf Blade attack. Ash earns the Balance Badge.

FORTREE CITY GYM

GYM LEADER: WINONA

WINONA VS. **ASH**

Ash once again goes against the grain and uses a type-disadvantaged Pokémon like Grovyle, which is weak against Flying-types like Altaria. In the end it works, as Grovyle uses Leaf Blade for the win!

WINONA VS. **ASH**

Winona sends out Swellow as her last Pokémon, while Ash chooses Grovyle, thinking his speed is an advantage. But all of Grovyle's jumping is no match for Swellow. Grovyle is hit with an Aerial Ace, an almost unavoidable attack, which does Grovyle in.

WINONA VS. **ASH**

Pikachu goes for Quick Attack while Swellow tries to keep its distance with Hydro Pump. Pikachu then electrifies the Hydro Pump, knocking both Pikachu and Swellow out.

WINONA VS. **ASH**

After a titanic clash in the air, Ash decides to have his Swellow use Wing Attack on the dusty ground, blinding Winona's Pokémon, allowing it to finish it off for the Feather Badge.

MOSSDEEP CITY GYM

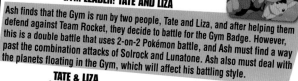

GYM LEADER: TATE AND LIZA

Ash finds that the Gym is run by two people, Tate and Liza, and after helping them defend against Team Rocket, they decide to battle for the Gym Badge. However, this is a double battle that uses 2-on-2 Pokémon battle, and Ash must find a way past the combination attacks of Solrock and Lunatone. Ash also must deal with the planets floating in the Gym, which will affect his battling style.

TATE & LIZA VS. **ASH**

The twins become effective through the use of their teamwork, but Ash steps his game up using combos of his own. He has Pikachu and Swellow combine their attacks, and give each other a protective Thunder armor, which breaks through the Light Screen and paves their way to victory and the Mind Badge!

SOOTOPOLIS CITY GYM

GYM LEADER: JUAN

Battling at the Sootopolis City Gym takes a lot of strength and tenacity. Not only is there a Double Battle to deal with where you must defeat both of your opponents' standing Pokémon to advance, but there is also a 3-on-3 battle where you use any of your surviving Pokémon from the previous rounds to take on Juan.

JUAN VS. **ASH**

Pikachu and Snorunt use the ice to get closer to Juan's Pokémon. It seems to work but Pikachu's Iron Tail and Snorunt's Headbutt can't match Sealeo's Aurora Beam and Seaking's Hyper Beam. Snorunt is unable to battle.

JUAN VS. **ASH**

Ash brings out Corphish to help Pikachu. Pikachu's Iron Tail takes out Seaking, leaving only Sealeo. When Juan uses Ice Ball for the third time, Pikachu's Thunder breaks the ball allowing Corphish to knock Sealeo out with Crabhammer!

JUAN VS. **ASH**

The battle switches to a more traditional one-on-one battle. When Grovyle uses Leaf Blade, Luvdisc's countering Sweet Kiss confuses Grovyle, who gets hit with a Water Gun and is knocked out.

JUAN VS. **ASH**

Corphish uses Crabhammer on top of the water and follows with ViceGrip. Corphish finishes it up with Crabhammer, which is super-effective.

JUAN VS. **ASH**

With only two Pokémon left, Juan chooses to go with Whiscash, who ends Corphish's night with a single Rock Smash!

JUAN VS. **ASH**

Whishcash uses Hyper Beam and the match seems lost, when suddenly Swellow comes back with an Aerial Ace and follows Whiscash into the water! Swellow follows with Aerial Ace to end the battle.

JUAN VS. **ASH**

Milotic's Hydro Pump versus Swellow's Aerial Ace doesn't give Ash the results he wanted. Milotic's follow-up attack Twister knocks Swellow out.

JUAN VS. **ASH**

With both battlers down to their last Pokémon, it is up to Pikachu. Thunder seems to harm Milotic, but Milotic uses Recover. Pikachu flips Milotic into the water, where a full-tilt Thunder attack finishes it. Ash earns the Rain Badge.

HOENN LEAGUE CHAMPIONSHIP

The Hoenn League Championship is Ever Grande City's star event and the gleam in every Hoenn Trainer's eye. As usual, a Trainer needs to earn eight badges for entry.

The Hoenn League Championship facilities are a sight to behold, featuring a main stadium surrounded by more stadiums, a Trainers' village, and its own Hoenn League Championship Pokémon Center.

OPENING CEREMONIES

To start off the tournament, a torch runner carries the flame of Moltres from Ever Grande City into the stadium, where it will be stored until the opening ceremonies. The ceremony itself, which features colorful balloons, the torchlighting, and appearances by the 256 qualifying competitors, doesn't begin until after the preliminary rounds have finished.

> Tyson is the torch runner, but Ash is selected to light the main stadium's torch in recognition of his help in defeating Team Rocket's latest attempt at torch thievery.

TOURNAMENT STRUCTURE

Cut-off for tournament registration is at 5 PM on the day before the preliminaries. With a field of over 600 entrants, the Hoenn League Championship's initial entry list will be chopped in half and then some before the tournament truly gets underway. Preliminary rounds trim down the field to 256 competitors through 1-on-1 battles where competitors register the Pokémon they plan to use.

After the preliminary rounds, Trainers must win all three double battle rounds of the Qualifying Tournament to join the 32 competitors advancing to the Victory Tournament. There's a day off following the completion of the Qualifying Tournament, allowing competitors to rest up and get in some last-minute training.

The Victory Tournament brings competitors to the main stadium for a full 6-on-6 battle on a stage that can rotate between Grass, Rock, Water, and Ice fields.

PRESIDENT GOODSHOW AND THE TORCH COMMITTEE

Professor Charles Goodshow, President of the Pokémon League Torch Committee, is a jovial old fellow who truly loves his job. His duty is to make sure the torch relay and lighting goes smoothly for each tournament; to make sure nothing is derailed even if the torch is stolen or extinguished, he's been known to carry a special canister with another flame of Moltres burning inside.

> The field type is selected randomly at the beginning of each match; one five-minute break is called as soon as a Trainer has three Pokémon unable to battle, and the field type switches again before the battle resumes.

ASH DEFEATS KATIE

Katie is a strategy-minded Trainer from Lilycove City who takes an early lead against Ash. But luck starts to turn against her when Corphish defeats her Golduck even while confused. Ash wins the day—although Katie makes him work for the win.

ASH DEFEATS MORRISON

Morrison is devastated to learn that he'll be paired up against his new buddy, and he almost loses the match by default when he can barely bring himself to call out his Pokémon. A quick lecture from Ash gets Morrison back into the game; although Ash still wins, the battle at least finishes as a fair fight.

Morrison

Morrison is a loud young Trainer from Verdanturf Town who easily matches Ash for sheer competitiveness. The two of them met before the Hoenn League Championship and they love to try and outdo each other. Just like Ash, he's also absent-minded when it comes to anything that doesn't involve Pokémon and battles—and Morrison doesn't have the advantage of Brock and Max to keep an eye on him. Morrison battles for fun, win or lose, and Ash is the first real friend he's ever battled.

TYSON DEFEATS ASH

In another close-fought battle between friendly rivals, even Tyson's powerhouse Metagross is taken down by Ash's quick strategizing. Tyson ekes out a win when both his Meowth and Ash's Pikachu are too exhausted to battle. Even though Tyson's Meowth is ready to collapse, Pikachu faints first.

Tyson

Hailing from Mauville City, Tyson is a calm, friendly Trainer with a passion for food. Like his personality, Tyson's battle strategy is carefully balanced, with a sound mix of offense and defense.

HOENN LEGENDARY POKÉMON

GROUDON • (GRAU-don)

Height	11'06" (3.5 m)	**Category**	Continent
Weight	2094.4 lbs (950.0 kg)	**Type**	Ground

The mighty king of Magma, Groudon weighs in at an enormous 2094 pounds, making it perhaps the heaviest Legendary Pokémon in existence. Extremely powerful, Groudon rages with the burning strength of newly formed land.

Worshipped for its power by the nefarious Team Magma, Groudon can create land. Groudon is a savior to flood victims because of its ability to evaporate water and create ground. Groudon is the opposite of majestic Kyogre, and the two have battled ceaselessly with neither yet laying claim to victory.

KYOGRE • (kai-OH-gurr)

Height	14'09" (4.5 m)	**Category**	Sea Basin
Weight	776.0 lbs (352.0 kg)	**Type**	Water

Majestic servant of the sea, Kyogre is the mythological Pokémon that expanded the seas by covering the lands with rain. Very large, Kyogre resembles a killer whale, and its most dominant features are its fins.

Sought greatly by Team Aqua, Kyogre can expand the oceans. Though large, Kyogre is nimble within the waves of its natural habitat—the sea.

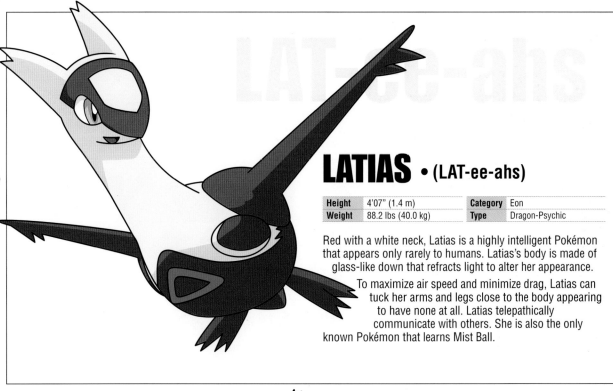

LATIAS • (LAT-ee-ahs)

Height	4'07" (1.4 m)	Category	Eon
Weight	88.2 lbs (40.0 kg)	Type	Dragon-Psychic

Red with a white neck, Latias is a highly intelligent Pokémon that appears only rarely to humans. Latias's body is made of glass-like down that refracts light to alter her appearance.

To maximize air speed and minimize drag, Latias can tuck her arms and legs close to the body appearing to have none at all. Latias telepathically communicate with others. She is also the only known Pokémon that learns Mist Ball.

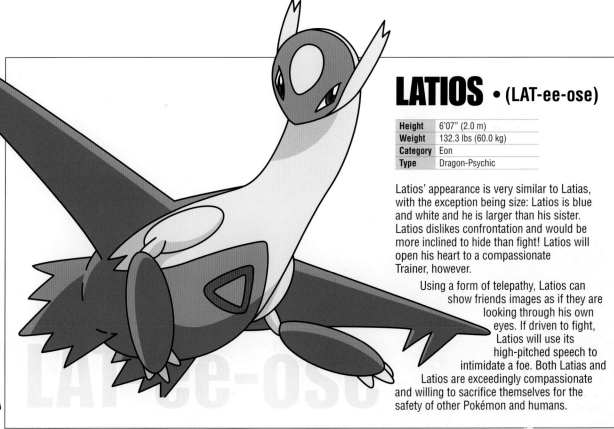

LATIOS • (LAT-ee-ose)

Height	6'07" (2.0 m)
Weight	132.3 lbs (60.0 kg)
Category	Eon
Type	Dragon-Psychic

Latios' appearance is very similar to Latias, with the exception being size: Latios is blue and white and he is larger than his sister. Latios dislikes confrontation and would be more inclined to hide than fight! Latios will open his heart to a compassionate Trainer, however.

Using a form of telepathy, Latios can show friends images as if they are looking through his own eyes. If driven to fight, Latios will use its high-pitched speech to intimidate a foe. Both Latias and Latios are exceedingly compassionate and willing to sacrifice themselves for the safety of other Pokémon and humans.

RAYQUAZA • (ray-KWAZ-uh)

Height	23'00" (7.0 m)	**Category**	Sky High
Weight	455.2 lbs (206.5 kg)	**Type**	Dragon-Flying

Rayquaza has lived for hundreds of millions of years in the ozone layer. This Dragon- and Flying-type has never touched the ground. Its constant movement has prevented it from being discovered until recently.

Very aggressive, Rayquaza is a powerful Pokémon. Large and sleek, it lacks wings or other propulsion, but it still flies. It does have rudder-like fins that appear periodically down its long green serpent-like body. It has no legs, but has short three-fingered hands and a large mouth to expel its awesome Hyper Beam.

REGICE • (REDGE-ice)

Height	5'11" (1.8 m)
Weight	385.8 lbs (175.0 kg)
Category	Iceberg
Type	Ice

Completely composed of Ice, Regice's body is so cold, not even magma can melt it. The super-chilled air wrapped around Regice is so cold that anyone who approaches it has a high probability of freezing. Like Regirock and Registeel, Regice has a series of small dots on its face that form a shape. Regice's looks like a plus sign.

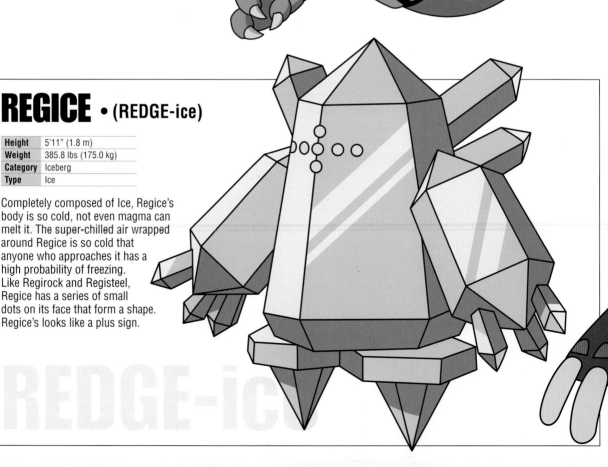

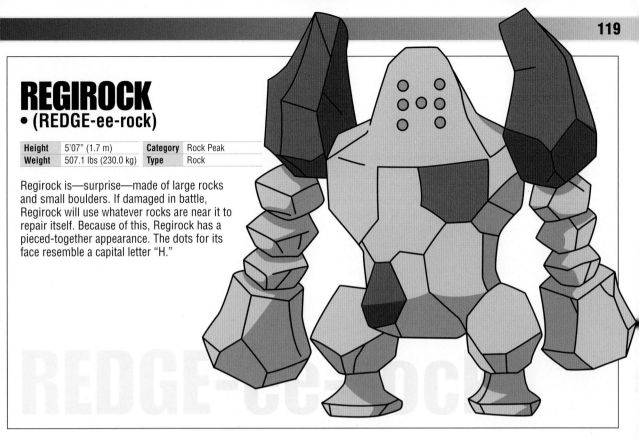

REGIROCK
• (REDGE-ee-rock)

Height	5'07" (1.7 m)	**Category**	Rock Peak
Weight	507.1 lbs (230.0 kg)	**Type**	Rock

Regirock is—surprise—made of large rocks and small boulders. If damaged in battle, Regirock will use whatever rocks are near it to repair itself. Because of this, Regirock has a pieced-together appearance. The dots for its face resemble a capital letter "H."

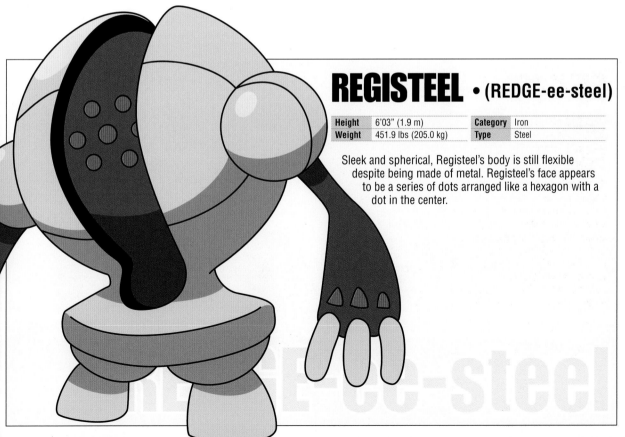

REGISTEEL • (REDGE-ee-steel)

Height	6'03" (1.9 m)	**Category**	Iron
Weight	451.9 lbs (205.0 kg)	**Type**	Steel

Sleek and spherical, Registeel's body is still flexible despite being made of metal. Registeel's face appears to be a series of dots arranged like a hexagon with a dot in the center.

DEOXYS • (dee-OCKS-iss)

Height	5'07" (1.7 m)	Category	DNA
Weight	134.0 lbs (60.8 kg)	Type	Psychic

Formed in a meteor while descending through the atmosphere, Deoxys is a mutated virus. Completely alien, this Psychic-type Pokémon can use any of four Formes: Normal Forme, Attack Forme, Defense Forme, and Speed Forme.

Completely versatile, Deoxys can adapt its form to any situation. Each of its three modified Formes changes its appearance. In Attack Forme, Deoxys' tentacle arms form a sharp point, just like its head. In Defense Forme, its head and body merge, almost as if it were a turtle withdrawing its head back into its shell. The Speed Forme is more slender and the back of its head swoops out to a point to reduce wind resistance and improve its aerodynamics.

NORMAL FORME

ATTACK FORME

DEFENSE FORME

SPEED FORME

HOENN MYTHICAL POKÉMON

JIRACHI • (jer-AH-chi)

Height	1'00" (0.3 m)	Category	Wish
Weight	2.4 lbs (1.1 kg)	Type	Steel-Psychic

Jirachi is asleep most of the time. It will only awake from its sleep if it is sung to with a voice of purity. Jirachi is a small Steel- and Psychic-type Pokémon.

Floating most of the time, Jirachi has stubby little legs. The only known Pokémon that can learn Doom Desire, Jirachi normally flees when in trouble. If forced to fight, it can use this exceedingly powerful Move.

HOENN POKÉMON

After traveling through the regions of Kanto and Johto, you will make Hoenn your next stop—home to the mighty Kyogre and Groudon!

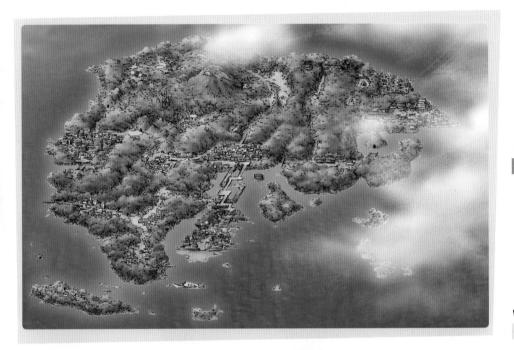

ABSOL
Height: 3'11" (1.2 m)
Weight: 103.6 lbs. (47.0 kg)

DARK

AGGRON

Height: 6'11" (2.1 m)
Weight: 793.7 lbs. (360.0 kg)

STEEL | ROCK

ALTARIA

Height: 3'07" (1.1 m)
Weight: 45.4 lbs. (20.6 kg)

DRAGON | FLYING

ANORITH

Height: 2'04" (0.7 m)
Weight: 27.6 lbs. (12.5 kg)

ROCK | BUG

ARMALDO

Height: 4'11" (1.5 m)
Weight: 150.4 lbs. (68.2 kg)

ROCK | BUG

ARON

Height: 1'04" (0.4 m)
Weight: 132.3 lbs. (60.0 kg)

STEEL | ROCK

AZURILL

Height: 0'08" (0.2 m)
Weight: 4.4 lbs. (2.0 kg)

NORMAL | FAIRY

BAGON

Height: 2'00" (0.6 m)
Weight: 92.8 lbs. (42.1 kg)

DRAGON

BALTOY

Height: 1'08" (0.5 m)
Weight: 47.4 lbs. (21.5 kg)

GROUND | PSYCHIC

BANETTE

Height: 3'07" (1.1 m)
Weight: 27.6 lbs. (12.5 kg)

GHOST

BARBOACH

Height: 1'04" (0.4 m)
Weight: 4.2 lbs. (1.9 kg)

WATER | GROUND

BEAUTIFLY

Height: 3'03" (1.0 m)
Weight: 62.6 lbs. (28.4 kg)

BUG | FLYING

BELDUM

Height: 2'00" (0.6 m)
Weight: 209.9 lbs. (95.2 kg)

STEEL | PSYCHIC

BLAZIKEN

Height: 6'03" (1.9 m)
Weight: 114.6 lbs. (52.0 kg)

FIRE | FIGHTING

BRELOOM

Height: 3'11" (1.2 m)
Weight: 86.4 lbs. (39.2 kg)

GRASS | FIGHTING

CACNEA

Height: 1'04" (0.4 m)
Weight: 113.1 lbs. (51.3 kg)

GRASS

CACTURNE

Height: 4'03" (1.3 m)
Weight: 170.6 lbs. (77.4 kg)

GRASS | DARK

CAMERUPT

Height: 6'03" (1.9 m)
Weight: 485.0 lbs. (220.0 kg)

FIRE | GROUND

CARVANHA

Height: 2'07" (0.8 m)
Weight: 45.9 lbs. (20.8 kg)

WATER | DARK

CASCOON

Height: 2'04" (0.7 m)
Weight: 25.4 lbs. (11.5 kg)

BUG

CASTFORM

Height: 1'00" (0.3 m)
Weight: 1.8 lbs. (0.8 kg)

NORMAL

CHIMECHO

Height: 2'00" (0.6 m)
Weight: 2.2 lbs. (1.0 kg)

PSYCHIC

CLAMPERL

Height: 1'04" (0.4 m)
Weight: 115.7 lbs. (52.5 kg)

WATER

CLAYDOL

Height: 4'11" (1.5 m)
Weight: 238.1 lbs. (108.0 kg)

GROUND | PSYCHIC

COMBUSKEN

Height: 2'11" (0.9 m)
Weight: 43.0 lbs. (19.5 kg)

FIRE | FIGHTING

CORPHISH

Height: 2'00" (0.6 m)
Weight: 25.4 lbs. (11.5 kg)

WATER

CRADILY

Height: 4'11" (1.5 m)
Weight: 133.2 lbs. (60.4 kg)

ROCK | GRASS

CRAWDAUNT

Height: 3'07" (1.1 m)
Weight: 72.3 lbs. (32.8 kg)

WATER | DARK

DELCATTY

Height: 3'07" (1.1 m)
Weight: 71.9 lbs. (32.6 kg)

NORMAL

DEOXYS

Height: 5'07" (1.7 m)
Weight: 134.0 lbs. (60.8 kg)

PSYCHIC

DUSCLOPS

Height: 5'03" (1.6 m)
Weight: 67.5 lbs. (30.6 kg)

GHOST

DUSKULL

Height: 2'07" (0.8 m)
Weight: 33.1 lbs. (15.0 kg)

GHOST

DUSTOX

Height: 3'11" (1.2 m)
Weight: 69.7 lbs. (31.6 kg)

BUG POISON

ELECTRIKE

Height: 2'00" (0.6 m)
Weight: 33.5 lbs. (15.2 kg)

ELECTRIC

EXPLOUD

Height: 4'11" (1.5 m)
Weight: 185.2 lbs. (84.0 kg)

NORMAL

FEEBAS

Height: 2'00" (0.6 m)
Weight: 16.3 lbs. (7.4 kg)

WATER

FLYGON

Height: 6'07" (2.0 m)
Weight: 180.8 lbs. (82.0 kg)

GROUND DRAGON

GARDEVOIR

Height: 5'03" (1.6 m)
Weight: 106.7 lbs. (48.4 kg)

PSYCHIC FAIRY

GLALIE

Height: 4'11" (1.5 m)
Weight: 565.5 lbs. (256.5 kg)

ICE

GOREBYSS

Height: 5'11" (1.8 m)
Weight: 49.8 lbs. (22.6 kg)

WATER

GROUDON

Height: 11'06" (3.5 m)
Weight: 2094.4 lbs. (950.0 kg)

GROUND

GROVYLE

Height: 2'11" (0.9 m)
Weight: 47.6 lbs. (21.6 kg)

GRASS

GRUMPIG

Height: 2'11" (0.9 m)
Weight: 157.6 lbs. (71.5 kg)

PSYCHIC

GULPIN

Height: 1'04" (0.4 m)
Weight: 22.7 lbs. (10.3 kg)

POISON

HARIYAMA

Height: 7'07" (2.3 m)
Weight: 559.5 lbs. (253.8 kg)

FIGHTING

HUNTAIL

Height: 5'07" (1.7 m)
Weight: 59.5 lbs. (27.0 kg)

WATER

ILLUMISE

Height: 2'00" (0.6 m)
Weight: 39.0 lbs. (17.7 kg)

BUG

JIRACHI

Height: 1'00" (0.3 m)
Weight: 2.4 lbs. (1.1 kg)

STEEL PSYCHIC

KECLEON

Height: 3'03" (1.0 m)
Weight: 48.5 lbs. (22.0 kg)

NORMAL

KIRLIA

Height: 2'07" (0.8 m)
Weight: 44.5 lbs. (20.2 kg)

PSYCHIC FAIRY

KYOGRE

Height: 14'09" (4.5 m)
Weight: 776.0 lbs. (352.0 kg)

WATER

LAIRON

Height: 2'11" (0.9 m)
Weight: 264.6 lbs. (120.0 kg)

STEEL ROCK

LATIAS

Height: 4'07" (1.4 m)
Weight: 88.2 lbs. (40.0 kg)

DRAGON | PSYCHIC

LATIOS

Height: 6'07" (2.0 m)
Weight: 132.3 lbs. (60.0 kg)

DRAGON | PSYCHIC

LILEEP

Height: 3'03" (1.0 m)
Weight: 52.5 lbs. (23.8 kg)

ROCK | GRASS

LINOONE

Height: 1'08" (0.5 m)
Weight: 71.6 lbs. (32.5 kg)

NORMAL

LOMBRE

Height: 3'11" (1.2 m)
Weight: 71.6 lbs. (32.5 kg)

WATER | GRASS

LOTAD

Height: 1'08" (0.5 m)
Weight: 5.7 lbs. (2.6 kg)

WATER | GRASS

LOUDRED

Height: 3'03" (1.0 m)
Weight: 89.3 lbs. (40.5 kg)

NORMAL

LUDICOLO

Height: 4'11" (1.5 m)
Weight: 121.3 lbs. (55.0 kg)

WATER | GRASS

LUNATONE

Height: 3'03" (1.0 m)
Weight: 370.4 lbs. (168.0 kg)

ROCK | PSYCHIC

LUVDISC

Height: 2'00" (0.6 m)
Weight: 19.2 lbs. (8.7 kg)

WATER

MAKUHITA

Height: 3'03" (1.0 m)
Weight: 190.5 lbs. (86.4 kg)

FIGHTING

MANECTRIC

Height: 4'11" (1.5 m)
Weight: 88.6 lbs. (40.2 kg)

ELECTRIC

MARSHTOMP

Height: 2'04" (0.7 m)
Weight: 61.7 lbs. (28.0 kg)

WATER | GROUND

MASQUERAIN

Height: 2'07" (0.8 m)
Weight: 7.9 lbs. (3.6 kg)

BUG | FLYING

MAWILE

Height: 2'00" (0.6 m)
Weight: 25.4 lbs. (11.5 kg)

STEEL | FAIRY

MEDICHAM

Height: 4'03" (1.3 m)
Weight: 69.4 lbs. (31.5 kg)

FIGHTING | PSYCHIC

MEDITITE

Height: 2'00" (0.6 m)
Weight: 24.7 lbs. (11.2 kg)

FIGHTING | PSYCHIC

METAGROSS

Height: 5'03" (1.6 m)
Weight: 1212.5 lbs. (550.0 kg)

STEEL | PSYCHIC

METANG

Height: 3'11" (1.2 m)
Weight: 446.4 lbs. (202.5 kg)

STEEL | PSYCHIC

MIGHTYENA

Height: 3'03" (1.0 m)
Weight: 81.6 lbs. (37.0 kg)

DARK

MILOTIC

Height: 20'04" (6.2 m)
Weight: 357.1 lbs. (162.0 kg)

WATER

MINUN

Height: 1'04" (0.4 m)
Weight: 9.3 lbs. (4.2 kg)

ELECTRIC

MUDKIP

Height: 1'04" (0.4 m)
Weight: 16.8 lbs. (7.6 kg)

WATER

NINCADA

Height: 1'08" (0.5 m)
Weight: 12.1 lbs. (5.5 kg)

BUG   GROUND

NINJASK

Height: 2'07" (0.8 m)
Weight: 26.5 lbs. (12.0 kg)

BUG   FLYING

NOSEPASS

Height: 3'03" (1.0 m)
Weight: 213.8 lbs. (97.0 kg)

ROCK

NUMEL

Height: 2'04" (0.7 m)
Weight: 52.9 lbs. (24.0 kg)

FIRE   GROUND

NUZLEAF

Height: 3'03" (1.0 m)
Weight: 61.7 lbs. (28.0 kg)

GRASS   DARK

PELIPPER

Height: 3'11" (1.2 m)
Weight: 61.7 lbs. (28.0 kg)

WATER   FLYING

PLUSLE

Height: 1'04" (0.4 m)
Weight: 9.3 lbs. (4.2 kg)

ELECTRIC

POOCHYENA

Height: 1'08" (0.5 m)
Weight: 30.0 lbs. (13.6 kg)

DARK

RALTS

Height: 1'04" (0.4 m)
Weight: 14.6 lbs. (6.6 kg)

PSYCHIC   FAIRY

RAYQUAZA

Height: 23'00" (7.0 m)
Weight: 455.2 lbs. (206.5 kg)

DRAGON   FLYING

REGICE

Height: 5'11" (1.8 m)
Weight: 385.8 lbs. (175.0 kg)

ICE

REGIROCK

Height: 5'07" (1.7 m)
Weight: 507.1 lbs. (230.0 kg)

ROCK

REGISTEEL

Height: 6'03" (1.9 m)
Weight: 451.9 lbs. (205.0 kg)

STEEL

RELICANTH

Height: 3'03" (1.0 m)
Weight: 51.6 lbs. (23.4 kg)

WATER   ROCK

ROSELIA

Height: 1'00" (0.3 m)
Weight: 4.4 lbs. (2.0 kg)

GRASS   POISON

SABLEYE

Height: 1'08" (0.5 m)
Weight: 24.3 lbs. (11.0 kg)

DARK   GHOST

SALAMENCE

Height: 4'11" (1.5 m)
Weight: 226.2 lbs. (102.6 kg)

DRAGON   FLYING

SCEPTILE

Height: 5'07" (1.7 m)
Weight: 115.1 lbs. (52.2 kg)

GRASS

SEALEO

Height: 3'07" (1.1 m)
Weight: 193.1 lbs. (87.6 kg)

ICE | WATER

SEEDOT

Height: 1'08" (0.5 m)
Weight: 8.8 lbs. (4.0 kg)

GRASS

SEVIPER

Height: 8'10" (2.7 m)
Weight: 115.7 lbs. (52.5 kg)

POISON

SHARPEDO

Height: 5'11" (1.8 m)
Weight: 195.8 lbs. (88.8 kg)

WATER | DARK

SHEDINJA

Height: 2'07" (0.8 m)
Weight: 2.6 lbs. (1.2 kg)

BUG | GHOST

SHELGON

Height: 3'07" (1.1 m)
Weight: 243.6 lbs. (110.5 kg)

DRAGON

SHIFTRY

Height: 4'03" (1.3 m)
Weight: 131.4 lbs. (59.6 kg)

GRASS | DARK

SHROOMISH

Height: 1'04" (0.4 m)
Weight: 9.9 lbs. (4.5 kg)

GRASS

SHUPPET

Height: 2'00" (0.6 m)
Weight: 5.1 lbs. (2.3 kg)

GHOST

SILCOON

Height: 2'00" (0.6 m)
Weight: 22.0 lbs. (10.0 kg)

BUG

SKITTY

Height: 2'00" (0.6 m)
Weight: 24.3 lbs. (11.0 kg)

NORMAL

SLAKING

Height: 6'07" (2.0 m)
Weight: 287.7 lbs. (130.5 kg)

NORMAL

SLAKOTH

Height: 2'07" (0.8 m)
Weight: 52.9 lbs. (24.0 kg)

NORMAL

SNORUNT

Height: 2'04" (0.7 m)
Weight: 37.0 lbs. (16.8 kg)

ICE

SOLROCK

Height: 3'11" (1.2 m)
Weight: 339.5 lbs. (154.0 kg)

ROCK | PSYCHIC

SPHEAL

Height: 2'07" (0.8 m)
Weight: 87.1 lbs. (39.5 kg)

ICE | WATER

SPINDA

Height: 3'07" (1.1 m)
Weight: 11.0 lbs. (5.0 kg)

NORMAL

SPOINK

Height: 2'04" (0.7 m)
Weight: 67.5 lbs. (30.6 kg)

PSYCHIC

SURSKIT
Height: 1'08" (0.5 m)
Weight: 3.7 lbs. (1.7 kg)

BUG | WATER

SWABLU

Height: 1'04" (0.4 m)
Weight: 2.6 lbs. (1.2 kg)

NORMAL | FLYING

SWALOT

Height: 5'07" (1.7 m)
Weight: 176.4 lbs. (80.0 kg)

POISON

SWAMPERT

Height: 4'11" (1.5 m)
Weight: 180.6 lbs. (81.9 kg)

WATER GROUND

SWELLOW

Height: 2'04" (0.7 m)
Weight: 43.7 lbs. (19.8 kg)

NORMAL FLYING

TAILLOW

Height: 1'00" (0.3 m)
Weight: 5.1 lbs. (2.3 kg)

NORMAL FLYING

TORCHIC

Height: 1'04" (0.4 m)
Weight: 5.5 lbs. (2.5 kg)

FIRE

TORKOAL

Height: 1'08" (0.5 m)
Weight: 177.2 lbs. (80.4 kg)

FIRE

TRAPINCH

Height: 2'04" (0.7 m)
Weight: 33.1 lbs. (15.0 kg)

GROUND

TREECKO

Height: 1'08" (0.5 m)
Weight: 11.0 lbs. (5.0 kg)

GRASS

TROPIUS

Height: 6'07" (2.0 m)
Weight: 220.5 lbs. (100.0 kg)

GRASS FLYING

VIBRAVA

Height: 3'07" (1.1 m)
Weight: 33.7 lbs. (15.3 kg)

GROUND DRAGON

VIGOROTH

Height: 4'07" (1.4 m)
Weight: 102.5 lbs. (46.5 kg)

NORMAL

VOLBEAT

Height: 2'04" (0.7 m)
Weight: 39.0 lbs. (17.7 kg)

BUG

WAILMER

Height: 6'07" (2.0 m)
Weight: 286.6 lbs. (130.0 kg)

WATER

WAILORD

Height: 47'07" (14.5 m)
Weight: 877.4 lbs. (398.0 kg)

WATER

WALREIN

Height: 4'07" (1.4 m)
Weight: 332.0 lbs. (150.6 kg)

ICE WATER

WHISCASH

Height: 2'11" (0.9 m)
Weight: 52.0 lbs. (23.6 kg)

WATER GROUND

WHISMUR

Height: 2'00" (0.6 m)
Weight: 35.9 lbs. (16.3 kg)

NORMAL

WINGULL

Height: 2'00" (0.6 m)
Weight: 20.9 lbs. (9.5 kg)

WATER FLYING

WURMPLE

Height: 1'00" (0.3 m)
Weight: 7.9 lbs. (3.6 kg)

BUG

WYNAUT

Height: 2'00" (0.6 m)
Weight: 30.9 lbs. (14.0 kg)

PSYCHIC

ZANGOOSE

Height: 4'03" (1.3 m)
Weight: 88.8 lbs. (40.3 kg)

NORMAL

ZIGZAGOON

Height: 1'04" (0.4 m)
Weight: 38.6 lbs. (17.5 kg)

NORMAL

SINNOH

Sinnoh is a vast region bisected by Mt. Coronet. Professor Rowan is the resident Pokémon professor, hailing from Sandgem Town. Sinnoh is an amazing place, and at the time when he first arrived, is the only region visited by Ash to have a substantial area covered in snow.

Though a large majority of Sinnoh is land, fresh-water lakes are prevelant within the region proper. Three rather important lakes are Verity in the west, Acuity in the north, and Valor in the east. These three lakes are home to Mesprit, Uxie, and Azelf, respectively. The entire northwest of the region is dominated by the Eterna Forest. Many Trainers, including Ash, have gotten lost in this massive forest.

Jubilife is the largest city in Sinnoh, and it is very modern. Hearthome City is an active city with many things to do. People from all over the world of Pokémon come to Hearthome to test their skill in the Tag Battle.

DAWN

After her 10th birthday, this spirited young girl left her home in Sinnoh's Twinleaf Town to see the world and become a great Pokémon Coordinator. She first met Ash after she and her Piplup helped save Ash's Pikachu, and since then she's traveled with Ash and Brock on their Sinnoh adventures, competing in Pokémon Contests along the way.

Pokétch

Dawn earned her Pokétch after helping stop Team Rocket pass out a wave of fake Pokétch. One of her newest Pokétch applications is the Coin Toss application, which she uses to help decide which way to go—or who gets to go first in a Pokémon Battle!

THE SURPRISING VOICE OF REASON

Dawn hasn't had quite as many adventures as Ash and Brock, but that often comes as an asset! For one thing, Dawn hasn't had nearly as much experience with Team Rocket and their various schemes. So when Team Rocket suggests that the "twerps" help them train Cacnea, Ash and Brock cheerfully agree to help—while Dawn is openly skeptical of any plan that helps makes the villains even stronger.

A SENSE OF STYLE

Dawn likes to dress up—so much so that her mother had to stop her from bringing a suitcase full of clothes on her journey! Being a Coordinator may involve looking good on stage, but Dawn is determined to stay stylish at all times, even if it means having Piplup use BubbleBeam to help fix her bedhead.

PIPLUP

Piplup, Dawn's First Partner Pokémon, is proud, sassy, and doesn't always follow Dawn's directions. Dawn met Piplup after it ran out of Professor Rowan's research center, and even though they didn't get along, they had to work together to escape some wild Ariados.

A CRISIS OF CONFIDENCE

Normally, Dawn is upbeat and cheerful—her catchphrase is "No need to worry!" But after two Contests in a row where she fails to advance beyond the first round, she starts to doubt whether she should even continue competing in Contests at all. Even the advice and encouragement of her rivals Zoey and Kenny aren't enough to keep her spirits up, though Dawn tries to hide her turmoil behind her usual happy demeanor. In Veilstone City, Dawn meets Maylene, a Gym Leader suffering from a similar crisis of confidence, and Dawn challenges her to a Gym battle. Dawn loses the match, but both she and Maylene regain their fighting spirit.

PACHIRISU

Pachirisu was so cute that Dawn just had to catch it after spotting it in the wild. But after an exhausting chase and capture, Dawn discovered that Pachirisu was too hyperactive to listen to any of her commands, and she reluctantly released it. Fortunately, she and Pachirisu were reunited, and this Electric-type Pokémon remains as energetic as ever—although its lack of control over its Discharge move still comes as a shock.

BUIZEL

Though stubborn Buizel started its journey with Dawn, along the road it found a true pal in Ash, so they arranged the perfect trade. Buizel battle its way through Competitions with Ash. In exchange, Ash's friend Aipom joined Dawn's Contest team.

DAWN'S BIG SECRET

All of Dawn's childhood friends called her "Dee-Dee," and she was determined to keep the reason a secret. But when Ursula's duo Plusle and Minun shocked her at a Pokémon competition in Daybreak Town, Dawn had no choice but to face her past and the hair-raising story behind her nickname. When Dawn was a little girl, she hugged her class' Pokémon pals Plusle and Minun so tightly that they zapped her to break loose. The charge covered Dawn's hair in sparkling glitter shocks, and a boy joked that she looked like she had "diamond dandruff." To tease her, classmates started calling her "Dee-Dee" for short. Every time she hears this embarrassing name, it makes her want to pull her hair out.

A LEGACY TO LIVE UP TO

Dawn's mother Johanna was a prize-winning Coordinator, and Dawn dreams of following in her footsteps. As a good luck charm, Dawn carries her mother's first Contest Ribbon with her on her journey.

A Full-Fledged Heroine

In addition to being a new Trainer to join Ash on his travels after he arrives in the Sinnoh region, Dawn represents a new development in the world of Pokémon. Ash lives for his quest to become a Pokémon Master, and although we've met his mother Delia, little else is known about his past. Ash was joined by Brock and Misty, both characters who have families and Gym Leader responsibilities to deal with. With May, Ash was joined by a new and more nuanced character: not only did she have a Gym Leader father to deal with, but she also had to handle the responsibility of looking after her little brother Max.

But perhaps more so than any of Ash's other travel companions, Dawn is a fully realized character. Like Brock, Misty, and May, Dawn has a family—her mother, Johanna—that weighs on her mind. As with May, we also see snippets of Dawn's history in flashbacks, including embarrassing moments from her childhood. But what sets Dawn apart is that we also see her childhood friends, including Leona, her friend since kindergarten.

Dawn's Pokémon

BUNEARY

Buneary was Dawn's first Pokémon capture, and it certainly wasn't an easy one. But it's more than happy to travel with Dawn and her friends, as it seems to have a real crush on Ash's Pikachu.

AIPOM

After Ash realized that his Aipom loved being in Contests, he traded it to Dawn in exchange for her Buizel. Aipom evolved into Ambipom and made its Contest debut with Dawn in the Solaceon Town Contest, but the pair didn't make it past the first round.

AMBIPOM

CYNDAQUIL

You wouldn't expect shy Cyndaquil to set a battle ablaze. But, when it gets fired up, so do the flames on its back. When Cyndaquil evolved into Quilava, Dawn felt she too had grown as a Coordinator.

PILOSWINE

SWINUB

This Pokémon has its nose to the ground for good reason. It can sniff out delicious food and a fresh spring buried deep in the dirt. Dawn trained with Swinub so much that it evolved not just once into Piloswine, but twice into Mamoswine!

MAMOSWINE

QUILAVA

TOGEKISS

Graceful Togekiss likes to play peacekeeper and appreciates those who share its love of harmony. Dawn had to open her heart and rethink her strategy so this Flying- and Fairy-type could soar in Contests.

PROFESSOR ROWAN

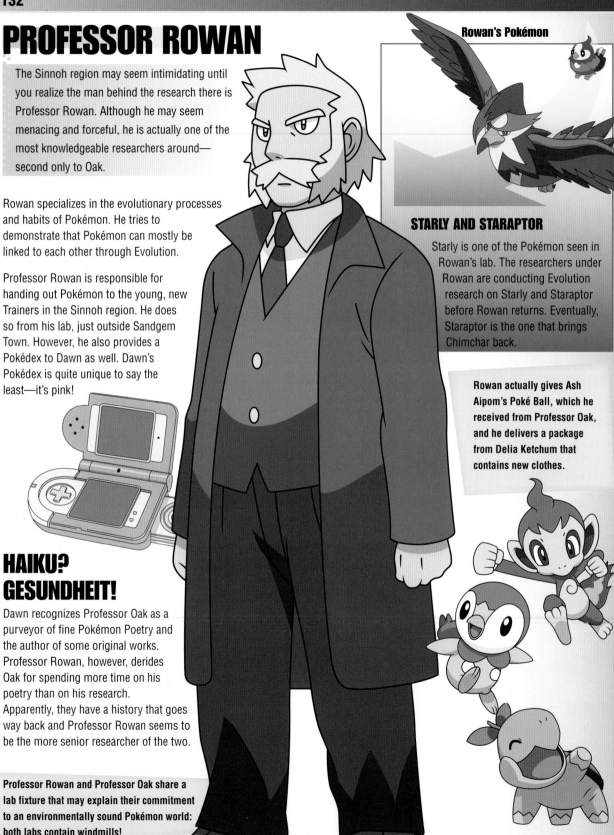

The Sinnoh region may seem intimidating until you realize the man behind the research there is Professor Rowan. Although he may seem menacing and forceful, he is actually one of the most knowledgeable researchers around—second only to Oak.

Rowan specializes in the evolutionary processes and habits of Pokémon. He tries to demonstrate that Pokémon can mostly be linked to each other through Evolution.

Professor Rowan is responsible for handing out Pokémon to the young, new Trainers in the Sinnoh region. He does so from his lab, just outside Sandgem Town. However, he also provides a Pokédex to Dawn as well. Dawn's Pokédex is quite unique to say the least—it's pink!

HAIKU? GESUNDHEIT!

Dawn recognizes Professor Oak as a purveyor of fine Pokémon Poetry and the author of some original works. Professor Rowan, however, derides Oak for spending more time on his poetry than on his research. Apparently, they have a history that goes way back and Professor Rowan seems to be the more senior researcher of the two.

Professor Rowan and Professor Oak share a lab fixture that may explain their commitment to an environmentally sound Pokémon world: both labs contain windmills!

Rowan's Pokémon

STARLY AND STARAPTOR

Starly is one of the Pokémon seen in Rowan's lab. The researchers under Rowan are conducting Evolution research on Starly and Staraptor before Rowan returns. Eventually, Staraptor is the one that brings Chimchar back.

Rowan actually gives Ash Aipom's Poké Ball, which he received from Professor Oak, and he delivers a package from Delia Ketchum that contains new clothes.

ZOEY

A Coordinator from Snowpoint City who is Dawn's friend as well as her rival, Zoey first met Dawn by chance in the Jubilife Contest. Zoey, who already had a Ribbon by that time, quickly fell into the role of Dawn's cool older friend (though Zoey's exact age is unknown). She's not afraid to stand up for herself or for Dawn. When Jessie challenges Dawn to a double battle, hoping to score an easy win on a novice, Zoey senses Jessie's trick and takes up the challenge herself.

Although Zoey always seems to have it together, she can admit that she gets nervous during Contests or upset about a loss. She doesn't measure her performance strictly in terms of Ribbons, though, and she won't let herself, or her friends, succumb to second-guessing after a loss. So after Dawn's disappointing performance in the Solaceon Contest, Zoey heads over to dispel Dawn's blues and get her back on the right track.

Two Degrees of Separation

Prior to the Jubilife Contest, both Zoey and Kenny competed in a Contest where Zoey beat Kenny and came out the winner—that's how Zoey won her first Ribbon. The two Coordinators didn't know each other before the Contest; although Zoey and Kenny have Dawn in common, up until now, Dawn has yet to meet up with both of them at the same time.

Zoey is serious about Contests, and she expects everyone else to be dedicated, too. She doesn't believe it's possible to excel at both Contests and Gym Battles. But after Nando defeats her in a Contest, she realizes that even a Coordinator can learn from Gym battling. She's the one who suggests that Ash trade his Contest-loving Aipom for Dawn's battle-loving Buizel.

Zoey's Pokémon

FINNEON

Zoey used Finneon in the Wallace Cup, and it later evolved into Lumineon.

LUMINEON

SHELLOS

After Dawn caught her Buizel, Zoey stuck around to do some more fishing and came up with this Shellos. She's used it as an effective Contest partner for Glameow. It later evolved into Gastrodon.

GASTRODON WEST

GLAMEOW

Like Dawn's other role model, her mother Johanna, Zoey also has a Glameow. Her Glameow can uncurl its tail and use it to strike, a move that catches opponents by surprise.

MISDREAVUS

She has used Misdreavus in the Jubilife Contest and the Wallace Cup. She does use it during the appeals round, with its highly effective Shock Wave attack. It later evolved into a Mismagius.

LEAFEON

This Grass-type can absorb the sun's energy for photosynthesis. Zoey boldly matched her pal Leafeon against Bug-type expert Nando and their bravery blossomed. Leafeon lead her to the Grand Festival's final round.

KIRLIA

When this Psychic- and Fairy-type gets happy vibes from its Trainer, it busts out its best dances moves. With Zoey, Kirlia got so much Contest time, it evolved into Gallade before the Grand Festival.

GALLADE

MISMAGIUS

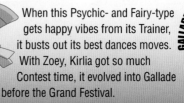

KENNY

A regular kid from Twinleaf Town, Kenny is a Pokémon Coordinator who's known Dawn since their nursery school days. He enjoys having a chance to reveal Dawn's embarrassing childhood moments to her new friends, too.

Even though Kenny loves to tease Dawn and occasionally puts on a cocky attitude, he's still a young boy who's not always as tough as he wants to appear. When he's trapped in the Solaceon Ruins along with Ash and Brock, he's terrified by the strangeness of the place until Ash reminds him to put on a brave face for his Pokémon.

Kenny's Pokémon

ALAKAZAM

Kenny uses it in the appeals round of Floaroma Contest.

PRINPLUP

Prinplup gets along fine with its Trainer, but it's a proud Pokémon and not always friendly toward everyone else. It later evolved into Empoleon.

EMPOLEON

MACHOKE

No task is too small and no weight is too big for muscle-bound Machoke. The Fighting–type is always there to lend Kenny a hand and lift up any heavy item. Machoke simply considers hard work to be the perfect workout.

FLOATZEL

The evolved form of Buizel, The Sea Weasel Pokémon is often spotted swimming in ports. Like a good lifeguard, if it sees someone drowning, Floatzel snaps into action to save him or her. Kenny can count on his pal Floatzel in or out of the water!

BRELOOM

After Kenny's Breloom uses Energy Ball in a friendly battle against Ash, Ash asks Kenny to help teach the move to his Turtwig.

NANDO

This self-styled Pokémon Bard adds a musical touch to almost everything he does, from conversations to Contests. He's exceedingly thoughtful and polite; in Pokémon battles, he even gives his Pokémon gentle requests instead of commands.

Despite his demeanor, he could be said to be a rival of both Ash and Dawn; unable to decide between pursuing Pokémon Contests or Gym battles, he battled both Trainers and was inspired to compete in Contests and Gym battles. Nando's plan seems to be paying off, as he's won at the Eterna Gym and earned two Ribbons—the second Ribbon was earned by defeating Zoey in the finals of the Hearthome Contest.

Nando's Pokémon

ROSELIA

Nando's Roselia evolved from a Budew during a battle with Ash's Pikachu. It later evolved into a Roserade.

ROSERADE

SUNFLORA

Nando and his Sunflora were mistakenly framed for stealing the Adamant Orb from the Eterna Historical Museum, but Sunflora helped track down the real perpetrators: Team Rocket.

KRICKETOT

This Bug-type's antennae can recreate the sweet sound of the xylophone when they clank together. Together with Altaria, Nando showcased its amazing musical abilities at the Grand Festival.

KRICKETUNE

When teamed with Sunflora's Grasswhistle, Kricketune can use Sing to put on a musical performance that will wow a Contest audience.

ALTARIA

The evolved form of Swablu, the Humming Pokémon wraps its fluffy wings around true friends and hums a heartfelt melody. It's no wonder Altaria found a deep connection with a sensitive poet like Nando!

LOPUNNY

The perfect pal for a guy who enters Pokémon Contests and Competitions, Lopunny has long, beautiful legs made for ballet and for kicking. Nando's Lopunny competed in the Grand Festival semi-finals against Zoey.

ARMALDO

The evolved form of Anorith, The Plate Pokémon is completely covered in a hard armor casing. It was one of the Pokémon Nando called upon to battle Ash in the Sinnoh League's opening round.

PAUL

On and off the battlefield, rival Pokémon Trainers are often friends, or at least good sports. Even Ash's first real rival, Gary Oak, is Ash's friend and ally as well. But Paul, a Trainer who treats Pokémon more like a game than a matter of living, feeling creatures, isn't here to be polite to anyone—least of all Ash. Paul is here to win.

Hailing from Veilstone City, Paul is a pragmatic, cold-hearted Trainer who believes in strength, victory, and not much else. He's no cheater, but to him, a win is a win regardless of whether it was won by kindness or cruelty. And kindness isn't in Paul's vocabulary: he expects 100% performance from his Pokémon at all times, never hesitating to criticize or release Pokémon who fail to fulfill expectations. Even at the moment of capture, Paul thinks only about what power a Pokémon has to offer, using his Pokédex to check the Pokémon he catches and keeping only Pokémon that meet his requirements. There's no room for weakness on his team.

Most Trainers want their Pokémon to avoid being hurt. But if he can get an advantage out of it, Paul orders his Pokémon to take damage during a battle; it's one of his ruthless but effective strategies.

Ash is determined to beat Paul and prove friendship and cooperation are the best ways to train Pokémon, but to his chagrin, his best results against Paul are only draws. Ash can barely even get Paul's attention, which only causes Ash's frustration to build. But on some level, Paul has been paying attention to Ash— Ash's Pokémon, that is. He couldn't care less about Ash's speeches on trust and friendship; instead, he's more interested in Pikachu's Volt Tackle.

WHEN A LIFE TOUCHES ANOTHER LIFE…

Cynthia, the top Trainer in Sinnoh, has seen Paul's behavior firsthand. But, unlike Ash, she doesn't react with outrage. She sees her younger self in Paul, a Trainer whose only thought is to become stronger, and gently urges him to think of his Pokémon not as tools but like people, each with their own unique personality. Although Ash and his friends remind Paul of Cynthia's lesson, it remains to be seen whether her words will have any effect.

Paul's Pokémon

ELEKID

Raised by Paul from an Elekid, Electabuzz has an attitude like its Trainer and an ongoing feud with Pikachu. It later evolved into an Electivire.

DRAPION

This prickly Pokémon was able to take out Ash's friends Buizel, Staraptor, and Torterra with Toxic Spikes during the Sinnoh League quarterfinals.

TURTWIG

Paul's First Partner Pokémon was a Turtwig. It's reached its final evolved form: a massive Torterra.

...SOMETHING NEW IS BORN?

Paul's Electabuzz seems to take after him; even when it was an Elekid. It doesn't get along with Ash's Pikachu, but in Veilstone City, Electabuzz had a chance to witness Ash's devotion toward his Pokémon. And as for Chimchar, Ash's support and kindess hasn't erased the memories of its brutal times with Paul. Chimchar still has some unfinished business to settle with its former Trainer.

FROSSLASS

After Ninjask was knocked out of the Sinnoh League quarterfinals, Froslass was brought onto the battlefield. Ash chose to send out Pikachu. Although Froslass is a force to be reckoned with, it was no match for the Mouse Pokémon.

URSARING

Caught in the Bewilder Forrest, Ursaring packs a mighty Hyper Beam. It takes on its former teammate Chimchar in a battle so brutal, it traumatizes Chimchar into unleashing its true power.

MURKROW

Paul caught his Murkrow during his travels outside the Sinnoh region. It evolves into Honchkrow in a battle with Gym Leader Maylene in Veilstone City.

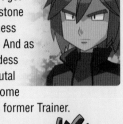

HONCHKROW

WEAVILE

This Weavile is another Pokémon Paul caught during his travels in the Sinnoh region.

GLISCOR

In a city on the route back to Veilstone City, Paul heard about a tough Gliscor and decided to catch it.

GASTRODON EAST

Paul's Gastrodon from the East Sea is a tough opponent. Paul picked it as his second Pokémon in the Sinnoh League Quarterfinals, but Ash's creative strategy eliminated it.

NINJASK

Paul caught Ninjask before Chimchar. But with Ash's training, the next time Ninjask saw Chimchar it had evolved into Infernape. Though Ninjask is known for its speed, it was no match for the Fire-type in the Sinnoh League quarterfinals.

LAIRON

After helping Lairon grow into its final evolution, Aggron, the Steel- and Rock-type Pokémon was Paul's first pick in the Full Battle with Ash and Pikachu in the Sinnoh League quarterfinals.

AGGRON

MAGMAR

This Magmar seems to have replaced Chimchar. Paul used it in his Veilstone Gym battle, exploiting Magmar's type advantage against Gym Leader Maylene's Lucario. It later evolved into a Magmortar.

MAGMORTAR

Chimchar

Is this the one that Paul let get away? Paul knew his Chimchar had amazing potential; when he first saw it in the wild, it unleashed an almost uncontrollable power to defeat a gang of Zangoose that had it cornered and scared. Thinking this power would be useful for the Pokémon League, Paul asked Chimchar to come with him. Chimchar believed it could become strong this way, but Paul's harsh training methods—far beyond anything he used on his other Pokémon—never managed to reawaken that power in Chimchar.

During the Hearthome City Tag Battle Tournament, Chimchar froze up when again confronted with a Zangoose—so Paul, disgusted, deliberately turned his back on his own Pokémon. Fortunately for Chimchar, after the battle it found a new, gentler Trainer in Ash. Paul has even seen Ash unlock Chimchar's true power, though it's still uncontrolled and dangerous.

MINDING HIS MANNERS

Paul may be mean, but he's not mean enough to think he can treat everyone that way. When it comes to Nurse Joy and other authority figures, such as Gym Leader Roark, Paul sometimes even says "thank you." And even though it may have been arrogant of Paul to challenge Cynthia, the Sinnoh Champion, he didn't give her attitude. After she decisively defeated him in battle, she made a number of suggestions which he reluctantly followed.

On the other hand, Paul will turn on anyone he doesn't respect, even a Gym Leader. After an easy victory over Veilstone Gym Leader Maylene, Paul didn't hesitate to insult her to her face.

Paul's most candid conversation to date is not with Ash, but with Brock. When Brock approached Paul with serious concerns about Chimchar's health, Paul explained how he met Chimchar and why he pushes Chimchar to the breaking point.

Reggie

Reggie is the complete opposite of his younger brother Paul. Mild-manned and pleasant, Reggie is a Pokémon breeder who is now back in Veilstone City. Like his brother Paul, Reggie traveled to other regions before returning to Sinnoh.

The display cases full of badges don't belong to Paul—they're Reggie's! Kanto, Johto, Hoenn, Sinnoh, and the Battle Frontier: Reggie's seen and battled it all.

Paul can leave some of his Pokémon with Reggie, then call to have Reggie send over whatever Pokémon he needs for a battle. Paul isn't any more outwardly friendly towards his brother than he is with anyone else, but he did tell Reggie about Ash and Pikachu's Volt Tackle.

TEAM GALACTIC

Move over, Team Rocket. There's a new team in town, and they mean business—serious, nasty business.

WHO ARE THESE PEOPLE?

What is Team Galactic up to? We never quite know until almost the end, when it may or may not be too late. Pokémon Trainers should be on their guard around this group. As far as we know, they are responsible for such heinous acts as the stealing of the Adamant Orb and the Lustrous Orb, riling up the Unown to obtain the Spear Key, trashing the train tracks to Lake Acuity, and other general malfeasance. But what do they want? Could it be something to do with Dialga and Palkia? Or do they just like the cool names associated with planets?

COMMANDER SATURN

We get the first whiff of wrongdoing when Commander Saturn orders Team Rocket to steal the Adamant Orb from the Eterna Museum. Later, Saturn kicks up a storm when he uses a Draco Plate, Iron Plate, and Splash Plate to unlock a strange, cube-shaped key that transforms space-time into reality. He unleashes his Bronzor's Confuse Ray on the Unown and wreaks havoc.

Known Pokémon

BRONZOR   **TOXICROAK**

COMMANDER MARS

The comely Commander Mars is more than just good looks—she is evil incarnate. She and Saturn try to steal the Lustrous Orb from Celestic Town. Later, she travels to Iron Island with the Spear Key to find the exact location of the Spear Pillar on Mt. Coronet. However, Riley and Lucario foil her plans.

Known Pokémon

PURUGLY   **BRONZOR**

COMMANDER JUPITER

Jupiter is given the role of protector and guardian in the Team Galactic organization. She protects Charon at the Fuego Ironworks as he works on the Red Chain project. She's also told to look after the capture of the Lake Guardians. Although she does manage to capture Looker, she is upset that Azelf, Mesprit, and Uxie decide to side with the good guys. Maybe it's the outfits.

Known Pokémon

SKUNTANK

COMMANDER CYRUS

Behind every good organization is one mean boss. Cyrus disguises himself as an upstanding and successful businessman who has built most of the buildings in the Sinnoh region. In reality, he is running the whole Team Galactic organization. He wants the Lake Guardians, and even sets Pokémon Hunter J out to get them. But when he finally realizes his dream of unlocking the space-time portal, the portal is destroyed and Cyrus disappears.

Known Pokémon

AZELF   **MESPRIT**   **UXIE**

DIALGA   **PALKIA**

CHARON

Charon is sort of like the IT guy for Team Galactic. He makes sure their evil plans follow the charts and schedules that are set on paper. Not so tough without the pocket protector, are we Charon?

Known Pokémon: None

TEAM ROCKET AND THE "TWERPS"

Team Rocket has bedeviled Ash and his friends since the beginning, but these Pokémon thieves can put their criminal instincts aside and work with the "twerps" when it's necessary. Especially James and Meowth, who are more kind-hearted than they look. Although Team Rocket usually doesn't take long to break the truce, they've cooperated with Ash and his friends on more occasions than one would think.

UNITED TO DEFEAT A COMMON FOE

Shortly after Ash and his friends land on Mandarin Island in the Orange Islands, Pikachu and Togepi suddenly turn on Ash and Misty. Meowth acts strangely and runs from Team Rocket, too. Butch and Cassidy are using a Drowzee to control all the Pokémon in the area; Jessie and James try to beat them and get Meowth back, but to no avail. Ash and his friends help patch up Jessie and James, then convince them to join the fight against Butch and Cassidy.

After Butch and Cassidy are busted, Team Rocket is up for a special award and the gratitude of the locals, but playing the hero would be bad for their reputation, so they skip out on the accolades.

SOMETIMES IT'S JUST THE RIGHT THING TO DO

When Brock helps Jaco the Pokémon breeder forge a working relationship with his Electrike, their hard work and dedication touches James and Meowth. The two Team Rocket members even stop Jessie in the middle of an attempt to steal Electrike, refusing to let her destroy the deepening partnership between Electrike and Jaco.

James and Meowth even volunteer to help Jaco and Electrike train; with their experience getting blasted by Pikachu, they're happy to provide moving targets for Electrike's Thunder attacks. They still can't resist the chance to try and steal Pikachu, but when Electrike evolves into Manectric and blasts them off with Thunder, they're just pleased that it's finally mastered its electric attack.

SOMETIMES THERE'S JUST NO OTHER CHOICE

When angry Ursaring (on a mating-season rampage) force both heroes and bad guys to scatter and regroup, Jessie finds herself with Brock and Ash, while James and Meowth end up with Misty. Everyone has to call a temporary truce if they want to make it out of the forest, and although Team Rocket's members can't quite put their criminal ways aside, seeing the way the other half lives causes Team Rocket to reflect on their own lives.

Team Rocket is awed by Brock's delicious cooking, and Jessie is also startled by Brock's generosity when their group bunks down for the night.

WE'RE JUST HERE FOR MORAL SUPPORT

When Ash and Pikachu first took on Lt. Surge at the Vermillion City Gym, Pikachu received a sound drubbing at the hands of Lt. Surge's Raichu. Pikachu remained determined to defeat Raichu under its own power. This courage is so touching to Team Rocket that they secretly root for Pikachu to win the rematch.

Team Rocket pulled for Chimchar in the Hearthome Tag Tournament; they'd seen how harshly Paul treated his Chimchar, and it was too much for even them to condone. Later, Meowth sees Chimchar struggle to adjust to Ash's kindness, and has a moonlight heart-to-heart with the troubled Fire-type.

Can You Keep a Secret?

Sometimes Team Rocket is absolutely, 100% sincere about asking for cooperation. When James' Chimecho falls ill, he takes it to his Nanny and Pop-Pop for treatment. He can't bear to tell the kindly couple what he does for a living, so he passes himself off as a company president. But May's sick Munchlax is also recuperating under Nanny and Pop-Pop's care, so James earnestly begs the twerps to help maintain his charade.

WANTED DANGEROUS
SINNOH'S MOST WANTED

Team Galactic and Team Rocket aren't the only threats to peace in Sinnoh—there are criminals both big and small, but one of the biggest of them all is the ruthless mercenary known as Pokémon Hunter J.

POKÉMON HUNTER J

Even the combined efforts of Officer Jenny and the Pokémon Rangers have yet to stop Pokémon Hunter J and her heartless business. No one knows her true identity, but they know her work: she's a Pokémon Hunter, a mercenary who captures Pokémon with the sole intent of selling them to willing buyers. She doesn't stop at capturing wild Pokémon, either—if she sees a Pokémon she needs or thinks she can sell at a good price, she'll take it and add it to her sales catalog regardless of whether it already has an owner.

What makes J particularly dangerous is that she's a pro at what she does. She takes the same business-like approach towards her clients as she does her targets. She never fawns over a client and won't hesitate to cut off any clients who break a deal. As for her targets, she treats valuable Pokémon with care, but shows no mercy toward anything without a resale value. Being a member of her crew is no guarantee of safe conduct, either; she once jettisoned an entire hangar of her ship, together with all the crew onboard.

Good vs. Evil

Ash and his friends have run into J more times than they care to think about. First, she grabbed Pikachu and they had to get it back along with a Trainer's stolen Gardevoir. Then she came after a group of Shieldon that Gary was studying, so they had to help. Finally, she was hired to steal a Riolu, and it took the help of Top Ranger Kellyn to assist Ash and his friends in getting Riolu back. Fortunately, although they haven't managed to stop her yet, Ash and his allies have thwarted her plan every time they've crossed paths.

TRICKS OF THE TRADE

Pokémon Hunter J's operation includes a fleet of vehicles and a giant airship that can cloak itself to avoid detection, but not all of her equipment is on such a large scale.

Her visor doubles as a data display, letting her view maps and live information that help track her targets.

The gauntlet on her left wrist fires a beam that can freeze Pokémon in stasis. Once a Pokémon is frozen, it can be transferred to a case for easier transport and storage.

Pokémon Hunter J doesn't do all the dirty work herself—she has an ample crew of subordinates who help run the ship and grab Pokémon. These minions have Golbat of their own, too.

Pokémon Hunter J's Pokémon
DRAPION, ARIADOS, & SALAMENCE

INSIDE THE POKÉMON LEAGUE

The Pokémon League doesn't often cross Trainer's minds, but it's the organizing body behind the system of Gyms and region-wide tournaments that every Trainer aspires to challenge. In addition, the League is also involved in the process of raising Pokémon to distribute to starting Trainers.

TOURNAMENT ORGANIZATION

The Pokémon League tournaments represent the pinnacle of achievement for Trainers everywhere, and it's important to make sure that everything goes off without a hitch. The League is involved in all aspects from the promulgation of rules and selection of referees to the torch relay that starts a tournament.

POKÉMON JUDGES

Being a referee for Pokémon battles involves more than just waving a few flags, and Hoenn's Bomba Island is where aspiring battle judges learn what it takes. There, the Pokémon Battle Judge Training School puts would-be judges through a rigorous curriculum; knowing how to call a match requires expert knowledge of Pokémon types, moves, and other characteristics,

which allows a judge to gauge whether a Pokémon is down for the count. Only the best of the best will be qualified and selected to referee actual Pokémon League tournaments.

Where Do First Partner Pokémon Come From?

New Trainers begin their adventures with one of three First Partner Pokémon from their region. But where do these First Partner Pokémon come from, and why are they all at the same strength? It's normally a well-kept secret, but the Pokémon League distributes Eggs to individuals who raise them as First Partner Pokémon. One such individual is Mr. Swampy, who raises Mudkip Eggs in a secluded part of Hoenn.

POKÉMON LEAGUE CERTIFICATION

In Kanto's Dark City, two unofficial Gyms—the Yas Gym and Kaz Gym—battled for supremacy in the belief that the winning Gym would receive official certication and make a fortune. Their activities gave all Pokémon Trainers a bad reputation in town, since the Gyms weren't content to just recruit passing Trainers to their cause. The Gyms' Trainers and Pokémon would brawl in the streets, unacceptable behavior for any respectable Gym.

A disguised Nurse Joy was one of the Pokémon League's official inspectors, and there was no chance she'd approve the Yas or Kaz Gyms. However, she gave them a chance to make amends: if they joined forces to repair all the damage they'd caused and learned how to be responsible Trainers, they might get a chance to start their Gym certification bid from scratch.

GYM INSPECTION AND CERTIFICATION

To get to a Pokémon League tournament, a Trainer needs badges. And to get badges, a Trainer needs to win challenges at an official Gym. That means the League has to oversee Gym approvals and certifications to make sure the process runs smoothly.

GYM INSPECTION

Once a Gym is certified and operational, it still has to face the might of the Pokémon Inspection Agency. The PIA has the power to shut down Gyms that are unclean, unsafe, or just not up to their standards.

SINNOH GYM BATTLES

The rules for Gym battles in Sinnoh aren't much different from the rules anywhere else; the standard Gym battle is a 3-on-3 match where only the challenger may substitute Pokémon. Win badges from eight Gyms, and you'll be eligible to compete in the Sinnoh League. Ash is determined to get those badges, and these are the Gyms he's visited so far.

ETERNA GYM

GYM LEADER: GARDENIA

GARDENIA VS. **ASH**

The Gym's open roof proves pivotal when the sun gives Cherubi more power.

GARDENIA VS. **ASH**

This matchup is about Ash's Turtwig's toughness. It battles through the same Leech Seed attack to win the match.

GARDENIA VS. **ASH**

Staravia outflies Cherubi's Leaf Blade and uses an ultra-fast Aerial Ace to send Cherubi packing.

GARDENIA VS. **ASH**

Still suffering from the previous battle's Leech Seed attack, Turtwig succumbs in one blow to Gardenia's Roserade.

GARDENIA VS. **ASH**

Ash knows Gardenia's Turtwig is as fast as his Staravia. But Staravia still finds itself on the losing end of a Leech Seed attack.

GARDENIA VS. **ASH**

Aipom starts with the flair of a Pokémon Contest entrance, and backs it up with a massive Swift for the win.

OREBURGH GYM

REMATCH **GYM LEADER: ROARK**

Gym Leaders 101

Being a Gym Leader means more than schooling Trainers on the battlefield. Ash wants to win against Roark to prove Paul's methods are wrong, and Ash takes on the Oreburgh Gym rematch with this in mind. Sensing something amiss, Roark approaches Ash during a training session and reminds him to focus on the Gym battle, not his battle to prove Paul wrong.

ROARK VS. **ASH**

Pikachu utilizes his speed and Iron Tail to frustrate Onix until Onix uses Rock Tomb to imprison Pikachu. Never one to give up, Ash uses Thunderbolt to escape and Iron Tail to finish it.

ROARK  VS. **ASH**

The fight is fairly even, with Geodude using Roll Out and Aipom using Swift. In the end, Aipom gets the best of Geodude, surprising Roark.

> Rampardos was originally a very special Cranidos—the first fossil Pokémon revived by the Fossil Restorer machine, and Roark's Pokémon ever since he was a kid.

ROARK VS. **ASH**

Rampardos makes quick work of an already tired Aipom. One hit and Aipom is unable to battle.

ROARK VS. **ASH**

Pikachu and Rampardos put each other to the test, meeting in the middle of the ring with a Volt Tackle and Headbutt. In the end, Rampardos was just too strong, flinging Pikachu against the rocky terrain of the Gym, securing the win.

ROARK VS. **ASH**

Rampardos' knowledge of Fire-type moves puts Turtwig at a big disadvantage, but Turtwig is well trained and strong. It uses Razor Leaf to secure the win and Ash's first badge in the Sinnoh region.

VEILSTONE GYM

GYM LEADER: MAYLENE

Gym Leaders 101

Gym Leaders and challengers have something to give each other. Maylene became unnerved by the realization that winning or losing a Gym battle can have a huge effect on a challenger. For Brock, the cumulative effect of all those battles and their lessons is important. In his opinion, challengers help shape a Gym Leader into someone better.

MAYLENE VS. **ASH**

Staravia comes back from the brink of defeat with Aerial Ace to defeat Machoke.

MAYLENE VS. **ASH**

Cleared of its Confusion, Staravia takes Meditite out with a Brave Bird attack.

MAYLENE VS. **ASH**

Meditite dodges everything Staravia throws, and Staravia has to return when it is too confused to continue.

MAYLENE VS. **ASH**

Ash's Staravia tries Brave Bird again but Lucario is ready. Its Metal Claw sends Staravia back to the Poké Ball.

MAYLENE VS. **ASH**

Chimcar suffers the same fate as Staravia, but Ash manages to retrieve it as well.

MAYLENE VS. **ASH**

Lucario's Bone Rush and Force Palm make quick work of the feisty Chimchar.

MAYLENE VS. **ASH**

Lucario and Buizel put on a show for the ages. They blast the roof off the Veilstone Gym and are both unable to battle. The match ends in a draw, but Maylene awards the Cobble Badge for the effort of Ash's Pokémon.

PASTORIA GYM

GYM LEADER: CRASHER WAKE

If Ash wants to make it to the finals, he'll have to get past Crasher Wake and his Water-type Gym. But first, Pikachu and Buizel must put aside their feud.

CRASHER WAKE VS. **ASH**

Despite the edge of Electric-type attacks, Pikachu starts out slow against Gyarados. This changes when Pikachu busts out Volt Tackle for the win.

CRASHER WAKE VS. **ASH**

Knowing Quagsire is strong against Electric-type attacks, Ash brings out Turtwig, which gets hammered by Sludge Bomb and is forced to retreat.

CRASHER WAKE VS. **ASH**

Buizel turns Quagsire's Ice Beam against it and throws a frozen Aqua Jet back at the dumbfounded Pokémon. Quagsire is swiftly defeated.

CRASHER WAKE VS. **ASH**

Floatzel, the evolved form of Buizel, easily turns away Buizel's Aqua Jet. After using Bulk Up to raise its attack and defense power, Floatzel parries with Buizel until it's knocked out of the battle.

CRASHER WAKE VS. **ASH**

Using a mix of Electric-type attacks, Pikachu comes close to losing. Unfortunately for Crasher, not close enough. Floatzel damages Pikachu, so Ash sends Buizel in to finish the match.

CRASHER WAKE VS. **ASH**

Buizel's Aqua Jet and Floatzel's Ice Fang clash as Buizel learns to use the cover of the pool once again to knock out Floatzel. Ash earns the Fen Badge.

HEARTHOME GYM

GYM LEADER: FANTINA

Fantina's penchant for Hypnosis has proven a problem for Ash before, and now he has a Gym badge at stake.

FATINA VS. **ASH**

Ash has not previously battled Gengar. When Gengar tries Hypnosis, Buizel stops it with Water Gun. Gengar goes to Nightshade, but Buizel's Water Pulse knocks out Gengar.

FATINA VS. **ASH**

Using Flame Wheel and Flamethrower as counter-shields against Psy Wave and Dark Pulse, Chimchar knocks out Fantina's second Pokémon.

FATINA VS. **ASH**

Drifblim, Fantina's heaviest hitter, uses Psychic and then Will-O-Wisp, creating a counter-shield. Ash's old nightmare, Hypnosis, paired with Ominous Wind knocks out Pikachu.

FATINA VS. **ASH**

Buizel spins an Aqua Jet to wipe out the Will-O-Wisp shield, but Fantina counters with Ominous Wind. Once again, her old standby, Hypnosis, combined with Psychic takes out Buizel.

FATINA VS. **ASH**

Chimchar uses Flamethrower to absorb Will-O-Wisp and break the counter-shield. When Fantina tries Hypnosis, Chimchar is ready with Flamethrower and knocks out Drifblim for the win. Ash nabs the Relic Badge.

CANALAVE GYM

GYM LEADER: BYRON

It's time for Ash to face Byron for the Mine Badge. But Byron's love of defense won't make this easy.

BYRON VS. **ASH**

Bronzor's Heatproof Ability nullifies Chimchar's Fire-type moves. Chimchar uses Dig and Flamethrower in response to Bronzor's Rain Dance. After using Flame Wheel, Chimchar is triumphant.

BYRON VS. **ASH**

Buizel should have the type advantage—it uses Water Gun against Steelix's Screech, but Screech immobilizes Buizel. This sets up a Bind/Iron Tail combo, which finishes off Buizel.

BYRON VS. **ASH**

Chimchar tries to use Dig, but Steelix's Iron Tail shakes the earth. This shaking causes Steelix to fall through gaps in the battlefield that Chimchar's Dig created. Chimchar's Flame Wheel then knocks out Steelix.

BYRON VS. **ASH**

Bastiodon is powerful, and Chimchar is running out of steam, so this skirmish seems pretty lopsided from the very beginning. When Chimchar is knocked out, Ash brings in Gliscor.

BYRON VS. **ASH**

The rookie Gliscor hangs in like a champ and it comes down to one last standoff. Bastiodon's Flash Cannon against Gliscor's Sand Attack/Fire Fang combo is the decider. Gliscor wins, and Ash wins the Mine Badge!

SNOWPOINT GYM

GYM LEADER: CANDICE

In a four-on-four battle, Ash uses a Grass-type Pokémon against the Gym's Ice-type Pokémon. This puts Ash at a disadvantage, but he must have something up his sleeve…

CANDICE **VS.** **ASH**

Sneasel easily skates across the ice to avoid Grotle's Energy Ball. After using Icy Wind, Grotle reveals its strategy: to use the Rock Climb Move to defeat Sneasel in midair.

CANDICE **VS.** **ASH**

Has Ash forgotten that Medicham is part Psychic-type, which shreds Flying-type Pokémon? It turns out that Medicham's Fire Punch is no match for Staraptor's Brave Bird.

CANDICE **VS.** **ASH**

Gliscor's snow-melting Fire Fang is very effective. Unfortunately, so is Snover's Ice Beam, which annihilates Gliscor. Several combo moves later, Gliscor is eliminated.

CANDICE **VS.** **ASH**

Candice uses snowy Moves to counter the fiery ones, creating a shield of mist on the battlefield. When the smoke clears, Snover is out, and Chimchar wins the round.

CANDICE **VS.** **ASH**

Chimchar gives it a solid Fire-type try, but Abomasnow easily deflects Flamethrower with Blizzard. Ash recalls Chimchar and sends out Staraptor…

CANDICE **VS.** **ASH**

…Ash's choice to bring out Staraptor turns out to be costly and a little arrogant, as Abomasnow defeats it in one move. Ash then sends out Grotle, hoping for a little revenge…

CANDICE **VS.** **ASH**

…Grotle is knocked out in one move, as well. Ash has no choice but to send out Chimchar. Surfing on an ice shard, Chimchar devastates Abomasnow with Flamethrower, and finishes it off with Flame Wheel. Ash earns the Icicle Badge.

SUNYSHORE GYM

GYM LEADER: VOLKNER

Volkner and Ash had to overcome a few obstacles before they could compete—like defeating Team Rocket after they stole the Sunyshore Tower. But now, they finally can have a good, old-fashioned Pokémon battle.

VOLKNER **VS.** **ASH**

Type advantage means nothing when a Gym Leader uses type moves as a defense, which does not bode well for Ash. Torterra rushes Electivire with Rock Climb. However, Electivire decisively knocks out Torterra with Ice Punch.

VOLKNER **VS.** **ASH**

After a quick succession of Fire and Ice punches, it looks like Pikachu is done… until Pikachu's Static Ability, which can temporarily paralyze an opponent, kicks in. Pikachu wins a lucky one.

VOLKNER **VS.** **ASH**

Jolteon shoots a series of Shadow Balls at Infernape, which sends them straight back with Mach Punch. Eventually, Infernape knocks out Jolteon with a well-timed punch.

VOLKNER **VS.** **ASH**

Pikachu's Iron Tail seemingly pummels Luxray into submission. But when Luxray uses Thunder Fang followed by Shockwave, it's lights out for Pikachu.

VOLKNER **VS.** **ASH**

Luxray's Thunder Fang and Shockwave combos toss Infernape like a ragdoll. Just when all seems lost, Infernape's Blaze Ability helps it defeat Luxray despite being low on health. Ash takes the Beacon Badge.

HEARTHOME TAG BATTLE TOURNAMENT

Hearthome City is the "City Where Hearts Meet" and if it takes a tag battle tournament to make Trainers' hearts meet, so much the better!

Hearthome City is famous for the Hearthome Tag Battle tournament, a three-day tournament that brings Trainers together in Hearthome Stadium.

The prize for each winner is the Soothe Bell, a bell with a beautiful sound that puts everyone's mind at ease who hears it.

Each contestant receives a numbered registration card. At the start of the tournament, all the Trainers are gathered in the Hearthome Stadium and the random pairings are displayed so they can find their tournament partner. Battles begin later that afternoon, giving Trainers some time to practice with their partner.

TOURNAMENT RULES:

- EACH TRAINER BATTLES WITH THE SAME PARTNER FOR THE ENTIRE TOURNAMENT.
- THE TOURNAMENT IS A TAG BATTLE EVENT, WITH EACH TRAINER USING ONE POKÉMON PER BATTLE.
- THERE ARE NO SUBSTITUTIONS AND NO TIME LIMITS DURING BATTLES.

The tournament MC is none other than Hearthome's own mayor, Enta.

Ash, Dawn, and Brock all enter the tournament. For Ash and Brock, the tournament is just another fun event, but for Dawn—who enters at Zoey's suggestion—it just might be a way to get her mind off her Hearthome Contest disappointment. Two of them will find new friendships and excitement in tag battle teamwork, but for one of them, the tag battle tournament turns out to be a bittersweet experience.

DAWN'S PARTNER: CONWAY

Conway is all about statistics and strategy: he's analyzed every league battle to develop a formula for battle victory. He's not nearly as confident with girls as he is with numbers, but despite his deliberate, geeky demeanor, he's a great partner for Dawn. His Slowking is optimized with defensive moves like Safeguard and Protect so Dawn can concentrate on attacking while Conway watches her back.

BROCK'S PARTNER: HOLLY

Holly is a cool older girl who makes it clear to Brock that she's just not that into him. But once she sees that Brock is more than just a skirt-chaser, she comes to respect him as a person and a tag battle partner. After Paul's Torterra deals her Farfetch'd a one-hit KO during the quarterfinal battles, Holly is deeply apologetic to Brock for letting him down; she leaves right after the tournament, vowing to become a better Trainer.

ASH'S PARTNER: PAUL

Paul and Ash are all too well acquainted by now, and Paul certainly isn't interested in playing nice for the sake of the tournament—he's only competing so he can train his Pokémon, especially Chimchar.

HEARTHOME TAG BATTLE TOURNAMENT RESULTS

NOTABLE BATTLES: DAY ONE

Dawn and Conway use Piplup and Slowking to defeat a female Trainer's Scyther and male Trainer's Koffing.

Brock and Holly use Sudowoodo and Wingull to defeat two male Trainers' Yanma and Bagon.

Ash and Paul use Pikachu and Chimchar to defeat two male Trainers' Magmar and Rhydon.

NOTABLE BATTLES: DAY TWO

Ash and Paul use Turtwig and Chimchar to defeat two male Trainers' Metagross and Zangoose.

Seeing Chimchar freeze in terror when confronted by Zangoose, Paul turns away in disgust and abandons it for good. After the battle, Ash takes in Chimchar as one of his own Pokémon.

QUARTERFINAL BATTLE: DAY THREE

Ash and Paul use Staravia and Torterra to defeat Brock's Croagunk and Holly's Farfetch'd. With Farfetch'd knocked out almost immediately, it's up to Brock and Croagunk to save the day. Croagunk single-handedly takes on Torterra, but Torterra's power proves to be too much.

FINAL BATTLE: DAY THREE

Ash and Paul use Chimchar and Elekid to defeat Dawn's Buizel and Conway's Heracross, winning the tournament.

During the battle, Elekid evolves into Electabuzz. Now that Paul has given up on Chimchar, this is the only tournament reward he cares about—later he even tosses his Soothe Bell prize at Ash, having no use for it.

SINNOH POKÉMON CONTESTS

Pokémon Contests everywhere share the same basic structure, but there are a few extra details a Coordinator needs to know if he or she wants to shine in the Sinnoh region.

WHAT'S THE SAME?

No matter where you are, the principle is the same: Pokémon Contests are judged on a contestant's ability to showcase his or her Pokémon in battles and individual appeals. Trainers from other regions will find the judging panel in Sinnoh to be a familiar sight. The panel members are, Mr. Contesta, Pokémon Contest Director and head of the judging committee; Mr. Sukizo, Head of the Pokémon Fan Club, and a "remarkable" man of few words; and the Nurse Joy from the Contest town or city.

WHAT'S CHANGED?

Handling the Contest MC duties in Sinnoh is Marian, who's just as lively as Contest MCs everywhere else.

As always, a Coordinator needs a Contest pass in order to enter competitions. These passes don't transfer between regions, but a Sinnoh Contest pass can be acquired at any Sinnoh region Contest Hall. Once a Coordinator's ID information is downloaded from his or her Pokédex and the Contest pass is printed, the newly registered Coordinator also receives a ribbon case, rulebook, Ball Capsule, and envelope containing starter seals.

Dress to Impress

Coordinators in Kanto and Hoenn are happy to compete in their everyday clothes, but in Sinnoh, Coordinators dress to the nines for every Contest. Some Coordinators, like Dawn, stick with the same basic outfit for each contest and alter their accessories, but Zoey prefers to wear different outfits for each Contest.

Colorful seals can be placed on the Ball Capsule. Each seal creates a different special effect when the Poké Ball is thrown using the Ball Capsule.

Sinnoh's Unofficial Contests

Contests aren't just for Sinnoh's big towns and cities! Other towns also host "unofficial" Contests—in other words, Contests where the prize isn't a ribbon that's valid towards entry in the Grand Festival. Dawn enters one such Contest on the way to Floaroma Town: the Contest is part of a village festival, and the prize is a year's worth of fruit.

All it takes is an audio/video truck, some outdoor bleachers, two judges, and voila! Instant Contest.

Jessie enters the Contest with Ash's Aipom, which he reluctantly lent her for the Contest after she saved its life. Aipom loves the Contest spotlight and it's doing so well with Jessie that Ash is afraid it might never want to return to him!

After the village Contest's first round, two Coordinators are selected for the final round—a standard five-minute Contest battle. This time, Jessie and Aipom easily defeat Dawn and her untried Pachirisu.

JUBILIFE CONTEST

Located in the heart of Jubilife City, the Jubilife Contest Hall is also conveniently close to a Pokémon Center.

The Jubilife Contest is Dawn's Contest debut, but Zoey's fourth Contest. It's also the Sinnoh Contest debut of Ash, indulging his Aipom's interest in Contests and Jessie, who takes the stage as her alter ego, the not-so-great Coordinator Jessilina.

For once in her life, Jessie fights fair, only to see Carnivine wither before the force of Zoey's Glameow and its attacks. Zoey wins the match, making this her second Ribbon.

FLOAROMA CONTEST

Scenic Floaroma Town is a testament to the wonders of the natural world. What better place for an event that showcases the natural beauty of Pokémon? But flowers are the last thing on the mind of Kenny, Dawn's childhood acquaintance, who enters this Contest for a chance to see her again.

In a battle between evolution stages that goes right down to the wire, Dawn's Piplup defeats Kenny's Prinplup.

Dawn is declared the winner. Kenny will just have to wait a little longer to earn his first Ribbon.

HEARTHOME CONTEST

In Hearthome City, the Contest format is in a double performance format. Dawn faces twice the competition from her rivals as well, since both Nando and Zoey are in town to enter the Contest. The Contest comes down to Zoey and Nando in the finals, with Nando surprising Zoey with a victory, earning his second Ribbon!

SOLACEON CONTEST

The Solaceon Contest draws a big crowd, as if there wasn't already enough pressure on Dawn to prove her Hearthome Contest defeat was just a fluke.

Convinced James and Meowth have a top-secret strategy to guarantee her the win, Jessie sails onstage and wins with confidence, not realizing she's just won her first Ribbon fair and square.

WALLACE CUP

Unlike most Contests, in the Wallace Cup, 16 contestants move on to the second round instead of eight.

Sootopolis Gym Leader, Champion Master of Hoenn, Top Contest Coordinator and Contest Master: Wallace is the cream of the Coordinator crop. Originally hailing from Hoenn, he's traveled both Hoenn and Kanto to promote his Wallace Cup Contest event. Now the Wallace Cup has come to the shores of Sinnoh's Lake Valor, where Wallace will sit in as a special judge.

Coordinator 101

Friendship is the key to success. Wallace has an important reminder for all Trainers—for a Pokémon to truly shine, it's the relationship between Trainer and Pokémon that's most important. Part of building that relationship is taking time out to interact with Pokémon beyond just training; play time is important too!

Ribbons Are a Girl's Best Friend

May still has the half of a Ribbon she won at Terracotta Town in a draw with Ash, and Dawn always carries her mother's first Ribbon with her. Both of them draw on these Ribbons for strength during their competitions—though for Dawn, a constant reminder of all she has to live up to can be a source of pressure as well as inspiration!

JOIN THE EVOLUTION

As we grow, travel, and learn, we begin to change: becoming wiser, stronger, and more capable. The same holds true for Pokémon. During the course of a Pokémon's life , it can change if it so chooses. The change is both in its physical appearance and its abilities—some even alter their type.

The number of stages and the kind of Evolution is dependent upon the Pokémon, but for the most part, Pokémon have three stages. The first form of Pokémon is its earliest. When Professors hand out First Partner Pokémon, they are always in their first stage. Through hard, consistent training, a Pokémon at an unannounced time begins to glow and change. When it is done, it is larger, looks more mature, and possesses one or more different Moves.

Not all Evolutions happen in the same way, or for the same reasons. Some Pokémon will change to one of several completely different forms based on the time of day when it begins the Evolution process. Likewise, if it evolves in one area versus another it could be totally different. Some stones cause Pokémon to evolve. There is no set way or time as a Trainer to know, you just have to be ready, flexible, and know your Pokémon inside and out.

It is important to note that not all Pokémon evolve and not all Pokémon, if they can evolve, want to. Pikachu is a good example. Pikachu could evolve into a Raichu, and has had an opportunity, but didn't want to. Ash, to his credit, supported Pikachu's decision.

Some Pokémon have a pre-evolved form. This is a baby form. The Pokémon is not ready to train or be trained. James' Mime Jr. or Brock's Bonsly are examples of this. They usually don't know much, but have one or two safety abilities: Mime Jr.'s Mimic or Bonsly's Fake Tears. It is enough to carry them through the world long enough for them to evolve into their normal adult form.

IT CAME FROM OUTER SPACE

The Pokémon world is teeming with life, but some of that life may have originated beyond the planet. Might there be other Pokémon yet to be discovered, somewhere out amongst the stars?

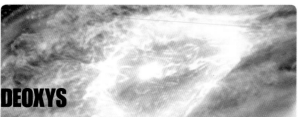

DEOXYS

If there's a top candidate for extraterrestrial Pokémon, Deoxys must be it—sightings of this rare Pokémon are tied to meteorite activity.

Deoxys provided a great deal of insight into its species; using Meowth as a voicebox, it told Max that its long journey was cold, lonely, and frightening.

Even after the meteorite landed, Deoxys remained alone in the meteorite. It didn't emerge full-fledged until the meteorite's core was transformed by a combination of solar wind activity and the meteorite's own energy. Due to the painful geomagnetic energy emanating from the meteorite, it had to flee its "cradle" and take refuge in an extradimensional space it created.

LUNATONE

Mary and Ken, also known as the Pokémon Mystery Club, have evidence that Lunatone is definitely an extraterrestrial. When a meteor struck the Hoenn region, these two aggressive investigators tracked down the crash site and witnessed a Lunatone emerge from the broken shards of the meteorite.

Solrock is another Pokémon that's rumored to come from somewhere beyond the planet. Not long after a meteorite impact, one village in Hoenn sees a Solrock in the area.

Meteorite Mysteries

Meteorites are objects of particular interest in the Pokémon world. In Sinnoh, Veilstone City is known for its meteorites—without them, the city wouldn't even exist! Before there was a city, there was a cluster of meteorites that were recognized as "guardians" since ancient times. Veilstone City was created by the people who flocked to the area, drawn by curiosity.

CLEFAIRY

Are Clefairy from outer space? If not, there must be a very good explanation for why the Clefairy have a spaceship that resembles a UFO. The spaceship doesn't run on pixie dust, either; the banks of equipment inside show it's clearly a sophisticated machine.

Clefairy's extraterrestrial connections may still be a secret to many, but it's no great secret that Clefairy can be found near Mt. Moon. Somewhere on the mountain is a huge meteor called the "Moon Stone."

On nights with a full moon, Clefairy and Clefable gather to dance around the Moon Stone as a form of prayer. It may be related to the Moon Stone's origins in outer space.

Cleffa, the pre-evolved form of Clefairy, seem to appear whenever there's a meteor shower. Some say it rides to earth on shooting stars; its body is shaped like a star, too!

WORKING SIDE-BY-SIDE

All across the world, people have partnered with Pokémon to accomplish vital tasks and jobs. For all the Trainers who focus on battles, there are likely just as many who work alongside their Pokémon in every sense of the word! From the Pokémon firefighting squads to Machoke that help with manual labor, from Nurse Joy and Chansey to Officer Jenny and Growlithe—there are many examples of these fruitful partnerships.

WHISTLE WHILE YOU WORK: LEDYBA

Lots of flowering plants depend on other creatures to spread their pollen, and that's where Arielle and her six Ledyba come in. Farmers can ask Arielle and her Pokémon to pollinate orchards like this stand of apple tree, ensuring that the trees will bear fruit.

Arielle uses a mixture of verbal commands and whistle notes to direct her Ledbya. The whistle has been passed down through generations of her family, but it's not the whistle that's special. Arielle raised her Lebyda from their infancy, and it's this lifelong relationship that allows them to work together so well.

BRIDGING TROUBLED WATERS: BIBAREL

When you need a stone bridge built, this Bibarel is your best bet. Other Pokémon can cut stone, but no regular Pokémon can do it with this trained Bibarel's precision and know-how. Under the direction

of Isis, an engineer, Bibarel uses its sharp teeth to swiftly cut rough blocks of stone down to exact specifications. It may not have an engineering degree, but Bibarel trained under a master before working with Isis.

THE ANSWER IS BLOWING ON THE WIND: HOPPIP

Mariah the weather forecaster uses all kinds of scientific instruments, but her seven Hoppip are a special help. Hoppip are so light that a strong wind can blow them miles away, and Mariah sometimes has to keep them in a netted enclosure so they don't fly off! But they're more than just a quick way to check wind speed—they can also sense imminent changes in the wind, and Mariah studies their behavior patterns in the hope that it will help meteorologists make weather predictions.

THE CUTTING EDGE: FARFETCH'D AND MAGMAR

Sylvester and his father are in the business of making purifying charcoal, a fuel that also cleanses the air and water. To do it, they rely on two things: top-quality wood from Ilex Forest, and help from Farfetch'd and Magmar.

The wood needs to be cut just so, and Farfetch'd can use its Cut move to chop a log into a perfect stack of wood. Then, Magmar turns up the heat to burn the wood into charcoal.

EXPRESS AIR MAIL: PIDGEY

For over 50 years, the carrier Pidgey of the Pidgey Carrier Express have delivered mail throughout the city and out to nearby islands that lack ferry service.

The Pidgey Express represents years of hard work and devotion, from raising the Pidgey and taking them up in a mini-blimp to show them their routes, to waiting up on stormy nights to make sure every last one comes home safe.

SINNOH LEGENDARY POKÉMON

AZELF • (AZ-elf)

Height	1'00" (0.3 m)	Category	Willpower
Weight	0.7 lbs (0.3 kg)	Type	Psychic

Azelf is known as "The Being of Willpower." It sleeps at the bottom of a lake to keep the world in balance. It is small and blue, with three small red gems—two on its tails and one on its forehead.

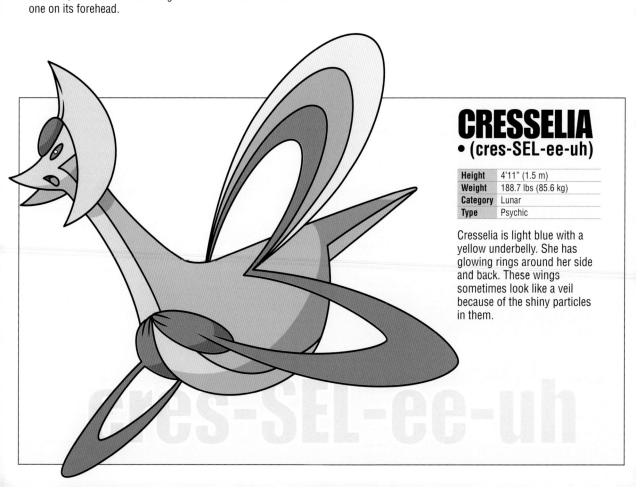

CRESSELIA
• (cres-SEL-ee-uh)

Height	4'11" (1.5 m)
Weight	188.7 lbs (85.6 kg)
Category	Lunar
Type	Psychic

Cresselia is light blue with a yellow underbelly. She has glowing rings around her side and back. These wings sometimes look like a veil because of the shiny particles in them.

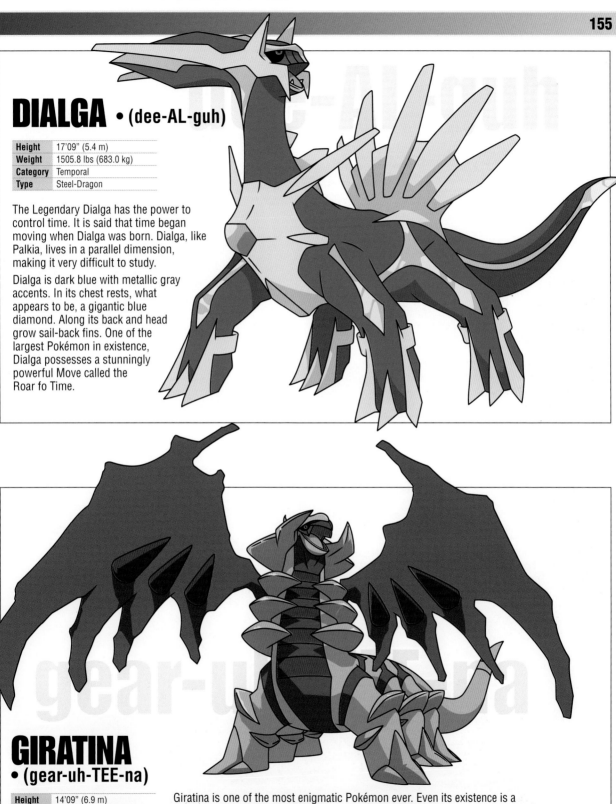

DIALGA • (dee-AL-guh)

Height	17'09" (5.4 m)
Weight	1505.8 lbs (683.0 kg)
Category	Temporal
Type	Steel-Dragon

The Legendary Dialga has the power to control time. It is said that time began moving when Dialga was born. Dialga, like Palkia, lives in a parallel dimension, making it very difficult to study.

Dialga is dark blue with metallic gray accents. In its chest rests, what appears to be, a gigantic blue diamond. Along its back and head grow sail-back fins. One of the largest Pokémon in existence, Dialga possesses a stunningly powerful Move called the Roar fo Time.

GIRATINA
• (gear-uh-TEE-na)

Height	14'09" (6.9 m)
Weight	1653.5 lbs (650.0 kg)
Category	Renegade
Type	Ghost-Dragon

Giratina is one of the most enigmatic Pokémon ever. Even its existence is a mystery—it is said to come from a world that mirrors our own. Its impressive height and ragged, horned wings make it a terrifying sight, and its six-legged body can appear in ancient cemeteries.

HEATRAN • (HEE-tran)

Height	5'07" (1.7 m)	Category	Lava Dome
Weight	948.0 lbs (430.0 kg)	Type	Fire-Steel

Born from fire, Heatran loves to dig into the walls and caverns of magma caves. It has immeasurably sharp claws extending from each of its feet. Heatran is a rarely seen Pokémon. This is not surprising, as it lives in active volcano craters.

MESPRIT • (MES-prit)

Height	1'00" (0.3 m)	Category	Emotion
Weight	0.7 lbs (0.3 kg)	Type	Psychic

Mesprit is known as "The Being of Emotion." It taught humans the nobility of sorrow, pain, and joy. Mesprit also has two red jewels on its tails and one on its forehead.

PALKIA • (PAL-kee-uh)

Height	13'09" (4.2 m)	Category	Spatial
Weight	740.8 lbs (336.0 kg)	Type	Water-Dragon

Palkia has the ability to distort space. It is said to live in a gap in the spatial dimension parallel to ours. Because of this, it is nearly impossible to get factual information about this Pokémon.

It has a long neck and formidable tail. Inset on its shoulders are two enormous pink spheres that resemble pearls.

REGIGIGAS
• (REDGE-ee-gee-gus)

Height	12'02" (3.7m)
Weight	925.9 lbs (420.0 kg)
Category	Colossal
Type	Normal

Sealed away in a statue, Regigigas awakens when Regirock, Regice, and Registeel are brought together. Regigigas is very similar to the other Regis in overall shape—Regigigas' dots are two parallel lines of gems.

This Legendary Pokémon was once rumored to have towed continents with ropes. It certainly is a strong Pokémon and truly a fear-inducing sight.

UXIE • (YUKE-see)

Height	1'00" (0.3 m)	Category	Knowledge
Weight	0.7 lbs (0.3 kg)	Type	Psychic

Uxie is known as "The Being of Knowledge." It is said that it can wipe out the memory of those who look into its eyes. Uxie's two tails have two red gems, while another sits in its forehead.

SINNOH MYTHICAL POKÉMON

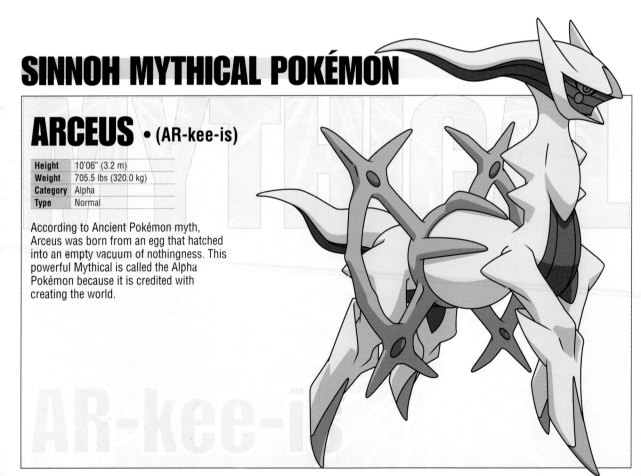

ARCEUS • (AR-kee-is)

Height	10'06" (3.2 m)
Weight	705.5 lbs (320.0 kg)
Category	Alpha
Type	Normal

According to Ancient Pokémon myth, Arceus was born from an egg that hatched into an empty vacuum of nothingness. This powerful Mythical is called the Alpha Pokémon because it is credited with creating the world.

DARKRAI • (DARK-rye)

Height	4'11" (1.5 m)
Weight	111.3 lbs (50.5 kg)
Category	Pitch-Black
Type	Dark

Dark and ominous, Darkrai lives up to its name. Legends say that on moonless nights, Darkrai lures people to sleep and gives them horrible nightmares.

Made of shadow and able to travel very fast, it can speak to humans. It has a flowing white mane.

MANAPHY • (man-UH-fee)

Height	1'00" (0.3 m)	Category	Seafaring
Weight	3.1 lbs (1.4 kg)	Type	Water

Manaphy, also known as the Prince of the Sea, acts as the leader of Pokémon from the ocean.

Very empathetic, it can change the perception of people through its Heart Swap technique, forcing people to look at things from other perspectives.

PHIONE • (fee-Oh-nay)

Height	1'04" (0.4 m)	Category	Sea Drifter
Weight	6.8 lbs (3.08 kg)	Type	Water

The Sea Drifter Pokémon floats through the warm blue waters of the ocean. A homebody at heart, no matter how far the waves may whisk this small swimmer away, it will always find its way back to the very place it was born.

SHAYMIN • (SHAY-min)

LAND FORME

Height	0'08" (0.2 m)	Category	Gratitude
Weight	4.6 lbs (2.09 kg)	Type	Grass

SKY FORME

Height	1'03" (0.38 m)	Category	Gratitude
Weight	11.4 lbs (5.17 kg)	Type	Grass-Flying

This shy form of Shaymin can easily camouflage itself in a field of special Sinnoh wildflowers called Gracedia that look just like the buds that bloom on its back. Shaymin has the incredible ability to clean its environment—the dirtier the job, the stronger Shaymin's Seed Flare gets. Although both Formes can purify toxins, they're polar opposites personality-wise. Each spunky Sky Forme was once a bashful Land Forme. Since Shaymin are known as The Gratitude Pokémon, the people of Sinnoh often give Gracedia bouquets as thank-you gifts.

LAND FORME

SKY FORME

SINNOH POKÉMON

Just north of Kanto and Johto is Sinnoh. Sinnoh is home to some of the most mysterious Pokémon—
Giratina and Darkrai!

ABOMASNOW

Height: 7'03" (2.2 m)
Weight: 298.7 lbs. (135.5 kg)

GRASS	ICE

AMBIPOM

Height: 3'11" (1.2 m)
Weight: 44.8 lbs. (20.3 kg)

NORMAL

ARCEUS

Height: 10'06" (3.2 m)
Weight: 750.5 lbs. (340.42 kg)

NORMAL

AZELF

Height: 1'00" (0.3 m)
Weight: 0.7 lbs. (0.3 kg)

PSYCHIC

BASTIODON

Height: 4'03" (1.3 m)
Weight: 329.6 lbs. (149.5 kg)

ROCK	STEEL

BIBAREL

Height: 3'03" (1.0 m)
Weight: 69.4 lbs. (31.5 kg)

NORMAL	WATER

BIDOOF

Height: 1'08" (0.5 m)
Weight: 44.1 lbs. (20.0 kg)

NORMAL

BONSLY

Height: 1'08" (0.5 m)
Weight: 33.1 lbs. (15.0 kg)

ROCK

BRONZONG

Height: 4'03" (1.3 m)
Weight: 412.3 lbs. (187.0 kg)

STEEL	PSYCHIC

BRONZOR

Height: 1'08" (0.5 m)
Weight: 133.4 lbs. (60.5 kg)

STEEL	PSYCHIC

BUDEW

Height: 0'08" (0.2 m)
Weight: 2.6 lbs. (1.2 kg)

GRASS	POISON

BUIZEL

Height: 2'04" (0.7 m)
Weight: 65.0 lbs. (29.5 kg)

WATER

BUNEARY

Height: 1'04" (0.4 m)
Weight: 12.1 lbs. (5.5 kg)

NORMAL

BURMY (PLANT CLOAK)

Height: 0'08" (0.2 m)
Weight: 7.5 lbs. (3.4 kg)

BUG

BURMY (SANDY CLOAK)

Height: 0'08" (0.2 m)
Weight: 7.5 lbs. (3.4 kg)

BUG

BURMY (TRASH CLOAK)

Height: 0'08" (0.2 m)
Weight: 7.5 lbs. (3.4 kg)

BUG

CARNIVINE

Height: 4'07" (1.4 m)
Weight: 59.5 lbs. (27.0 kg)

GRASS

CHATOT

Height: 1'08" (0.5 m)
Weight: 4.2 lbs. (1.9 kg)

NORMAL   FLYING

CHERRIM

Height: 1'08" (0.5 m)
Weight: 20.5 lbs. (9.3 kg)

GRASS

CHERUBI

Height: 1'04" (0.4 m)
Weight: 7.3 lbs. (3.3 kg)

GRASS

CHIMCHAR

Height: 1'08" (0.5 m)
Weight: 13.7 lbs. (6.2 kg)

FIRE

CHINGLING

Height: 0'08" (0.2 m)
Weight: 1.3 lbs. (0.6 kg)

PSYCHIC

COMBEE

Height: 1'00" (0.3 m)
Weight: 12.1 lbs. (5.5 kg)

BUG   FLYING

CRANIDOS

Height: 2'11" (0.9 m)
Weight: 69.4 lbs. (31.5 kg)

ROCK

CRESSELIA

Height: 4'11" (1.5 m)
Weight: 188.7 lbs. (85.6 kg)

PSYCHIC

CROAGUNK

Height: 2'04" (0.7 m)
Weight: 50.7 lbs. (23.0 kg)

POISON   FIGHTING

DARKRAI

Height: 4'11" (1.5 m)
Weight: 111.3 lbs. (50.5 kg)

DARK

DIALGA

Height: 17'09" (5.4 m)
Weight: 1505.8 lbs. (683.0 kg)

STEEL   DRAGON

DRAPION

Height: 4'03" (1.3 m)
Weight: 135.6 lbs. (61.5 kg)

POISON   DARK

DRIFBLIM

Height: 3'11" (1.2 m)
Weight: 33.1 lbs. (15.0 kg)

GHOST   FLYING

DRIFLOON

Height: 1'04" (0.4 m)
Weight: 2.6 lbs. (1.2 kg)

GHOST   FLYING

DUSKNOIR

Height: 7'03" (2.2 m)
Weight: 235.0 lbs. (106.6 kg)

GHOST

ELECTIVIRE

Height: 5'11" (1.8 m)
Weight: 305.6 lbs. (138.6 kg)

ELECTRIC

EMPOLEON

Height: 5'07" (1.7 m)
Weight: 186.3 lbs. (84.5 kg)

WATER   STEEL

FINNEON

Height: 1'04" (0.4 m)
Weight: 15.4 lbs. (7.0 kg)

WATER

FLOATZEL

Height: 3'07" (1.1 m)
Weight: 73.9 lbs. (33.5 kg)

WATER

FROSLASS

Height: 4'03" (1.3 m)
Weight: 58.6 lbs. (26.6 kg)

ICE   GHOST

GABITE

Height: 4'07" (1.4 m)
Weight: 123.5 lbs. (56.0 kg)

DRAGON   GROUND

GALLADE

Height: 5'03" (1.6 m)
Weight: 114.6 lbs. (52.0 kg)

PSYCHIC   FIGHTING

GARCHOMP

Height: 6'03" (1.9 m)
Weight: 209.4 lbs. (95.0 kg)

DRAGON   GROUND

GASTRODON (EAST SEA)

Height: 2'11" (0.9 m)
Weight: 65.9 lbs. (29.9 kg)

WATER   GROUND

GASTRODON (WEST SEA)

Height: 2'11" (0.9 m)
Weight: 65.9 lbs. (29.9 kg)

WATER   GROUND

GIBLE

Height: 2'04" (0.7 m)
Weight: 45.2 lbs. (20.5 kg)

DRAGON | GROUND

GIRATINA

Height: 14'09" (4.5 m)
Weight: 1653.5 lbs. (750.0 kg)

GHOST | DRAGON

GLACEON

Height: 2'07" (0.8 m)
Weight: 57.1 lbs. (25.9 kg)

ICE

GLAMEOW

Height: 1'08" (0.5 m)
Weight: 8.6 lbs. (3.9 kg)

NORMAL

GLISCOR

Height: 6'07" (2.0 m)
Weight: 93.7 lbs. (42.5 kg)

GROUND | FLYING

GROTLE

Height: 3'07" (1.1 m)
Weight: 213.8 lbs. (97.0 kg)

GRASS

HAPPINY

Height: 2'00" (0.6 m)
Weight: 53.8 lbs. (24.4 kg)

NORMAL

HEATRAN

Height: 5'07" (1.7 m)
Weight: 948.0 lbs. (430.0 kg)

FIRE | STEEL

HIPPOPOTAS

Height: 2'07" (0.8 m)
Weight: 109.1 lbs. (49.5 kg)

GROUND

HIPPOWDON

Height: 6'07" (2.0 m)
Weight: 661.4 lbs. (300.0 kg)

GROUND

HONCHKROW

Height: 2'11" (0.9 m)
Weight: 60.2 lbs. (27.3 kg)

DARK | FLYING

INFERNAPE

Height: 3'11" (1.2 m)
Weight: 121.3 lbs. (55.0 kg)

FIRE | FIGHTING

KRICKETOT

Height: 1'00" (0.3 m)
Weight: 4.9 lbs. (2.2 kg)

BUG

KRICKETUNE

Height: 3'03" (1.0 m)
Weight: 56.2 lbs. (25.5 kg)

BUG

LEAFEON

Height: 3'03" (1.0 m)
Weight: 56.2 lbs. (25.5 kg)

GRASS

LICKILICKY

Height: 5'07" (1.7 m)
Weight: 308.6 lbs. (140.0 kg)

NORMAL

LOPUNNY

Height: 3'11" (1.2 m)
Weight: 73.4 lbs. (33.3 kg)

NORMAL

LUCARIO

Height: 3'11" (1.2 m)
Weight: 119.0 lbs. (54.0 kg)

FIGHTING | STEEL

LUMINEON

Height: 3'11" (1.2 m)
Weight: 52.9 lbs. (24.0 kg)

WATER

LUXIO

Height: 2'11" (0.9 m)
Weight: 67.2 lbs. (30.5 kg)

ELECTRIC

LUXRAY

Height: 4'07" (1.4 m)
Weight: 92.6 lbs. (42.0 kg)

ELECTRIC

MAGMORTAR

Height: 5'03" (1.6 m)
Weight: 149.9 lbs. (68.0 kg)

FIRE

MAGNEZONE

Height: 3'11" (1.2 m)
Weight: 396.8 lbs. (180.0 kg)

ELECTRIC | STEEL

MAMOSWINE

Height: 8'02" (2.5 m)
Weight: 641.5 lbs. (291.0 kg)

ICE | GROUND

MANAPHY

Height: 1'00" (0.3 m)
Weight: 3.1 lbs. (1.4 kg)

WATER

MANTYKE

Height: 3'03" (1.0 m)
Weight: 143.3 lbs. (65.0 kg)

WATER | FLYING

MESPRIT

Height: 1'00" (0.3 m)
Weight: 0.7 lbs. (0.3 kg)

PSYCHIC

MIME JR.

Height: 2'00" (0.6 m)
Weight: 28.7 lbs. (13.0 kg)

PSYCHIC | FAIRY

MISMAGIUS

Height: 2'11" (0.9 m)
Weight: 9.7 lbs. (4.4 kg)

GHOST

MONFERNO

Height: 2'11" (0.9 m)
Weight: 48.5 lbs. (22.0 kg)

FIRE | FIGHTING

MOTHIM

Height: 2'11" (0.9 m)
Weight: 51.4 lbs. (23.3 kg)

BUG | FLYING

MUNCHLAX

Height: 2'00" (0.6 m)
Weight: 231.5 lbs. (105.0 kg)

NORMAL

PACHIRISU

Height: 1'04" (0.4 m)
Weight: 8.6 lbs. (3.9 kg)

ELECTRIC

PALKIA

Height: 13'09" (4.2 m)
Weight: 740.8 lbs. (336.0 kg)

WATER | DRAGON

PHIONE

Height: 1'04" (0.4 m)
Weight: 6.8 lbs. (3.1 kg)

WATER

PIPLUP

Height: 1'04" (0.4 m)
Weight: 11.5 lbs. (5.2 kg)

WATER

PORYGON-Z

Height: 2'11" (0.9 m)
Weight: 75.0 lbs. (34.0 kg)

NORMAL

PRINPLUP

Height: 2'07" (0.8 m)
Weight: 50.7 lbs. (23.0 kg)

WATER

PROBOPASS

Height: 4'07" (1.4 m)
Weight: 749.6 lbs. (340.0 kg)

ROCK | STEEL

PURUGLY

Height: 3'03" (1.0 m)
Weight: 96.6 lbs. (43.8 kg)

NORMAL

RAMPARDOS

Height: 5'03" (1.6 m)
Weight: 226.0 lbs. (102.5 kg)

ROCK

REGIGIGAS

Height: 12'02" (3.7 m)
Weight: 925.9 lbs. (420.0 kg)

NORMAL

RHYPERIOR

Height: 7'10" (2.4 m)
Weight: 623.5 lbs. (282.8 kg)

GROUND | ROCK

RIOLU

Height: 2'04" (0.7 m)
Weight: 44.5 lbs. (20.2 kg)

FIGHTING

ROSERADE

Height: 2'11" (0.9 m)
Weight: 32.0 lbs. (14.5 kg)

GRASS | POISON

ROTOM

Height: 1'00" (0.3 m)
Weight: 0.7 lbs. (0.3 kg)

ELECTRIC | GHOST

SHAYMIN (LAND FORME)

Height: 0'08" (0.2 m)
Weight: 4.6 lbs. (2.09 kg)

GRASS

SHAYMIN (SKY FORME)

Height: 1'03" (0.38 m)
Weight: 11.4 lbs. (5.17 kg)

GRASS | FLYING

SHELLOS (EAST SEA)

Height: 1'00" (0.3 m)
Weight: 13.9 lbs. (6.3 kg)

WATER

SHELLOS (WEST SEA)

Height: 1'00" (0.3 m)
Weight: 13.9 lbs. (6.3 kg)

WATER

SHIELDON

Height: 1'08" (0.5 m)
Weight: 125.7 lbs. (57.0 kg)

ROCK | STEEL

SHINX

Height: 1'08" (0.5 m)
Weight: 20.9 lbs. (9.5 kg)

ELECTRIC

SKORUPI

Height: 2'07" (0.8 m)
Weight: 26.5 lbs. (12.0 kg)

POISON | BUG

SKUNTANK

Height: 3'03" (1.0 m)
Weight: 83.8 lbs. (38.0 kg)

POISON | DARK

SNOVER

Height: 3'03" (1.0 m)
Weight: 111.3 lbs. (50.5 kg)

GRASS | ICE

SPIRITOMB

Height: 3'03" (1.0 m)
Weight: 238.1 lbs. (108.0 kg)

GHOST | DARK

STARAPTOR

Height: 3'11" (1.2 m)
Weight: 54.9 lbs. (24.9 kg)

NORMAL | FLYING

STARAVIA

Height: 2'00" (0.6 m)
Weight: 34.2 lbs. (15.5 kg)

NORMAL | FLYING

STARLY

Height: 1'00" (0.3 m)
Weight: 4.4 lbs. (2.0 kg)

NORMAL | FLYING

STUNKY

Height: 1'04" (0.4 m)
Weight: 42.3 lbs. (19.2 kg)

POISON | DARK

TANGROWTH

Height: 6'07" (2.0 m)
Weight: 283.5 lbs. (128.6 kg)

GRASS

TOGEKISS

Height: 4'11" (1.5 m)
Weight: 83.8 lbs. (38.0 kg)

FLYING | FAIRY

TORTERRA

Height: 7'03" (2.2 m)
Weight: 683.4 lbs. (310.0 kg)

GRASS | GROUND

TOXICROAK

Height: 4'03" (1.3 m)
Weight: 97.9 lbs. (44.4 kg)

POISON | FIGHTING

TURTWIG
Height: 1'04" (0.4 m)
Weight: 22.5 lbs. (10.2 kg)

GRASS

UXIE

Height: 1'00" (0.3 m)
Weight: 0.7 lbs. (0.3 kg)

PSYCHIC

VESPIQUEN
Height: 3'11" (1.2 m)
Weight: 84.9 lbs. (38.5 kg)

BUG | FLYING

WEAVILE
Height: 3'07" (1.1 m)
Weight: 75.0 lbs. (34.0 kg)

DARK | ICE

WORMADAM
(SANDY CLOAK)

Height: 1'08" (0.5 m)
Weight: 14.3 lbs. (6.5 kg)

BUG | GRASS

WORMADAM
(PLANT CLOAK)
Height: 1'08" (0.5 m)
Weight: 14.3 lbs. (6.5 kg)

BUG | GRASS

WORMADAM
(TRASH CLOAK)

Height: 1'08" (0.5 m)
Weight: 14.3 lbs. (6.5 kg)

BUG | GRASS

YANMEGA
Height: 6'03" (1.9 m)
Weight: 113.5 lbs. (51.5 kg)

BUG | FLYING

UNOVA

Unova is a region known for two opposite environments: bustling cities and beautiful forests.

On his journey, Ash traveled through big hubs like artsy Nacrene City, shopping paradise Striaton City, movie-making Virbank City, business center Castelia City, and the incredible metropolis of Nimbasa City.

If you need to escape the crowds, Unova has plenty of places perfect for a retreat. From seaside hot spot Undella Town to the vast Pinwheel Forrest filled with wild Pokémon, nature abounds in Unova!

There are also incredible places to visit for brave history buffs, as Unova is the setting for many stories in Pokémon mythology. Adventurous Ash boldly passed through booby traps to visit legendary locations like Milos Island, the Ancient Ruins, Dragonspiral Tower, the Abyssal Ruins, and the White Ruins.

PROFESSOR JUNIPER

Professor Juniper might be young, but don't underestimate her because of her age. Professor Oak tells Ash that she is one of the most important Pokémon researchers. She has focused her studies on finding out more about Pokémon origins.

Professor Juniper is the first person to welcome Ash to Unova. She conducts her research all over the region, but her main lab is in Nuvema Town. Every new Trainer in Unova visits this friendly scientist's spot to receive a Pokémon—Tepig, Snivy, or Oshawott—and a brand new Pokédex. But Professor Juniper doesn't just help Trainers begin their journey; she is always just an Xtransceiver video chat away if they ever need her!

In fact, she and Ash become such good pals after competing in the Unova League that he heads straight to Nuvema Town to visit her. He wouldn't think of leaving the region without saying goodbye and getting her advice.

COMPUTER WHIZ

Professor Juniper often builds specialized technology to aid her studies. She invented a Pokémon Trading Device to create an Evolution Exchange between her friend Karrablast and Bianca's buddy Shelmet. The incredible machine helps them evolve into Accelgor and Escavalier once they hit the battlefield.

Juniper built a mobile lab in Area 1 to study the electrified, floating stones in Chargestone Cave.

From all the way over in Nuvema Town, she could track the weird energy causing the Venipede to stampede Castelia City.

Perhaps her most incredible device was the Pokémon Restoration Machine that harnessed Musharna's Dream Energy to bring the ancient Archen back to life from the 100-million-year-old Plume Fossil.

The Power of Pikachu

When Professor Juniper first sees Pikachu, she can't contain her excitement! In Unova, Pikachu are so rare that she can't wait to bring it to her lab to study it. And while Pikachu is happy to show off its strength, it's even happier to have her help when a visit from the Legendary Zekrom shorts its power.

THE GIFT OF FRIENDSHIP

When Ash leaves Professor Juniper's lab, Oshawott also slips out to follow him on his journey. After days of traveling side by side, Oshawott asks to officially come along for the ride. But when Ash tosses his Poké Ball, he realizes Oshawott is one of Juniper's Pokémon. Ash does the right thing and calls the Professor to let her know what happened. She is so moved by Oshawott's story that she gifts Ash its Poké Ball, and the two become friends forever!

PROFESSOR CEDRIC JUNIPER

Professor Juniper's dad, Cedric, is also a professor. But he doesn't contain his research to a lab; he's an eccentric archaeologist always on the road and ready for adventure! If you're lucky enough to go exploring with him, come prepared to think quickly. You never know when he'll send you head-first into trouble just for the excitement of it all, as Ash, Iris, and Cilan discovered.

If you're brave and bold enough to follow his lead (or perhaps his mislead), Professor Cedric can show you spectacular places and things you've only read about in history books, such as the Golden Dark Stone from the Black Chapter of Pokémon Mythology or the Light Stone from the White Chapter of Pokémon Mythology. Professor Cedric Juniper certainly has a confusing way with words. Even though he is incredibly knowledgeable about ancient Pokémon scripts, he is harder to read than the symbols of a dead language. He'll be the first to tell you that the number one rule for adventure with Professor Cedric Juniper is: "Act after I finish my thought!" If unheeded, you might just find yourself falling into a pitfall of his personality and an ancient booby trap.

BIANCA

Bubbly Bianca is a ball of energy bouncing around Unova. A Pokémon Trainer who also assists Professor Juniper, she meets Ash on a mission to deliver him a new badge case. However, it was easier to find Ash in all of Unova than it is to find the box in her purse! Bianca is very scatter-brained. However, what she lacks in organization, she makes up for in enthusiasm. Eventually, she is able to secure all eight Gym badges needed to battle in the Unova League Championship!

MUSCLE IN ON

If you're a muscle-bound Fighting-type, Bianca won't be shy about seeing just how strong you are. At the Clubsplosion battle, she went around squeezing all the upper arms she could. However, perhaps she shouldn't get so touchy-feely when she's so out-matched. Scraggy wasn't shy about head-butting her when she asked it to flex.

Bianca's Pokémon

SHELMET > TRADES FOR KARRABLAST

Using Professor Juniper's patented Pokémon Trading Device combined with a fun battle, Bianca trades her shy Shelmet for Karrablast. Then, they battle so Shelmet can officially evolve into an awesome, yet angry, Escavalier. Professor Juniper suggests they then have a Tag Battle with Ash and Cilan so Escavalier can blow off some steam and also bond with Bianca—and it works! With Escavalier by her side, Bianca wins enough Gym badges to qualify for the Unova League.

ESCAVALIER

Foot, Meet Mouth

Oblivious and impatient, Bianca often steps on people's toes. She loves to jump in during a battle and bark orders over other Trainers' instructions. Eager Bianca is anxious for ways to prove herself, but she usually does more harm than good. For example, when she thinks Emolga is hiding in a bush, Bianca has Pignite set it on fire. But it turns out the shrub is really a giant Scolipede! Then, bumbling Bianca has Minccino stop it with Hyper Voice, but that also backfires when it annoys an angry Galvantula. Good thing her friends Ash, Iris, and Cilan are there to step in and help her out of sticky situations. They've done that more than once… and they're always happy to help a friend!

MINCCINO

Bianca first sees Minccino when it swoops in to steal Ash's shiny badge case. When she goes to catch the Chinchilla Pokémon, Pignite is blown away by the petite cutie's big Hyper Voice and strong Tickle. However, Bianca accidentally gets her wish when Minccino spots another shiny object—her dirty Poké Ball. Minccino comes over to clean it, and it gets caught.

PIGNITE

Bianca's First Partner Pokémon, Pignite, is always ready to battle for its buddy, competing with anyone from Gym Leader Elesa to Bianca's own dad… She would be even more lost without her First Partner Pokémon! And it evolved into an incredibly strong Emboar that wowed everyone when they won the second round of the Clubsplosion tournament against tough Trainer Trip and Conkeldurr. Bianca called upon Emboar again during the Unova League. Although it was able to defeat Cameron's Samurott, he won the round with speedy Riolu. Still, Bianca knows she has a fiery battle buddy in Emboar!

EMBOAR

PROFESSOR FENNEL

Professor Fennel is a scientist from Striaton City. She studies dreams and the hidden powers they possess.

Ash, Cilan, and Iris first meet Professor Fennel at the Pokémon Center when a pink mist covers the city, causing all the Pokémon to fall asleep. Together, they help everyone wake up to the real problem, Team Rocket, and reunite Fennel with her long lost friend, the Musharna.

WHEN DREAMS BECOME A NIGHTMARE

Professor Fennel's Pokémon

MUSHARNA

MUNNA

Professor Fennel used to work at the Dreamyard, a Pokémon energy research facility just outside of her hometown. Her mission was to find a way to harness Musharna's Dream Mist to create a clean energy source for Unova. Unfortunately, Professor Fennel's dreams were cut short by a huge explosion at the lab. She still works tirelessly to learn more about dreams and how they can make an impact.

The Pokémon Fossil Restoration Machine

Designed by Professor Fennel, this incredible piece of technology can create a complete DNA map from a Fossil and then magically hatch it into a new life. Unfortunately, this super computer was destroyed shortly after it restored Archen. Some seeds trapped in the Plume Fossil rock grew so strong that they burst clean through the machine.

IRIS

A Trainer from the Village of Dragons—an entire town in Unova devoted to Dragon-type Pokémon—Iris dreams of someday becoming a Dragon Master. To begin her journey, the village's Elder presents her with an Axew to care for, and it's that very Axew that accidentally introduces her to Ash.

When Ash spots Axew in the forest, he naturally wants to catch the awesome Dragon-type. Ash tosses his Poké Ball, but his aim is off, and it bonks Iris directly on the head. Luckily, once Iris sees Ash's adorable pal Pikachu, she doesn't stay angry about his accidental wallop for long. From that moment, Iris and Ash are always together, if only so they can tease each other. Iris always tells Ash, "You're such a kid!" However, she is truly thrilled to travel with Ash through her home region, Unova and the Decolore Islands. When their boat docks in Vermilion City, Iris bids her friend Ash a fond farewell as she heads to Blackthorn City to train with Gym Leader Clair.

Putting the Sense in Sensitive

People from the Village of Dragons are famous for having incredible eyesight, and Iris is no exception. She practically has built-in binoculars! Iris can see things far in the distance that her friends can't spot.

Just like her favorite Dragon-type Pokémon, she can't stand the cold and she's afraid of Ice-types. She gets chills just looking at Georgia's Beartic.

Iris's Pokémon

EXCADRILL

Iris and Drilbur were unstoppable in battle. After 98 straight wins, Drilbur evolved into Excadrill, winning the Village of Dragons' Competition. For their 100th battle, Iris and Excadrill met Drayden, the famous Dragon Master. Upon defeat, Excadrill lost confidence and wouldn't battle again. Iris patiently helped it regain its strength to become the powerful Pokémon it is today!

EMOLGA

Almost everyone falls in love with Iris' female Emolga, an Electric- and Flying-type with an amazing Attract. It uses this adoration to its advantage—this trickster always angles for food. In fact, Emolga first spotted Iris because she was carrying a bunch of fruit. Bianca immediately wanted to catch Emolga, but Emolga chose Iris because she was more interested in caring for it than catching it.

MAKE LIKE A TREE AND LEAVE

If you don't see Iris on the ground, look up! Iris loves to climb trees and swing on vines. She can trek fast on treetops, and she's such an expert, she even taught Dawn how to escape some angry Onix using her tricks of the tree travelin' trade.

THE DOCTOR IS IN

Iris might save you a trip to the Pokémon Center because she's a whiz at making herbal remedies for Pokémon. She knows which plants make the perfect medicine, and with Axew's help, she finds the proper herbs for her all-natural cures. Iris takes great care of her Pokémon patients by spoon-feeding them her remedies. Both Pansage and Scraggy have had speedy recoveries from surprise attacks thanks to Iris.

A RISING STAR

Iris thirsts for adventure and hungers to learn all about Pokémon—that's why she's on the road with Ash! Just before they met, Iris ran away from one of the most prestigious private schools in Unova, the Opelucid Academy, after a tough Pokémon battle with its principal local Gym Leader, Drayden. Ready to carve her own path to becoming a Dragon Master, Iris set off on her journey with Axew.

Brave and eager for new experiences, Iris isn't afraid to challenge anyone to a battle, including Elite Four member and Dragon-type expert Cynthia. All her practice pays off when she and Excadrill defeat Ash and Pikachu to win Don George's Club Battle Tournament and a Top-Class Driftveil Wing Set! She also makes it all the way to the semi-finals of the highly contested Pokémon World Tournament Junior Cup. Iris is certainly a Trainer to watch!

Oddly enough, the person who has his eye on her career is Drayden. Although Iris thought she was rebelling by leaving school, it turns out that Drayden had already talked to the Village of Dragons' Elder about having Iris eventually take his place as the Opelucid City Gym Leader. Perhaps someday she'll be the keeper of the Legend Badge!

AXEW

Like Pikachu, Iris's friend Axew is always out of its Poké Ball. It often rides in her big hair. Axew is a lover, not a fighter. Iris tries hard to help her pal trust its abilities. They both have a lot to learn and they're doing it together, sometimes even in mid-battle! When Iris and Axew overcome their shyness to challenge Elite Four member Cynthia, Axew unleashes its first Giga Impact because it's inspired by its opponent and fellow Dragon-type, Garchomp.

DRAGONITE

When a flock of Pidove gets caught in its battle with Hydreigon, Dragonite risks its safety to protect them. Unfortunately, Hydreigon's attacks send Dragonite crashing into a power plant, which shuts off electricity where Iris is visiting Elite Four Member Cynthia. When Officer Jenny asks for help, Iris steps up. She rescues the injured Dragonite. Grateful Dragonite asks to join Iris on her journey. Iris has had a real pal ever since!

CILAN

Cilan and his brothers Chili and Cress are the three Striaton City Gym Leaders. Ash and Iris meet Cilan when he spots their amazing Axew and Pikachu. At first, he doesn't let on that he's a Gym Leader, so when Ash asks for directions to the Gym, Cilan decides to have a little fun and escort him there. Boy, is Ash surprised when he walks in the door—not only is Cilan the Gym Leader, he is also a triplet! Ash could choose to battle any one of the three Gym Leader brothers for the Insect Badge, but adventurous Ash opts to battle all three. After watching all the matches full of Ash's brand of surprising moves, Cilan is captivated by his battle style. He then asks to join the Trainer on his journey! Cilan then followed Ash from Unova through the Decolore Islands. After all their adventures together, Cilan was so inspired, he decided he was ready to try his hand at a fishing contest in the Hoenn Region. So, the pals parted ways when they reached Vermillion City.

Food for Thought

The only thing Cilan loves more than Pokémon is food! With so much experience working in a restaurant, Cilan really knows his way around the kitchen. This excellent chef is always whipping up delicious meals and funny food puns for his friends. He talks about almost everything as if he can eat it, especially battles! He rhapsodizes about a match's aroma and recipe as if it's a dish being cooked. You know things are heating up when Cilan exclaims, "The time for the battle to be served is here!"

Cilan isn't just a great Gym Leader; he has also earned quite the reputation as a perceptive Pokémon Connoisseur.

MR. NICE GUY

Cool, calm, and collected, Cilan is always nice, even to his rivals. He's so compassionate that he can help stop a fight, and he always stands up for what is right. Even when Burgundy is a bad sport after she loses their rematch and taunts him before the Clubsplosion tournament, he compliments her strengths and encourages her to keep training. But his kind words just rub her the wrong way, and she remains rude about wanting to someday defeat him. No matter, Cilan would never stoop to a bully's level and tease back. He's too good for bad words.

DOWN TO A SCIENCE

Cilan has an appetite for information and is also an expert in many areas of study, from classic movies to solving mysteries to scientific facts. He doesn't just evaluate Pokémon; he also likes to suss out every situation.

On a visit to Virbank City, Cilan points out all the famous places where scenes from his favorite movies were filmed!

When a cute Cubchoo goes missing, Cilan turns into the perfect private eye. He sniffs out the clues and acts like a detective to help reunite the Pokémon with its Trainer.

Cilan also loves to read science books. He simply thinks everything can be explained by reason and often tries to find the scientific truth behind Iris' sixth sense claims.

IT RUNS IN THE FAMILY

Cilan is a triplet. His brothers Chili and Cress complete the trio, and together they run the Striaton Gym, which is also a fancy restaurant! Some would say three Gym Leaders are like too many cooks in the kitchen, but they know how to work together and support each other. And just like the dishes they serve in their restaurant, each has his own flavor.

Cilan's Pokémon

PANSAGE

Pansage is Cilan's best buddy. They think alike and both have green, poofy hair. Like Cilan, Pansage never loses its cool. Even when Dwebble lashed out at it, Pansage knew the Pokémon was just scared and didn't strike back.

DWEBBLE

Cilan first spots Dwebble carving itself a new stone home. But the minute it moves in, three Dwebble bullies steal it. Cilan and his pals help Dwebble recover its rock. Now there's one more thing Dwebble hopes never to lose: its new friend Cilan.

CYNTHIA

A Sinnoh region Champion and member of the Elite Four, Cynthia is a celebrity known all over for her incredible battles. She keeps a vacation place in the beautiful tourist destination of Undella Town. There, she can get a little R&R, and she loves to host guests. She has a big home in Unova and an even bigger heart!

When Ash bumps into his old chum Cynthia in line for a sweet Bearticone in Lacunosa Town, she generously offers him and his friends a place to stay in her mansion. She also encourages Ash, Cilan, and Iris to enter the Pokémon World Tournament Junior Cup, a competition that she is set to open with an exhibition match.

NURTURE IS HER NATURE

Cynthia considers herself the caretaker of her friends and Pokémon. When she almost runs into a sick Meloetta in the middle of the street, Cynthia pulls her car over to save the poor Pokémon and knows just what will heal it: an Oran

Berry. When Team Rocket captures Meloetta, Cynthia has everyone hop on her boat to go rescue it. There's no mountain too high, no valley too low to keep Cynthia from helping a friend in need.

LEARN TO PLAY BY HEART

Aspiring Dragon Master Iris challenges Cynthia and her Dragon-type Garchomp to a battle. Iris knows she has a lot to learn, and the Sinnoh Champion couldn't be a better teacher. Since Cynthia and Garchomp are so inspiring to watch in action, they really make an impact (or rather, Giga Impact) on Axew and Iris. In this very match, Axew was able to use the Normal-type for the first time.

All Sweetness and Light

At the Pokémon World Tournament Junior Cup, Cynthia and Garchomp perform in an exciting exhibition battle with Caitlin and her Gothitelle from the Unova Elite Four. Both ladies begin the battle with good sportsmanship by complimenting each other's strengths and reputations. And when these two powerhouses unite, the battle is nothing short of explosive! The combination of Garchomp's Draco Meteor and Gothitelle's Thunderbolt covers the entire stadium in stunning fireworks. The match might be deemed a draw, but this battle is truly art.

JERVIS

Jervis is the typical butler: refined, a little stuffy, and always available to serve. He first meets Ash and company at Cynthia's villa in Undella Town. Besides chauffeuring the slickest wheels in Unova, Jervis also dispenses advice about Pokémon and the dangers of certain environments. If you're rich enough to pick one up, you should definitely get yourself a butler.

CAITLIN

We first meet Caitlin, a member of the Elite Four and the White Rose Fairy, during the first round jostling for the Junior Cup. She's a little stuck-up and cute, but her opponent Cynthia is having none of it. In a battle of Garchomp versus Gothitelle, Garchomp's mighty Dragon Punch almost shatters Caitlin's confidence, but the match ends in a draw.

OLD FRIENDS AND NEW

DAWN

A surprise was waiting for Ash at Cynthia's seaside vacation spot in Undella Town: Dawn, his old friend from Sinnoh!

Ash is so excited to catch up with Dawn, and Cilan and Iris are also thrilled to finally meet the Pokémon Coordinator they've heard so much about. Pokémon Connoisseur Cilan immediately challenges Dawn and Piplup to a battle so he can evaluate them, and he is obviously impressed with their unity on and off the field. Cilan's cooking reminds Dawn of the good old days with Brock, now studying to be a Pokémon Doctor.

GIRL POWER

Dawn finds a special friend in Ash's Unova travel buddy, Iris. They bond over their experiences traveling with Ash and can laugh at his habits.

Nothing can come between these new buddies, even in a head-to-head battle at the Pokémon World Tournament Junior Cup! Despite Dragonite ignoring Iris' instruction, they win the quarter finals against Mamoswine and Dawn. Like a good sport, Dawn congratulates Iris and makes her feel better about her struggles with stubborn Dragonite.

MIXING OIL AND WATER-TYPES

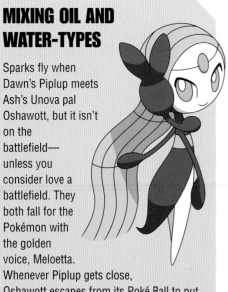

Sparks fly when Dawn's Piplup meets Ash's Unova pal Oshawott, but it isn't on the battlefield—unless you consider love a battlefield. They both fall for the Pokémon with the golden voice, Meloetta. Whenever Piplup gets close, Oshawott escapes from its Poké Ball to put Piplup in its place. But Meloetta can unite even these tough rivals simply by singing its beautiful songs. In the end, Oshawott is sad to see Dawn and Piplup leave Unova to participate in the Wallace Cup. With a little patience and a whole lot of fun together, even foes can turn into friends!

IT'S SO HARD TO SAY GOODBYE

When Dawn is ready to continue on to Johto, Ash doesn't want to say so long to his old pal—well, at least not until they have a chance to battle! In Cynthia's backyard battlefield, Ash and Pikachu take on Dawn and Quilava. But Cynthia calls the match a draw since they are both such talented Trainers who have clearly learned a lot from each other. Hey, that's what friends are for!

PROFESSOR OAK

Along with Ash's mom, Professor Oak travels with Ash from their home in the Kanto region to Unova. There, he introduces Ash to another important Pokémon researcher, his colleague Professor Juniper. They regularly consult each other on scientific matters, and Professor Oak often finds himself in the region. In fact, Ash bumps into Professor Oak at a fair about the Kanto region in Unova. After seeing him give a lecture on Pokémon, Ash gets nostalgic for his early days as a Trainer and does a Pokémon exchange to see his old chum Charizard.

No matter where Ash travels, Professor Oak is there to encourage him and care for the Pokémon he catches. Ash is lucky to have a true friend and mentor in Professor Oak.

FERRIS

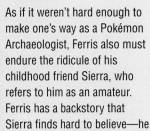

As if it weren't hard enough to make one's way as a Pokémon Archaeologist, Ferris also must endure the ridicule of his childhood friend Sierra, who refers to him as an amateur. Ferris has a backstory that Sierra finds hard to believe—he once traveled back in time and met a Tirtouga in trouble. When Team Rocket shows up to steal a fossil he discovers and has Dr. Zager revive it, he renews his friendship with the newly released Tirtouga inside the fossil.

RIDLEY

A descendent of the protectors of the ancient Temple and Reveal Glass, Ridley is Meloetta's personal bodyguard. Over the centuries, many villains have tried to capture this Pokémon. To keep Meloetta safe, Ridley and his people have gone into hiding deep in the forest. But one day, while wandering in a field of white flowers, Jessie, James, and Meowth capture Meloetta. Before Ridley and his buddy Golurk can stop them, Yamask covers them in dark smoke and escapes. Luckily, thanks to their deep connection, Ridley senses when Meloetta is nearby, and he tracks Meloetta to Cynthia's vacation home.

SIERRA

Sierra is kind of a pain—she seems to take joy in ridiculing her childhood friend Ferris. She refuses to believe that he traveled to the past via a Time Gate he discovered during their romps through Twist Mountain as children. She becomes a believer when she sees his relationship with the revived Tirtouga.

TRIP

Trip is a force to be reckoned with both on and off the battlefield. A real loner, Trip is the opposite of Ash, his biggest rival in Unova. Trip isn't interested in making friends. Impatient and ambitious, Trip claims he doesn't have time for emotions. He wants to think only logically, no matter who or what he could hurt, like when he wanted to battle the Venipede stampede as Burgh and Ash tried to herd them. Trip only cares about one thing: becoming a Pokémon Champion.

Trip met Ash on the first day of his journey as a Trainer, while picking out his First Partner Pokémon, Snivy, at Professor Juniper's lab . Even before he has a moment to practice with Snivy, Trip already brags that he'll beat Ash, and he does. This early loss motivates Ash throughout Unova to train hard to finally beat Trip. He gets his chance in the first round of the Unova League!

TRANQUILL

In Trip's six-on-six battle with Ash at the Pokémon Battle Club, Tranquill wins rounds against Oshawott and Tepig. But it's no match for Ash's Pikachu! However, when there's trouble, Trip and Tranquill team up with Ash to herd the Venipede stampede in Castelia City.

LAMPENT

While Burgh prefers to reason with the Venipede stampeding Castelia City, Trip instructs the Ghost- and Fire-type to attack from the air. Rather than let Trip ruin the peace talks, Ash jumps in front of the Venipede to protect them.

FRILLISH

In Ash's second battle against Trip, Frillish easily wins the round against Pidove and Snivy. No one can touch its Cursed Body!

A CHANGE WOULD DO YOU GOOD

Although Trip starts out as real jerk, he has a change of heart along his Unova journey. After finally getting the chance he dreamed of as a little boy, a battle with his idol Alder, something in him shifts. Because the battle is his reward for winning the Pokémon World Tournament Junior Cup, Trip goes in with confidence that he'll crush the Unova Champion—but he loses. The experience seems to teach Trip how to be humble. He finally sees Alder's wise words in action and how his morals make him a Champion Trainer. When Ash next sees Trip at the Unova League, he's a changed man. They face off in the first round, and up until the very last second, it looks like Trip and Serperior will cinch the match. However, Ash and Pikachu are a team with an incredible bond, and with an impressive combination of Electro Ball and Thunderbolt, they finally beat Trip. Ash is even more surprised when Trip shakes his hand and wishes him luck. After this battle with the great Grass-type, it's clear that Trip truly turns over a new leaf.

KNOW THE SCORE

Whenever Ash runs into Trip, Ash does his best to impress him. But Trip always one-ups Ash, literally. In Nimbasa City, when Ash wins his fourth Gym badge, Trip already has his fifth. When Ash asks for a rematch with Trip at the Pokémon Battle Club in Luxuria Town, Trip has six Pokémon, and Ash has only five. Trip is hard to beat! But it's a struggle just to convince him to battle unless he deems you worthy.

R-E-S-P-E-C-T

The first handful of times Ash encounters Trip, he isn't afraid to say what he thinks, though his thoughts typically aren't very nice. He puts the "brutal" in brutal honesty. When the Unova League Champion, Alder, says that building friendships with your Pokémon is more important than their strength in battle, Trip scoffs at him for being a sap. Even Trip's personal hero is a target for his sharp tongue, but Trip's favorite victim is Ash. Trip calls him a backwoods hick from the "boonies" of the Kanto region. When Ash loses their first rematch, Trip calls Ash and his Pokémon "losers." Trip also thinks everything is below him and just plain "basic." Since he considers himself a winner, he doesn't handle losing well. When Bianca and Emboar win their round in the Clubsplosion tournament, Trip just storms out. The truth is, Trip is a great Trainer, but he's a bad sport.

SNIVY

Trip's Snivy is so smart that it wins its first battle against Ash and Pikachu. The next time Ash runs into Trip, it has already evolved into Servine. When they meet again at the Pokémon World Tournament Junior Cup, Servine has evolved again into the powerhouse Serperior. The Grass-type wins against Cilan and goes on to win the finals against Ash. But when Ash and Pikachu get a rematch in the Unova League, it's a fight to the finish and Pikachu squeaks out a win!

VANILLITE

When Ash and Iris accidentally interrupt Trip and Vanillite's attempt to catch a wild Palpitoad, Ash convinces Trip to battle him for a third time. Trip tries Ash's "off the wall battle style" by choosing Vanillite to battle Tepig, but the round ends in a draw.

TIMBURR

This Fighting-type is tough, but Ash, Bianca, and Cilan all get their chance. Against Ash, Trip notices Oshawott can't control its Aqua Jet because its eyes are closed. This helps Ash's training, but it doesn't help Trip; Timburr loses the round. Against Cilan, Trip calls on his pal, which is now Gurdurr. However, Cilan ultimately wins the round. Gurdurr evolves again into a cool Conkeldurr. But when Bianca's Emboar wins the Clubsplosion tournament's second round by using its pillars against it, Trip is extra embarrassed. Trip thinks this pal let him down, but a good Trainer knows he's the one letting his Pokémon down by being a bad sport.

ALDER

Outgoing and adventurous, Alder is treated like a rock star in Unova. Hordes of Trainers ask the Champion Master of the Unova region for his autograph. His biggest fan is Trip, who has dreamed of battling Alder since he met him as a child. When Trip sees him again in Nimbasa City, though, he's frustrated by Alder's hippie attitude. Don't let Alder's calm and considerate manner fluster you, too. With his buddy Bouffalant, he can crush a battle opponent in one swift move, as he showed Trip at the World Tournament Junior Cup. With his lighthearted outlook, Alder makes everything look easy.

Alder is generous with his fans. He might be bad at remembering names—just ask Tristan and Ashton, otherwise known as Trip and Ash—but Alder is always up for a battle challenge. He might not be able to stay awake for it, as Ash found out when Alder started snoring in the middle of their battle. Alas, Alder is tired because he's a busy man who can always be counted on to save the day!

A MAN WITH A MESSAGE

Years ago, Alder told Trip that it was important to grow strong. But really, he feels training is more complex. Years later, Alder added to his statement, saying that it's not just about strength; it's also about knowing when to show it. Slowly, he's showing Trip the true way to train, leading by example. A big-hearted Champion, Alder stands for justice and compassion. His goal is simple—to unite people and Pokémon.

And Alder is a man of his word. When a Gigalith was on a rampage through Nimbasa City, he refused to let Officer Jenny and Herdier battle it back. Instead, he put his life in danger to reason with the angry Pokémon. Because he did, he discovered that the Pokémon was injured and needed help.

A Ladies' Man

Alder has quite the reputation for being a flirt. Alder enjoys chatting up the women he meets, especially Officer Jenny, Nurse Joy, and even Elite Four Champion Cynthia. Really, his true love is his best friend and battle buddy, Bouffalant!

CAMERON

Cameron can come off as a doofus. His blunders include miscalculating the number of badges needed to enter the Unova Championships, getting lost with Ash on his way to complete his final badge, and arriving too late to compete in the Pokémon World

Tournament Junior Cup. Nevertheless, he proves that you should never underestimate a Trainer with desire in his heart, becoming a formidable rival to Ash. Using evolved and powerful Pokémon like Hydreigon, Samurott, and eventually Lucario, Cameron takes down Ash and knocks him out of the final four tournament, which he later loses to Virgil.

DRAYDEN

Iris has a big task at hand—she's going to compete against her mentor and Dragon Master Drayden, the leader of the Opelucid City Gym. She admits that when she was first enrolled in the Opelucid City training program, she left because she was homesick and never finished her training. When Drayden later defeats her, he softens the blow by telling Iris that he wants her to one day become the Opelucid City Gym Leader.

VIRGIL

Virgil is part of the Pokémon Rescue Squad, a group founded by his father Jeff and brother Davy, that is dedicated to saving people and Pokémon from sticky situations. In fact, he met Ash and Iris when they accidentally got caught in a rockslide on their way to Vertress City. Luckily, Virgil was there in a flash and had his pal Espeon use Psychic to lift them back to safer ground.

Espeon is one of Virgil's eight Team Eevee members. Virgil's Rescue Squad crew includes Eevee and all seven of its evolutions, hence the name. Needless to say, Virgil is an Eevee expert!

Shortly after meeting Ash, Virgil got another distress call. Wild Cryogonal had frozen the lake water, the control room, and the power source at the local dam. Of course, Ash, Iris, and Cilan wanted to help the Pokémon Rescue Squad's efforts! Together with Virgil and Davy, they got to the bottom of the problem, a small Cryogonal was trapped behind some pipes. Eevee snapped into action using Dig to burrow a rescue tunnel. Then, Pikachu paired up with Team Eevee's Jolteon to recharge the emergency batteries and get the power back on. The Pokémon Rescue Squad saved the day again with the help of their new friends! But before Ash, Cilan, and Iris said goodbye to Virgil to head to the Unova League, they discovered they'd see him there too! The Evolution Pokémon expert had earned all eight gym badges and was all set to enter the big tournament.

Virgil and his well-trained roster of Eevee and its evolved forms wound up making a huge splash at the championship. Virgil impressed everyone with his battle style and heart. So, it was no surprise when this talented Trainer went on to win the Unova League!

BURGUNDY

While waiting in a long line to be evaluated by a Pokémon Connoisseur, Burgundy beckons Ash to let her give him a reading. But instead of giving Ash pointers, Burgundy takes the opportunity to sling insults. She tells Ash that all of his Pokémon are horrible, and unless he ditches them, he won't be anything but a loser. However, in reality, Burgundy is a big faker. She's a beginning Connoisseur, Rank C, and she doesn't have the credentials to call it like she sees it. As an A-ranked Connoisseur, Cilan is happy to call her out! But it seems Burgundy feels like Cilan did that a long time ago, as Burgundy has a beef with the Striaton City Gym Leader that goes back to her childhood. After Burgundy tried and failed to earn the Trio Badge, Cilan commented that she didn't care for her Pokémon properly. And ever since that fateful battle, she has been planning her revenge!

Food for Thought

Like a typical Connoisseur, Burgundy likes to compare things to food. She also likes to pepper her speech with French words. But no matter what she's saying, her bad temper often boils over.

MISS UNDERSTOOD

Just like their first meeting, Burgundy thinks Cilan is always insulting her pride when he is really offering constructive criticism and encouragement. After all, that's the job of a Connoisseur! Even when Burgundy tells him off before big battle events like the Pokémon World Tournament Junior Cup and the Clubsplosion tournament, Cilan calmly assures her that he believes she can win. But his kind words of support only make her angrier. Cilan has already inspired her to become a Connoisseur, so maybe she'll someday pick up his good sportsmanship. Until then, she'd rather join Georgia, Iris' foe, on the sidelines of the battlefield, so they can both rant about their rivals like sore losers.

GEORGIA

Georgia is spunky and full of attitude. Always ready to attack and quick to snap back, she has almost as much bite as the Dragon-types she's obsessed with battling (and her mouth might be full of more hot air). No matter the challenge, she is confident she can show her strength, or at least talk a good game.

The Dragon Buster

Georgia coined the term "Dragon Buster" to describe her main interest: defeating Dragon-types on the battlefield. She's especially interested in  battling Trainers from the Village of Dragons because she once lost a battle there, and her ego has never recovered from it. She considers her number one enemy to be Iris, and she isn't shy about telling Iris this at competitions like the Clubsplosion tournament and the Pokémon World Tournament Junior Cup just to show her up. But truly, her mouth is mightier than her battle moves. At the Pokémon World Tournament Junior Cup, the two rivals are pitted against each other in the first round. And although Dragonite doesn't listen to Iris' instructions, it knocks out Georgia's Pokémon pal Beartic with a terrific Thunder Punch.

STEPHAN

With a striped red tank and spiky red hair, it's hard to miss Stephan, but it's very easy to mispronounce his name. No one can ever get it right, much to Stephan's dismay. When Stephan, along with his pal Sawk, climbed the entire Mistralton Tower carrying a Litwick to win the Wishing Bell Festival, his prize was a chance to ring the lucky bell to make a wish. Forget money, fame, or even Pokémon power; Stephan simply wanted people to pronounce his name properly.

However, if you just say the word "battle," Stephan won't care what you call him as long as you call on him. A regular contestant at the competitions in Unova, he's a good sport about his name and playing the game. And he's always down to practice, too! At the Clubsplosion battle, he and Ash trained their Pokémon side by side. His hard work paid off when he hit a back-to-back winning streak. After his triumph at the Wishing Bell Festival, Stephan and Sawk swept the whole Clubsplosion competition, even defeating Montgomery and tough guy Throh! So, Ash isn't surprised when he runs into Stephan again at the Unova League in Vertress City. In fact, the two are randomly matched up to battle in the third round. Ash wins the heated three-on-three battle to advance onto the quarterfinals. But like a good sport, Stephan stays in the stands to root for all of his friends through the tournament.

Training Technology

Crafty Stephan powers up his Electric-type Pokémon with a modified bicycle that he made. It stores energy with every pedal and can really charge up attacks for a battle!

Stephan's Pokémon

BLITZLE

ZEBSTRIKA

LIEPARD

SAWK

LUKE

Luke is a Trainer who loves Pokémon, but his true passion is making movies. In fact, he only enters the Pokémon Club Battle tournament in Nimbasa City to study moves for filming his action sequences. However, while competing in the tournament, Luke can't resist filming every moment to make a documentary of the event, too.

Luke's passion for filmmaking pays off. Not only does he win a film festival with the first movie he made starring Ash, Iris, and Cilan—*The Legend of the Pokémon Knight*—he is also one of the few directors chosen to shoot a movie for the new Pokéstar Studio's film competition. Along with his pals and favorite cast, he makes an action-packed flick that captures the top prize! And what does he win? The chance to make another movie at Pokéstar Studios, a dream come true for this talented director!

ZORUA—A STAR IS FORMED

Luke works at the local movie theater in Nimbasa Town, which is where he met his favorite actress Pokémon, Zorua. It had morphed to look like the star of the movie that was playing, and Luke thought the real actress was sitting in the audience. Because Zorua can shape-shift, its imitations are uncanny!

Ash, Cilan, and Iris first met Zorua when it was pretending to be Pikachu, and not even Ash could tell them apart. Zorua is a real star that usually plays all the roles in Luke's movies. However, it was a good thing Luke cast Ash, Cilan, and Iris in *The Legend of the Pokémon Knight*. When Team Rocket showed up to snatch Zorua, our heroes snapped into action to give the film a happy ending.

But no one wants Zorua more than Bianca! She's obsessed with the Tricky Fox Pokémon and constantly pestering Luke to trade Zorua for Pignite. Zorua can't stand Bianca and always finds a way to slip out of her super-tight hugs. Zorua never wants to leave its buddy Luke, but it has also found a good friend in Iris. Whenever the Dragon Buster Georgia bullies Iris, Zorua changes form into a Georgia puppet so Iris can give her a taste of her own teasing.

Luke's Pokémon

LEAVANNY

ZORUA

GOLETT

LARVESTA

TEAM ROCKET

Jessie, James, and Meowth have turned over a new leaf and are striving to be taken seriously. They've set their sights on the treasures of Unova to complete their most dastardly deeds for their boss yet! They have new outfits, new mission statements, new rides—like a helicopter and a submarine—and a whole new stealth style. They're looking to climb the ladder of the Team Rocket organization, and Giovanni couldn't be prouder of their progress. In Unova, they pull off all kinds of elaborate plans, from breaking into the Nacrene City Museum, to nabbing enough Roggenrola for Dr. Zager's cannon, to stealing secret data from the Dream Yard, to capturing Meloetta's song. Perhaps they've been successful thanks to their support in Unova from scientific genius Dr. Zager and protective Pierce. But luckily, Ash and his friends are always there to foil their plans, even if their new helicopter won't blast off.

Best Friends Foe-ever?

Strangely enough, Jessie, James, and Meowth find allies in the twerps once Team Plasma's evil plans come into play. As they say, the enemy of your enemy is your friend. However, it seems they'll never stop trying to steal Ash's best pal Pikachu, or the rest of his Pokémon, for that matter—some things never change.

DR. ZAGER

Behind the bushy silver hair and a monocle is one of the greatest scientific minds in Unova. Unfortunately, he uses his brain not for good, but for Team Rocket's evil. Since Pierce introduced them at the research lab, Jessie, James, and Meowth look to this mad scientist for instructions and information.

The tech wiz behind Team Rocket, Dr. Zager proves that knowledge is power. He's had a hand in all kinds of nefarious plans, like creating the Roggenrola cannon, snatching the Meteonite, stealing Professor Fennel's research to build his own Pokémon Restoration Machine, and helping to capture the Legendary Pokémon Landorus, Thundurus, and Tornadus.

Dr. Zager also solves complex equations and problems for his boss, Giovanni, to help him become all too powerful. But when Giovanni's aims spiral out of control in Operation Tempest, and the Reveal Glass turns him into a tyrant that wants to destroy Unova, Dr. Zager steps in as the voice of reason to stop him. This level-headed evildoer has his limits—he wants to control Unova, but he knows that he won't have anything to control if it is destroyed. After calming Giovanni down, he stays loyal to his boss and continues his research to empower Team Rocket to rule the region.

GIOVANNI

Giovanni has done a formidable job over the years of staying out of the limelight. But in Unova, he's forced to make an appearance when his usually inept Team Rocket finally locates a Meloetta. He wants to launch Operation Tempest, a misguided attempt to corral Tornadus, Thundurus, and Landorus and to rule Unova. He doesn't just show up and spread good cheer to everyone, either—he finally battles Ash face to face, where his Persian defeats Pikachu. When he finally commands the Reveal Glass, which unlocks the forces of nature, he ends up going insane and tries to encase Unova in ice. Some guys just can't be trusted with a little power. Team Rocket saves him, reversing years of *him* saving *them*, and he's convinced to give up his nefarious plans. Back to the drawing board, Giovanni.

PIERCE

A key secret operative in the Team Rocket gang, Pierce is on the pulse of all their plans to steal Meteonite. Smart and slippery, he gives out assignments, keeps tabs on their minions, and steps in to abort a mission when necessary.

To aid his work, Pierce wears a special ring that's capable of projecting classified information to debrief members of Team Rocket. With his detailed instructions, Jessie, James, and Meowth are able to break into the Antimony Research Lab to hack their servers and steal the data on Meteonite. Then, together with his colleague Dr. Zager, Pierce locates even more powerful Meteonite for their evil mission.

But when things get too sticky, it's Pierce who helps Jessie, James, and Meowth make a quick escape before Officer Jenny can arrest them at the Dream Yard.

TEAM PLASMA

GHETSIS

The mysterious head of the Team Plasma organization, Ghetsis is shady through and through. Between his secret communiques with Aldith and Colress, his Top Secret Project G and Project F, and his connection to N and the Seven Sages, Ghetsis has only evil on his mind. Evil and the control of Reshiram, that is.

COLRESS

Colress works at the behest of Ghetsis, but for a lackey, he still has some pretty evil tricks up his sleeve. His claim to fame is using EM waves to control Pokémon minds, which he uses on Pikachu. Thankfully, Ash's love for his Pokémon trumps EM waves and Pikachu is freed. Fighting against Colress is Team Rocket, which foils his plans not once but twice. Later, Colress builds a better machine that ends up controlling Pokémon with a single burst.

SCHWARZ AND WEISS

Schwarz and Weiss make Jessie and James look good. As part of Team Plasma, their first job was to capture a Braviary, which they immediately fumbled on the one-yard line. When they pursued the mysterious N, Ash and friends came to help, and Schwarz and Weiss were immediately forced to battle. Their Seviper and Zangoose were no match for Pikachu, Excadrill, and Braviary.

N

The mysterious N has a symbiotic relationship with all Pokémon—it even appears as if he can understand them when they speak. After meeting up with Ash and his friends, and trusting their intentions, N decides to accompany the team to the White Ruins and help them with their plan to stop Team Plasma.

ALDITH

Aldith is a company grunt. Her purpose is to make sure Colress is in line with the whole "taking over Unova" thing. She doesn't like the fact that Colress is more interested in the true Power of Pokémon; she just wants to make sure Ghetsis has his vision realized. She is also a commando, leading teams in battle against Ash and friends, and then against Team Rocket.

UNOVA LEAGUE

Ash arrived in Vertress City ready to compete in the biggest championship in the region—The Unova League. In order to qualify to enter, each Trainer must have earned eight gym badges in Unova. One hundred and twenty-eight Trainers have all registered with the hopes of winning the coveted title. The competition is stiff! Ash, Stephan, Bianca, Virgil, Cameron, and Ash's biggest rival, Trip, have all registered. This is going to be one heated contest. But Ash, just like the first letter of his name, is ready to bring his A-game.

To signal the start, announcer Freddy the Scoop rides into the arena on a parachute. But the biggest drop is the news he brings. It seems the Trainers will have to battle it out first in a qualifying round with only one Pokémon. The choice is clear for Ash, his best friend Pikachu.

Vertress City's Officer Jenny lights the Unova League Flame Cauldron to officially begin the competition.

PRELIMINARY ROUND

All 128 Trainers have been paired up to battle in the preliminary round. The winning 64 Trainers will make the cut, which means only half of all the Trainers will qualify to compete in the Unova League. Those aren't great odds, but Stephan and Zebstrika, Bianca and Emboar, Virgil and Vaporeon, and Cameron and Ferrothorn all successfully earn their place in the next round.

To earn his place, Ash will have to beat a big rival—Trip, a Trainer he has battled and lost to before. Trip chose strong Serperior to start. Ash calls on his best friend Pikachu as planned, but that also puts him at a Type disadvantage since Electric-type moves are weak against Grass-types. At first, they're both so speedy, they're dodging each other's Attacks. However, when Serperior is able to land a fierce combination of Dragon Tail and Wrap, it has Pikachu trapped. Trip is now confident that the win will be his, but Ash isn't ready to give up. He asks Pikachu to power up Electro Ball and add an Iron Tail whip. With the double blow, Pikachu turns the round around and leaves Serperior unable to battle. Ash wins the qualifying match and officially earned his place at the Unova League Tournament!

OPENING ROUND

In this round, each Trainer gets to choose two Pokémon. The 64 qualifying Trainers are paired up for battle. It looks like Bianca and Cameron are up first! Bianca calls on her Bug/Steel-type friend, Escavalier. Cameron chooses his Water-type pal Samurott. Bianca used Iron Defense three times to up Escavalier's defense power. However, it seems her strategy is missing an offense. So, Samurott was able to win the round with a double Razor Shell throw. Next, Bianca calls on her Fire-type buddy Emboar. It is able to stop Samurott with a combination of Arm Thrust and Hammer Arm hits. However, when Cameron chooses his second Pokémon, Riolu, its incredible Vacuum Wave punch wins him the round. Ash, Stephan, and Virgil all win their matches too!

But before the next round, Iris' pal Axew goes missing. The friends drop everything and band together to find the lost little Dragon-type. Any Trainer great enough to make it to the Unova League knows it's all about teamwork!

THIRD ROUND

Ash and his good friend Stephan are randomly paired up to have the 3-on-3 battle in the third round, but they won't let their friendship get in the way of their bid for the title. Stephan starts with Liepard, Ash chooses Krookodile. It's a Dark-type vs. Dark-type battle, so the Trainer's true strategy will shine. Ash wisely had Krookodile use Dig to dodge Liepard's Double Team trick. A fierce swipe of Dragon Claw left Liepard unable to battle, but Krookodile took a lot of damage.

So, when Stephan calls on his second Pokémon, Electric-type, Zebstrika, Ash chooses his Water/Ground-type pal Palpitoad. Ash might have picked a Pokémon with a strong type advantage, but he didn't count on Zebstrika's speed. After a heated match, they're both left unable to battle.

For his third and final Pokémon pick, Stephan chooses Fighting-type Sawk. He is showing no signs of letting up! Ash calls on his Bug/Grass-type buddy, Leavanny. The battle is so heated Leavanny activates its Special Ability, Swarm, to increase its power. Then, Leavanny is even able to stop Sawk's big Bulk Up by wrapping it in String Shot. However, it accidentally cuts through its own threads with an X-Scissor slice and frees Sawk. With one crazy Karate Chop by Sawk, Leavanny is left unable to battle.

Krookodile comes back to battle. Now, it has a big type disadvantage and looks tired, but looks can be deceiving. The Intimidation Pokémon is ready to rumble! Sawk swings Close Combat and Dragon Claw, but it's no match for Krookodile's surprising and awesome Aerial Ace Attack. In one fell swoop from high in the sky, Sawk is left unable to battle. With that, Ash has won the round and will advance to the quarterfinals. Like a good sport, Stephan congratulates his buddy Ash on his smart battle strategy.

QUARTERFINALS

Ash is again paired up for a six-on-six battle with another friend. This round, it's Cameron. He was so excited for the match the night before that Cameron couldn't sleep a wink and instead went for a long run. When they step onto the battlefield the next day, Ash completely understands his motivation. It's a big match for both of them! And Cameron has brought a surprise secret weapon to the quarterfinals—Hydreigon, the Brutal Pokémon. They say two heads are better than one and this Pokémon has three!

Ash chooses Boldore to step onto the battlefield. It fires Rock Blast and Flash Cannon, but it can barely make a dent. Hydreigon bombards Boldore with its fierce Tri Attack, tough Dragon Rush, and finishes the round with a shocking Dragon Pulse.

Next, Ash calls on Oshawott to battle the powerful Hydreigon. Oshawott gives the match its all. Ash has it hold its Hydro Pump splash strong. Then, Oshawott gets close to the three-headed Pokémon with Tackle and adds Razor Shell slashes, but surprisingly, it isn't enough to overwhelm the Brutal Pokémon. Then, with a strong combination of Double Hit and Dragon Rush, Hydreigon wins the round.

Hydreigon seems unstoppable, but Ash never gives up. He chooses a third Pokémon, his Fire-type pal Pignite. It scores a direct hit with its scorching Flamethrower. Amazingly enough, when Pignite adds a Brick Break hit, Hydreigon is left unable to battle. What unbelievable power Pignite possesses! With that, Ash has scored his first win in the quarterfinals, but the battle isn't over yet.

Cameron calls on Grass/Steel-type Pokémon Ferrothorn, but it has a serious type disadvantage. It fires Pin Missile, Mirror Shot, and takes a swipe with Metal Claw. But Pignite is so fired up that with a double blast of Fire-type moves Flamethrower and Flame Charge, it wins the round.

For his third Pokémon, Cameron chooses a Pokémon with the type advantage, Samurott. Pignite musters up the energy to use some of its best moves, a fiery Flamethrower and a Brick Break chop, but it's too tired to really give it full force. So, with combination of a Hydro Pump blast and an Aqua Jet wallop, Pignite is left unable to battle. Samurott has won the round.

Ash chooses his best friend Pikachu next. Quick on its feet, Samurott deflects Pikachu's Electric-type attacks with Razor Shell. But when Pikachu whacks Iron Tail, it wins the round and evens the score.

Next, Cameron chooses Water/Flying-type Swanna. It takes to the battlefield, or rather to the sky, as it plans to attack from above. Speedy Pikachu is able to avoid Swanna's repeated Pluck. With a bright Electro Ball, Swanna is left unable to battle. Pikachu has won another round.

Cameron calls on his fifth Pokémon, Fighting-type Riolu. So, Ash swaps Pikachu out for Normal/Flying-type, Unfezant. But any aerial advantage it might have is immediately squashed as limber Riolu jumps on Unfezant's back to pin it down. Unfezant is eventually able to break out of its hold, but it cannot withstand Riolu's swirling Circle Throw. Riolu wins the round!

So, Ash calls on his sixth and final Pokémon, smart Snivy. The battle between Snivy and Riolu is so heated, it creates not only an incredible show but also an awesome transformation! Cameron can't believe his eyes as he watches his friend Riolu, right in the middle of the arena, evolve into Lucario, the powerful Aura Pokémon! With its newfound strength and its new forceful Aura Sphere, Lucario wins the round!

Now, it comes down to Pikachu. Ash brings back his best friend to battle Lucario. Pikachu is always up for a challenge and this battle will sure put it to the test. When Lucario unleashes its infamous Aura Sphere, Pikachu counters with an Electro Ball blast. Both Pokémon bring such power to the match that it becomes a battle of wills. The fight rages on. When Pikachu uses an Iron Tail hit, Lucario matches it with Copycat. Both Pokémon look like they're down for the count. But amazingly enough, they both get back up and back into it. Again, Pikachu fires Electro Ball and Lucario shoots Aura Sphere. This time, it's not a draw. Brave Pikachu is left unable to battle. Lucario and Cameron advance to the next round in the Unova League. Although Ash is knocked out of the competition, he is so proud of his Pokémon pals and, above all, happy to watch his friend Cameron continue on in the tournament.

SEMI-FINALS

In the semi-final round, Cameron and Lucario will face Virgil and his three remaining Pokémon: Espeon, Flareon, and Eevee, key members of the Pokémon Rescue Squad's Team Eevee. Lucario seemed unstoppable, but Fire-type Flareon has a strong type advantage. Lucario hangs tough through Flareon's fierce Flamethrower. But when it adds a Fire Blast kapow, Lucario is finally unable to battle. Virgil has won the round and advances to the Finals. Cameron, Ash, Cilan, and Iris are all excited to root for their pal in the tournament's big showdown.

FINALS

In the Finals, Virgil and Team Eevee face a tough Trainer named Dino and his Dragon-type buddy Druddigon. Cleverly, Eevee uses Dig to dodge Druddigon's Dragon Rage. Then, Eevee fights back with an Iron Tail wallop and a smooth move that scores a direct hit, Trump Card. Druddigon is left unable to battle. It's official, Virgil has won the Unova League! Ash can't wait to congratulate his incredible pal on his big win and his even bigger heart.

UNOVA GYM BATTLES

In Unova, Ash once again proves his dedication to becoming a great Pokémon Trainer. Sometimes he needs a rematch or even to meet a pre-battle challenge, but Ash shows that persistence and hard work pay off when he ultimately earns his eight badges from Unova Gym Leaders.

STRAITON GYM

GYM LEADERS: CHILI, CRESS, and CILAN

Even though it takes only one win to earn the Trio Badge, Ash boldly decides to battle all three Gym Leaders!

 CHILI VS. ASH

Chili thinks Ash is brave for sending a Fire-type against a Fire-type, a true test of strength. Pansear has an awesome Dig, but Ash has Tepig grab Pansear by the tail and then use Ember and Tackle to win the round!

CRESS VS. ASH

In this round, Pikachu has the type advantage, but Panpour wins the round with a strong combo of Mud Sport and Water Gun.

CILAN VS. ASH

Again, Ash picks a Pokémon with a type disadvantage, and things look bleak when Oshawott can't even aim its Water Gun. But Ash's pal deflects Pansage's powerful Solar Beam with Scalchop, the tide turns, and Ash wins the round and the Trio Badge!

CASTELIA GYM

GYM LEADER: BURGH

 BURGH VS. ASH

Dwebble's shell is especially light, so it can move so fast that even speedy Tepig is no match for it. Dwebble wins the round with Rock Wrecker.

 BURGH VS. ASH

In true Ash fashion, he goes for a Bug-type vs. Bug-type battle. Dwebble's shell and Protect keep it safe at first, but Sewaddle is in it to win it. After a tough Tackle, Sewaddle snags the victory with Razor Leaf.

 BURGH VS. ASH

With Whirlipede's Solar Beam, Sewaddle looks to be down for the count. But the light blast's power helps it evolve into Swadloon. In its new form, Swadloon wins the round with an amazing Energy Ball.

 BURGH VS. ASH

When Swadloon gets wrapped up in Leavanny's String Shot, Ash wisely has it use Razor Leaf to break free. But when Leavanny quickly follows up with Hyper Beam, Swadloon is unable to battle back.

 BURGH VS. ASH

Leavanny wraps up Pikachu's tail in String Shot so it can't aim its Thunderbolt. Ash has Pikachu spin around in Leavanny's Leaf Storm to cut the thread. Pikachu then unleashes Thunder Bolt, Iron Tail, and a big Electro Ball. Ash earns the Insect Badge!

NACRENE GYM

GYM LEADER: LENORA

 LENORA VS. ASH

Lillipup's tricky Roar forces Ash to trade out Pokémon quickly.

 LENORA VS. ASH

Watchog's Mean Look traps Oshawott on the field. It tries to defend itself with Scalchop, but Watchog's Electric-type attacks are so strong it wins the round with Thunderbolt.

 LENORA VS. ASH

Tepig's Ember has no effect on Lillipup. So, Lenora and Lillipup easily win the battle with Take Down.

After Training with Don George at the Pokémon Battle Club, Ash returned to the Nacrene City Gym to challenge Lenora to a rematch.

 LENORA VS. ASH

Lenora had Herdier use Mean Look to switch out the Pokémon on the battlefield.

 LENORA VS. ASH

Ash expects Lenora to use her classic combo of Roar and Mean Look. But she also has Watchog use Confuse Ray so Oshawott can't aim Aqua Jet. When Watchog's Thunderbolt hits Oshawott's Aqua Jet, both Pokémon are knocked out.

 LENORA VS. ASH

Tepig proves that it trains hard, as its attacks are faster and stronger than ever. Herdier has a great Giga Impact, but Tepig wins the round with fiery Ember and Flame Charge, and Ash earns the Basic Badge.

DRIFTVEIL GYM

GYM LEADER: CLAY

Clay gives Ash a challenge before they even step onto the battlefield—he must bring back a bag of Revival Herbs in order to try for the Quake Badge in the underground mine gym.

CLAY **VS.** **ASH**

Oshawott breaks through the swirling dirt of Krokorok's Sandstorm with a spinning Aqua Jet. Then it shoots Aqua Jet through the Dig holes to catch Krokorok off guard. Oshawott throws in Razor Shell to win the round!

CLAY **VS.** **ASH**

Ash picks Snivy for its type advantage and his plan works. Once Snivy's Attract puts Palpitoad in a trance, it wins the round with its great Grass-type attacks: Vine Whip, Leaf Blade, and Lead Storm.

CLAY

Since Palpitoad is also a Water-type, the playing field is pretty even. But once Oshawott drops its Scalchop, Palpitoad is able to win the round with Rock Smash.

Clay's Excadrill helped him dig the very mine in which they're battling. When Snivy's Attract fails, it tries Leaf Storm twice. It's no match for the strong Excadrill, who wins with Rapid Spin and Horn Drill.

CLAY **VS.** **ASH**

Just when it looks like Roggenrola is about to get knocked out, it evolves into Boldore. Excadrill's and Boldore's Rock Smashes go head to head. Boldore's new form gives it the strength to win Ash the Quake Badge.

NIMBASA GYM

GYM LEADER: ELESA

ELESA **VS.** **ASH**

Speedy Zebstrika dominates the round with Double Kick and Quick Attack. But when Palpitoad uses Supersonic, the switch is flipped and it wins the round with a combo of Mud Shot and Hydro Pump.

ELESA **VS.** **ASH**

Ash blanks on Grass-types' disadvantage against Flying-types. Realizing his error, he starts on the offensive. But Emolga is unfazed by Snivy's attempts; it strikes with Acrobatics until it emerges victorious.

ELESA **VS.** **ASH**

Emolga confuses Palpitoad with Aerial Ace and Attract, so it's too trapped in a daze to use Supersonic. With one more Aerial Ace, Emolga wins the round.

ELESA **VS.** **ASH**

The fans see Elesa as the clear winner, but Pikachu begs Ash to go in and shake things up. Though Emolga's and Pikachu's Electro Balls cancel each other out, Pikachu's powerful Quick Attack knocks out Emolga.

ELESA **VS.** **ASH**

Tynamo uses Tackle to bury Pikachu in the ground and pummels it while it's trapped. Amazingly, Pikachu pulls itself out. Ash has it spray the stadium with Thunderbolt to recharge its energy. Pikachu wins the battle with a double Iron Tail. Ash earns the Bolt Badge.

MISTRALTON GYM

GYM LEADER: SKYLA

SKYLA **VS.** **ASH**

Ground-type attacks have no effect on a Flying-type, but Ash loves a challenge, so he chooses Krokorok. Although Krokorok hides with Dig, it can't run from Swoobat's attacks. It wins with an awesome Air Cutter.

SKYLA **VS.** **ASH**

Unfezant is the evolved form of Tranquill, so the scales are tipped in Skyla's favor right from the start. Before Tranquill really begins battling, Ash takes his tired friend off the field.

SKYLA **VS.** **ASH**

Thanks to a trick Skyla learned from her Grandfather Miles, Pikachu's Electric-type moves have no effect on Swanna. Skyla wins with Swanna's trio of signature moves: Bubble Beam, Hurricane, and Brave Bird.

Skyla prefers her imaginary form of fighting, Air Battles, but Ash convinces her to get her head out of the clouds and accept his challenge for the Jet Badge.

SKYLA **VS.** **ASH**

Ash sticks to strange tactics, pitting Flying-type against Flying-type. Swoobat's Air Cutter and Tranquill's Gust are at a stalemate. But Tranquill's speed and its amazingly powerful Air Cutter win the round.

SKYLA **VS.** **ASH**

Pikachu is excited to electrify the battle and turn things around for Ash. Pikachu waits for Unfezant to get close before it uses Iron Tail, then it follows up with a big Electro Ball to win the round.

SKYLA **VS.** **ASH**

This battle is so heated, Tranquill evolves into Unfezant. The flying skill of Ash's female Unfezant allows it to stay on Swanna's tail. It attacks twice with Brave Bird and Aerial Ace to win Ash the Jet Badge.

ICIRRUS GYM

GYM LEADER: BRYCEN

BRYCEN VS. **ASH**

Vanillish uses a combo of Astonish and Blizzard to freeze out Krokorok. Ash asks it to return before things get even more slippery.

BRYCEN VS. **ASH**

Scraggy tries to stop Cryogonal's Rapid Spin with Focus Blast, but it breaks out an amazing Aurora Beam and wins the round.

BRYCEN VS. **ASH**

Pignite begins the battle with Flame Charge, but Beartic blows out its fire with Brine. Then, Beartic combines Icicle Crash and a surprising Aerial Ace to win the round.

BRYCEN VS. **ASH**

For its first Gym Battle, Scraggy puts its all into High Jump and Headbutt, but Vanillish just floats away. Finally, Scraggy breaks through Vanillish's Blizzard with Focus Blast and delivers a Headbutt to win the round.

BRYCEN VS. **ASH**

Brycen begins by using Cryogonal's Reflect to cut Pignite's Attack Power in half. But Pignite slices through Cryogonal's superb Rapid Spin with Fire Pledge and wins the round.

BRYCEN VS. **ASH**

Brycen and Beartic seem unstoppable, but Krokorok is determined. Ash borrows a move he saw in the Clubsplosion Tournament. He has Krokorok grab big chunks of Stone Edge and meet Beartic in midair before it can unleash Aerial Ace. Ash wins the battle and the Freeze Badge!

VERBANK GYM

GYM LEADER: ROXIE

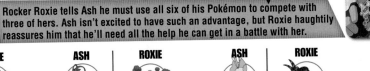

Rocker Roxie tells Ash he must use all six of his Pokémon to compete with three of hers. Ash isn't excited to have such an advantage, but Roxie haughtily reassures him that he'll need all the help he can get in a battle with her.

ROXIE VS. **ASH**

Boldore sets the stage with Sandstorm, but Koffing quickly blows it away with Clear Smog. After a couple Gyro Ball blasts, Boldore is quickly out of the battle.

ROXIE VS. **ASH**

Unfezant uses Gust to fan away Koffing's Will-O-Wisp, but it isn't so lucky when it comes to stopping Koffing's killer Gyro Ball. Unfezant is knocked out.

ROXIE VS. **ASH**

Ash chooses Leavanny, a Grass-type with a clear disadvantage. But after watching Koffing in action, he has a plan! After wrapping Koffing in String Shot, Leavanny uses Energy Ball to eliminate its foe.

ROXIE VS. **ASH**

Leavanny gets hit with Toxic, and it's just a matter of time before it's unable to battle. Leavanny tries to keep fighting, but it's officially out after a slap of Sludge Bomb.

ROXIE VS. **ASH**

Pignite uses a triple threat of Flame Charge, Flamethrower, and Fire Pledge to win the round! But Scolipede's Toxic poisons Pignite, so Roxie generously shares a Pecha Berry to get Pignite ready for another round.

ROXIE VS. **ASH**

Ash has Pignite go on the offensive to stave off Garbodor's powerful Poison-type attacks. But after a huge Hyper Beam hit, Pignite is unable to battle.

ROXIE VS. **ASH**

Ash has Palpitoad sling Mud Shot, but Garbodor counters with a toxic Gunk Shot and a double dose of Venoshock. Palpitoad is then unable to keep battling the Poison-type opponent.

ROXIE VS. **ASH**

Pikachu dodges Garbodor and lands a Thunderbolt and Iron Tail. Once Garbodor lands a few Gunk Shots, Pikachu loses the momentum. But Ash and Pikachu find a second wind when they hear their friends cheering. Pikachu uses Static and then a bold Electro Ball to win the Toxic Badge for Ash.

DON GEORGE

Ash first meets Don George in Accumula Town. Iris tells Ash that if he's looking to train hard and battle hard, Don George's Pokémon Battle Club is the place to be in Unova! But there isn't just one…

Cousins, Identical Cousins

There are Pokémon Battle Clubs all across the Unova region. Each one is run by a Don George, identical cousins with the same name. Being a great coach must be genetic, as each Don George can bring out the confident battle spirit in every Pokémon and Trainer with his specialized training.

Get Your Battle On

The Pokémon Battle Club isn't just a place to get expert training—hey, it's called a Battle Club for a reason! Trainers can post and search for challengers on the Battle Club's electronic bulletin board, and then use their battlefield for the match. It's a one-stop battlin' shop!

Soft Side

Don George might be big, burly tough guy, but he's also a total softy. Passionate about Pokémon and training, he can't help but cry happy tears when the moment strikes him. For example, when Don George thinks a mysterious Pokémon poking around his storage room is actually the first Umbreon ever spotted, he gets all choked up. But nothing tops his blubbering while watching the final match of his Club Battle. That round between Iris and Ash is a real fight to the finish, and to Don George, nothing is more beautiful than an amazing battle.

CLUBSPLOSION TOURNAMENT

Trainers and spectators alike are excited to enter the Pokémon Club Battle Stadium for this tournament because it is known for its rounds of amazing hand-to-hand combat between Fighting-type Pokémon. A tournament tradition, Don George presents the winner with the grand prize of a year's supply of all six Pokémon vitamin drinks: HP Up, Calcium, Zinc, Carbos, Protein, and Iron—guaranteed to boost any Pokémon's power. Undoubtedly, Ash, Iris, and Cilan are there to battle it out, but so are their rivals Trip, Georgia, and Burgundy. Stephan and Bianca also register for the competition. Although the fiercest foes in this tournament seem to be Montgomery and his terrifyingly tough Throh, the underdogs Stephan and Sawk surprise everyone when they win with Close Combat!

CLUB BATTLE

Nimbasa Town's Don George hosts the famous Club Battle, a tournament that draws Trainers from all over Unova. The competition is stiff, but the prize is light as a feather, seven to be exact. The winner, Iris, received the seven feather "Top-Class Driftveil Wing Set," a rare set that contains Health, Muscle, Resist, Genius, Clever, Swift, and Pretty Wings. But the competition was tough, and Iris had to prove herself in front of fellow competitors Ash, Cilan, Burgundy, Bianca, Dino, Antonio, Stephan, Georgia, and Trip.

FREDDY "THE SCOOP" O'MARTIAN

Did you know that the announcer at Pokémon tournaments has a name? That's right, it's Freddy the Scoop. The one thing you can say about Freddy is that he's always ready to add a little dramatic flair to any battle. You don't think so? Try imagining a battle narrated by anyone else. That's what we thought. He's co-hosted events with both Don George of Nimbasa and Alder, the Unova Champ.

PLACES TO VISIT

Here is a small sampling of the many special sites and attractions that call Unova home. A visit to this bustling region reveals many other cities, towns, and points of interest. Unova truly offers something exciting to any Trainer or sightseer!

CASTELIA CITY

This city by the sea has so many skyscrapers, and even more people and Pokémon! At the heart of this city is Central Plaza, a beautiful public park with a famous fountain. Foodies are known to flock to this town to taste the icy sweet treats at Castelia Cone.

NIMBASA CITY

The sister city to Castelia boasts the acclaimed brothers Ingo and Emmet, also known as the Subway Bosses. Their rails connect every corner of the city. All you have to do is hop on the right line to get to one of Nimbasa's amazing attractions. You can ride the famous Ferris Wheel, watch the street artists in Performers Square, see a concert at the Musical Theater, catch a game at the Big Stadium, or even play a game yourself at the Small Court.

MILOS ISLAND

Off the coast of Driftveil City lies Milos Island, a natural wonderland that is the only source of Revival Herbs, a special cure with incredible healing powers for Pokémon. A sacred spot to visit, there is an impressive shrine to Landorus, the Mythical Pokémon and guardian of the island that created the abundance of greenery. There are also two very important obelisks that keep Legendary Pokémon Thundurus and Tornadus separated so they cannot fight again.

According to The Ancient Legend of Milos Island, long ago, their epic battle terrorized the island. Landorus swooped in to restore order and replenished the land with Revival Herbs.

NACRENE CITY

Nacrene City is known in Unova as the center of creativity because so many artists call it home. There is a multitude of statues and public art all over the city, but perhaps the best place for art fanatics to visit is the Nacrene City Museum. It's full of interesting artifacts and it also houses an incredible library. Be careful which book you take off the shelf, because it might be the secret key that unlocks the door to the Nacrene Gym, which is actually hidden inside the museum.

HERO'S RUIN

The Hero's Ruin has two parts: Black and White. The White Ruins are at the Dragon Spiral Tower, the tallest tower in Unova. The entrance is covered in hieroglyphics. Although the ruins' builders are a mystery, the site is known to possess the Light Stone, a precious and powerful treasure connected to the Legendary Pokémon Reshiram. According to the White Chapter of Pokémon Mythology, when a person searching deeply for truth arrives at the White Ruins, Reshiram will appear to battle the hero as a test of his or her strength and heart.

According to the Black Chapter of Pokémon Mythology, the Black Ruins are said to be the place where the Hero first met the Legendary Pokémon, Zekrom. To deter trespassers, it is full of booby-traps, from faulty bridges to false entrances to rolling rocks. As if those weren't scary enough, scores of Cofagrigus and Sigilyph guard the entire site. Tight security keeps intruders away from its sacred treasure, the Golden Dark Stone, which is connected to Zekrom.

DECOLORE ISLANDS

Located off the coast of Unova is a group of lush green lands known as the Decolore Islands. Here are some spots that travelers in the know love to visit, just keep your eyes peeled for pirates!

HONEY ISLAND

If you have a sweet tooth, Honey Island is the place for you! It takes its name from the famous sweet honey the local Combee produce. Honey Island is also known for having delicious deserts.

SCALCHOP ISLAND

Dewott and Oshawott are the Pokémon that populate this special place that celebrates Scalchops. In fact, the locals are such big fans of the flying object, the island hosts the Scalchop King Competition in which contestants try their hand to win the Golden Scalchop. Amazingly enough, Ash and Oshawott were declared the winners! This meant Oshawott had to stay on Scalchop Island to perform his official Kingly duties with his crush, The Scalchop Queen, Osharina. Ash is happy for his pal, but sad to say goodbye. Luckily, Oshawott decides to continue on the journey with Ash when Osharina makes it known that she'd prefer the King to be a Dewott named Caesar.

GRAND SPECTRALA ISLAND

A great place to stop for a bite to eat and visit Nurse Joy at the Pokémon Center. When the tide is low, you can walk across the sand to the Grand Spectrala Islet.

TOROM ISLAND

Look out for blackouts on this island. It's full of Rotom with appetites for electricity and they can snack all day! Ash and his friends run into Professor Oak about town in Torom Island. He is there to try to catch Rotom for a research project he's working on about Pokémon and their relationship to electrical devices.

WAYFARER ISLAND

A great place for Pokémon watching, Wayfarer Island is a well-known rest stop for Pokémon on the move of migration. While visiting, Ash, Iris, and Cilan spotted Caterpie, Metapod, Butterfree, Swanna, Altaria, Swellow, and Swablu.

CAPACIA ISLAND

Lovely Capacia Island is adorned with flowers, fruit, and sometimes, even alien Pokémon! Ash and his pals got the chance to see Beheeyem's flying saucer on the island and help them repair it.

HARVEST ISLAND

It's hard to imagine today because Harvest Island is covered in delicious fruit, but legend has it, that at one time, there was only

one fruit tree left. Two Pokémon fought over it until a brave boy divided the fruit and gave half to each one, asking them to share. Peace was then restored to the island. Now, the Grand Harvest Festival is held to commemorate the legend and the island's bounty. This holiday brings locals together to celebrate and it's also the day that Ash, Cilan, and Iris met Alexa, the journalist from Kalos. Even more notably, it's the island where Ash and his pal Pignite won the Pokémon Sumo Contest. Luckily, Ash's new pal Alexa was there to capture it with her camera.

CAVE ISLAND

This island lives up to its name. Its giant cave is home to many kinds of wild Pokémon including a Druddigon with unusual coloring.

PALADIN ISLAND

According to legend, an incredible battle between the strongest Trainer from Unova and the strongest Trainer from Sinnoh happened long ago on Paladin Island. An impressive lighthouse was built to mark the spot of the epic match. Coincidentally, Cilan finds himself being challenged to a very important battle on the island too! An Ice-type expert named Morana has come with her tough Pokémon pal, Abomasnow, to demand a match with the gym leader. But the stakes are more than just a gym badge, she wants the whole Striaton City Gym! She has already won rounds with Chili and Cress, and all she has to do now is defeat Cilan. However, Pansage and Cilan are such a strong team that its Solar Beam and heart can break through any ice sent by Abomasnow. Together, they are able to defeat Morana right there on Paladin Island.

ALEXA

With Helioptile, Gogoat, and Noivern by her side, this journalist is on an incredible journey. She is always chasing a story and thereby adventure. Whether her news beat is ancient fossils or futuristic robots, Alexa is never without her enthusiasm or her camera.

Ash first met Alexa at Grand Harvest Festival in the Decolore Islands. She was there to cover the festivities and Ash was the one making a scene. When he spotted her pal Helioptile, he thought it was wild and tried to catch it. What he caught instead was a big zap of electricity! Alexa ran over to see what the commotion was and instead became instant friends with Ash. She was so impressed by his zest for life, she decided to briefly follow him on his journey. Together they traveled through the Decolore Islands, back to Kanto, and onto Kalos. Alexa often meets up with Ash and his crew throughout the region to cheer them on!

RIGHTEOUS REPORTER

Journalistic integrity is her utmost concern. Alexa always tries to seek out stories, but she knows there are more important things than a big scoop. Alexa feels her job is to inform and protect the public. She won't tell news that's better left a secret for people and Pokémon alike. When she found a treasure map that led to a chest full of Evolution Stones on a deserted Decolore Island, she feared reporting the story would put the precious stones in danger of falling into the wrong hands. So, she deleted her entire recording.

When Clembot was accused of vandalism, reporter Alexa was there to help prove its innocence. She followed the trail of clues to reveal the real perpetrator—the evil replica Dark Clembot and its even more evil creator, robotics expert, Doctor Belmondo. With Alexa and her camera around, the truth will always be exposed!

THE SUPER SANTALUNE SISTERS

Alexa is from one talented family! Her sister is Viola, the Santalune City Gym Leader. Just like her sister Alexa, Viola is never without her camera. Alexa prefers video, but Viola is all about photography. When Ash battles Viola, you bet Alexa is there in the stands to watch the match and rematch unfold. In fact, Alexa offers to help Ash train with her and Noivern before he challenges her sister again. That's a true pal!

IN TOP FORM

Sometimes, you can tell where a Pokémon is from just by looking at it. A few special Pokémon come in different forms to reflect the environment in which they were born.

BURMY/WORMADAM

Even if it's born where there's seemingly nothing around to wrap itself up in, Burmy always comes covered in a cloak based on its surroundings: plant, sandy, or trash. Male Burmy shed these cloaks when they evolve into Mothim. However, female Burmy evolve into Wormadam and keep their colorful cloaks.

SHELLOS/GASTRODON

There are two forms of the Sea Slug Pokémon: East Sea and West Sea. Color-coded and easy to spot, those from the East Sea are turquoise, while those from the West are pink.

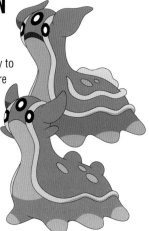

DEERLING/SAWSBUCK

The Season Pokémon change forms four times a year with the weather: Winter, Spring, Summer, and Fall. So, if you need to know the time of year, all you need to do is use your eyes and sometimes even your nose to find the answer. Deerling's fur changes color and scent, while the plants in Sawsbuck's horns bloom accordingly.

BASCULIN

With either red or blue lines running down their backs, Basculin are always ready to earn their stripes in battle. And boy do they live up to their species name—the two forms of the Hostile Pokémon don't get along and will often start attacking each other immediately.

MELOETTA

When Meloetta is about to battle, it changes form and color from green to orange. But if Meloetta really wants to change, it can become completely invisible to the naked eye. Unfortunately, Team Rocket has special goggles to help them spot it.

TOGETHER THROUGH THICK AND THIN

Meloetta has a special place in its heart for Ash. When they first met, he rescued it from a falling piece of a set in the Pokéstar Studios prop room, but then Meloetta disappeared. The next time Ash saw Meloetta was when it wandered into the middle of the road. He helped care for it with Cynthia. Then, Meloetta followed Ash on the entire airplane ride to Undella Town, but he didn't know it was there because it was playing invisible. But once Meloetta materialized, Ash was so excited to have this new friend along for all the fun! And ever since, no matter who is in trouble, they've had each other's backs.

Fine Tune

Piplup and Oshawott fall in love with Meloetta's beautiful voice and spirit. But when they fight over its attention, Meloetta can calm their jealousy with a ditty. Meloetta's song is so soothing, it even had the strength to stop a pack of angry Onix in their tracks.

WHAT IS A POKÉMON CONNOISSEUR?

This career path began in the Unova region. Pokémon Connoisseurs advise Trainers on how to build strong relationships with Pokémon. To be a Pokémon Connoisseur, one must go to a special school and study hard to possess, as Cilan puts it, the "knowledge and experience to judge the compatibility between Trainers and their Pokémon." Then, the Pokémon Connoisseur Association ranks the would-be Connoisseurs based on their abilities. The classes from lowest to highest are C, B, A, and S.

You must have at least an A ranking to give consultations to the public at a Poké Mart. A-ranked Cilan is the first Pokémon Connoisseur Ash has ever met. So, although he's a Grass-type expert, Cilan had to carefully study all types of Pokémon and personalities.

UNOVA LEGENDARY POKÉMON

COBALION • (koh-BAY-lee-un)

Height	6'11" (2.1 m)	Category	Iron Will
Weight	551.2 lbs (250.0 kg)	Type	Steel-Fighting

Cobalion's body and heart might be made of steel, but it has a soft spot for its fellow Pokémon. It will stand up against any bully, even humans. But if a Pokémon is the one misbehaving, a single look from the Iron Will Pokémon is enough to force the culprit to remember its manners instantly.

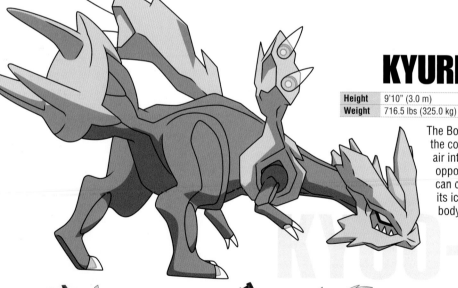

KYUREM • (KYOO-rem)

Height	9'10" (3.0 m)	Category	Boundary
Weight	716.5 lbs (325.0 kg)	Type	Dragon-Ice

The Boundary Pokémon can blow quite the cold wind. Its chilly energy can turn air into ice and freeze out its opponents. However, its frosty ability can completely backfire. Once, when its icy power sprang a leak, Kyurem's body was frozen solid.

BLACK KYUREM

BLACK KYUREM OVERDRIVE MODE

WHITE KYUREM

WHITE KYUREM OVERDRIVE MODE

LANDORUS • (LAN-duh-rus)

Height	4'11" (1.5 m)	Category	Abundance
Weight	149.9 lbs (68.0 kg)	Type	Ground-Flying

Landorus soars through the sky, but its impact is felt deep in the ground. The energy in its tail is the best fertilizer. Almost instantly, the Abundance Pokémon can turn any dirt into a field full of crops that are bigger and taller than anyone can grow by hand. That's why Landorus is also known as "The Guardian of the Fields."

THERIAN FORME

RESHIRAM
• (RESH-i-ram)

Height	10'06" (3.2 m)	Category	Vast White
Weight	727.5 lbs (330.0 kg)	Type	Dragon-Fire

Don't be fooled by the Vast White Pokémon's cool appearance—it is white hot. When its long tail fires up a flame, it can turn anything it touches into ash. Reshiram can heat up more than just a battle. If its torch-like tail really gets cooking, the heat can grow so great that it causes temperatures to rise across the world.

RESHIRAM OVERDRIVE MODE

TERRAKION • (tur-RAK-ee-un)

Height	6'03" (1.9 m)
Weight	573.2 lbs (260.0 kg)
Category	Cavern
Type	Rock-Fighting

Terrakion is so tough it can tackle a solid brick wall and cause it to crumble. Fearless and righteous, the Cavern Pokémon used its strength to put a stop to a human war that had caused a group of Pokémon to lose their homes.

THUNDURUS • (THUN-duh-rus)

Height	4'11" (1.5 m)	Category	Bolt Strike
Weight	134.5 lbs (61.0 kg)	Type	Electric-Flying

Whoever said, "Lightning doesn't strike twice," never met Thundurus! The Bolt Strike Pokémon can shoot lightning from each one of the spikes on its tail for a grand total of six giant sparks. If this Pokémon gets fired up, it can cause quite a blaze on the ground from way up in the sky.

THERIAN FORME

TORNADUS • (tohr-NAY-dus)

Height	4'11" (1.5 m)	Category	Cyclone
Weight	138.9 lbs (63.0 kg)	Type	Flying

Covered in a cloud of energy, Tornadus can fly at an incredibly fast 200 miles per hour. Its speed alone can blow a fierce breeze strong enough to destroy buildings below. The Cyclone Pokémon can also tap down a terribly tough wind with energy in its tail.

THERIAN FORME

VIRIZION • (vih-RY-zee-un)

Height	6'07" (2.0 m)	Category	Grassland
Weight	440.9 lbs (200.0 kg)	Type	Grass-Fighting

Legend has it that Virizion is always there to battle on behalf of a friend, even if the enemy is human. Its trusty blades are built-in, and Virizion's horns are as sharp as a sword. It moves so fast that the Grassland Pokémon can mow down anything that gets in its way.

ZEKROM • (ZECK-rahm)

Height	9'06" (2.9 m)
Weight	760.6 lbs (345.0 kg)
Category	Deep Black
Type	Dragon-Flying

This deep black Pokémon flies through the skies, easily disguised in a cloak of thunderclouds. Just like a bolt of lightning, Zekrom can create quite a zap with the electric generator in its tail. In fact, it is so powerful that it once took Professor Juniper's computer system completely offline.

ZEKROM OVERDRIVE MODE

UNOVA MYTHICAL POKÉMON

GENESECT • (JEN-uh-sekt)

Height	4'11" (1.5 m)	Category	Paleozoic
Weight	181.9 lbs (82.5 kg)	Type	Bug-Steel

The Paleozoic Pokémon roamed the land roughly 300 million years ago. It was just a fossil until Team Plasma brought the Pokémon back to life and attached a powerful cannon to its body.

RESOLUTE FORME

KELDEO • (KELL-dee-oh)

Height	4'07" (1.4 m)	Category	Colt
Weight	106.9 lbs (48.5 kg)	Type	Water-Fighting

Nothing makes Keldeo stronger than its determination. When it sets its mind to something, its body fills with power and it grows so fast that its incredible leaps become impossible to follow.

MELOETTA • (mell-oh-ET-tuh)

Height	2'00" (0.6 m)	Category	Melody
Weight	14.3 lbs (6.5 kg)	Type	Normal-Psychic

A Pokémon with a golden voice, it's called the Melody Pokémon. Behind its beautiful ditty lies an incredibly potent power. When it works in harmony with the Reveal Glass in the ancient Undersea Temple, Meloetta's tune is the key to summon the three powers of nature: Landorus, Thundurus, and Tornadus. In fact, that was Giovanni's plan when his Team Rocket goons helped him capture Meloetta. Luckily, Ash, Iris, Cilan, and Cynthia thwarted his attempt.

PIROUETTE FORME

VICTINI • (vik-TEE-nee)

Height	1'04" (0.4 m)	Category	Victory
Weight	8.8 lbs (4.0 kg)	Type	Psychic-Fire

Victini might look tiny, but it can bring a big success. This Pokémon is a powerhouse that can jumpstart any battle with its endless supply of energy. Plus, it's happy to share its strength! If Victini pays you a visit, consider it your lucky day. The Victory Pokémon is known for turning any Trainer it chooses into a winner.

vik-TEE-nee

UNOVA POKÉMON

The distant region of Unova is home to Reshiram and Zekrom. According to legend, these two Pokémon originated from a single dragon and were pitted against each other during an ancient battle.

ACCELGOR

Height: 2'07" (0.8 m)
Weight: 55.8lbs. (25.3 kg)

BUG

ALOMOMOLA

Height: 3'11" (1.2 m)
Weight: 69.7 lbs. (31.6 kg)

WATER

AMOONGUSS

Height:2'01" (0.6 m)
Weight: 23.1 lbs. (10.5 kg)

GRASS   POISON

ARCHEN

Height: 1'08" (0.5 m)
Weight: 20.9 lbs. (9.5 kg)

ROCK   FLYING

ARCHEOPS

Height: 4'07" (1.4 m)
Weight: 70.5 lbs. (32.0 kg)

ROCK   FLYING

AUDINO

Height: 3'07" (1.1 m)
Weight: 68.3 lbs. (31.0 kg)

NORMAL

AXEW

Height: 2'00" (0.6 m)
Weight: 39.7lbs. (18.0 kg)

DRAGON

BASCULIN

Height: 3'03" (1.0 m)
Weight: 39.7 lbs. (18.0 kg)

WATER

BEARTIC

Height: 8'06" (2.6 m)
Weight: 573.2 lbs. (260.0 kg)

ICE

BEHEEYEM

Height: 3'03" (1.0 m)
Weight: 76.1 lbs. (34.5 kg)

PSYCHIC

BISHARP

Height: 5'03" (1.6 m)
Weight: 154.3 lbs. (70.0 kg)

| DARK | STEEL |

BLITZLE

Height: 2'07" (0.8 m)
Weight: 65.7 lbs. (29.8 kg)

ELECTRIC

BOLDORE

Height: 2'11" (0.9 m)
Weight: 224.9 lbs. (102.0 kg)

ROCK

BOUFFALANT

Height: 5'03" (1.6 m)
Weight: 208.6 lbs. (94.6 kg)

NORMAL

BRAVIARY

Height: 4'11" (1.5 m)
Weight: 90.4 lbs. (41.0 kg)

| NORMAL | FLYING |

CARRACOSTA

Height: 3'11" (1.2 m)
Weight: 178.6 lbs. (81.0 kg)

| WATER | ROCK |

CHANDELURE

Height: 3'03" (1.0 m)
Weight: 75.6 lbs. (34.3 kg)

| GHOST | FIRE |

CINCCINO

Height: 1'08" (0.5 m)
Weight: 16.5 lbs. (7.5 kg)

NORMAL

COBALION

Height: 6'11" (2.1 m)
Weight: 551.2 lbs. (250.0 kg)

| STEEL | FIGHTING |

COFAGRIGUS

Height: 5'07" (1.7 m)
Weight: 168.7 lbs. (76.5 kg)

GHOST

CONKELDURR

Height: 4'07" (1.4 m)
Weight: 191.8 lbs. (87.0 kg)

FIGHTING

COTTONEE

Height:1'00" (0.3 m)
Weight: 1.3 lbs. (0.6 kg)

| GRASS | FAIRY |

CRUSTLE

Height: 4'07" (1.4 m)
Weight: 440.9 lbs. (200.0 kg)

| BUG | ROCK |

CRYOGONAL

Height: 3'07" (1.1 m)
Weight: 326.3 lbs. (148.0 kg)

ICE

CUBCHOO

Height: 1'08" (0.5 m)
Weight: 18.7 lbs. (8.5 kg)

ICE

DARMANITAN

Height: 4'03" (1.3 m)
Weight: 204.8 lbs. (92.9 kg)

FIRE

DARUMAKA

Height: 2'00" (0.6 m)
Weight: 82.7 lbs. (37.5 kg)

FIRE

DEERLING

Height: 2'00" (0.6 m)
Weight: 43.0 lbs. (19.5 kg)

| NORMAL | GRASS |

DEINO

Height: 2'07" (0.8 m)
Weight: 38.1 lbs. (17.3 kg)

| DARK | DRAGON |

DEWOTT

Height: 2'07" (0.8 m)
Weight: 54.0 lbs. (24.5 kg)

WATER

DRILBUR

Height: 1'00" (0.3 m)
Weight: 18.7 lbs. (8.5 kg)

GROUND

DRUDDIGON

Height: 5'03" (1.6 m)
Weight: 306.4 lbs. (139.0 kg)

DRAGON

DUCKLETT

Height: 1'08" (0.5 m)
Weight: 12.1 lbs. (5.5 kg)

WATER	FLYING

DUOSION

Height: 2'00" (0.6 m)
Weight: 17.6 lbs. (8.0 kg)

PSYCHIC

DURANT

Height: 1'00" (0.3 m)
Weight: 72.8 lbs. (33.0 kg)

BUG	STEEL

DWEBBLE

Height: 1'00" (0.3 m)
Weight: 32.0 lbs. (14.5 kg)

BUG	ROCK

EELEKTRIK

Height: 3'11" (1.2 m)
Weight: 22.0 lbs. (48.5 kg)

ELECTRIC

EELEKTROSS

Height: 6'01" (2.1 m)
Weight: 177.5 lbs. (80.5 kg)

ELECTRIC

ELGYEM

Height: 1'08" (0.5 m)
Weight: 19.8 lbs. (9.0 kg)

PSYCHIC

EMBOAR

Height: 5'03" (1.1 m)
Weight: 330.7 lbs. (30.0 kg)

FIRE	FIGHTING

EMOLGA

Height: 1'04" (1.6 m)
Weight: 11.0 lbs. (150.0 kg)

ELECTRIC	FLYING

ESCAVALIER

Height: 3'03" (1.0 m)
Weight: 72.8 lbs. (33.0 kg)

BUG	STEEL

EXCADRILL

Height: 2'04" (0.7 m)
Weight: 89.1 lbs. (40.4 kg)

GROUND	STEEL

FERROSEED

Height: 2'00" (0.6 m)
Weight: 41.4 lbs. (18.8 kg)

GRASS	STEEL

FERROTHORN

Height: 3'03" (1.0 m)
Weight: 242.5 lbs. (110.0 kg)

GRASS	STEEL

FOONGUS

Height: 0'08" (0.2 m)
Weight: 2.2 lbs. (1.0 kg)

GRASS	POISON

FRAXURE

Height: 3'03" (1.0 m)
Weight: 79.4 lbs. (36.0 kg)

DRAGON

FRILLISH (FEMALE)

Height: 3'11" (1.2 m)
Weight: 72.8 lbs. (33.0 kg)

WATER	GHOST

FRILLISH (MALE)

Height: 3'11" (1.2 m)
Weight: 72.8 lbs. (33.0 kg)

WATER	GHOST

GALVANTULA

Height: 2'07" (0.8 m)
Weight: 31.5 lbs. (14.3 kg)

BUG	ELECTRIC

GARBODOR

Height: 6'03" (1.9 m)
Weight: 236.6 lbs. (107.3 kg)

POISON

GENESECT

Height: 4'11" (1.5 m)
Weight: 181.9 lbs. (82.5 kg)

BUG STEEL

GIGALITH

Height: 5'07" (1.7 m)
Weight: 573.2 lbs. (260.0 kg)

ROCK

GOLETT

Height: 3'03" (1.0 m)
Weight: 202.8 lbs. (92.0 kg)

GROUND GHOST

GOLURK

Height: 9'02" (2.8 m)
Weight: 727.5 lbs. (330.0 kg)

GROUND GHOST

GOTHITA

Height: 1'04" (0.4 m)
Weight: 12.8 lbs. (5.8 kg)

PSYCHIC

GOTHITELLE

Height: 4'11" (1.5 m)
Weight: 97.0 lbs. (44.0 kg)

PSYCHIC

GOTHORITA

Height: 2'04" (0.7 m)
Weight: 39.7lbs. (18.0 kg)

PSYCHIC

GURDURR

Height: 3'11" (1.2 m)
Weight: 40.0 lbs. (88.2 kg)

FIGHTING

HAXORUS

Height: 5'11" (1.8 m)
Weight: 232.6 lbs. (105.5 kg)

DRAGON

HEATMOR

Height: 4'07" (1.4 m)
Weight: 127.9 lbs. (58.0 kg)

FIRE

HERDIER

Height: 2'11" (0.9 m)
Weight: 32.4 lbs. (14.7 kg)

NORMAL

HYDREIGON

Height: 5'11" (1.8 m)
Weight: 352.7 lbs. (160.0 kg)

DARK DRAGON

JELLICENT (FEMALE)

Height: 7'03" (202 m)
Weight: 297.6 lbs. (135.0 kg)

WATER GHOST

JELLICENT (MALE)

Height: 7'03" (202 m)
Weight: 297.6 lbs. (135.0 kg)

WATER GHOST

JOLTIK

Height: 0'04" (0.1 m)
Weight: 1.3 lbs. (0.6 kg)

BUG ELECTRIC

KARRABLAST

Height: 1'08" (0.5 m)
Weight: 13.0 lbs. (5.9 kg)

BUG

KELDEO

Height: 4'07" (1.4 m)
Weight: 106.9 lbs. (48.5 kg)

WATER FIGHTING

KLANG

Height: 2'00" (0.6 m)
Weight: 112.4 lbs. (51.0 kg)

STEEL

KLINK

Height: 1'00" (0.3 m)
Weight: 46.3 lbs. (21.0 kg)

STEEL

KLINKLANG

Height: 2'00" (0.6 m)
Weight: 178.6 lbs. (81.0 kg)

STEEL

KROKOROK

Height: 3'03" (1.0 m)
Weight: 73.6 lbs. (33.4 kg)

GROUND DARK

KROOKODILE

Height: 4'11" (1.5 m)
Weight: 212.3 lbs. (96.3 kg)

GROUND DARK

KYUREM

Height: 9'10" (3.0 m)
Weight: 716.5 lbs. (325.0 kg)

DRAGON ICE

LAMPENT

Height: 2'00" (0.6 m)
Weight: 28.7 lbs. (13.0 kg)

GHOST FIRE

LANDORUS

Height: 4'11" (1.5 m)
Weight: 149.9 lbs. (68.0 kg)

GROUND FLYING

LARVESTA

Height: 3'07" (1.1 m)
Weight: 63.5 lbs. (28.8 kg)

BUG FIRE

LEAVANNY

Height: 3'11" (1.2 m)
Weight: 45.2 lbs. (20.5 kg)

BUG GRASS

LIEPARD

Height: 3'07" (1.1 m)
Weight: 82.7lbs. (37.5 kg)

DARK

LILLIGANT

Height: 3'07" (1.1 m)
Weight: 35.9 lbs. (16.3 kg)

GRASS

LILLIPUP

Height: 1'04" (0.4 m)
Weight: 9.0 lbs. (4.1 kg)

NORMAL

LITWICK

Height: 1'00" (0.3 m)
Weight: 6.8 lbs. (3.1 kg)

GHOST FIRE

MANDIBUZZ

Height: 3'11" (1.2 m)
Weight: 87.1 lbs. (39.5 kg)

DARK FLYING

MARACTUS

Height: 3'03" (1.0 m)
Weight: 61.7 lbs. (28.0 kg)

GRASS

MELOETTA

Height: 2'00" (0.6 m)
Weight: 14.3 lbs. (6.5 kg)

NORMAL PSYCHIC

MIENFOO

Height: 2'11" (0.9 m)
Weight: 44.1 lbs. (20.0 kg)

FIGHTING

MIENSHAO

Height: 4'07" (1.4 m)
Weight: 78.3 lbs. (35.5 kg)

FIGHTING

MINCCINO

Height: 1'04" (0.4 m)
Weight: 12.8 lbs. (5.8 kg)

NORMAL

MUNNA

Height: 2'00" (0.6 m)
Weight: 51.4 lbs. (23.3 kg)

PSYCHIC

MUSHARNA

Height: 3'07" (1.1 m)
Weight: 133.4 lbs. (60.5 kg)

PSYCHIC

OSHAWOTT
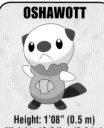
Height: 1'08" (0.5 m)
Weight: 13.0 lbs. (5.9 kg)
WATER

PALPITOAD

Height: 2'07" (0.8 m)
Weight: 37.5 lbs. (17.0 kg)
WATER GROUND

PANPOUR

Height: 2'00" (0.6 m)
Weight: 29.8 lbs. (13.5 kg)
WATER

PANSAGE

Height: 2'00" (0.6 m)
Weight: 23.1 lbs. (10.5 kg)
GRASS

PANSEAR

Height: 2'00" (0.6 m)
Weight: 24.3 lbs. (11.0 kg)
FIRE

PATRAT

Height: 1'08" (0.5 m)
Weight: 25.6 lbs. (11.6 kg)
NORMAL

PAWNIARD

Height: 1'08" (0.5 m)
Weight: 22.5 lbs. (10.2 kg)
DARK STEEL

PETILIL

Height: 1'08" (0.5 m)
Weight: 14.6 lbs. (6.6kg)
GRASS

PIDOVE

Height: 1'00" (0.3 m)
Weight: 4.6 lbs. (2.1 kg)
NORMAL FLYING

PIGNITE
Height: 3'03" (1.0 m)
Weight: 122.4 lbs. (55.5 kg)
FIRE FIGHTING

PURRLOIN

Height: 1'04" (0.4m)
Weight: 22.3 lbs. (10.1 kg)
DARK

RESHIRAM

Height: 10'6" (3.2 m)
Weight: 727.5 lbs. (330.0 kg)
DRAGON FIRE

REUNICLUS

Height: 3'03" (1.0 m)
Weight: 44.3 lbs. (20.1 kg)
PSYCHIC

ROGGENROLA

Height: 1'04" (0.4 m)
Weight: 39.7 lbs. (18.0 kg)
ROCK

RUFFLET

Height: 1'08" (0.5 m)
Weight: 23.1 lbs. (10.5 kg)
NORMAL FLYING

SAMUROTT

Height: 4'11" (1.5 m)
Weight: 208.6 lbs. (94.6 kg)
WATER

SANDILE

Height: 2'04" (0.7 m)
Weight: 33.5 lbs. (15.2 kg)
GROUND DARK

SAWK

Height: 4'07" (1.4 m)
Weight: 112.4 lbs. (51.0 kg)
FIGHTING

SAWSBUCK

Height: 6'03" (1.9 m)
Weight: 203.9 lbs. (92.5 kg)
NORMAL GRASS

SCOLIPEDE

Height: 8'02" (2.5 m)
Weight: 442.0 lbs. (200.5 kg)
BUG POISON

SCRAFTY

Height: 3'07" (1.1 m)
Weight: 66.1 lbs. (30.0 kg)

| DARK | FIGHTING |

SCRAGGY

Height: 2'00" (0.6 m)
Weight: 26.0 lbs. (11.8 kg)

| DARK | FIGHTING |

SEISMITOAD

Height: 4'11" (1.5 m)
Weight: 136.7 lbs. (62.0 kg)

| WATER | GROUND |

SERPERIOR

Height: 10'10" (3.3 m)
Weight: 138.9 lbs. (63.0 kg)

| GRASS |

SERVINE

Height: 2'07" (0.8 m)
Weight: 35.3 lbs. (16.0 kg)

| GRASS |

SEWADDLE

Height: 1'00" (0.3 m)
Weight: 5.5 lbs. (2.5 kg)

| BUG | GRASS |

SHELMET

Height: 1'04" (0.4 m)
Weight: 17.0 lbs. (7.7 kg)

| BUG |

SIGILYPH

Height: 4'07" (1.4 m)
Weight: 30.9 lbs. (14.0 kg)

| PSYCHIC | FLYING |

SIMIPOUR

Height: 3'03" (1.0 m)
Weight: 63.9 lbs. (29.0 kg)

| WATER |

SIMISAGE

Height: 3'07" (1.1 m)
Weight: 67.2 lbs. (30.5 kg)

| GRASS |

SIMISEAR

Height: 3'03" (1.0 m)
Weight: 61.7 lbs. (28.0 kg)

| FIRE |

SNIVY

Height: 2'00" (0.6 m)
Weight: 17.9 lbs. (8.1 kg)

| GRASS |

SOLOSIS

Height: 1'00" (0.3 m)
Weight: 2.2 lbs. (1.0 kg)

| PSYCHIC |

STOUTLAND

Height: 3'11" (1.2 m)
Weight: 134.5 lbs. (61.0 kg)

| NORMAL |

STUNFISK

Height: 6'03" (0.7 m)
Weight: 573.2 lbs. (11.0 kg)

| GROUND | ELECTRIC |

SWADLOON

Height: 1'08" (0.5 m)
Weight: 16.1 lbs. (7.3 kg)

| BUG | GRASS |

SWANNA

Height: 4'03" (1.3 m)
Weight: 53.4lbs. (24.2 kg)

| WATER | FLYING |

SWOOBAT

Height: 2'11" (0.9 m)
Weight: 23.1 lbs. (10.5 kg)

| PSYCHIC | FLYING |

TEPIG

Height: 1'08" (0.5 m)
Weight: 21.8 lbs. (9.9 kg)

| FIRE |

TERRAKION

Height: 6'03" (1.9 m)
Weight: 573.2 lbs. (260.0 kg)

| ROCK | FIGHTING |

THROH

Height: 4'03" (1.3 m)
Weight: 122.4 lbs. (55.5 kg)

| FIGHTING |

THUNDURUS

Height: 4'11" (1.5 m)
Weight: 134.5 lbs. (61.0 kg)

| ELECTRIC | FLYING |

TIMBURR

Height: 2'00" (0.6 m)
Weight: 27.6 lbs. (12.5 kg)

| FIGHTING |

TIRTOUGA

Height: 2'04" (0.7 m)
Weight: 36.4 lbs. (16.5 kg)

| WATER | ROCK |

TORNADUS

Height: 4'11" (1.5 m)
Weight: 138.9 lbs. (63.0 kg)

| FLYING |

TRANQUILL

Height: 2'00" (0.6 m)
Weight: 33.1 lbs. (15.0kg)

NORMAL   FLYING

TRUBBISH

Height: 2'00" (0.6 m)
Weight: 68.3 lbs. (31.0 kg)

POISON

TYMPOLE

Height: 1'08" (0.5 m)
Weight: 9.9 lbs. (4.5 kg)

WATER

TYNAMO

Height: 1'04" (0.2 m)
Weight: 11.7 lbs. (0.3 kg)

ELECTRIC

UNFEZANT (FEMALE)

Height: 3'11" (1.2 m)
Weight: 63.9 lbs. (29.0 kg)

NORMAL   FLYING

UNFEZANT (MALE)

Height: 3'11" (1.2 m)
Weight: 63.9 lbs. (29.0 kg)

NORMAL   FLYING

VANILLISH

Height: 3'07" (1.1 m)
Weight: 90.4 lbs. (41.0 kg)

ICE

VANILLITE

Height: 1'04" (0.4 m)
Weight: 12.6 lbs. (5.7 kg)

ICE

VANILLUXE

Height: 4'03" (1.3 m)
Weight: 126.8 lbs. (57.5 kg)

ICE

VENIPEDE

Height: 1'04" (0.4 m)
Weight: 11.7 lbs. (5.3 kg)

BUG   POISON

VICTINI

Height: 1'04" (0.4 m)
Weight: 8.8 lbs. (4.0 kg)

PSYCHIC   FIRE

VIRIZION
Height: 6'07" (2.0 m)
Weight: 440.9 lbs. (200.0 kg)

GRASS   FIGHTING

VOLCARONA

Height: 50'3" (1.6 m)
Weight: 101.4 lbs. (46.0 kg)

BUG   FIRE

VULLABY
Height: 1'08" (0.5 m)
Weight: 19.8 lbs. (9.0 kg)

DARK   FLYING

WATCHOG

Height: 3'07" (1.1 m)
Weight: 59.5 lbs. (27.0 kg)

NORMAL

WHIMSICOTT

Height: 2'04" (0.7 m)
Weight: 14.6 lbs. (6.6 kg)

GRASS   FAIRY

WHIRLIPEDE

Height: 3'11" (1.2 m)
Weight: 129.0 lbs. (58.5 kg)

BUG   POISON

WOOBAT

Height: 1'04" (0.4 m)
Weight: 4.6 lbs. (2.1 kg)

PSYCHIC   FLYING

YAMASK

Height: 1'08" (0.5 m)
Weight: 3.3 lbs. (1.5 kg)

GHOST

ZEBSTRIKA

Height: 5'03" (1.6 m)
Weight: 175.3 lbs. (79.5 kg)

ELECTRIC

ZEKROM

Height: 9'06" (2.9 m)
Weight: 760.6 lbs. (345.0 kg)

DRAGON   ELECTRIC

ZOROARK

Height: 5'03" (1.6 m)
Weight: 178.8 lbs. (81.1 kg)

DARK

ZORUA

Height: 2'04" (0.7 m)
Weight: 27.6 lbs. (12.5 kg)

DARK

ZWEILOUS

Height: 4'07" (1.4 m)
Weight: 110.2 lbs. (50.0 kg)

DARK   DRAGON

KALOS

The Kalos region is renowned for its unusual shape. From afar, it looks like a star! It has five points, but three main sub regions: Central, Coastal, and Mountain.

Connecting Kalos' cities and towns is a network of rivers. So, it's no wonder that the region also has a lot of wildlife in its lush forests.

In the heart of Kalos is lovely Lumiose City. It is a town known for its art and architecture like it's most famous landmark, the incredibly tall Prism Tower. The sparkling structure draws tourists from near and far to admire its beauty.

THE THREE SUBREGIONS OF KALOS

CENTRAL KALOS

Let your nose lead you to Central Kalos. It's full of flowering plants and Princess Allie's mansion, The Parfum Palace! The local greenery gets plenty of water thanks to all the rivers that cross through Central Kalos. All the waterways also make it fun to sail around this section by boat. Just south of Lumiose City, this part of the region holds the hubs Santalune City and Vaniville Town.

COASTAL KALOS

A sea lover's paradise, the ocean runs along the west side of Kalos. The locals really love their ocean views and they can't seem to get too close to the coast. For example, if you're looking to challenge the Shalour City Gym Leader Korrina, you'll have to wait until low tide to even be able to enter the gym at the Tower of Mastery. But the sea isn't Coastal Kalos' only treasure. The shores of Coastal Kalos are covered in cliffs and rocks, and some of them hold extremely valuable stones. Many Trainers, looking for Mega Stones and other rare rocks, journey to the famous Geosenge Town.

MOUNTAIN KALOS

Coastal Kalos might boast about its rocks and boulders, but if you like to hike to high peaks, Mountain Kalos can't be beat! Although, perhaps it's even more fun to go down the mountainsides on skis. The eastern part of this region gets plenty of snow thanks to its chilly climate. It might be easy to stay cool temperature-wise, but if you make it over to this section's marshes, you might find yourself in hot water. Supposedly, the bogs in the northeast are haunted. Consider yourself warned.

MEGA EVOLUTION

A new, even more powerful form of Evolution has been discovered—Mega Evolution. Pokémon researchers have found that this incredible state makes Pokémon stronger, faster, tougher, and, in some cases, even unstoppable. However, unlike other forms of Evolution, it is temporary. A Pokémon can solely power up with Mega Evolution during battle. Afterward, it returns to its previous form.

Only a select group of Pokémon species possess the power to Mega Evolve like Blastoise, Audino, and Venusaur. The first Mega Evolved Pokémon Ash spotted was a Mega Blaziken—and not a moment too soon! Ash was falling off of Prism Tower when Mega Blaziken zoomed over and caught him in mid-air.

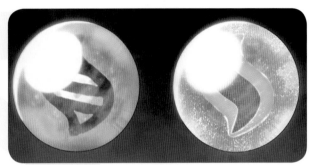

Although there is no denying the power of Mega Evolution, its details are still largely undiscovered. Researchers like Professor Sycamore of Kalos are working tirelessly to uncover more of Mega Form's mysteries. Here is what we have been able to learn so far.

Beyond even the ability to Mega Evolve, a Pokémon and Trainer must also hold three things:

First, a Trainer must have a Key Stone. Although the shiny orb is worn in an item of clothing like a glove, a belt, a hat, or even an earring, fashion is not its primary function. The Key Stone connects the Trainer and Pokémon partner in special communication, no words necessary. The Trainer can see things through their Pokémon pal's eyes and sense their emotions. Amazingly enough, the Key Stone also acts like a tracking device. Should their Pokémon pal ever get lost, the Trainer can see exactly where it went.

A Key Stone really comes in handy when villains like Team Rocket are around! Jessie, James, and Meowth tried to kidnap Gardevoir mid-battle, but their plans were in vain. Diantha, the Champion of The Kalos Region, can help Gardevoir Mega Evolve, so she was able to track them down in no time. Jessie, James, and Meowth are no match for a Mega Evolved Pokémon!

Secondly, a Trainer must journey to find another special stone, but this one is very specific. Each Mega Evolving Pokémon needs its own Mega Stone present to Mega Evolve. For example, Pidgeot needs Pidgeotite, Scizor needs Scizorite, and Lopunny needs Lopinnite. This link in the Mega Evolutionary chain is so potent, that a Mega Stone can only be held by someone worthy of its capabilities. No amount of money will buy one. Villains can't steal one. And for that matter, average Trainers can't even touch one—which brings us to the third and final thing a Trainer must possesses.

Lastly, and most importantly, Trainer and Pokémon must share a deep bond. They must cheer each other on, both on and off the battlefield. They have to be the kind of best friends that can read each other's minds and have each other's backs. They have to put the work into teamwork. Then, and only then, can they begin their journey to find a hidden Mega Stone.

The ancestors of Shalour City Gym Leader Korrina are famous figures in Mega Evolution. Even with her important bloodline, she did not assume she could just waltz right up with Lucario and grab the Lucarionite. She vowed to win 100 battles in a row before she would even travel to Geosenge Town to search for the Mega Stone. Ash was so impressed with her record that when she hit her mark, he helped her locate Lucarionite in a cave.

THE CHART OF MEGA EVOLUTION

POKÉMON	MEGA STONE	MEGA-EVOLVED FORM

ABOMASNOW
Grass Ice

ABOMASITE

MEGA ABOMASNOW
Grass Ice

ABSOL
Dark

ABSOLITE

MEGA ABSOL
Dark

AERODACTYL
Rock Flying

AERODACTYLITE

MEGA AERODACTYL
Rock Flying

AGGRON
Steel Rock

AGGRONITE

MEGA AGGRON
Steel

ALAKAZAM
Psychic

ALAKAZITE

MEGA ALAKAZAM
Psychic

POKÉMON	MEGA STONE	MEGA-EVOLVED FORM

ALTARIA
Dragon Flying

ALTARIAMITE

MEGA ALTARIA
Dragon Fairy

AMPHAROS
Electric

AMPHAROSITE

MEGA AMPHAROS
Electric Dragon

AUDINO
Normal

AUDINITE

MEGA AUDINO
Normal Fairy

BANETTE
Ghost

BANNETTITE

MEGA BANETTE
Ghost

BEEDRILL
Bug Poison

BEEDRILLITE

MEGA BEEDRILL
Bug Poison

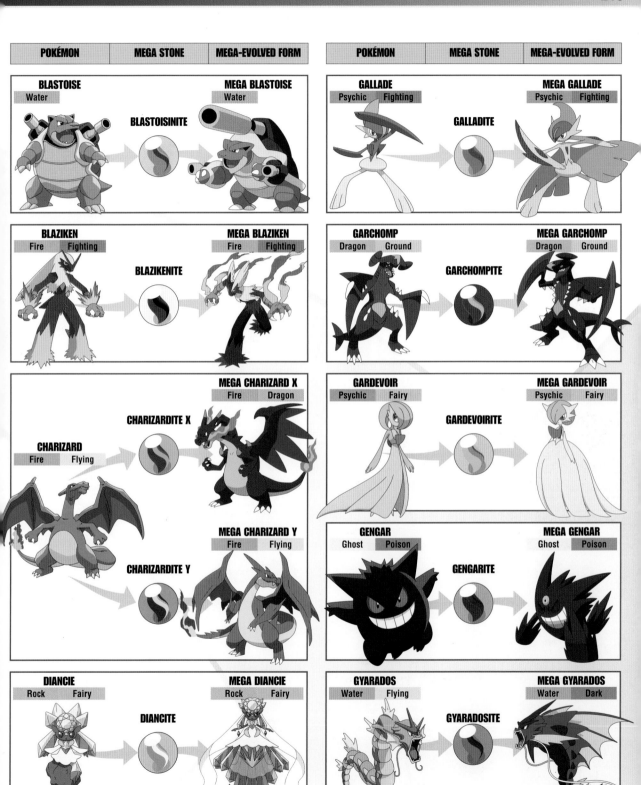

POKÉMON	MEGA STONE	MEGA-EVOLVED FORM

BLASTOISE
Water

BLASTOISINITE

MEGA BLASTOISE
Water

BLAZIKEN
Fire · Fighting

BLAZIKENITE

MEGA BLAZIKEN
Fire · Fighting

CHARIZARD
Fire · Flying

CHARIZARDITE X

MEGA CHARIZARD X
Fire · Dragon

CHARIZARDITE Y

MEGA CHARIZARD Y
Fire · Flying

DIANCIE
Rock · Fairy

DIANCITE

MEGA DIANCIE
Rock · Fairy

POKÉMON	MEGA STONE	MEGA-EVOLVED FORM

GALLADE
Psychic · Fighting

GALLADITE

MEGA GALLADE
Psychic · Fighting

GARCHOMP
Dragon · Ground

GARCHOMPITE

MEGA GARCHOMP
Dragon · Ground

GARDEVOIR
Psychic · Fairy

GARDEVOIRITE

MEGA GARDEVOIR
Psychic · Fairy

GENGAR
Ghost · Poison

GENGARITE

MEGA GENGAR
Ghost · Poison

GYARADOS
Water · Flying

GYARADOSITE

MEGA GYARADOS
Water · Dark

POKÉMON	MEGA STONE	MEGA-EVOLVED FORM	POKÉMON	MEGA STONE	MEGA-EVOLVED FORM

HERACROSS
| Bug | Fighting |

HERACRONITE

MEGA HERACROSS
| Bug | Fighting |

MAWILE
| Steel | Fairy |

MAWILITE

MEGA MAWILE
| Steel | Fairy |

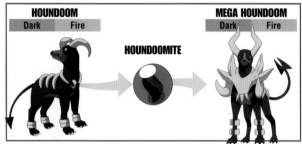

HOUNDOOM
| Dark | Fire |

HOUNDOOMITE

MEGA HOUNDOOM
| Dark | Fire |

MEDICHAM
| Fighting | Psychic |

MEDICHAMITE

MEGA MEDICHAM
| Fighting | Psychic |

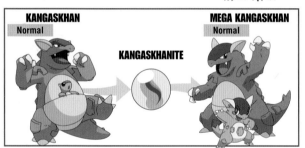

KANGASKHAN
| Normal |

KANGASKHANITE

MEGA KANGASKHAN
| Normal |

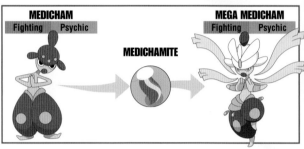

LUCARIO
| Fighting | Steel |

LUCARIONITE

MEGA LUCARIO
| Fighting | Steel |

MEWTWO
| Psychic |

MEWTWONITE X

MEGA MEWTWO X
| Psychic | Fighting |

MEWTWONITE Y

MEGA MEWTWO Y
| Psychic |

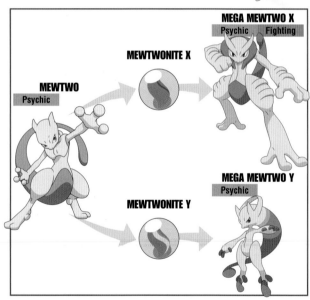

MANECTRIC
| Electric |

MANECTITE

MEGA MANECTRIC
| Electric |

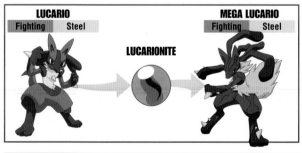

PIDGEOT
| Normal | Flying |

PIDGEOTITE

MEGA PIDGEOT
| Normal | Flying |

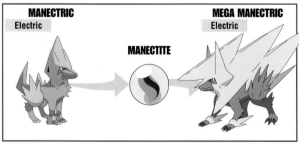

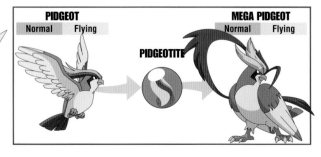

POKÉMON	MEGA STONE	MEGA-EVOLVED FORM
PINSIR Bug	PINSIRITE	**MEGA PINSIR** Bug Flying
SABLEYE Dark Ghost	SABLENITE	**MEGA SABLEYE** Dark Ghost
SCIZOR Bug Steel	SCIZORITE	**MEGA SCIZOR** Bug Steel
SHARPEDO Water Dark	SHARPEDONITE	**MEGA SHARPEDO** Water Dark
SLOWBRO Water Psychic	SLOBRONITE	**MEGA SLOWBRO** Water Psychic

POKÉMON	MEGA STONE	MEGA-EVOLVED FORM
STEELIX Steel Ground	STEELIXITE	**MEGA STEELIX** Steel Ground
TYRANITAR Dark Rock	TYRANITARITE	**MEGA TYRANITAR** Dark Rock
VENUSAUR Grass Poison	VENUSAURITE	**MEGA VENUSAUR** Grass Poison
GROUDON Ground	RED ORB	**PRIMAL GROUDON** Ground
KYOGRE Water	BLUE ORB	**PRIMAL KYOGRE** Water

PROFESSOR SYCAMORE

You can find cool Professor Sycamore at his Lumiose City Lab. It's a special place that is so much more than just where new Trainers in Kalos can pick up their First Partner Pokémon—Chespin, Fennekin, and Froakie. His lab has an incredible Pokémon habitat that friends like Psyduck, Marill, Azurill, Caterpie, Weedle, Zigzagoon, Combee, Helioptile, and Linoone all call home too. Professor Sycamore loves to spend time caring for and observing the Pokémon there. His specialty is Mega Evolution. In fact, he's the leading expert in the field.

Although he loves research and studying data in his lab, he isn't exactly a homebody. The Professor loves to travel around the region to attend Pokémon Showcases, conduct his research in the field, and even run a fun Pokémon Summer Camp that Ash and his friends attended.

A FRIEND INDEED

They say a friend in need is a friend indeed. The way Ash first met Professor Sycamore, he knew he was someone he could really count on! But friendship is a two-way street. Ash proved himself to be a fantastic friend too!

Even though Froakie was injured, it hopped in to help Ash battle back Team Rocket. So, afterward, Ash and his pals rushed Froakie to Professor Sycamore's lab nearby. The Professor was happy to help nurse his old friend Froakie back to good health. Not only did this experience create a friendship between the Professor and Ash, but it bonded the troubled Froakie, who had been returned by a few Trainers, to Ash too. Before Ash could leave Professor Sycamore's lab, Froakie asked Ash with a Poké Ball to be its Trainer. Now, with Froakie's stamp of approval, Professor Sycamore saw that Ash was someone he could really count on too! And that's what friendship is all about.

A MEGA FRIENDSHIP

Professor Sycamore's best friend is devoted Garchomp, always by his side. They have a deep bond that goes all the way back to when the Professor first met his pal, Gible. Together with Professor Sycamore's guidance, it evolved from Gible to Gabite to Garchomp and even Mega Garchomp.

SOPHIE & COSETTE

Professor Sycamore has two right hands—assistants that Is! He really relies on his trusty helpers, Sophie and Cosette. They're happy to watch over the lab and Pokémon when Professor Sycamore is out and about, but they often travel together as a team. They are counselors at his Summer Camp and avid Pokémon Showcase fans.

CLEMONT

Clemont is the Lumiose City Gym Leader and an Electric-type expert, but perhaps he is best known for his inventions. In fact, before Ash meets Clemont, he meets Clembot, the robot that guards Clemont's Gym at Prism Tower. And it is one tough gatekeeper! If a challenger hasn't won at least four badges in Kalos, it will greet them in two ways: with an electric zap and then an ejection that sends the visitor flying. So, Ash actually met Clemont when he broke Ash's ejection fall with another one of his inventions, a giant inflatable pillow. Whatever the situation, Clemont has a gadget!

Ash is always happy to have a kind, smart guy like Clemont with him on his journey through Kalos. Clemont decided to join Ash after watching him heroically save Professor Sycamore's friend Garchomp when Team Rocket used a special control collar to send it on a rampage. Impressed with his bravery and his skills, Clemont knew he could learn a lot from Ash.

And there's always more to learn! So, after an epic battle against Team Rocket at the Power Plant, Clemont and Ash briefly parted ways so he could go back to his Gym in Lumiose City and focus on training. Clemont knew Ash would return to Lumiose City and challenge him for the Voltage Badge and he wanted to be ready! But nothing could prepare Clemont for Ash's incredible battle skills. After awarding Ash the Voltage Badge, he again joined him on his journey through Kalos.

SHOWERED WITH POWER

Clemont attended a very prestigious school that focused on Electric-type Pokémon. He graduated with top honors and is one of their most famous graduates because he made quite an impact on the community. Back in his school days, while taking a walk, Clemont stumbled upon an exhausted Shinx. He rushed it to the local Pokémon Center where Nurse Joy explained that she often sees tired, local Electric-type Pokémon because there is something in the environment that drains them. Clever Clemont was determined to help! He decided to use his brainpower to invent and build a special recharging chamber that rains electricity. He called it the Clemontic Shower! Still to this day, his invention stands in the city for all Electric-type Pokémon to use. In fact, when they were in town, Ash's pal Pikachu and Bonnie's buddy Dedenne got the chance to enjoy a recharge in Clemont's invention.

MAN VS MACHINE

Just like his school days, Clemont loves solving problems with inventions. He has lots of tricks up his sleeve, or in this case, bots in his backpack. Clemontic Gear, as he likes to call his collection of gadgetry, boasts a wide range of helpful and sometimes explosive mechanisms. Here are some of his latest and greatest:

Clemont often uses his mechanical Aipom Arm to lift and grab things. Sometimes that thing is his little sister Bonnie when she's doing something embarrassing, like trying to ask Viola to be his girlfriend!

220

Clemont's first Pokéstar Shooter was better at causing a scene than filming one. Instead of being a portable camera, it was a mobile one that chased the star, Serena. But Clemont made some tweaks and the second edition is picture perfect. Clemont's Pokéstar Shooter Mark Two is a great camera for the budding PokéVision director. All you need to add is, "Action!"

Clemont might have had his Flower Arranger One go out with a bang, literally. But Clemont's Snow-Flower Finder has the power to sniff out even the faintest floral scent in the air, even if it's buried under a mound of snow. Luckily, it helped find a special bloom just in time to heal a sick Snover.

When Clemont makes a machine for dancing, it seems to work better as fireworks. His Not a Very Good Dancer Automated Good Dancing Device and Only Lonely Dancing Robo-Partner give the very definition of an explosive performance. But Clemont proves he can get into the groove with the Mini Music Box he creates for the special Pledging Tree Festival in Coumarine City. It features a fine tune and his Pokémon pals Chespin, Luxio and Bunnelby enjoying the melody inside.

Clemont's contraptions might not always work perfectly, but that only encourages him to use his brain to fix it or create a new gizmo. Bigger than even than the explosions Clemont's faulty thingamajigs can cause is his heart. And even more than for his machines, he has a big soft spot for his little sister Bonnie who is always by his side.

DOWN TO A SCIENCE

Clemont might be known for his mechanical skills. But he also excels at chemistry, in the kitchen. Chef Clemont knows how to combine all the right ingredients into a delicious meal!

CLEMONT'S POKÉMON

LUXRAY

Clemont was thrilled to be reunited with his Pokémon pal from the past, Shinx, who had since evolved into Luxio. But Luxio was still hurt because it thought Clemont had abandoned it. Clemont took the opportunity to set the record straight. The truth is, he couldn't find Shinx when he was heading out of town. But now that they're back together, Clemont never wants to be apart again! During a battle with tricky Team Rocket at the Kalos Power Plant, it evolves into Luxray and saves the day!

BUNNELBY

Clemont first met Bunnelby when it stole his snack—which is typically not a great way to make a friend. When Clemont followed it back to its home in an abandoned subway car, he realized the Pokémon needed his help. He and Bonnie nursed it back to health after a skirmish. Clemont also got the subway car moving with his Clemontic Gear Running Generator and together with Bunnelby, they drove its home to a safe place at the end of the line. Happy to have helped, Clemont and Bonnie said goodbye to their new friend. Before Clemont got very far, Bunnelby came running after them and asked Clemont to join him on his journey.

CHESPIN

Chespin has an appetite for battle and pastries! In fact, Clemont first met Chespin when it had a mouthful of macaroons. It can sniff out treats anywhere, which can be helpful or completely selfish. But it battles as boldly as it snacks! Just after meeting Clemont, the two teamed up to save Professor Sycamore and destroy Team Rock's robot, Mega-Mega Meowth. Bonded by the battle, Chespin asked to join Clemont on his journey and they've been together ever since!

DEDENNE

A big berry introduced Bonnie to Dedenne as the tiny Pokémon fell out of a tree and landed on her head. It was love at first bop! But since Bonnie's not old enough to be a Trainer, she begged her big brother to catch Dedenne. Seeing that Clemont and his sister are true friends, Dedenne decides to join him on his journey.

Clemont has left a few of his Pokémon pals back at the Lumiose City Gym to help stand guard with his robo-twin, Clembot: Magnemite, Magnetite, and Heliolisk.

BONNIE

Clemont's little sister is too young to be a Pokémon Trainer, but that doesn't stop her from getting in on all the action! Whether it's refereeing a match or giving Pikachu a bath, she just loves spending time with Pokémon! In fact, she begged her brother to catch Dedenne so she could take care of it. Dedenne likes to stay by their side and rides out of its Poké Ball in Bonnie's backpack. She is so looking forward to training Dedenne when she is old enough! She also cares for a Zygarde Core she nicknamed Squishy.

Sometimes, Bonnie gets so excited when she sees a new Pokémon that it scares them. When she first met Ash's pal Pikachu, she gave it such a tight hug, it zapped her. But soon Pikachu was able to see taht she's just a little girl with a big heart that can't help herself around cute Pokémon.

But the only thing she loves more than Pokémon is her big brother Clemont. Like a blonde shadow, she follows him around wherever he goes—including on his journey with Ash. She is so proud of him and his inventions! Well, the ones that work. And one works perfectly on her. You see, Bonnie wants to help find Clemont a nice girl to marry and often asks point blank if they're interested in her brother. Clemont gets so embarrassed, he lifts her into the air with his robot Aipom Arm.

MEYER

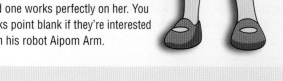

Clemont and Bonnie's dad Meyer runs an electronics shop. However, he is better known as a superhero called The Blaziken Mask. Wherever there is trouble, you can spot his orange cape! The Blaziken Mask always brings his Mega Evolving Blaziken sidekick with him. But most importantly, he is always there in the knick of time to help. When Ash fell off the Prism Tower, The Blaziken Mask amazingly caught him in mid-air. When Team Rocket stole Professor Sycamore's best friend Garchomp and his Key Stone, The Blaziken Mask swooped in and shared his Key Stone so Professor Sycamore could block their trickery. When Team Rocket framed Clembot for causing trouble at local stores, The Blaziken Mask helped clear its name.

But underneath his fierce superhero image, Meyer is a big mush. He cries with joy when Clemont and Bonnie do things that make him proud—like follow Ash on his journey. And the truth is, he's way too loving a dad to let his kids completely go. So, he often hops on his motorcycle with Ampharos and drives over to check up on them. They're always happy to see their dad, especially when The Blaziken Mask is there to save the day!

SERENA

The daughter of a famous Rhyhorn Racer named Grace, Serena was trying very hard to live up to her heritage. Her mom had her practice and practice, but it didn't seem to be helping. Serena was sick of getting thrown off of Rhyhorn every time she tried to ride. She felt lost. But there was one person she knew she had to find—her old friend Ash.

OLD FRIENDS, NEW ADVENTURE

While watching TV with her mom, she spotted Ash bravely trying to save Garchomp from atop the Prism Tower. She couldn't believe it was Ash, the boy she met back at Professor Oak's Summer Camp. In fact, back at camp, Ash had used a handkerchief to bandage her injured knee and she still had that hanky! So, Serena left home to set out to find him. When she did, he was in the middle of trying to earn the Bug Badge from the Gym Leader of Santalune City, Viola. Although Ash didn't remember her, Serena's memory served them both well. She reminded Ash what he had told her, "Don't give up until it's over." Serena's words of encouragement gave Ash the advantage he needed in his rematch, true grit. From then on, Serena has been there for Ash as he travels through Kalos. And for whatever details from camp Ash has forgotten, he and Serena have made many more new memories together on their latest journey.

SHE'S GOT STYLE

Serena loves to create incredible outfits with her Pokémon! Since beginning her journey with Ash, she's found two fun ways to express her love of playing dress up—Pokémon Showcases and PokéVision videos. Serena and her Pokémon feel great when they know they are looking good. Her fashion sense adds to all of their confidence!

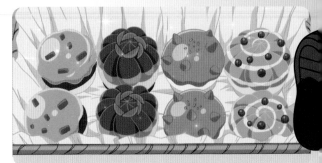

SMART COOKIE

In addition to Serena's many talents, she's also one of the best bakers. She is known for her yummy Poké Puffs and macaroons. So when they come hot out of the oven, be sure to snag one before Ash's chum Chespin scarfs all the sweets down.

SECOND NATURE

When Serena finally figured out what she wanted to pursue, competing in Pokémon Showcases, she thought the hard part was over. But boy, was she mistaken! Becoming a Pokémon Performer takes a lot of training, hard work, and even tripping up—like Fennekin did on its pink ribbon at their first Pokémon Showcase in Coumarine City. Serena might have stumbled at the start, but she didn't give up. She summoned her strength and used her heart and her smarts to become a wonderful Pokémon Performer with the help of her talented Pokémon pals. Together, they have since won three Princess Keys—Dendemille, Anistar, and Fleurrh!

SERENA'S POKÉMON

BRAIXEN

Professor Sycamore's lab was her first stop when she was trying to locate Ash. She got more than just clues there, she got her furry friend Fennekin too! Fennekin worked hard to become a fabulous Pokémon Performer at Pokémon Showcases. During a battle with the Fighting Type Pokémon, Serena's encouragement made all the difference and it evolved into Braixen.

PANCHAM

If Pancham had a middle name, it would be trouble. It loves to cause a scene! Serena first spotted Pancham when it interrupted a Pokémon Showcase performance. Then, it stole Ash's hat, Clemont's glasses, and Serena's heart. Serena could see how much Pancham liked attention and liked to perform. And Pancham could see that Serena understood that it put the act in acting out. So, Pancham agreed to battle her and Fennekin to join her on her journey.

SYLVEON

Serena met Sylveon when it was a wild Eevee who loved to dance. Unfortunately, Team Rocket saw her magical moves and decided to capture the tiny dancer. But Serena stepped up to save The Evolution Pokémon. Impressed with her caring heart, Eevee then decided to join Serena on her journey. Serena's support really transformed Eevee. During a tag battle with Ash at a dance party thrown by Pokémon Showcase Emcee Monsieur Pierre, Eevee evolved into Sylveon.

POKÉMON PERFORMERS

Pokémon Performers are Trainers with a very special skill set—they have a talent for showbiz! They step out onto the stage with their Pokémon and do coordinated dances. Their teamwork and footwork are so impressive!

Pokémon Performers also take pride in their outfits. They have a flare for fashion! Pokémon Performers create special ensembles and accessories to add some razzle dazzle to their rhythm. Dressing up helps Pokémon Performers get excited and get into the groove. When they feel like they look their best, they perform best!

There is no greater entertainment for Pokémon and performing art fans like a Pokémon Showcase, where Pokémon Performers meet and compete. The prize for winning a Pokémon Showcase is a Princess Key. Or, if it's a Master Class, it can be a title like Kalos Queen and matching tiaras. It all depends on the Showcase and the showmanship.

There are Rookie Class Pokémon Showcases in Lagoon Town, Coumarine City, Dendemille Town, Anistar City, Couriway Town, and Fleurrh City. There is a Master Class Pokémon Showcase in Gloire City. In order for a Trainer to earn a spot at the Master Class, they must first obtain three Princess Keys. When a Pokémon Performer earns their first Princess Key, they are also awarded a special Key Ring to display their prizes.

Serena, Shauna, Miette, Nini, and Aria are all Pokémon Performers who entertain audiences with their Pokémon partners.

WATCH & LEARN: POKÉVISION

Pokémon Performers don't need to wait for a Pokémon Showcase to have an audience. They post PokéVision videos about themselves, their Pokémon, and their style, for all to see! This helps build their fan following. The top ten videos can always be viewed at Pokémon Centers around Kalos.

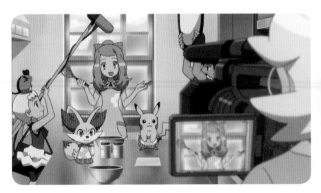

Serena was inspired by Aria to make her first PokéVision video in Lumiose City. She borrowed a camera to capture her and Fennekin's friendship. Together they played and baked Poké Puffs. Ash and Clemont also worked on their own videos. But Team Rocket disguised as "Pokémon Rocketeers" tried to shut down production and steal the stars, Fennekin, Pikachu, and Dedenne. Amazingly enough, Serena stepped up and her Fire-type pal was able to use Flamethrower for the first time to fend off the terrible trio. Fennekin wasn't going to let anyone get in Serena's way of PokéVision Super Stardom!

Serena and Fennekin's video got a lot of plays! By the time they got to Professor Sycamore's Summer Camp, Serena had a fan base. Fellow camper, Shauna, had seen their video and was star struck by Serena! She is such a talented PokéVision star, she also directed her Team Froakie pals—Ash, Clemont, and Bonnie, in an award-winning video later that week.

YUMMY POKÉ PUFFS

Pokémon Performers are also known for being the best bakers. They love making their partners tasty Poké Puffs. Something sweet is always a treat, especially after a day of training!

Serena is certain her Poké Puffs are the best! But she had to put it to the test. She has some stiff competition from her fellow Pokémon Performers. When a sneaky Slurpuff ate an entire batch of her Poké Puffs, its Trainer Miette said she wasn't impressed. Miette wanted to settle the score and prove she was the better baker. So, she challenged Serena to enter a baking contest with her to prove who was really number one. Serena was happy to bake a new batch of her Poké Puffs to try to win the prize and show up Miette. But here was only one problem—neither one of them won the contest. So, instead they decided they could both be the best at sportsmanship. They parted with a handshake ready to meet again at a Pokémon Showcase.

ARIA: THE KALOS QUEEN

Aria is one talented Pokémon Performer, both on camera and in person. She's famous for winning the Gloire Master Class and the title, Kalos Queen. She also has quite a following for her PokéVision videos. In fact, one of Aria's videos inspired Serena to make her own! Serena really looks up to Aria and it's no wonder if you've ever seen her perform with her super-skilled buddy Braxien.

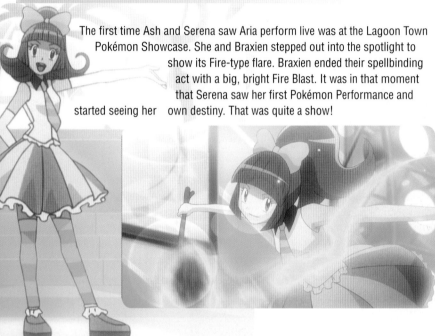

The first time Ash and Serena saw Aria perform live was at the Lagoon Town Pokémon Showcase. She and Braxien stepped out into the spotlight to show its Fire-type flare. Braxien ended their spellbinding act with a big, bright Fire Blast. It was in that moment that Serena saw her first Pokémon Performance and started seeing her own destiny. That was quite a show!

JUST DANCE

Aria was the belle of the ball at Pokémon Showcase Emcee Monsieur Pierre's party. She started the dance floor and even took a twirl with Ash. The only ones who love dancing more than Aria are her Pokémon!

SAY CHEESE

In addition to her title, Aria arguably also has an award-winning smile. Her cheerful personality comes through in her performances. She is so full of joy, she makes so many people and Pokémon happy! Her PokéVision videos are popular because her positive energy is infectious. A true entertainer, she always shows off her pearly whites as well as her talented Pokémon.

POKÉMON GROOMERS

On the way to Cyllage Town, Ash and his pals come across a town with a famous Pokémon Groomer named Sherman and his assistant Jessica. A Pokémon Groomer artfully brushes, styles, and cares for Pokémon in their salon. Sherman's favorite Pokémon to pamper is Furfrou.

KORRINA

Bold Korrina knows how to make an entrance! Always racing around on her roller skates, she has a need for speed because she's very driven. It's clear Korrina has got spunk. It's no wonder she's a Fighting-type expert. She wanted to get all the way to 100 straight wins before she looks in Geosenge Town for the special Mega Evolution stone for Lucario, Lucarionite.

When Korrina spotted Ash on a forest path, she immediately challenged him to a battle. Korrina and her pal Lucario had just won 98 battles in a row. Ash and Pikachu helped her reach her goal with her final two battles. Korrina and Lucario won number 99 against Ash and Pikachu with an incredible Bone Rush. Then, Ash and Korrina teamed up for a tag battle against Jessie and James to earn her 100th straight win. Ash and his pals felt so invested in Korrina's desire to help her best friend Lucario Mega Evolve, they then joined her on her journey to Geosenge Town.

But that wasn't the last time Ash and Korrina crossed paths. When Ash arrived in Shalour City, he headed to the Tower Of Mastery to challenge its Gym Leader, Korrina. He got the chance to a battle his friend again, but this time it was for the coveted Rumble Badge.

Korrina's Fighting-Type Pokémon Pals:

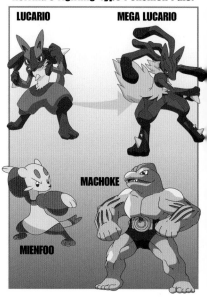

GURKINN

Korrina's grandfather Gurkinn is a Mega Evolution guru. But he's also quite the prankster. He sneakily sent Blaziken out to challenge Korrina and Lucario before she was able to take the Lucarionite from the inside the cave. But it isn't just valuables he's protecting. Gurkinn claimed the Scroll of Secrets was a document with important information on Mega Evolution. Korrina, Ash, and his friends did everything to keep it out of Team Rocket's hands. But when they blasted the villains off, they learned the real secret: the scroll was just a letter with Gurkinn's common-sense life advice. However, one thing is definitely true—he and his granddaughter Korrina are descendants of the man who discovered Mega Evolution. Their ancestor and his Lucario were the first to ever reach this Form. So, in honor of their heritage, Korrina and Gurkinn train with Lucario too. In fact, it was Gurkinn who gave Korrina her Key Stone to help inspire her to work hard to help her best buddy Lucario Mega Evolve.

DIANTHA

The multi-talented Champion of the Kalos Region and Elite Four Member, Diantha, is also a very famous actress. But she isn't faking anything when she steps on the battlefield with her partner, a Gardevoir that can Mega Evolve. When Ash first met superstar Diantha, he couldn't resist the chance to challenge her. Unfortunately, Team Rocket broke up their battle by trying to steal Gardevoir. So, Ash vowed to work hard to beat the Kalos League and get his chance at a rematch with Diantha.

RIVALS

ALAIN

Fascinated by Mega Evolution, Alain is on a journey to learn everything he can about the mysterious transformation. In fact, he meets Ash while studying his Greninja during a battle with Sawyer and Sceptile. Alain himself trains hard with an amazing Mega Evolving Charizard. So Team Flare better beware, they don't stand a chance against Alain.

TIERNO

Trainer Tierno and his best friend Squirtle dance to the beat of their own drummer. And boy have they got rhythm! They step in time together when they face a foe. These two dancers are light on their feet and never miss a beat in battle. So, it's no wonder Tierno was able to help his pal evolve to Wartole and then Blastoise. After seeing their moves at Professor Sycamore's Pokémon Summer Camp, Ash too tried to learn their fancy footwork. But Tierno keeps a unique tempo that can't be repeated. Tierno also trains with his Pokémon pals Ludicolo, Hitmontop, Politoed, and Raichu.

SANPEI

From Ninja Village, Sanpei is a very special and wise ninja. Ash is so impressed by Sanpei and his friend Frogadier's Quick   Attack, he asks
                                                for a lesson.
                                                 Patient and
                                                  caring,
Sanpei is always will to share his knowledge with Ash. And Ash is always willing to help Sanpei, whether it's battling back Team Rocket or ninjas. The two have each other's backs. It's no wonder with that kind of loyalty and work ethic that Sanpei was able to help Frogadier evolve into Greninja.

SAWYER

Sawyer is always scribbling down his thoughts and observations in a notebook. But he didn't notice that the Laverre City Gym was closed. Funnily enough, neither did Ash and that's exactly how the two met. Although, at first, Sawyer had not earned a gym badge from Clemont or Valerie, he kept working and making notes. Eventually, he became a Trainer to watch! With his help, Begon evolved into Shelgon. Also, while locked in battle with Ash, Treecko evolved into Grovyle. Then, when Ash ran into Sawyer again, it had evolved into Sceptile. It seems studious Sawyer's note taking is a strategy that's paying off big time! Ash and his friends are certainly happy to have him around to battle back Team Flare.

SHAUNA

A Pokémon Performer and regular at Pokémon Showcases, Shauna dreams of becoming the Kalos Queen! Shauna first met Serena at Professor Sycamore's Summer Camp, but she already knew her from her hit PokéVision video. A first, she put Serena on a pedestal because she was a celebrity, but over the course of the camp they truly bonded as friends. Energetic and passionate, Shauna is always there to support Serena on her journey. And she's quite an inspiration! In fact, it was Shauna who first took Serena and her friends to see a Pokémon Showcase. At Coumarine City, Shauna won her first Princess Key with an amazing performance by Flabébé and Bulbasaur. But when Serena won Dendemille Showcase, Shauna was a good sport and a good friend. She was so happy for Serena! It's no wonder an amazing pal like Shauna was able to help her buddy Bulbasaur evolve into incredible Ivysaur.

MIETTE

Miette thinks she's the best. She brags about her Poké Puffs so much that both she and Serena enter a baking contest to settle the score. Although neither one of their Poké Puffs wins, there is another prize Miette has set her sights on—Ash! Miette can tell that Serena has a secret crush on her travel buddy and she would just love to blab about it. Serena is so embarrassed, she doesn't even say a word when Miette asks Ash to be her date to Monsieur Pierre's dance party to make her jealous. It seems like Miette's main goal is to get whatever Serena wants.

NINI

Outside of Coumarine City, Serena met Nini—a Pokémon Performer about to enter her first Pokémon Showcase, just like her! The two hit it off and decided to practice together. From that day on, they often see each other at Showcases from Anistar City to Couriway Town. Nini keeps busy training with her pals Smoochum and Farfetch'd.

TREVOR

Trainer Trevor works hard with his best buddy Charmander. But even more than battle, Trevor loves taking photos. He's always got his camera out to catch a snap of a new or unusual Pokémon. Amazingly enough, he's even gotten a shot of the illusive Legendary Pokémon Moltres!

SKY BATTLES

In majestic Kalos Canyon, a very unique kind of battle is waged. It's not on the rocks. It's not on the ground. It's up in the air! These impressive Sky Battles use special wing suits that send Trainers soaring with their Flying-type Pokémon.

When Ash first sees a Sky Battle in action, he can't wait to try it himself. After a quick lesson with Serena and Clemont, he accepts a battle challenge from Sky Trainer Moria. She's so good, she's also an instructor. But Ash isn't intimidated, he's excited for the chance to take his battle style to the skies!

At first, Ash calls upon his friend Fletchling. But Moria's battle buddy, a top-notch Talonflame, isn't interested in battling a Pokémon so little and inexperienced. Fletchling is bummed because it wants to show Talonflame what it's got. So, Moria places a bet—if Hawlucha wins a battle against Talonflame, Fletchling will get the chance to battle them. So with that wager, Ash's pal Hawlucha steps up, or rather flies in.

Although Hawlucha is a Flying-type, it can only glide, which puts it at a disadvantage in a Sky Battle. Talonflame's air game is strong that with an amazing combination of Steel Wing and Karate Chop, Hawlucha is left unable to battle. Just when it looks like Fletchling's dream of a Sky Battle definitely isn't going to happen, Team Rocket shows up.

The terrible trio of Jesse, James, and Meowth, have come to poach Pokémon. Brave Fletchling stands up to their foes and sends them blasting off. Everyone can see that although Fletchling is small, its heart is big. Moria and Talonflame are so impressed by its bravery, they offer to battle the fierce Flying-type.

The battle between Talonflame and Fletchling was so heated that Fletchling awesomely evolved into Fletchinder, the Ember Pokémon. With its newfound strength and determination, Fletchinder won the round with a fiery Flame Charge. Even more importantly, Fletchinder proved once and for all that you can't judge the power of a Pokémon by its size.

PROFESSOR SYCAMORE'S SUMMER CAMP

One week every summer, Professor Sycamore hosts a special Summer Camp for Pokémon Trainers in the Kalos Region. Located in Coastal Kalos, the camp is right in the mountains overlooking the ocean. Ash, Clemont, and Serena couldn't wait to attend! Together, their bunk was known as Team Froakie. As a cabin, they competed in a bunch of fun challenges. The winning team from the week will earn their place in the Summer Camp Hall of Fame, an honor previously held by Kalos superstars like Diantha.

The first day of camp, Ash, Serena, and Clemont met a group of friends just like them: Tierno, Shauna, and Trevor, better known around camp as Team Squirtle. When Professor Sycamore asked all the campers to pair up for a practice battle, it was an easy match. Ash and Froakie had a Water-type battle with Tierno and Squirtle. Ash was amazed by Tierno and Squirtle's stylish synchronized battle dance. Serena and Fennekin battled Shauna and Bulbasaur. During their match, Shauna taught Serena about Pokémon Performers. It was the first time Serena had heard of such a path for Pokémon fans. Clemont and Chespin try to battle Trevor and Charmander, but Chespin was too scared to spark the Fire-type. Hopefully all of the practice and training they'll get at summer camp will give Chespin more confidence.

The next morning, Serena woke up ready to hit the ground running, literally! She led her Team Froakie friends on a jog along the beach. Afterward, there was a camp-wide fishing contest that put Tierno, Shauna, and Trevor, A.K.A. Team Squirtle, in the lead. Then, at the dining hall, Professor Sycamore announced their next challenge: each team will make a PokéVision video. Serena is quick on her feet to come up with a good storyline. She plans to direct her Team Froakie friends in a video focused on their Pokémon pals and delicious Poké Puffs. With the help of Fire-type Fennekin, Serena baked the perfect Poké Puffs. Now, all they needed was a place to film.

While Team Froakie was location scouting through the woods, Serena accidentally slipped off the side of a cliff. Ash bravely tried to save her, but they both went tumbling down the side of a mountain. While Clemont and Bonnie run to get help, Ash and Serena discuss their dreams. Ash has traveled through six regions and trained tirelessly in the hopes of become a Pokémon Master. Serena, on the other hand, has been wandering aimlessly looking to find her path, her true passion. Her future has been weighing heavily on her mind.

Luckily, Professor Sycamore was there to save them in no time. Strangely enough, he brought the kitchen staff, which was actually Team Rocket in disguise, to help rescue them. Now back safely a top the mountain, Serena stepped up as director and helped her Team Froakie film their PokéVision video masterpiece! Later that day, Professor Sycamore screened all the teams' videos. To Ash, Clemont, Bonnie, and even Serena's surprise, Team Froakie won first place!

However, before they knew it, it was time for another activity at Professor Sycamore's jam-packed Summer Camp of fun. The teams were set to compete in Pokémon Orienteering—part scavenger hunt, part obstacle course, part race, and 100% awesome challenge. It's no wonder it's Professor Sycamore's favorite camp activity! Campers follow a map that leads them to different parts of the forest where they're have to complete different tasks as quickly as possible. For each successfully finished task, the team is rewarded with a special stamp. The campers found themselves scaling mountains, running, and even jumping so high they were nearly flying! But perhaps the biggest challenge in Pokémon Orienteering was the unexpected one. When a thick fog covered the forest, Bonnie and Pikachu got separated from their team. Worse yet, unable to see, the pair got in quite a bit of trouble. First, Bonnie accidentally angered a swarm of Beedrill. Then, they ran into some Amoongus who used Spore to put the two to sleep. But instead of resting her head on a pillow, Bonnie took a nap on Drifloon who carried her up, up, and away.

Meanwhile, Ash, Clemont, and Serena were frantically trying to find Bonnie and Pikachu. When Team Squirtle catches wind of the situation, they selflessly decide to forget about the competition and help the rescue effort. Together as one team, they finally find Bonnie and Pikachu. Although the teams had forgone winning the Pokémon Orienteering award, they were rewarded with something even rarer. Through the fog, a rainbow-colored Pokémon appears. It made all the flowers around it bloom! Could it have been the Legendary Pokémon, Xerneas?! Before anyone can take out their Pokédex to figure out who it was, the stunning Pokémon scampers away. What a sight!

On the last day of Summer Camp there was a big Team Battle competition—a completely new way of battling for Ash and his friends. Trevor explained that Team Battles are when groups of 3, 5, or 7 Trainers team up and create their battle strategy and combination moves together. For example, Team Froakie made a round winning combination when they had Pikachu blast Electro Ball, Fennekin use Head Power, and Bunnelby add Dig. With powerful moves like that, it's no wonder Team Froakie made it all the way to the finals. Their dreams of being in the Hall Of Fame were within reach, they just had to win one more round! But Team Rocket decided it was the perfect time to steal Pokémon.

Jessie, James, and Meowth pretended to be Nurse Joy's helpers. They offered to take Team Froakie's friends into the Pokémon Center for a check up. However, when their fake out is discovered, Team Rocket was sent blasting off by Fennekin, Bunnelby, Pikachu, and Froakie.

But there was no rest for the weary! Back at camp, it was time for the final round of the competition. Team Froakie would be battling their friends Team Squirtle for the title. Tierno began the match by setting the pace with his battle dance. Fennekin could not stop the energetic Squirtle with Hidden Power and it was left unable to battle. Bulbasaur unleashed Solar Beam, but with the help of Chespin's Vine Whip, Pikachu dodged it. Then, Pikachu used Thunderbolt to knock Charmander out of the round. Both teams were then down one Pokémon, but the battle had really just begun!

With a combination of Chespin's Vine Whip and Pikachu's Electro Ball, Bulbasaur was no longer able to battle. Then, Pikachu mustered up a massive Thunderbolt zap that stopped Squirtle and won the round. Team Froakie won the Team Battle Competition and sealed their place in the Summer Camp Hall of Fame!

Like good sports, Tierno, Shauna, and Trevor congratulated their friends and rivals Ash, Serena, and Clemont. Ash complimented Tierno on his battle rhythm. Later that night, after the closing ceremony fireworks, Tierno stayed up late to teach Ash his trademark moves. And then, with heartfelt goodbyes, the teams realized they're really going to miss their camp friends. Ash, Tierno, Serena, Shauna, Clemont, and Trevor hope they will cross paths again in Kalos, but their special camp memories will always be with them.

SKY RELAY

A Pokémon Sky Relay is a unique marathon in mid-air. It is a race between teams that have three flying Pokémon each. On the road to Anistar City, Ash was lucky enough to stumble upon one just in time to enter! The heavy favorite for the competition was the winner from the previous Sky Relay, Orson. He was there to defend his title, but Ash was still excited to give his all with Fletchinder, Hawlucha, and Noibat. At first, Ash had beginner's luck and his friend Fletchinder took the lead! However, the competition was about to get more heated. Team Rocket sneakily entered the Sky Relay to mess with the twerp and his team. They had their mechanical Pelipper attack Ash's pal Hawlucha. But fortunately, their robot broke down revealing their plot and they were disqualified in the middle of the race. Now it was up to Ash's friend Noibat to try to close the gap. It had to make up for all the time Team Ash lost battling back Team Rocket. Noibat focused and flew brilliantly, but it was not experienced with flying against the wind gusts in the valley. Starly from Team Orson maintained the lead and earned its team a second win. Incredibly enough, because of its hard work and dedication, Noibat flew in for second place. Ash was so proud of his team and so happy they got the chance to compete in the high-flying fun that is a Sky Relay.

COOL PLACES IN KALOS

PLEDGING TREE IN COUMARINE CITY

In the center of Coumarine City grows a terrifically tall tree that was planted by a Trainer and Pokémon pal in honor of their lasting friendship. It started as a sapling and grew to be the biggest tree in town. It's a tree that is so fantastic it has its own festival! Locals gather to decorate and celebrate its majesty by exchanging presents with their friends.

Ash, Serena, Clemont, and Bonnie happened to be in town on the holiday and decided to make each other great gifts. But before they even got to open them, greedy Team Rocket swooped in to try to steal them all! The crew snapped into action to battle them back. And boy was it worth it when they opened their presents! Ash had gathered their Pokémon pals a bunch of berries. Serena made Fennekin and Pancham cool accessories. Clemont made a music box with Fennekin, Bunnelby, Chespin, and Luxio. Bonnie drew a picture of all of her friends. But perhaps the most special gift came all the way from Serena's mom, Grace. She sent her daughter the gift of encouragement, a new dress for her next Pokémon Showcase!

BATTLE CHATEAU

Just outside of Cyllage City is a mansion made for matches, the Battle Chateau. Trainers from all around Kalos flock to the Battle Chateau to challenge each other to, well, as the name promises, battle! With every win, the victor earns a title from Baron to Grand Duke. Ash, Serena, Clemont, and Bonnie we're lucky enough to watch an amazing round between two gym leaders, Duke Grant with Onix and Duchess Viola with Surskit. Amazingly enough, when Grant won the round with Onix's powerful combination of Rock Tomb and Flash Cannon, he was promoted to the highest possible title—Grand Duke. With the help of his pal Pikachu, Ash too was able to win a battle and earn a title while he was visiting. You can now call him Baron Ash!

CUSSLER

Off the Murraille Coast lies a sunken ship full of treasure. The luxury liner met a terrible fate when it accidentally crashed into an iceberg and sank into the sea. In its heyday, the Cussler was a famous and fancy cruise ship that used to carry many guests. Now that it lies at the bottom of the ocean, it still draws a crowd, just of Water-type Pokémon. Ash and his pals are lucky enough to get a tour of the vessel from a couple of underwater archeologists.

GRACE TOWER

Are you curious about Alien Pokémon from space? Then Grace Mountain in the place for you! Supposedly, there have been many UFO sightings from atop this rocky mountain. It's a natural wonder that is known for the supernatural. But if you're a skeptic of life in outer space, there's still something special for you down on the ground. At the base of Grace Tower live many wild Malamar, Flabébé, Inkay, Ledyba, and Bidoof.

REFLECTION CAVE

This famous cave is covered in mirror-like crystal. But before you go fixing your hair in your reflection, beware! As Ash learned, your mirror reflection can come alive too! Or should we say two? Once sucked into the Mirror World, there is a double of you, your friends, and everything you know…Except, they're all their total opposites. Happy turns to sad. Good turns to bad. If you don't escape by sunset, you'll be trapped in the Mirror World

forever. Luckily, thanks to the help of their pals, Ash and Pikachu were able to bust through a portal before it was too late.

TEAM FLARE: MEMBERS

Team Rocket isn't the only group causing trouble. In Kalos, really make it double. Team Flare is a secretive organization, but one thing is clear, their carefully laid plans are totally evil. Team Flare's fiery red uniforms and unusual eyeglasses are easy to spot, but no one can see their sneak attacks coming. Be sure to keep a watch out for...

ALAIN

Ash knows Alain as the Trainer with an incredible Mega Evolving Charizard. When Alain encountered Ash and his amazing Greninja, he challenged them to a battle. In fact, they have battled not once, but twice for practice. Little does Ash know, he really has a much bigger fight with this Team Flare henchman. Their paths keep running into each other and soon or later, the truth about his involvement with Team Flare will come out.

LYSANDRE

The leader of Team Flare, Lysandre runs his ruthless Operation Z from a secret hideout in Kalos. He monitors every move of two Zygarde Cores he calls Z1 and Z2. Lysandre will stop at nothing until he is successful in his evil mission, but he doesn't fight any of the real battles himself. Like a coward, he prefers to stay in his lab and rely on Xerosic and his Team Flare grunts to carry out his commands.

MABLE, CELOSIA, BRYONY, AND ALIANA

The top Team Flare henchwomen are happy to do the dirty work on the ground. Wherever there's a chance to catch Z1 or Z2, they're there backed by a group of Pokémon and Team Flare goons to use their might to capture the Zygarde Cores at any cost.

XEROSIC

Team Flare's mad scientist concocts robots, tracking devices, ray guns, and more all to aid Team Flare's fight. Called "Doctor" by his peers, he is Lysandre's right hand man. Xerosic is a key to Operation Z. It's just too bad he uses his talents creating technology for evil instead of good.

TEAM FLARE MISSION

Ash, Clemont, Serena, and Bonnie first encountered Team Flare when they tried to poach Bonnie's new Pokémon pal Squishy. Since it seems like Squishy hopped in Bonnie's backpack to escape the clutches of its fiery foes, they are very protective of their little green friend.

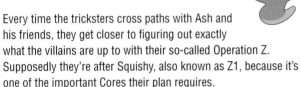

Every time the tricksters cross paths with Ash and his friends, they get closer to figuring out exactly what the villains are up to with their so-called Operation Z. Supposedly they're after Squishy, also known as Z1, because it's one of the important Cores their plan requires.

In fact, Team Flare has set up surveillance in Terminus Cave. So, when Ash and his friends visit the landmark with Squishy, they unwittingly alert Team Flare. While Squishy is bathing in a glowing lake deep inside the cave, the red goons attack. Squishy senses their presence and becomes invisible to protect itself. However, Team Flare's ray guns are clever enough to find and catch it in an orange trap.

Before Ash, Clemont, Serena, and Bonnie can fight back, another villainous crew arrived on the scene—Team Rocket. While the two evil Teams battled each other with insults, Squishy seized the opportunity to commune with a fellow Forme, all of the Zygarde Cells around. Suddenly, before everyone's eyes, it turned into Zygarde 10% Forme. Squishy grew fangs, four legs, and could run up to 60 mph. Not only that, but it's new found power rustled the cave rocks into an earthquake. Squishy was then able to make its escape from Terminus Cave and the clutches of Team Flare.

But Squishy isn't all the fiery crew is out to capture, they're also after Squishy's Zygarde Core companion, Z2. The two Pokémon are able to communicate telepathically. But no amount of warning can protect them from Team Flare.

When Z2 was surrounded by Team Flare and Team Rocket, it amazingly enough was able to absorb enough Zygarde Cells around it to become Zygarde 50% Forme. The giant is able to move massive mountainous rocks. But even that couldn't stop the attack. When Team Flare calls on their friends Alain and Mega-Evolving Charizard, they're able to distract the Legendary Pokémon Zygarde with an epic battle. Although Zygarde's strength and will are winning the round, it's so focused on fighting its foe, it doesn't see the Team Flare goons firing their ray guns at it. Trapped in the orange zap, Team Flare was then able to capture Z2. Although, they are separated, Squishy can tell that Z2 is in serious trouble.

Who knows what villainy Team Flare has in store?! It's up to Ash, Clemont, Serena, and Bonnie to protect Squishy, and therein the world, from Team Flare!

KALOS GYM BATTLES

From the moment Ash arrived in Kalos, he has had one goal—to earn eight gym badges to score a place to compete in the Kalos League! So far, he has received seven on his journey and he's working hard to complete his goal. For the opportunity of a gym battle, Ash proves he'll climb any mountain, even literally when he goes to battle for the Cliff Badge in Cyllage City. In Kalos, Ash shows teamwork and determination can take you to new heights!

SANTALUNE CITY

GYM LEADER: VIOLA

Ash is amazed to discover that the photographer who took a picture of him and his pal Pikachu is actually Alexa's sister, Gym Leader Viola!

VIOLA VS. **ASH**

Surskit's Ice Beam is so chilling it freezes over the battlefield and then even stops Pikachu's Electro Ball blast and Thunderbolt Zap in mid-air. Surskit then seals its win with Signal Beam.

VIOLA VS. **ASH**

Flying-type Fletchling has two big advantages—it's type and it soars above that tricky icy battlefield. Surskit tries to trap it in Sticky Web, but Fletchling dodges it with Double Team. It finishes the round by firing a fierce Razor Wing.

VIOLA VS. **ASH**

Both Vivillon and Fletchling will fight in flight, but not for long. Vivillon uses Psychic to send Fletchling crashing down to the ground. Then it adds a Gust wind to send it straight into a Sticky Web. While Fletchling is trapped, Vivillon sends a bright Solar Beam to win the battle for Viola.

SANTALUNE CITY GYM

REMATCH

GYM LEADER: VIOLA

Thanks to some training advice from Alexa, Ash confidently returns to the Santalune Gym to challenge Viola to a rematch.

VIOLA VS. **ASH**

Before Surskit can freeze the battlefield with Ice Beam, Pikachu jumps on it to redirect the spray from the floor to the ceiling. It was a clever idea but unfortunately, it only makes the ice rain down onto the battlefield. But Pikachu is prepared for anything. It whips its tail to cut through the ice layer and stake it's place in the solid ground. Then, it shoots a big Thunderbolt burst to win the round.

VIOLA VS. **ASH**

Fletchling trained hard to be ready for it's round. It recovers from Vivillon's confusing Psychic and rides Gust like it's a kite. But when Vivillon hits it with Sleep Powder it is too tired to dodge a Solar Beam blast and is left unable to battle.

VIOLA VS. **ASH**

Ash wisely has Pikachu uses Electro Ball on itself to break Vivillon's powerful Sleeping Powder Spell. Then, Pikachu fires another Electro Ball at Vivillon. The blast knocks Vivillon's wing into some ice, which leaves it struggling to stay in the air. Pikachu adds a Thunderbolt zap to win Ash the match and the Bug Badge.

CYLLAGE CITY

GYM LEADER: GRANT

The Cyllage Gym is atop a mountain. There are two ways to get there: by elevator or by climbing. Ash starts out on the right foot and impresses Grant by climbing his way up. To the gym leader, taking the harder route signifies an enlightened challenger who understands the importance of inner peace.

 GRANT VS. **ASH**

Froakie dodges Onix's Rock Tomb rain by jumping up the giant Pokémon's back in a move Ash created called the "Rock Tomb Climb." Froakie winds up all the way on Onix's face. From close range, it fires Water Pulse to win the round.

GRANT VS. **ASH**

Froakie uses its Rock Tomb Climb to hop on the swirling stones from Tyrunt's Rock Tomb. But when Tyrunt jumps high into the air and drops Draco Meteor, Froakie is left unable to battle.

 GRANT VS. **ASH**

Fletchling starts with Razor Wing, but Tyrunt's Crunch treats it like lunch and eats the Attack. Worse yet, Tyrunt's ability to jump counters any aerial advantage Fletchling might have. In fact, Tyrunt wallops Fletchling with Dragon Tail in mid-air to win the round.

 GRANT VS.   **ASH**

Tyrunt tries Draco Meteor, but as the fireballs fall, Pikachu climbs them with Ash's patented "Draco Meteor Climb." Tyrunt then tries shooting Rock Tomb, but Pikachu hits the stones with Iron Tail and knocks a rock straight into Tyrunt's mouth. With a Thunderbolt flash Pikachu wins the match and Ash is awarded the Cliff Badge.

SHALOUR CITY

GYM LEADER: KORRINA

Ash has studied his buddy Tierno's battle dance step for step in the hopes that the technique will help him earn the Rumble Badge.

KORRINA	ASH	KORRINA	ASH	KORRINA	ASH	KORRINA	ASH

 VS.   VS.   VS.

Ash begins the battle by clapping a beat for Hawlucha to move its feet. Although it seems to be in the battle groove, Mienfoo's precise movements are prevailing. So, mid-battle Ash drops the dancing act. Back to their own unique style, Hawlucha is able to dodge Mienfoo's High Jump Kick and it wins the round with a fierce combination of Karate Chop and Flying Press.

Machoke is so strong it stops Fletchinder's Steel Wing by holding it with its bare hands. It then pauses to fire up Focus Blast, but Fletchinder uses the time wisely to quickly shoot Flame Charge. The searing Attack wins Fletchinder the match.

Amazingly enough, Fletchinder is able to block Mega Lucario's Aura Sphere with a strong Steel Wing. But under the cover of smoke, Mega Lucario sneaks up behind Fletchinder and wallops it with a powered up Punch to win the round.

Mega Lucario blocks Hawlucha's Flying Press with Bone Rush. Then, Mega Lucario's launches an Aura Sphere with such force, Hawlucha slams into the gym wall and is unable to continue battling.

KORRINA	ASH

 VS.

Pikachu had never been able to beat Lucario, and now it's in its Mega Evolved form! But Ash is a man with a plan. He has Pikachu use Iron Tail to whack away Mega Lucario's Aura Sphere ball and block Bone Rush. Then, it lands a direct and amazing Thunderbolt blast to win the round and Ash the Rumble Badge.

COUMARINE CITY

GYM LEADER: RAMOS

When Ash arrives at the Coumarine Gym ready to battle, old man Ramos has other plans for the day— a tea party and some gardening. This leisurely approach challenges Ash, but he soon shows Ramos he is ready to battle!

RAMOS	ASH	RAMOS	ASH	RAMOS	ASH	RAMOS	ASH

 VS.   VS.   VS.

Fletchinder has a strong type advantage, but Jumpluff powers up its Speed with Sunny Day. So Fletchinder realizes it's in a race. With its body covered in Flame Charge, it scores a quick hit that leaves Jumpluff unable to battle.

Fletchinder's will won't let Weepinbell's Poison Powder zap all of its energy. It continues to try Flame Charge. But Weepinbell waits until it gets close to grab its wing and tosses it to the ground with Slam. Fletchinder is finally left unable battle.

Hawlucha has the type advantage, but when it gets hit with Poison Powder its energy is drained. Hawlucha musters up the strength to hit Weepinbell with a High Jump Kick. However, while it's close to its foe, Weepinbell seizes the opportunity to use its signature Slam to win the round.

Weepinbell is up to its usual Poison Powder, but Frogadier has a trick up his sleeve, or should we say scarf? Frogadier uses his Gummy Frubbles like a mask to block the sleepy stuff. Then, it finishes the round by cutting to the chase with Aerial Ace.

RAMOS	ASH

 VS.

Frogadier tries to cut Gogoat's Razor Leaf tornado with Aerial Ace, but it rises and falls right on Frogadier. Then, Gogoat drains Frogadier's energy with Leech Seed and the match looks like it's coming to an end. But Pikachu jumps in and rallies Ash, who in turn re-energizes Frogadier with his confident cheer. When Gogoat surrounds Frogadier in a swirling Razor Leaf, Ash instructs his pal to stop struggling to try and smash single leaves. He asks Frogadier to close his eyes and follow its instinct. Amazingly enough, it is then able to strategically slash through the storm with Aerial Ace. When it adds a Water Pulse burst, it wins the match and Ash the Plant Badge.

LUMIOSE CITY

GYM LEADER: CLEMONT

Clemont temporarily stopped traveling with Ash just to prepare for this special gym battle with his buddy. They're both in top form, but only one will come out on top. Serena, Bonnie, Fennekin, Dedenne, Pancham, Chespin, and even Meyer are there to watch the incredible match between these friends unfold.

CLEMONT VS. **ASH**

Bunnelby uses a clever combination, it powered up Wild Charge then it hid underground with Dig. This allowed Bunnelby to avoid a counter attack while it's dealing with recoil damage. It's clear Clemont has been training hard! But Pikachu is prepared. When Bunnelby uses Dig again, Pikachu gets it out by breaking the ground with Iron Tail. Then, it slaps Bunnelby with another Iron Tail, which leaves it unable to battle.

CLEMONT VS. **ASH**

Heliolisk is so fast that Goodra can't follow it with its eyes. So, it's easily able to blast a bright Flash and use a Dragon Tail smack. When Heliolisk uses Paralysis to stop Goodra in its tracks, Ash has his pal return to its Poké Ball.

CLEMONT VS. **ASH**

By choosing Hawlucha, Ash has turned the round into a speed battle where he has the type advantage. But Heliolisk's blinding Flash and Parabolic Charge blasts nearly knock out Hawlucha. When Heliolisk goes to shine Flash again, Ash thinks fast and has Hawlucha use High Jump Kick in close range to win the round.

CLEMONT VS. **ASH**

Hawlucha makes the first move and scores a direct hit swooping in with Flying Press, but its lead doesn't last long. Luxray energizes the battlefield and its attacks with Electric Terrain. With one run in of Luxray's extra powerful Wild Charge, Hawlucha is left unable to battle.

CLEMONT VS. **ASH**

The Electric Terrain, still buzzing on the battlefield, will power up Pikachu too, but it doesn't seem to help against Clemont's sound strategy. Luxray uses electric Fang to bite right through Pikachu's Thunderbolt. Luxray then runs a back-to-back jolt of Wild Charge to win the round.

CLEMONT VS. **ASH**

Goodra steps back on the battlefield still weak with Paralysis. But Ash has a plan, and an amazing one at that! He has Goodra use Rain Dance to activate its Hydration Ability to restore its strength and the battlefield. Luxray anxiously ambushes Goodra with Thunder Fang, Wild Charge, and Swift, but Ash has Goodra buy itself time with defensive moves while it powers up Bide. When Goodra finally unleashes a big, red Bide blast, Luxray is left unable to battle. Ash has won the Voltage Badge from his buddy Clemont!

LAVERRE CITY

GYM LEADER: VALERIE

At her Fashion Show, Ash watched designer and Gym Leader Valerie easily defeat Sawyer and Bagon with her super Fairy-type friend Spritzee. So, Ash knows eccentric Valerie is going to be full of surprises. He plans to stay alert and trust his gut to earn his sixth gym badge.

Fun fact: Valerie speaks Pokémon! She isn't totally fluent, but she can understand most of what her Pokémon pals say and talk back.

VALERIE VS. **ASH**

Sylveon catches Fletchinder in its ribbons, swings it around the room, and then surrounds it with a Fairy Wind tornado. It looks like an impossible hold to slip out of, but Ash cleverly has Fletchinder fire up Flame Charge to break free. Then, it swoops in with Steel Wing to win the round.

VALERIE VS. **ASH**

Spritzee starts out by covering the battlefield with a glowing Trick Room, a Psychic move that puts the battlers in a box and slows down speedy attacks. Inside, Spritzee slams Fletchling with direct hits of Dazzling Gleam and Gyro Ball. But Ash bides his time having Fletchinder use Flame Charge in the hopes it will power up its Attacks when Trick Room disappears. But he waited too long, Spritzee finishes the battle with a big ball of powerful pink Moon Blast.

VALERIE VS. **ASH**

Spritzee again boxes in the battlefield with Trick Room. Ash has Hawlucha slow down and carefully track Spritzee's every move. So, when it spins straight at Hawlucha with Gyro Ball, Hawlucha simply catches it in its arms. Then Hawlucha uses the momentum to twirl its X-Scissor and cut through Spritzee's bright Dazzling Gleam to destroy the Trick Room. Back on the regular battlefield, Hawlucha is now free to quickly use a surprisingly speedy High Jump Kick to win the round! Ash has earned the Fairy Badge.

DOUBLE BATTLE ANISTAR CITY

GYM LEADER: OLYMPIA

Gym Leader Olympia can see into the future, but does it hold a Psychic Badge for Ash? He'll need all of his brainpower to win a double battle against this wise gym leader. Professor Sycamore and his friends are there to cheer him on.

OLYMPIA VS. **ASH**

Meowstic combine Helping Hand and Future Site to make the first move on the celestial battlefield, but Ash plans to end the battle before Future Site falls down from the sky. That's wishful thinking as Meowstic easily dodge Talonflame and Frogadier's Attacks. As it turns out, the male Meowstic's Ability is Prankster, which lets it use the support move Light Screen before a foe Attacks to protect its female friend. But Meowstic aren't relying on defense, they fire a purple Psyshock beam. Talonflame and Frogadier can't dodge them because Psyshock follows their every flinch. Now it's clear the female Meowstic has the ability of Keen Eye, which makes it nearly impossible for an opponent to dodge an Attack. These Meowstic are truly double trouble! Before Ash can even try to make another move, Future Site rains down on the battlefield. Things have gone from bad to worse, but Ash never gives up! He starts thinking and fast. It becomes clear to Ash that his strategy needs to focus on teamwork. This is a double battle after all!

So, when Meowstic launch another Future Site, Ash has Pikachu tap its tail to keep track of the time it takes to resurface. When Meowstic launch another Psyshock stream, Frogadier hops on Talonflame's back to dodge it together. Then, at the last second, Talonflame takes a nosedive so Meowstic are attacked by their own Psyshock Attack. With that clever move, Ash has turned the tide of the battle!

Next, Ash has Frogadier and Talonflame each grab Meowstic. Timekeeper Pikachu warns that their Future Site is about to rain down rocks. So, the team tosses Meowstic into the stone hail. They take a direct hit, but Meowstic aren't going to give up that easily. They send another round of Psyshock. Frogadier quickly hops on Talonflame's back again to use Cut to stop the slithering purple beam. Then, Talonflame swoops in with a fiery Flame Charge to deliver a blow so strong it knocks out the male Meowstic.

Next, Frogadier works up a powerful ball of Water Pulse. It uses it like a shield to stop the female Meowstic's Psyshock. Frogadier stays strong and gives it everything it's got and eventually a Water Pulse blast overpowers Meowstic's Psyshock beam. Meowstic is left unable to battle. Ash is so proud of his Pokémon pals! Even Olympia admits she is impressed. With determination and cooperation, Ash has earned the Psychic Badge.

KALOS LEGENDARY POKÉMON

XERNEAS • (ZURR-nee-us)
THE LIFE POKÉMON

Height	9'10" (3.0 m)	Category	Life
Weight	474.0 lbs (215.0 kg)	Type	Fairy

Forget naps, Xerneas is an excellent sleeper. Legend has it that Xerneas morphed into the shape of a tree to take a thousand-year-long nap. But it possesses a great amount of vitality. It is said that the Life Pokémon can give the gift of immortality. And that's not all the light it possesses! Every color in the rainbow is reflected in this Fairy-type's dazzling horns.

YVELTAL • (ee-VELL-tall)
THE DESTRUCTION POKÉMON

Height	19'0" (5.8 m)	Category	Destruction
Weight	447.5 lbs (203.0 kg)	Type	Dark-Flying

Giant Yveltal has an impressive wingspan, but beware if it is showing its size off. When it opens its arms and tail out to reveal a bright red radiance, it has the ability to absorb the life force of living things. This glow is a no go.

ZYGARDE • (ZY-gard)
THE ORDER POKÉMON

Height	16'05" (5.0 m)	Category	Order
Weight	672.4 lbs (305.0 kg)	Type	Dragon-Ground

This solitary Pokémon prefers to stay out of sight, hidden in a cave deep in the mountains. There's no need to go searching for this Legendary Pokémon. It will reveal itself when it feels it is needed to restore order to the world. Thought of as the protector of the environment, Zygarde has the unbelievable ability to completely heal a threatened ecosystem.

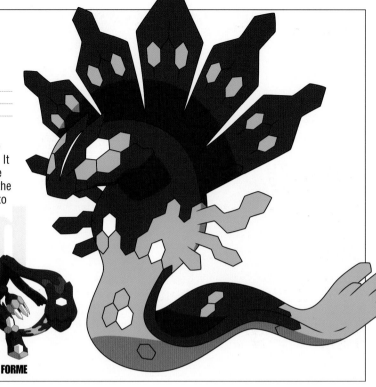

CORE FORME   **10 PERCENT FORME**   **COMPLETE FORME**

KALOS MYTHICAL POKÉMON

DIANCIE • (die-AHN-see)
THE JEWEL POKÉMON

Height	2'04" (0.7 m)	Category	Jewel
Weight	19.4 lbs (8.8 kg)	Type	Rock-Fairy

Sparkling Diancie is said to be the most gorgeous Pokémon of all. Pretty in pink, it is covered in gleaming jewels. But its power of bling doesn't end with its body jewelry. The Jewel Pokémon has a magic touch! Diancie can take ordinary carbon out of thin air and turn it into diamonds. While that is impressive, perhaps it's best known for it's beautiful transformation. There are ancient tales that tell of the most stunning sight to behold—Carbink's shift to Diancie.

HOOPA • (HOO-puh)
THE MISCHIEF POKÉMON

Height	1'08" (0.5 m)	**Category**	Mischief
Weight	19.8 lbs (9.0 kg)	**Type**	Psychic-Ghost

Hide your gold! Hide your silver! Heck, hide anything shiny you've got from Hoopa. This Mythical Pokémon has a reputation for taking what it wants and what it wants is riches. The Mischief Pokémon isn't your average petty thief. It is one terrifically powerful Pokémon. In fact, legend has it that Hoopa once stole an entire castle just to get at all the priceless treasures inside. Hoopa's strength knows no bounds, but it's weakness is greed.

UNBOUND

VOLCANION • (vol-KAY-nee-un)
THE STEAM POKÉMON

Height	5'07" (1.7 m)	**Category**	
Weight	429.9 lbs (195.0 kg)	**Type**	Fire-Water

You can't get more opposite types than Water and Fire. But sometimes something that seems so wrong can be totally right, even completely awesome! Case in point, the first Pokémon ever discovered to be a Fire *and* Water-type. It's an unbeatable combination that creates a powerful force of nature—steam. Right inside its belly, it uses fire to boil water instantly. Then, it can shoot the steam out of the arm on its back. The pressure is so powerful, it can blast a whole mountain out of its way. But it really feels its true foes are humans. So, you do not want to get too close to the Steam Pokémon, people.

KALOS POKÉMON

The star shaped Kalos region is rich in natural forests that many wild Pokémon call home. Perhaps its two most famous residents are The Life Pokémon, Xerneas, and The Destruction Pokémon, Yveltal.

CENTRAL KALOS

ABRA

Height: 2'11" (0.9 m)
Weight: 43.0 lbs. (19.5 kg)

PSYCHIC

AEGISLASH (BLADE FORME)

Height: 5'07" (1.7 m)
Weight: 116.8 lbs. (53.0 kg)

STEEL GHOST

AEGISLASH (SHIELD FORME)

Height: 5'07" (1.7 m)
Weight: 116.8 lbs. (53.0 kg)

STEEL GHOST

ALAKAZAM

Height: 4'11" (1.5 m)
Weight: 105.8 lbs. (48.0 kg)

PSYCHIC

AROMATISSE

Height: 2'07" (0.8 m)
Weight: 34.2 lbs. (15.5 kg)

FAIRY

AUDINO

Height: 3'07" (1.1 m)
Weight: 68.3 lbs. (31.0 kg)

NORMAL

AXEW

Height: 2'00" (0.6 m)
Weight: 39.7 lbs. (18.0 kg)

DRAGON

AZUMARILL

Height: 2'07" (0.8 m)
Weight: 62.8 lbs. (28.5 kg)

WATER FAIRY

AZURILL

Height: 0'08" (0.2 m)
Weight: 4.4 lbs. (2.0 kg)

NORMAL FAIRY

BEEDRILL

Height: 3'03" (1.0 m)
Weight: 65.0 lbs. (29.5 kg)

BUG POISON

BELLOSSOM

Height: 1'04" (0.4 m)
Weight: 12.8 lbs. (5.8 kg)

GRASS

BIBAREL

Height: 3'03" (1.0 m)
Weight: 69.4 lbs. (31.5 kg)

NORMAL WATER

BIDOOF

Height: 1'08" (0.5 m)
Weight: 44.1 lbs. (20.0 kg)

NORMAL

BLASTOISE

Height: 5'03" (1.6 m)
Weight: 188.5 lbs. (85.5 kg)

WATER

BRAIXEN

Height: 3'03" (1.0 m)
Weight: 32.0 lbs. (14.5 kg)

FIRE

BUDEW

Height: 0'08" (0.2 m)
Weight: 2.6 lbs. (1.2 kg)

GRASS POISON

BULBASAUR

Height: 2'04" (0.7 m)
Weight: 15.2 lbs. (6.9 kg)

GRASS POISON

BUNNELBY

Height: 1'04" (0.4 m)
Weight: 11.0 lbs. (5.0 kg)

NORMAL

BURMY

Height: 0'08" (0.2 m)
Weight: 7.5 lbs. (3.4 kg)

BUG

BURMY (PLANT CLOAK)

Height: 0'08" (0.2 m)
Weight: 7.5 lbs. (3.4 kg)

BUG

BURMY
(SANDY CLOAK)

Height: 0'08" (0.2 m)
Weight: 7.5 lbs. (3.4 kg)

BUG

BURMY
(TRASH CLOAK)

Height: 0'08" (0.2 m)
Weight: 7.5 lbs. (3.4 kg)

BUG

BUTTERFREE

Height: 3'07" (1.1 m)
Weight: 70.5 lbs. (32.0 kg)

BUG   FLYING

CARVANHA

Height: 2'07" (0.8 m)
Weight: 45.9 lbs. (20.8 kg)

WATER   DARK

CATERPIE

Height: 1'00" (0.3 m)
Weight: 6.4 lbs. (2.9 kg)

BUG

CHARIZARD

Height: 5'07" (1.7 m)
Weight: 199.5 lbs. (90.5 kg)

FIRE   FLYING

CHARMANDER

Height: 2'00" (0.6 m)
Weight: 18.7 lbs. (8.5 kg)

FIRE

CHARMELEON

Height: 3'07" (1.1 m)
Weight: 41.9 lbs. (19.0 kg)

FIRE

CHESNAUGHT

Height: 5'03" (1.6 m)
Weight: 198.4 lbs. (90.0 kg)

GRASS   FIGHTING

CHESPIN

Height: 1'04" (0.4 m)
Weight: 19.8 lbs. (9.0 kg)

GRASS

COMBEE

Height: 1'00" (0.3 m)
Weight: 12.1 lbs. (5.5 kg)

BUG   FLYING

CORPHISH

Height: 2'00" (0.6 m)
Weight: 25.4 lbs. (11.5 kg)

WATER

CRAWDAUNT

Height: 3'07" (1.1 m)
Weight: 72.3 lbs. (32.8 kg)

WATER   DARK

CROAGUNK

Height: 2'04'' (0.7 m)
Weight: 50.7 lbs. (23.0 kg)

POISON   FIGHTING

CROBAT

Height: 5'11" (1.8 m)
Weight: 165.3 lbs. (75.0 kg)

POISON   FLYING

DELCATTY

Height: 3'07" (1.1 m)
Weight: 71.9 lbs. (32.6 kg)

NORMAL

DELPHOX

Height: 4'11" (1.5 m)
Weight: 86.0 lbs. (39.0 kg)

FIRE   PSYCHIC

DIANCIE

Height: 2'04" (0.7 m)
Weight: 19.4 lbs. (8.8 kg)

ROCK   FAIRY

DIGGERSBY

Height: 3'03" (1.0 m)
Weight: 93.5 lbs. (42.4 kg)

NORMAL   GROUND

DODRIO

Height: 5'11" (1.8 m)
Weight: 187.8 lbs. (85.2 kg)

NORMAL   FLYING

DODUO

Height: 4'07" (1.4 m)
Weight: 86.4 lbs. (39.2 kg)

NORMAL   FLYING

DOUBLADE

Height: 2'07" (0.8 m)
Weight: 9.9 lbs. (4.5 kg)

STEEL   GHOST

DUCKLETT

Height: 1'08" (0.5 m)
Weight: 12.1 lbs. (5.5 kg)

WATER   FLYING

DUNSPARCE

Height: 4'11" (1.5 m)
Weight: 30.9 lbs. (14.0 kg)

NORMAL

ESPURR

Height: 1'00" (0.3 m)
Weight: 7.7 lbs. (3.5 kg)

PSYCHIC

EXPLOUD

Height: 4'11" (1.5 m)
Weight: 185.2 lbs. (84.0 kg)
NORMAL

FARFETCH'D
Height: 2'07" (0.8 m)
Weight: 33.1 lbs. (15.0 kg)
NORMAL   FLYING

FENNEKIN

Height: 1'04" (0.4 m)
Weight: 20.7 lbs. (9.4 kg)
FIRE

FLABÉBÉ
Height: 0'04" (0.1 m)
Weight: 0.2 lbs. (0.1 kg)
FAIRY

FLETCHINDER

Height: 2'04" (0.7 m)
Weight: 35.3 lbs. (16.0 kg)
FIRE   FLYING

FLETCHLING

Height: 1'00" (0.3 m)
Weight: 3.7 lbs. (1.7 kg)
NORMAL   FLYING

FLOETTE

Height: 0'08" (0.2 m)
Weight: 2.0 lbs. (0.9 kg)
FAIRY

FLORGES

Height: 3'07" (1.1 m)
Weight: 22.0 lbs. (10.0 kg)
FAIRY

FRAXURE

Height: 3'03" (1.0 m)
Weight: 79.4 lbs. (36.0 kg)
DRAGON

FROAKIE

Height: 1'00" (0.3 m)
Weight: 15.4 lbs. (7.0 kg)
WATER

FROGADIER

Height: 2'00" (0.6 m)
Weight: 24.0 lbs. (10.9 kg)
WATER

FURFROU

Height: 3'11" (1.2 m)
Weight: 61.7 lbs. (28.0 kg)
NORMAL

FURRET

Height: 5'11" (1.8 m)
Weight: 71.6 lbs. (32.5 kg)
NORMAL

GALLADE

Height: 5'03" (1.6 m)
Weight: 114.6 lbs. (52.0 kg)
PSYCHIC   FIGHTING

GARDEVOIR

Height: 5'03" (1.6 m)
Weight: 106.7 lbs. (48.4 kg)
PSYCHIC   FAIRY

GLOOM
Height: 2'07" (0.8 m)
Weight: 19.0 lbs. (8.6 kg)
GRASS   POISON

GOGOAT

Height: 5'07" (1.7 m)
Weight: 200.6 lbs. (91.0 kg)
GRASS

GOLBAT
Height: 5'03" (1.6 m)
Weight: 121.3 lbs. (55.0 kg)
POISON   FLYING

GOLDEEN
Height: 2'00" (0.6 m)
Weight: 33.1 lbs. (15.0 kg)
WATER

GOLDUCK
Height: 5'07" (1.7 m)
Weight: 168.9 lbs. (76.6 kg)
WATER

GRENINJA

Height: 4'11" (1.5 m)
Weight: 88.2 lbs. (40.0 kg)
WATER   DARK

GULPIN

Height: 1'04" (0.4 m)
Weight: 22.7 lbs. (10.3 kg)
POISON

GYARADOS

Height: 21'04" (6.5 m)
Weight: 518.1 lbs. (235.0 kg)
WATER   FLYING

HAXORUS

Height: 5'11" (1.8 m)
Weight: 232.6 lbs. (105.5 kg)
DRAGON

HONEDGE

Height: 2'07" (0.8 m)
Weight: 4.4 lbs. (2.0 kg)
STEEL   GHOST

HOOPA

Height: 1'08" (0.5 m)
Weight: 19.8 lbs. (9.0 kg)

PSYCHIC   GHOST

HOPPIP

Height: 1'04" (0.4 m)
Weight: 1.1 lbs. (0.5 kg)

GRASS   FLYING

ILLUMISE

Height: 2'00" (0.6 m)
Weight: 39.0 lbs. (17.7 kg)

BUG

IVYSAUR

Height: 3'03" (1.0 m)
Weight: 28.7 lbs. (13.0 kg)

GRASS   POISON

JUMPLUFF

Height: 2'07" (0.8 m)
Weight: 6.6 lbs. (3.0 kg)

GRASS   FLYING

KADABRA

Height: 4'03" (1.3 m)
Weight: 124.6 lbs. (56.5 kg)

PSYCHIC

KAKUNA

Height: 2'00" (0.6 m)
Weight: 22.0 lbs. (10.0 kg)

BUG   POISON

KECLEON

Height: 3'03" (1.0 m)
Weight: 48.5 lbs. (22.0 kg)

NORMAL

KIRLIA

Height: 2'07" (0.8 m)
Weight: 44.5 lbs. (20.2 kg)

PSYCHIC   FAIRY

LEDIAN

Height: 4'07" (1.4 m)
Weight: 78.5 lbs. (35.6 kg)

BUG   FLYING

LEDYBA

Height: 3'03" (1.0 m)
Weight: 23.8 lbs. (10.8 kg)

BUG   FLYING

LINOONE

Height: 1'08" (0.5 m)
Weight: 71.6 lbs. (32.5 kg)

NORMAL

LITLEO

Height: 2'00" (0.6 m)
Weight: 29.8 lbs. (13.5 kg)

FIRE   NORMAL

LOUDRED

Height: 3'03" (1.0 m)
Weight: 89.3 lbs. (40.5 kg)

NORMAL

LUCARIO

Height: 3'11" (1.2 m)
Weight: 119.0 lbs. (54.0 kg)

FIGHTING   STEEL

MAGIKARP

Height: 2'11" (0.9 m)
Weight: 22.0 lbs. (10.0 kg)

WATER

MARILL

Height: 1'04" (0.4 m)
Weight: 18.7 lbs. (8.5 kg)

WATER   FAIRY

MASQUERAIN

Height: 2'07" (0.8 m)
Weight: 7.9 lbs. (3.6 kg)

BUG   FLYING

MEDICHAM

Height: 4'03" (1.3 m)
Weight: 69.4 lbs. (31.5 kg)

FIGHTING   PSYCHIC

MEDITITE

Height: 2'00" (0.6 m)
Weight: 24.7 lbs. (11.2 kg)

FIGHTING   PSYCHIC

MEOWSTIC ♀

Height: 2'00" (0.6 m)
Weight: 18.7 lbs. (8.5 kg)

PSYCHIC

MEOWSTIC ♂

Height: 2'00" (0.6 m)
Weight: 18.7 lbs. (8.5 kg)

PSYCHIC

METAPOD

Height: 2'04" (0.7 m)
Weight: 21.8 lbs. (9.9 kg)

BUG

MINUN

Height: 1'04" (0.4 m)
Weight: 9.3 lbs. (4.2 kg)

ELECTRIC

MOTHIM

Height: 2'11" (0.9 m)
Weight: 51.4 lbs. (23.3 kg)

BUG   FLYING

MUNCHLAX

Height: 2'00" (0.6 m)
Weight: 231.5 lbs. (105.0 kg)

NORMAL

NINCADA

Height: 1'08" (0.5 m)
Weight: 12.1 lbs. (5.5 kg)

BUG   GROUND

NINJASK

Height: 2'07" (0.8 m)
Weight: 26.5 lbs. (12.0 kg)

BUG   FLYING

ODDISH

Height: 1'08" (0.5 m)
Weight: 11.9 lbs. (5.4 kg)

GRASS   POISON

PANCHAM

Height: 2'00" (0.6 m)
Weight: 17.6 lbs. (8.0 kg)

FIGHTING

PANGORO

Height: 6'11" (2.1 m)
Weight: 299.8 lbs. (136.0 kg)

FIGHTING   DARK

PANPOUR

Height: 2'00" (0.6 m)
Weight: 29.8 lbs. (13.5 kg)

WATER

PANSAGE

Height: 2'00" (0.6 m)
Weight: 23.1 lbs. (10.5 kg)

GRASS

PANSEAR

Height: 2'00" (0.6 m)
Weight: 24.3 lbs. (11.0 kg)

FIRE

PICHU

Height: 1'00" (0.3 m)
Weight: 4.4 lbs. (2.0 kg)

ELECTRIC

PIDGEOT

Height: 4'11" (1.5 m)
Weight: 87.1 lbs. (39.5 kg)

NORMAL   FLYING

PIDGEOTTO

Height: 3'07" (1.1 m)
Weight: 66.1 lbs. (30.0 kg)

NORMAL   FLYING

PIDGEY

Height: 1'00" (0.3 m)
Weight: 4.0 lbs. (1.8 kg)

NORMAL   FLYING

PIKACHU

Height: 1'04" (0.4 m)
Weight: 13.2 lbs. (6.0 kg)

ELECTRIC

PLUSLE

Height: 1'04" (0.4 m)
Weight: 9.3 lbs. (4.2 kg)

ELECTRIC

PSYDUCK

Height: 2'07" (0.8 m)
Weight: 43.2 lbs. (19.6 kg)

WATER

PYROAR ♀

Height: 4'11" (1.5 m)
Weight: 179.7 lbs. (81.5 kg)

FIRE   NORMAL

PYROAR ♂

Height: 4'11" (1.5 m)
Weight: 179.7 lbs. (81.5 kg)

FIRE   NORMAL

QUILLADIN

Height: 2'04" (0.7 m)
Weight: 63.9 lbs. (29.0 kg)

GRASS

RAICHU

Height: 2'07'' (0.8 m)
Weight: 66.1 lbs. (30.0 kg)

ELECTRIC

RALTS

Height: 1'04" (0.4 m)
Weight: 14.6 lbs. (6.6 kg)

PSYCHIC   FAIRY

RIOLU

Height: 2'04" (0.7 m)
Weight: 44.5 lbs. (20.2 kg)

FIGHTING

ROSELIA

Height: 1'00" (0.3 m)
Weight: 4.4 lbs. (2.0 kg)

GRASS   POISON

ROSERADE

Height: 2'11" (0.9 m)
Weight: 32.0 lbs. (14.5 kg)

GRASS   POISON

SCATTERBUG

Height: 1'00" (0.3 m)
Weight: 5.5 lbs. (2.5 kg)

BUG

SCOLIPEDE

Height: 8'02" (2.5 m)
Weight: 442.0 lbs. (200.5 kg)

BUG   POISON

SCRAFTY

Height: 3'07" (1.1 m)
Weight: 66.1 lbs. (30.0 kg)

DARK   FIGHTING

SCRAGGY

Height: 2'00'' (0.6 m)
Weight: 26.0 lbs. (11.8 kg)

DARK   FIGHTING

SEAKING

Height: 4'03" (1.3 m)
Weight: 86.0 lbs. (39.0 kg)

WATER

SENTRET

Height: 2'07" (0.8 m)
Weight: 13.2 lbs. (6.0 kg)

NORMAL

SHARPEDO

Height: 5'11" (1.8 m)
Weight: 195.8 lbs. (88.8 kg)

WATER   DARK

SHEDINJA

Height: 2'07" (0.8 m)
Weight: 2.6 lbs. (1.2 kg)

BUG   GHOST

SIMIPOUR

Height: 3'03" (1.0 m)
Weight: 63.9 lbs. (29.0 kg)

WATER

SIMISAGE

Height: 3'07" (1.1 m)
Weight: 67.2 lbs. (30.5 kg)

GRASS

SIMISEAR

Height: 3'03" (1.0 m)
Weight: 61.7 lbs. (28.0 kg)

FIRE

SKIDDO

Height: 2'11" (0.9 m)
Weight: 68.3 lbs. (31.0 kg)

GRASS

SKIPLOOM

Height: 2'00" (0.6 m)
Weight: 2.2 lbs. (1.0 kg)

GRASS   FLYING

SKITTY

Height: 2'00" (0.6 m)
Weight: 24.3 lbs. (11.0 kg)

NORMAL

SLURPUFF

Height: 2'07" (0.8 m)
Weight: 11.0 lbs. (5.0 kg)

FAIRY

SMEARGLE

Height: 3'11" (1.2 m)
Weight: 127.9 lbs. (58.0 kg)

NORMAL

SNORLAX

Height: 6'11" (2.1 m)
Weight: 1014.1 lbs. (460.0 kg)

NORMAL

SPEWPA

Height: 1'00" (0.3 m)
Weight: 18.5 lbs. (8.4 kg)

BUG

SPRITZEE

Height: 0'08" (0.2 m)
Weight: 1.1 lbs. (0.5 kg)

FAIRY

SQUIRTLE

Height: 1'08" (0.5 m)
Weight: 19.8 lbs. (9.0 kg)

WATER

SURSKIT

Height: 1'08" (0.5 m)
Weight: 3.7 lbs. (1.7 kg)

BUG   WATER

SWALOT

Height: 5'07" (1.7 m)
Weight: 176.4 lbs. (80.0 kg)

POISON

SWANNA

Height: 4'03" (1.3 m)
Weight: 53.4 lbs. (24.2 kg)

WATER   FLYING

SWIRLIX

Height: 1'04" (0.4 m)
Weight: 7.7 lbs. (3.5 kg)

FAIRY

TALONFLAME

Height: 3'11" (1.2 m)
Weight: 54.0 lbs. (24.5 kg)

FIRE   FLYING

TOXICROAK

Height: 4'03" (1.3 m)
Weight: 97.9 lbs. (44.4 kg)

POISON   FIGHTING

VENIPEDE

Height: 1'04" (0.4 m)
Weight: 11.7 lbs. (5.3 kg)

BUG | POISON

VENUSAUR

Height: 6'07" (2.0 m)
Weight: 220.5 lbs. (100.0 kg)

GRASS | POISON

VESPIQUEN

Height: 3'11" (1.2 m)
Weight: 84.9 lbs. (38.5 kg)

BUG | FLYING

VILEPLUME

Height: 3'11" (1.2 m)
Weight: 41.0 lbs. (18.6 kg)

GRASS | POISON

VIVILLON

Height: 3'11" (1.2 m)
Weight: 37.5 lbs. (17.0 kg)

BUG | FLYING

VOLBEAT

Height: 2'04" (0.7 m)
Weight: 39.0 lbs. (17.7 kg)

BUG

VOLCANION

Height: 5'07" (1.7 m)
Weight: 429.9 lbs. (195.0 kg)

FIRE | WATER

WARTORTLE

Height: 3'03" (1.0 m)
Weight: 49.6 lbs. (22.5 kg)

WATER

WEEDLE

Height: 1'00" (0.3 m)
Weight: 7.1 lbs. (3.2 kg)

BUG | POISON

WHIRLIPEDE

Height: 3'11" (1.2 m)
Weight: 129.0 lbs. (58.5 kg)

BUG | POISON

WHISMUR

Height: 2'00" (0.6 m)
Weight: 35.9 lbs. (16.3 kg)

NORMAL

WORMADAM
(PLANT CLOAK)

Height: 1'08" (0.5 m)
Weight: 14.3 lbs. (6.5 kg)

BUG | GRASS

WORMADAM
(SANDY CLOAK)

Height: 1'08" (0.5 m)
Weight: 14.3 lbs. (6.5 kg)

BUG | GRASS

WORMADAM
(TRASH CLOAK)

Height: 1'08" (0.5 m)
Weight: 14.3 lbs. (6.5 kg)

BUG | GRASS

ZIGZAGOON
Height: 1'04" (0.4 m)
Weight: 38.6 lbs. (17.5 kg)

NORMAL

COASTAL KALOS

ZUBAT

Height: 2'07" (0.8 m)
Weight: 16.5 lbs. (7.5 kg)

POISON | FLYING

ABSOL
Height: 3'11" (1.2 m)
Weight: 103.6 lbs. (47.0 kg)

DARK

AERODACTYL
Height: 5'11" (1.8 m)
Weight: 130.1 lbs. (59.0 kg)

ROCK | FLYING

ALOMOMOLA
Height: 3'11" (1.2 m)
Weight: 69.7 lbs. (31.6 kg)

WATER

AMAURA

Height: 4'03" (1.3 m)
Weight: 55.6 lbs. (25.2 kg)

ROCK | ICE

AMPHAROS

Height: 4'07'' (1.4 m)
Weight: 135.6 lbs. (61.5 kg)

ELECTRIC

ARTICUNO

Height: 5'07" (1.7 m)
Weight: 122.1 lbs. (55.4 kg)

ICE | FLYING

AURORUS

Height: 8'10" (2.7 m)
Weight: 496.0 lbs. (225.0 kg)

ROCK | ICE

BAGON

Height: 2'00" (0.6 m)
Weight: 92.8 lbs. (42.1 kg)

DRAGON

BARBARACLE

Height: 4'03" (1.3 m)
Weight: 211.6 lbs. (96.0 kg)

ROCK WATER

BINACLE

Height: 1'08" (0.5 m)
Weight: 68.3 lbs. (31.0 kg)

ROCK WATER

BOLDORE

Height: 2'11" (0.9 m)
Weight: 224.9 lbs. (102.0 kg)

ROCK

CARBINK

Height: 1'00" (0.3 m)
Weight: 12.6 lbs. (5.7 kg)

ROCK FAIRY

CHATOT

Height: 1'08" (0.5 m)
Weight: 4.2 lbs. (1.9 kg)

NORMAL FLYING

CHIMECHO

Height: 2'00" (0.6 m)
Weight: 2.2 lbs. (1.0 kg)

PSYCHIC

CHINCHOU

Height: 1'08" (0.5 m)
Weight: 26.5 lbs. (12.0 kg)

WATER ELECTRIC

CHINGLING

Height: 0'08" (0.2 m)
Weight: 1.3 lbs. (0.6 kg)

PSYCHIC

CLAMPERL

Height: 1'04" (0.4 m)
Weight: 115.7 lbs. (52.5 kg)

WATER

CLAUNCHER

Height: 1'08" (0.5 m)
Weight: 18.3 lbs. (8.3 kg)

WATER

CLAWITZER

Height: 4'03" (1.3 m)
Weight: 77.8 lbs. (35.3 kg)

WATER

CLOYSTER

Height: 4'11" (1.5 m)
Weight: 292.1 lbs. (132.5 kg)

WATER ICE

CORSOLA

Height: 2'00" (0.6 m)
Weight: 11.0 lbs. (5.0 kg)

WATER ROCK

CRUSTLE

Height: 4'07" (1.4 m)
Weight: 440.9 lbs. (200.0 kg)

BUG ROCK

CUBONE

Height: 1'04" (0.4 m)
Weight: 14.3 lbs. (6.5 kg)

GROUND

DEDENNE

Height: 0'08" (0.2 m)
Weight: 4.9 lbs. (2.2 kg)

ELECTRIC FAIRY

DRAGALGE

Height: 5'11" (1.8 m)
Weight: 179.7 lbs. (81.5 kg)

POISON DRAGON

DRIFBLIM

Height: 3'11" (1.2 m)
Weight: 33.1 lbs. (15.0 kg)

GHOST FLYING

DRIFLOON

Height: 1'04" (0.4 m)
Weight: 2.6 lbs. (1.2 kg)

GHOST FLYING

DUOSION

Height: 2'00" (0.6 m)
Weight: 17.6 lbs. (8.0 kg)

PSYCHIC

DWEBBLE

Height: 1'00" (0.3 m)
Weight: 32.0 lbs. (14.5 kg)

BUG ROCK

EEVEE

Height: 1'00" (0.3 m)
Weight: 14.3 lbs. (6.5 kg)

NORMAL

ELECTRIKE

Height: 2'00" (0.6 m)
Weight: 33.5 lbs. (15.2 kg)

ELECTRIC

EMOLGA

Height: 1'04" (0.4 m)
Weight: 11.0 lbs. (5.0 kg)

ELECTRIC FLYING

ESPEON

Height: 2'11" (0.9 m)
Weight: 58.4 lbs. (26.5 kg)

PSYCHIC

EXEGGCUTE

Height: 1'04" (0.4 m)
Weight: 5.5 lbs. (2.5 kg)

GRASS | PSYCHIC

EXEGGUTOR

Height: 6'07" (2.0 m)
Weight: 264.6 lbs. (120.0 kg)

GRASS | PSYCHIC

FERROSEED

Height: 2'00" (0.6 m)
Weight: 41.4 lbs. (18.8 kg)

GRASS | STEEL

FERROTHORN

Height: 3'03" (1.0 m)
Weight: 242.5 lbs. (110.0 kg)

GRASS | STEEL

FLAAFFY

Height: 2'07" (0.8 m)
Weight: 29.3 lbs. (13.3 kg)

ELECTRIC

FLAREON

Height: 2'11" (0.9 m)
Weight: 55.1 lbs. (25.0 kg)

FIRE

GIGALITH

Height: 5'07" (1.7 m)
Weight: 573.2 lbs. (260.0 kg)

ROCK

GLACEON

Height: 2'07" (0.8 m)
Weight: 57.1 lbs. (25.9 kg)

ICE

GOLETT

Height: 3'03" (1.0 m)
Weight: 202.8 lbs. (92.0 kg)

GROUND | GHOST

GOLURK

Height: 9'02" (2.8 m)
Weight: 727.5 lbs. (330.0 kg)

GROUND | GHOST

GOREBYSS

Height: 5'11" (1.8 m)
Weight: 49.8 lbs. (22.6 kg)

WATER

GRANBULL

Height: 4'07" (1.4 m)
Weight: 107.4 lbs. (48.7 kg)

FAIRY

GRUMPIG

Height: 2'11" (0.9 m)
Weight: 157.6 lbs. (71.5 kg)

PSYCHIC

HARIYAMA

Height: 7'07" (2.3 m)
Weight: 559.5 lbs. (253.8 kg)

FIGHTING

HAWLUCHA

Height: 2'07" (0.8 m)
Weight: 47.4 lbs. (21.5 kg)

FIGHTING | FLYING

HELIOLISK

Height: 3'03" (1.0 m)
Weight: 46.3 lbs. (21.0 kg)

ELECTRIC | NORMAL

HELIOPTILE

Height: 1'08" (0.5 m)
Weight: 13.2 lbs. (6.0 kg)

ELECTRIC | NORMAL

HERACROSS

Height: 4'11" (1.5 m)
Weight: 119.0 lbs. (54.0 kg)

BUG | FIGHTING

HIPPOPOTAS

Height: 2'07" (0.8 m)
Weight: 109.1 lbs. (49.5 kg)

GROUND

HIPPOWDON

Height: 6'07" (2.0 m)
Weight: 661.4 lbs. (300.0 kg)

GROUND

HORSEA

Height: 1'04" (0.4 m)
Weight: 17.6 lbs. (8.0 kg)

WATER

HOUNDOOM

Height: 4'07" (1.4 m)
Weight: 77.2 lbs. (35.0 kg)

DARK | FIRE

HOUNDOUR

Height: 2'00" (0.6 m)
Weight: 23.8 lbs. (10.8 kg)

DARK | FIRE

HUNTAIL

Height: 5'07" (1.7 m)
Weight: 59.5 lbs. (27.0 kg)

WATER

INKAY

Height: 1'04" (0.4 m)
Weight: 7.7 lbs. (3.5 kg)

DARK | PSYCHIC

JOLTEON

Height: 2'07" (0.8 m)
Weight: 54.0 lbs. (24.5 kg)

ELECTRIC

KANGASKHAN

Height: 7'03" (2.2 m)
Weight: 176.4 lbs. (80.0 kg)

NORMAL

KINGDRA

Height: 5'11" (1.8 m)
Weight: 335.1 lbs. (152.0 kg)

WATER | DRAGON

KROKOROK

Height: 3'03" (1.0 m)
Weight: 73.6 lbs. (33.4 kg)

GROUND | DARK

KROOKODILE

Height: 4'11" (1.5 m)
Weight: 212.3 lbs. (96.3 kg)

GROUND | DARK

LANTURN

Height: 3'11" (1.2 m)
Weight: 49.6 lbs. (22.5 kg)

WATER | ELECTRIC

LAPRAS

Height: 8'02" (2.5 m)
Weight: 485.0 lbs. (220.0 kg)

WATER | ICE

LEAFEON

Height: 3'03" (1.0 m)
Weight: 56.2 lbs. (25.5 kg)

GRASS

LUNATONE

Height: 3'03" (1.0 m)
Weight: 370.4 lbs. (168.0 kg)

ROCK | PSYCHIC

LUVDISC

Height: 2'00" (0.6 m)
Weight: 19.2 lbs. (8.7 kg)

WATER

MACHAMP

Height: 5'03" (1.6 m)
Weight: 286.6 lbs. (130.0 kg)

FIGHTING

MACHOKE

Height: 4'11" (1.5 m)
Weight: 155.4 lbs. (70.5 kg)

FIGHTING

MACHOP

Height: 2'07" (0.8 m)
Weight: 43.0 lbs. (19.5 kg)

FIGHTING

MAKUHITA

Height: 3'03" (1.0 m)
Weight: 190.5 lbs. (86.4 kg)

FIGHTING

MALAMAR

Height: 4'11" (1.5 m)
Weight: 103.6 lbs. (47.0 kg)

DARK | PSYCHIC

MANECTRIC

Height: 4'11" (1.5 m)
Weight: 88.6 lbs. (40.2 kg)

ELECTRIC

MANTINE

Height: 6'11" (2.1 m)
Weight: 485.0 lbs. (220.0 kg)

WATER | FLYING

MANTYKE

Height: 3'03" (1.0 m)
Weight: 143.3 lbs. (65.0 kg)

WATER | FLYING

MAREEP

Height: 2'00" (0.6 m)
Weight: 17.2 lbs. (7.8 kg)

ELECTRIC

MAROWAK

Height: 3'03" (1.0 m)
Weight: 99.2 lbs. (45.0 kg)

GROUND

MAWILE

Height: 2'00" (0.6 m)
Weight: 25.4 lbs. (11.5 kg)

STEEL | FAIRY

MIENFOO

Height: 2'11" (0.9 m)
Weight: 44.1 lbs. (20.0 kg)

FIGHTING

MIENSHAO

Height: 4'07" (1.4 m)
Weight: 78.3 lbs. (35.5 kg)

FIGHTING

MILTANK

Height: 3'11" (1.2 m)
Weight: 166.4 lbs. (75.5 kg)

NORMAL

MIME JR.

Height: 2'00" (0.6 m)
Weight: 28.7 lbs. (13.0 kg)

PSYCHIC | FAIRY

MOLTRES

Height: 6'07" (2.0 m)
Weight: 132.3 lbs. (60.0 kg)

| FIRE | FLYING |

MR. MIME

Height: 4'03" (1.3 m)
Weight: 120.1 lbs. (54.5 kg)

| PSYCHIC | FAIRY |

NIDOKING

Height: 4'07" (1.4 m)
Weight: 136.7 lbs. (62.0 kg)

| POISON | GROUND |

NIDOQUEEN

Height: 4'03" (1.3 m)
Weight: 132.3 lbs. (60.0 kg)

| POISON | GROUND |

NIDORAN ♀

Height: 1'04" (0.4 m)
Weight: 15.4 lbs. (7.0 kg)

| POISON |

NIDORAN ♂

Height: 1'08" (0.5 m)
Weight: 19.8 lbs. (9.0 kg)

| POISON |

NIDORINA (FEMALE)

Height: 2'07" (0.8 m)
Weight: 44.1 lbs. (20.0 kg)

| POISON |

NIDORINO (MALE)

Height: 2'11" (0.9 m)
Weight: 43.0 lbs. (19.5 kg)

| POISON |

NOSEPASS

Height: 3'03" (1.0 m)
Weight: 213.8 lbs. (97.0 kg)

| ROCK |

OCTILLERY

Height: 2'11" (0.9 m)
Weight: 62.8 lbs. (28.5 kg)

| WATER |

ONIX

Height: 28'10" (8.8 m)
Weight: 463.0 lbs. (210.0 kg)

| ROCK | GROUND |

PACHIRISU

Height: 1'04" (0.4 m)
Weight: 8.6 lbs. (3.9 kg)

| ELECTRIC |

PELIPPER

Height: 3'11" (1.2 m)
Weight: 61.7 lbs. (28.0 kg)

| WATER | FLYING |

PINSIR

Height: 4'11" (1.5 m)
Weight: 121.3 lbs. (55.0 kg)

| BUG |

PROBOPASS

Height: 4'07" (1.4 m)
Weight: 749.6 lbs. (340.0 kg)

| ROCK | STEEL |

QWILFISH

Height: 1'08" (0.5 m)
Weight: 8.6 lbs. (3.9 kg)

| WATER | POISON |

RELICANTH

Height: 3'03" (1.0 m)
Weight: 51.6 lbs. (23.4 kg)

| WATER | ROCK |

REMORAID

Height: 2'00" (0.6 m)
Weight: 26.5 lbs. (12.0 kg)

| WATER |

REUNICLUS

Height: 3'03" (1.0 m)
Weight: 44.3 lbs. (20.1 kg)

| PSYCHIC |

RHYDON

Height: 6'03" (1.9 m)
Weight: 264.6 lbs. (120.0 kg)

| GROUND | ROCK |

RHYHORN

Height: 3'03" (1.0 m)
Weight: 253.5 lbs. (115.0 kg)

| GROUND | ROCK |

RHYPERIOR

Height: 7'10" (2.4 m)
Weight: 623.5 lbs. (282.8 kg)

| GROUND | ROCK |

ROGGENROLA

Height: 1'04" (0.4 m)
Weight: 39.7 lbs. (18.0 kg)

| ROCK |

SABLEYE

Height: 1'08" (0.5 m)
Weight: 24.3 lbs. (11.0 kg)

| DARK | GHOST |

SALAMENCE

Height: 4'11'' (1.5 m)
Weight: 226.2 lbs. (102.6 kg)

| DRAGON | FLYING |

SANDILE

Height: 2'04" (0.7 m)
Weight: 33.5 lbs. (15.2 kg)

GROUND DARK

SAWK

Height: 4'07" (1.4 m)
Weight: 112.4 lbs. (51.0 kg)

FIGHTING

SEADRA

Height: 3'11" (1.2 m)
Weight: 55.1 lbs. (25.0 kg)

WATER

SEVIPER

Height: 8'10" (2.7 m)
Weight: 115.7 lbs. (52.5 kg)

POISON

SHELGON

Height: 3'07" (1.1 m)
Weight: 243.6 lbs. (110.5 kg)

DRAGON

SHELLDER

Height: 1'00" (0.3 m)
Weight: 8.8 lbs. (4.0 kg)

WATER

SIGILYPH

Height: 4'07" (1.4 m)
Weight: 30.9 lbs. (14.0 kg)

PSYCHIC FLYING

SKRELP

Height: 1'08" (0.5 m)
Weight: 16.1 lbs. (7.3 kg)

POISON WATER

SKUNTANK

Height: 3'03" (1.0 m)
Weight: 83.8 lbs. (38.0 kg)

POISON DARK

SLOWBRO

Height: 5'03" (1.6 m)
Weight: 173.1 lbs. (78.5 kg)

WATER PSYCHIC

SLOWKING

Height: 6'07" (2.0 m)
Weight: 175.3 lbs. (79.5 kg)

WATER PSYCHIC

SLOWPOKE

Height: 3'11" (1.2 m)
Weight: 79.4 lbs. (36.0 kg)

WATER PSYCHIC

SNUBBULL

Height: 2'00" (0.6 m)
Weight: 17.2 lbs. (7.8 kg)

FAIRY

SOLOSIS

Height: 1'00" (0.3 m)
Weight: 2.2 lbs. (1.0 kg)

PSYCHIC

SOLROCK

Height: 3'11" (1.2 m)
Weight: 339.5 lbs. (154.0 kg)

ROCK PSYCHIC

SPOINK

Height: 2'04" (0.7 m)
Weight: 67.5 lbs. (30.6 kg)

PSYCHIC

STARAPTOR
Height: 3'11" (1.2 m)
Weight: 54.9 lbs. (24.9 kg)

NORMAL FLYING

STARAVIA
Height: 2'00" (0.6 m)
Weight: 34.2 lbs. (15.5 kg)

NORMAL FLYING

STARLY

Height: 1'00" (0.3 m)
Weight: 4.4 lbs. (2.0 kg)

NORMAL FLYING

STARMIE
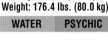
Height: 3'07" (1.1 m)
Weight: 176.4 lbs. (80.0 kg)

WATER PSYCHIC

STARYU

Height: 2'07" (0.8 m)
Weight: 76.1 lbs. (34.5 kg)

WATER

STEELIX

Height: 30'02" (9.2 m)
Weight: 881.8 lbs. (400.0 kg)

STEEL GROUND

STUNKY

Height: 1'04" (0.4 m)
Weight: 42.3 lbs. (19.2 kg)

POISON DARK

SWELLOW
Height: 2'04" (0.7 m)
Weight: 43.7 lbs. (19.8 kg)

NORMAL FLYING

SWOOBAT

Height: 2'11" (0.9 m)
Weight: 23.1 lbs. (10.5 kg)

PSYCHIC FLYING

SYLVEON

Height: 3'03" (1.0 m)
Weight: 51.8 lbs. (23.5 kg)
FAIRY

TAILLOW

Height: 1'00" (0.3 m)
Weight: 5.1 lbs. (2.3 kg)
NORMAL | FLYING

TAUROS

Height: 4'07" (1.4 m)
Weight: 194.9 lbs. (88.4 kg)
NORMAL

TENTACOOL

Height: 2'11" (0.9 m)
Weight: 100.3 lbs. (45.5 kg)
WATER | POISON

TENTACRUEL

Height: 5'03" (1.6 m)
Weight: 121.3 lbs. (55.0 kg)
WATER | POISON

THROH

Height: 4'03" (1.3 m)
Weight: 122.4 lbs. (55.5 kg)
FIGHTING

TYRANTRUM

Height: 8'02" (2.5 m)
Weight: 595.2 lbs. (270.0 kg)
ROCK | DRAGON

TYRUNT

Height: 2'07" (0.8 m)
Weight: 57.3 lbs. (26.0 kg)
ROCK | DRAGON

UMBREON

Height: 3'03" (1.0 m)
Weight: 59.5 lbs. (27.0 kg)
DARK

VAPOREON

Height: 3'03" (1.0 m)
Weight: 63.9 lbs. (29.0 kg)
WATER

WAILMER

Height: 6'07" (2.0 m)
Weight: 286.6 lbs. (130.0 kg)
WATER

WAILORD

Height: 47'07" (14.5 m)
Weight: 877.4 lbs. (398.0 kg)
WATER

WINGULL

Height: 2'00" (0.6 m)
Weight: 20.9 lbs. (9.5 kg)
WATER | FLYING

WOBBUFFET

Height: 4'03" (1.3 m)
Weight: 62.8 lbs. (28.5 kg)
PSYCHIC

WOOBAT

Height: 1'04" (0.4 m)
Weight: 4.6 lbs. (2.1 kg)
PSYCHIC | FLYING

WYNAUT

Height: 2'00" (0.6 m)
Weight: 30.9 lbs. (14.0 kg)
PSYCHIC

YANMA

Height: 3'11" (1.2 m)
Weight: 83.8 lbs. (38.0 kg)
BUG | FLYING

YANMEGA

Height: 6'03" (1.9 m)
Weight: 113.5 lbs. (51.5 kg)
BUG | FLYING

ZANGOOSE

Height: 4'03" (1.3 m)
Weight: 88.8 lbs. (40.3 kg)
NORMAL

ZAPDOS

Height: 5'03" (1.6 m)
Weight: 116.0 lbs. (52.6 kg)
ELECTRIC | FLYING

MOUNTAIN KALOS

ABOMASNOW

Height: 7'03" (2.2 m)
Weight: 298.7 lbs. (135.5 kg)
GRASS | ICE

ACCELGOR

Height: 2'07" (0.8 m)
Weight: 55.8 lbs. (25.3 kg)
BUG

AGGRON

Height: 6'11" (2.1 m)
Weight: 793.7 lbs. (360.0 kg)
STEEL | ROCK

ALTARIA

Height: 3'07" (1.1 m)
Weight: 45.4 lbs. (20.6 kg)
DRAGON | FLYING

AMOONGUSS

Height: 2'00" (0.6 m)
Weight: 23.1 lbs. (10.5 kg)
GRASS | POISON

ARBOK

Height: 11'06" (3.5 m)
Weight: 143.3 lbs. (65.0 kg)

POISON

ARIADOS

Height: 3'07" (1.1 m)
Weight: 73.9 lbs. (33.5 kg)

BUG   POISON

ARON

Height: 1'04" (0.4 m)
Weight: 132.3 lbs. (60.0 kg)

STEEL   ROCK

AVALUGG

Height: 6'07" (2.0 m)
Weight: 1113.3 lbs. (505.0 kg)

ICE

BANETTE

Height: 3'07" (1.1 m)
Weight: 27.6 lbs. (12.5 kg)

GHOST

BARBOACH

Height: 1'04" (0.4 m)
Weight: 4.2 lbs. (1.9 kg)

WATER   GROUND

BASCULIN

Height: 3'03" (1.0 m)
Weight: 39.7 lbs. (18.0 kg)

WATER

BEARTIC

Height: 8'06" (2.6 m)
Weight: 573.2 lbs. (260.0 kg)

ICE

BELLSPROUT

Height: 2'04" (0.7 m)
Weight: 8.8 lbs. (4.0 kg)

GRASS   POISON

BERGMITE

Height: 3'03" (1.0 m)
Weight: 219.4 lbs. (99.5 kg)

ICE

BISHARP

Height: 5'03" (1.6 m)
Weight: 154.3 lbs. (70.0 kg)

DARK   STEEL

BONSLY

Height: 1'08" (0.5 m)
Weight: 33.1 lbs. (15.0 kg)

ROCK

BUIZEL

Height: 2'04" (0.7 m)
Weight: 65.0 lbs. (29.5 kg)

WATER

CARNIVINE

Height: 4'07" (1.4 m)
Weight: 59.5 lbs. (27.0 kg)

GRASS

CHANDELURE

Height: 3'03" (1.0 m)
Weight: 75.6 lbs. (34.3 kg)

GHOST   FIRE

CONKELDURR

Height: 4'07" (1.4 m)
Weight: 191.8 lbs. (87.0 kg)

FIGHTING

CRYOGONAL

Height: 3'07" (1.1 m)
Weight: 326.3 lbs. (148.0 kg)

ICE

CUBCHOO

Height: 1'08" (0.5 m)
Weight: 18.7 lbs. (8.5 kg)

ICE

DEINO

Height: 2'07" (0.8 m)
Weight: 38.1 lbs. (17.3 kg)

DARK   DRAGON

DELIBIRD

Height: 2'11" (0.9 m)
Weight: 35.3 lbs. (16.0 kg)

ICE   FLYING

DIGLETT

Height: 0'08" (0.2 m)
Weight: 1.8 lbs. (0.8 kg)

GROUND

DITTO

Height: 1'00" (0.3 m)
Weight: 8.8 lbs. (4.0 kg)

NORMAL

DRAGONAIR

Height: 13'01" (4.0 m)
Weight: 36.4 lbs. (16.5 kg)

DRAGON

DRAGONITE

Height: 7'03" (2.2 m)
Weight: 463.0 lbs. (210.0 kg)

DRAGON   FLYING

DRAPION

Height: 4'03" (1.3 m)
Weight: 135.6 lbs. (61.5 kg)

POISON   DARK

DRATINI

Height: 5'11" (1.8 m)
Weight: 7.3 lbs. (3.3 kg)

DRAGON

DRUDDIGON

Height: 5'03" (1.6 m)
Weight: 306.4 lbs. (139.0 kg)

DRAGON

DUGTRIO

Height: 2'04" (0.7 m)
Weight: 73.4 lbs. (33.3 kg)

GROUND

DURANT

Height: 1'00" (0.3 m)
Weight: 72.8 lbs. (33.0 kg)

BUG STEEL

EKANS

Height: 6'07" (2.0 m)
Weight: 15.2 lbs. (6.9 kg)

POISON

ELECTRODE

Height: 3'11" (1.2 m)
Weight: 146.8 lbs. (66.6 kg)

ELECTRIC

ESCAVALIER

Height: 3'03" (1.0 m)
Weight: 72.8 lbs. (33.0 kg)

BUG STEEL

FEAROW

Height: 3'11" (1.2 m)
Weight: 83.8 lbs. (38.0 kg)

NORMAL FLYING

FLOATZEL

Height: 3'07" (1.1 m)
Weight: 73.9 lbs. (33.5 kg)

WATER

FLYGON

Height: 6'07" (2.0 m)
Weight: 180.8 lbs. (82.0 kg)

GROUND DRAGON

FOONGUS

Height: 0'08" (0.2 m)
Weight: 2.2 lbs. (1.0 kg)

GRASS POISON

GABITE

Height: 4'07" (1.4 m)
Weight: 123.5 lbs. (56.0 kg)

DRAGON GROUND

GARBODOR

Height: 6'03" (1.9 m)
Weight: 236.6 lbs. (107.3 kg)

POISON

GARCHOMP

Height: 6'03'' (1.9 m)
Weight: 209.4 lbs. (95.0 kg)

DRAGON GROUND

GASTLY

Height: 4'03" (1.3 m)
Weight: 0.2 lbs. (0.1 kg)

GHOST POISON

GENGAR

Height: 4'11" (1.5 m)
Weight: 89.3 lbs. (40.5 kg)

GHOST POISON

GEODUDE

Height: 1'04" (0.4 m)
Weight: 44.1 lbs. (20.0 kg)

ROCK GROUND

GIBLE

Height: 2'04" (0.7 m)
Weight: 45.2 lbs. (20.5 kg)

DRAGON GROUND

GLIGAR

Height: 3'07" (1.1 m)
Weight: 142.9 lbs. (64.8 kg)

GROUND FLYING

GLISCOR

Height: 6'07" (2.0 m)
Weight: 93.7 lbs. (42.5 kg)

GROUND FLYING

GOLEM

Height: 4'07" (1.4 m)
Weight: 661.4 lbs. (300.0 kg)

ROCK GROUND

GOODRA

Height: 6'07" (2.0 m)
Weight: 331.8 lbs. (150.5 kg)

DRAGON

GOOMY

Height: 1'00" (0.3 m)
Weight: 6.2 lbs. (2.8 kg)

DRAGON

GOTHITA
Height: 1'04" (0.4 m)
Weight: 12.8 lbs. (5.8 kg)

PSYCHIC

GOTHITELLE

Height: 4'11" (1.5 m)
Weight: 97.0 lbs. (44.0 kg)

PSYCHIC

GOTHORITA

Height: 2'04" (0.7 m)
Weight: 39.7 lbs. (18.0 kg)

PSYCHIC

GOURGEIST

Height: 2'11" (0.9 m)
Weight: 27.6 lbs. (12.5 kg)

GHOST | GRASS

GRAVELER

Height: 3'03" (1.0 m)
Weight: 231.5 lbs. (105.0 kg)

ROCK | GROUND

GURDURR

Height: 3'11" (1.2 m)
Weight: 88.2 lbs. (40.0 kg)

FIGHTING

HAUNTER

Height: 5'03" (1.6 m)
Weight: 0.2 lbs. (0.1 kg)

GHOST | POISON

HEATMOR

Height: 4'07" (1.4 m)
Weight: 127.9 lbs. (58.0 kg)

FIRE

HONCHKROW

Height: 2'11" (0.9 m)
Weight: 60.2 lbs. (27.3 kg)

DARK | FLYING

HOOTHOOT

Height: 2'04" (0.7 m)
Weight: 46.7 lbs. (21.2 kg)

NORMAL | FLYING

HYDREIGON

Height: 5'11" (1.8 m)
Weight: 352.7 lbs. (160.0 kg)

DARK | DRAGON

IGGLYBUFF

Height: 1'00" (0.3 m)
Weight: 2.2 lbs. (1.0 kg)

NORMAL | FAIRY

JIGGLYPUFF

Height: 1'08" (0.5 m)
Weight: 12.1 lbs. (5.5 kg)

NORMAL | FAIRY

JYNX

Height: 4'07" (1.4 m)
Weight: 89.5 lbs. (40.6 kg)

ICE | PSYCHIC

KARRABLAST

Height: 1'08" (0.5 m)
Weight: 13.0 lbs. (5.9 kg)

BUG

KLEFKI

Height: 0'08" (0.2 m)
Weight: 6.6 lbs. (3.0 kg)

STEEL | FAIRY

LAIRON

Height: 2'11" (0.9 m)
Weight: 264.6 lbs. (120.0 kg)

STEEL | ROCK

LAMPENT

Height: 2'00" (0.6 m)
Weight: 28.7 lbs. (13.0 kg)

GHOST | FIRE

LARVITAR

Height: 2'00" (0.6 m)
Weight: 158.7 lbs. (72.0 kg)

ROCK | GROUND

LICKILICKY

Height: 5'07" (1.7 m)
Weight: 308.6 lbs. (140.0 kg)

NORMAL

LICKITUNG

Height: 3'11" (1.2 m)
Weight: 144.4 lbs. (65.5 kg)

NORMAL

LIEPARD

Height: 3'07" (1.1 m)
Weight: 82.7 lbs. (37.5 kg)

DARK

LITWICK

Height: 1'00" (0.3 m)
Weight: 6.8 lbs. (3.1 kg)

GHOST | FIRE

LOMBRE

Height: 3'11" (1.2 m)
Weight: 71.6 lbs. (32.5 kg)

WATER | GRASS

LOTAD

Height: 1'08" (0.5 m)
Weight: 5.7 lbs. (2.6 kg)

WATER | GRASS

LUDICOLO

Height: 4'11" (1.5 m)
Weight: 121.3 lbs. (55.0 kg)

WATER | GRASS

MAGCARGO

Height: 2'07" (0.8 m)
Weight: 121.3 lbs. (55.0 kg)

FIRE | ROCK

MAGNEMITE

Height: 1'00" (0.3 m)
Weight: 13.2 lbs. (6.0 kg)

ELECTRIC   STEEL

MAGNETON

Height: 3'03" (1.0 m)
Weight: 132.3 lbs. (60.0 kg)

ELECTRIC   STEEL

MAGNEZONE

Height: 3'11" (1.2 m)
Weight: 396.8 lbs. (180.0 kg)

ELECTRIC   STEEL

MAMOSWINE

Height: 8'02" (2.5 m)
Weight: 641.5 lbs. (291.0 kg)

ICE   GROUND

MEWTWO

Height: 6'07" (2.0 m)
Weight: 269.0 lbs. (122.0 kg)

PSYCHIC

MIGHTYENA

Height: 3'03" (1.0 m)
Weight: 81.6 lbs. (37.0 kg)

DARK

MURKROW

Height: 1'08" (0.5 m)
Weight: 4.6 lbs. (2.1 kg)

DARK   FLYING

NOCTOWL

Height: 5'03" (1.6 m)
Weight: 89.9 lbs. (40.8 kg)

NORMAL   FLYING

NOIBAT
Height: 1'08" (0.5 m)
Weight: 17.6 lbs. (8.0 kg)

FLYING   DRAGON

NOIVERN

Height: 4'11" (1.5 m)
Weight: 187.4 lbs. (85.0 kg)

FLYING   DRAGON

PATRAT

Height: 1'08" (0.5 m)
Weight: 25.6 lbs. (11.6 kg)

NORMAL

PAWNIARD

Height: 1'08" (0.5 m)
Weight: 22.5 lbs. (10.2 kg)

DARK   STEEL

PHANTUMP

Height: 1'04" (0.4 m)
Weight: 15.4 lbs. (7.0 kg)

GHOST   GRASS

PILOSWINE

Height: 3'07" (1.1 m)
Weight: 123.0 lbs. (55.8 kg)

ICE   GROUND

POLITOED

Height: 3'07" (1.1 m)
Weight: 74.7 lbs. (33.9 kg)

WATER

POLIWAG

Height: 2'00" (0.6 m)
Weight: 27.3 lbs. (12.4 kg)

WATER

POLIWHIRL

Height: 3'03" (1.0 m)
Weight: 44.1 lbs. (20.0 kg)

WATER

POLIWRATH

Height: 4'03" (1.3 m)
Weight: 119.0 lbs. (54.0 kg)

WATER   FIGHTING

POOCHYENA

Height: 1'08" (0.5 m)
Weight: 30.0 lbs. (13.6 kg)

DARK

PUMPKABOO

Height: 1'04" (0.4 m)
Weight: 11.0 lbs. (5.0 kg)

GHOST   GRASS

PUPITAR

Height: 3'11" (1.2 m)
Weight: 335.1 lbs. (152.0 kg)

ROCK   GROUND

PURRLOIN

Height: 1'04" (0.4 m)
Weight: 22.3 lbs. (10.1 kg)

DARK

QUAGSIRE

Height: 4'07" (1.4 m)
Weight: 165.3 lbs. (75.0 kg)

WATER   GROUND

ROTOM

Height: 1'00" (0.3 m)
Weight: 0.7 lbs. (0.3 kg)

ELECTRIC   GHOST

SANDSHREW

Height: 2'00" (0.6 m)
Weight: 26.5 lbs. (12.0 kg)

GROUND

SANDSLASH

Height: 3'03" (1.0 m)
Weight: 65.0 lbs. (29.5 kg)

GROUND

SCIZOR

Height: 5'11" (1.8 m)
Weight: 260.1 lbs. (118.0 kg)

BUG STEEL

SCYTHER

Height: 4'11" (1.5 m)
Weight: 123.5 lbs. (56.0 kg)

BUG FLYING

SHELMET

Height: 1'04" (0.4 m)
Weight: 17.0 lbs. (7.7 kg)

BUG

SHUCKLE

Height: 2'00" (0.6 m)
Weight: 45.2 lbs. (20.5 kg)

BUG ROCK

SHUPPET

Height: 2'00" (0.6 m)
Weight: 5.1 lbs. (2.3 kg)

GHOST

SKARMORY

Height: 5'07" (1.7 m)
Weight: 111.3 lbs. (50.5 kg)

STEEL FLYING

SKORUPI

Height: 2'07" (0.8 m)
Weight: 26.5 lbs. (12.0 kg)

POISON BUG

SLIGGOO

Height: 2'07" (0.8 m)
Weight: 38.6 lbs. (17.5 kg)

DRAGON

SLUGMA

Height: 2'04" (0.7 m)
Weight: 77.2 lbs. (35.0 kg)

FIRE

SMOOCHUM

Height: 1'04" (0.4 m)
Weight: 13.2 lbs. (6.0 kg)

ICE PSYCHIC

SNEASEL

Height: 2'11" (0.9 m)
Weight: 61.7 lbs. (28.0 kg)

DARK ICE

SNOVER

Height: 3'03" (1.0 m)
Weight: 111.3 lbs. (50.5 kg)

GRASS ICE

SPEAROW

Height: 1'00" (0.3 m)
Weight: 4.4 lbs. (2.0 kg)

NORMAL FLYING

SPINARAK

Height: 1'08" (0.5 m)
Weight: 18.7 lbs. (8.5 kg)

BUG POISON

SPINDA

Height: 3'07" (1.1 m)
Weight: 11.0 lbs. (5.0 kg)

NORMAL

STUNFISK

Height: 2'04" (0.7 m)
Weight: 24.3 lbs. (11.0 kg)

GROUND ELECTRIC

SUDOWOODO

Height: 3'11" (1.2 m)
Weight: 83.8 lbs. (38.0 kg)

ROCK

SWABLU

Height: 1'04" (0.4 m)
Weight: 2.6 lbs. (1.2 kg)

NORMAL FLYING

SWINUB
Height: 1'04" (0.4 m)
Weight: 14.3 lbs. (6.5 kg)

ICE GROUND

TEDDIURSA

Height: 2'00" (0.6 m)
Weight: 19.4 lbs. (8.8 kg)

NORMAL

TIMBURR

Height: 2'00" (0.6 m)
Weight: 27.6 lbs. (12.5 kg)

FIGHTING

TORKOAL

Height: 1'08" (0.5 m)
Weight: 177.2 lbs. (80.4 kg)

FIRE

TRAPINCH

Height: 2'04" (0.7 m)
Weight: 33.1 lbs. (15.0 kg)

GROUND

TREVENANT

Height: 4'11" (1.5 m)
Weight: 156.5 lbs. (71.0 kg)

GHOST GRASS

TRUBBISH

Height: 2'00" (0.6 m)
Weight: 68.3 lbs. (31.0 kg)

POISON

TYRANITAR

Height: 6'07" (2.0 m)
Weight: 445.3 lbs. (202.0 kg)

ROCK | DARK

URSARING

Height: 5'11" (1.8 m)
Weight: 277.3 lbs. (125.8 kg)

NORMAL

VANILLISH

Height: 3'07" (1.1 m)
Weight: 90.4 lbs. (41.0 kg)

ICE

VANILLITE

Height: 1'04" (0.4 m)
Weight: 12.6 lbs. (5.7 kg)

ICE

VANILLUXE

Height: 4'03" (1.3 m)
Weight: 126.8 lbs. (57.5 kg)

ICE

VIBRAVA

Height: 3'07" (1.1 m)
Weight: 33.7 lbs. (15.3 kg)

GROUND | DRAGON

VICTREEBEL

Height: 5'07" (1.7 m)
Weight: 34.2 lbs. (15.5 kg)

GRASS | POISON

VOLTORB

Height: 1'08" (0.5 m)
Weight: 22.9 lbs. (10.4 kg)

ELECTRIC

WATCHOG

Height: 3'07" (1.1 m)
Weight: 59.5 lbs. (27.0 kg)

NORMAL

WEAVILE

Height: 3'07" (1.1 m)
Weight: 75.0 lbs. (34.0 kg)

DARK | ICE

WEEPINBELL

Height: 3'03" (1.0 m)
Weight: 14.1 lbs. (6.4 kg)

GRASS | POISON

WHISCASH

Height: 2'11" (0.9 m)
Weight: 52.0 lbs. (23.6 kg)

WATER | GROUND

WIGGLYTUFF

Height: 3'03" (1.0 m)
Weight: 26.5 lbs. (12.0 kg)

NORMAL | FAIRY

WOOPER

Height: 1'04" (0.4 m)
Weight: 18.7 lbs. (8.5 kg)

WATER | GROUND

XERNEAS
Height: 9'10" (3.0 m)
Weight: 474.0 lbs. (215.0 kg)

FAIRY

YVELTAL
Height: 19'00" (5.8 m)
Weight: 447.5 lbs. (203.0 kg)

DARK | FLYING

ZOROARK
Height: 5'03" (1.6 m)
Weight: 178.8 lbs. (81.1 kg)

DARK

ZORUA
Height: 2'04" (0.7 m)
Weight: 27.6 lbs. (12.5 kg)

DARK

ZWEILOUS
Height: 4'07" (1.4 m)
Weight: 110.2 lbs. (50.0 kg)

DARK | DRAGON

ZYGARDE
(50 PERCENT FORME)

Height: 16'05" (5.0 m)
Weight: 672.4 lbs. (305.0 kg)

DRAGON | GROUND

ALOLA

Alola means "sharing" and this friendly region is full of people who will share their food, stories, and adventures with you. Melemele Island has stunning beaches, beautiful forests, and warm seas teeming with life—and rare Pokémon! The region is made up of islands, such as Akala with its fiery Wela Volcano, and Poni Island with its ancient ruins, places of myth, and mystery. It's the perfect place for Ash's journey of discovery to continue.

THE POKÉMON SCHOOL

Ash's holiday in Alola turns into a great adventure when his mom enrolls him into the Pokémon school. Headmaster Samson Oak runs the school, and is rarely seen without his Pokémon Komala which spends its whole life asleep! Samson loves to speak in Pokémon puns, so "Bewear" his sense of humor! Ash's teacher is Professor Kukui, who has a secret life as a famous masked wrestler. Kukui lets Ash and Pikachu live in his home.

SCHOOL EVENTS

Life at the school is never just about studying in class, there's a whole host of games and challenges to get everyone learning by doing. There's the annual pancake race, Pokémon dancing, and fun events like a trip to a pop concert to see DJ Leo and his Dugtrio. Famous Alolan personalities visit the school like top Pokémon Base player, Uloulo. Field trips are a regular part of the curriculum. Ash and his pals went on a field trip to Akala Island where they joined in the Fire Festival. They even saved the famous Wela Crown after it had been taken by Marowak, a feisty Pokémon who was then collected by Kiawé. A camping trip to a creepy forest was also a great way to bond and face cool challenges like finding all the ingredients for a classic Alolan stew.

POKÉ CLASS

Professor Kukui makes sure every day is full of interest with his offbeat approach to teaching. There is little studying of textbooks, as pupils face intriguing tests and challenges. For example, Lillie was given a rare Poké egg to look after, to help her overcome her fear of touching Pokémon. It emerged as an Ice-type Vulpix called Snowy, and they became best friends. Another class challenge was Kukui's project to make the students swap their Pokémon. Ash was given Snowy, and Lillie received Pikachu in return. This helped the students appreciate the strengths and weaknesses of their friends' Pokémon. Harder for Ash than a duel was having to speak in front of the class and explain what he had learned. A little help from the all-knowing Rotomdex helped him through.

Z-MOVES

The most exciting thing about becoming a Pokémon Trainer in the Alola region is the discovery of Z-Moves. These allow the Trainer to achieve a whole new level of power. To perform a Z-Move, you need to have a Z-Ring. Ash is given one by Alola's island deity, Tapu Koko. Z-Rings contain Z-Crystals that come in many types. An Electric-type can unleash the Gigavolt Havoc attack. A Water-type Z-Crystal can unlock Hydro Vortex and Rock-type can produce the earth-shattering Continental Crush!

ASH'S ISLAND TRIALS

To use Z-Moves, a Pokémon Trainer must pass the Island Challenge, by beating the island Kahunas in a series of duels. On Melemele island, Ash faced Kahuna Hala in a duel at the Ruins of Conflict. Here, Ash learned that in Z-Moves the Trainer and Pokémon become one. Ash won the battle and Hala gave him a Fightinium Z-Crystal. Tapu Koko also gave him an Electrium-type Crystal, so he could perform Electric-Moves with Pikachu.

Ash's next challenge was with Olivia, the Akala Island Kahuna. They dueled at the Ruins of Life, the shrine of Tapu Lele. Using his Pokémon Rowlet and Rockruff, Ash won the duel and Olivia presented him with a Rockium-Z, a Rock-type Z-Crystal he could use with Rockruff to unlock great moves like Continental Crush.

Ash's next challenge was on Ula'ula Island, where he met the grouchy Kahuna, Nanu. Nanu, also the local cop, liked a quiet life and pretended at first he was not the Kahuna. When Ash kept pestering him, he beat Ash in a duel and said he was not ready for the trial. Ash stayed on and trained. Here he became friends with Acerola, Nanu's niece, and she helped him set up a new challenge. Ash beat Team Rocket in a pre-trial battle, in which Pikachu defeated Mimikyu by producing a ten million volt thunderbolt! In his rematch with Nanu, Ash used Continental Crush to beat Nanu's Black Hole Eclipse. He won the duel and Nanu gave him a Lycanium-Z Crystal for moves with Lycanroc.

Gladion, Lillie's brother, used the Z-Move Continental Crush to send Team Rocket blasting off again.

Ash and Pikachu used the Z-Move Gigavolt Havoc in his gym battle against Misty when he visited Kanto.

Lana and Popplio used the Z-Move Hydro Vortex when sharing power with Necrozma.

THE ISLANDS OF ALOLA

The Alola region isn't one big land mass, it's a fascinating and beautiful area made up of four different islands, each one with its own special Pokémon and claims to fame. Ash is based on Melemele Island, but his adventures take him to many exotic places.

MELEMELE

The main island of the Alola region, sunny, tropical Melemele is a popular holiday resort. It has the biggest shopping mall, the largest street markets, and the greatest sports arenas. It is also a land of lush forests and boasts miles of golden beaches. Once there, it's a tough place to leave, as Ash would agree!

ULA'ULA

This pretty island is home to the spectacular Ruins of Abundance. It is also the site of Mount Lanakila, Alola's highest peak. The Sitrus berries that grow here are famous for restoring strength.

AKALA ISLAND

Famed for its fiery Wela Volcano, this island is home to a proud and passionate people. Its volcanic soil is rich and fertile, making it the perfect place for farming and producing delicious Moomoo Milk! Every year at the Fire Festival, the Island Kahuna awards special Pokémon the Volcano Crown, which increases their power.

PONI ISLAND

Full of a sense of enchantment and the atmosphere of ancient days, this island is home to the Altar of the Sunne, the vast area of ruined temples that once were the site of an ancient battle between the Island Guardians and the Ultra Beasts. The Island Totems come here when they need to summon the Legendary Pokémon, Solgaleo. This island appeared to Ash in a dream about the Legendary Pokémon, Solgaleo, and so, even on his first visit, it was familiar to him.

ISLAND TOTEMS

These remarkable beings are known as Island Guardians. They have protected the Alola region for untold ages, uniting in times of trouble to focus their powers through the Altar of the Sunne. If a stranger of great potential visits, like Ash, the totems will guide him. In unusual cases they will even give a Z-Ring to a chosen Trainer to help them become even more powerful. They are curious, swift to reward and to punish!

TAPU KOKO

Height	5'11" (1.8 m)
Weight	42.2 lbs (20.5 kg)
Category	Land Spirit
Type	Electric Fairy

TAPU LELE

Height	3'11" (1.2 m)
Weight	41.0 lbs (18.6 kg)
Category	Land Spirit
Type	Psychic Fairy

TAPU BULU

Height	6'03" (1.9 m)
Weight	100.3 lbs (45.5 kg)
Category	Land Spirit
Type	Grass Fairy

TAPU FINI

Height	4'03" (1.3 m)
Weight	47.7 lbs (21.2 kg)
Category	Land Spirit
Type	Water Fairy

ISLAND KAHUNAS

These island leaders are preservers of tradition. They live to serve the island and its people, officiating at festivals. Only an Island Kahuna can take a Pokémon Trainer through the island trials to gain their Z-Ring, and master Z-Moves.

HALA

Hala is the Kahuna of Melemele Island. Shrewd and experienced, he tests the wisdom of young Trainers before letting them take the island challenge.

OLIVIA

Olivia is the Kahuna of Akala Island. Quick to laugh or cry, she is full of emotion—and rather clumsy!

NANU

Nanu is the Kahuna of Ula'ula Island. Keen for a quiet life he likes to avoid his duties, but can be kind-hearted, too.

DELICACIES OF THE REGION

Life in Alola is all about sharing, and nothing sums that up more than Alolans' attitude toward food. Alolans express their friendship by offering snacks and even feasts to visitors. Sold from street stalls, Alolan treats will have visitors coming back time after time.

MALASADA

These sweet treats are a kind of doughnut, one of the most popular items in the region. Team Rocket even take to selling their own brand.

ALOLAN STEW

This traditional spicy dish can be very hot, so beware! A special yellow nectar, loved by Orocorio Pokémon is needed for the perfect recipe.

KIAWE'S MOOMOO MILK ICE CREAM

Moomoo Milk is a popular refreshing drink of Alola, and it can be turned into yummy ice cream. Ash and Sophocles love Kiawé's family ice cream the best.

ASH'S ALOLA FRIENDS

Ash makes friends wherever he goes with his big heart, reckless courage, and touching affection for Pikachu. Ash knows that sometimes the people that tease and test you first of all make the best pals later. Even an enemy can become a pal! Whether they are Pokémon or human, every new friend brings new adventure, new challenges, and new kinds of fun.

KIAWE

Brave-hearted and skilled in Z-Moves, Kiawe has a warrior spirit. He works on his family farm on Akala Island, and does daily Moomoo Milk deliveries. His Pokémon is Turtonator.

LANA

A lover of the sea, Lana likes to spend time on the beach with her Pokémon Popplio. She is very fond of Ash but hates it when her sisters say Ash is her boyfriend!

LILLIE

Studious and kind, Lillie struggled to touch Pokémon for a long time. Sometimes testy with her work-obsessed mother, she lives in a mansion with her butler Hobbes and Snowy, her Pokémon.

MALLOW

A keen chef, Mallow works at Aina's Kitchen, her family restaurant where the gang love to hang out. Her Pokémon is Bounsweet who evolves into Steenee then Tsareena.

SOPHOCLES

Crazy about gadgets, Sophocles sometimes gets his Pokémon Togedemaru to power his computer. Sophocles is a frank talker and occasionally puts his foot in it with his pals.

MALLOW

LANA

KIAWE

LILLIE

SOPHOCLES

ASH'S ALOLA FOES

Where there is sun there are always shadows, and the beauty of Alola attracts the bad guys as well as the good. Giovanni, the boss of Team Rocket sends his agents in search of Pokémon the likes of which have never been collected before. Naturally, Ash and his friends will have to cope with their crazy antics along the way, and some other unfriendly faces, too.

TEAM ROCKET

Jessie thinks she is a Flower of Evil and James claims to be a Master of Darkness. In fact they are rather prone to blasting off in defeat. In Alola, however, they gain a Z-Ring and discover a rare Meowth. Plus, they sell doughnuts on the street!

TEAM ROCKET POKÉMON

MEOWTH

A cool cat that aims high. Sadly, its masters always bring it low. A rare talking Pokémon.

WOBBUFFET

A Psychic-type, that does nothing but shout its name. Wobbuffet is enthusiastic company and never complains.

MIMIKYU

Mimikyu frightens Meowth with scary talk and hates Pikachu. A Ghost- and Fairy-type, it is tough in a fight!

MAREANIE

A Poison- and Water-type, Mareanie has fallen in love with James and loves to give his head an adoring squeeze.

BEWEAR

This strong-armed Pokémon adopts Team Rocket and keeps making them blast off back to its lair!

TEAM SKULL

A gang of troublemakers. Their leader is Tupp. Rapp is the one with pink hair and Zipp just agrees with Tupp all the time.

VIREN

The boss of Rainbow Happy Resorts is known as Mr. Greedy-Creep by Ash. He runs the cheating Revengers wrestling team.

AETHER PARADISE

This man-made island is a research center for the protection and rearing of Pokémon. Here, Pokémon of every type are studied by scientists from all over the world. The center features a conservation area, and re-creations of every environment that Pokémon are found in, to make them feel at home. Equally, every care is taken to put its human occupants at ease, with labs, libraries, and rest and relaxation facilities of every kind. A resource for everyone in Alola, its doors are always open to students and Trainers of Pokémon to share the wealth of knowledge accumulated there.

THE AETHER FOUNDATION

This sophisticated organization spares no expense in assembling the greatest minds and the most advanced technology to learn all there is to know about Pokémon. But there is a more secretive side to their work, investigating the mysterious creatures known as Ultra Beasts, and the wormholes in the fabric of reality that they travel through. Four years ago, the Ultra Beast known as the UB01 Symbiont appeared here. As so little is known of these creatures, the Foundation developed anti Ultra-Beast Pokémon to defend against them. The Synthetic Pokémon, Type: Null, was created for this purpose, evolving into Gladion's Pokémon, Silvally.

PROFESSOR BURNET

An outgoing personality, Professor Burnet is a top wormhole expert. Married to Prof. Kukui, her research skills make her vital to the mission to understand Ultra Beasts.

LUSAMINE

Lillie's mother is the head of the Foundation and leads the emergency response to Ultra Beasts. A driven personality, she is rarely off her phone.

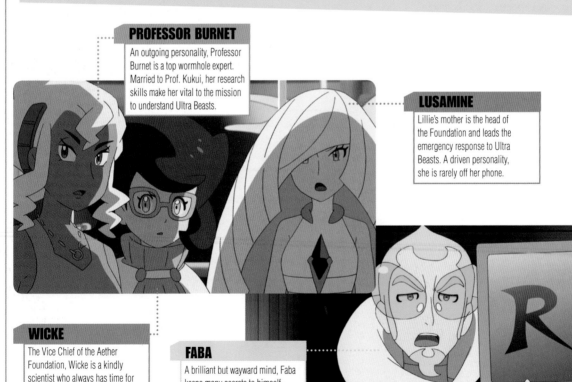

WICKE

The Vice Chief of the Aether Foundation, Wicke is a kindly scientist who always has time for everyone. She gives tours to visiting students.

FABA

A brilliant but wayward mind, Faba keeps many secrets to himself. Ambitious, he will do anything to further his research, even if it means putting others in peril.

ULTRA CRISES

The scientists at the Aether Foundation dealt with a series of incredible events when Ultra Beasts started to visit Alola. Years before, in his experiments with wormholes, Faba summoned the UB Symbiont that scared Lillie and made her unable to touch Pokémon. Later, when Faba sought to impress his boss Lusamine by summoning another UB Symbiont, it carried her away through the wormhole.

Nebby's power fascinated Faba.

To save Lusamine, Ash and his friends traveled to the Altar of the Sunne. Here, Nebby evolved into Solgaleo and carried Ash and his friends through the wormhole. They soon found that the UB symbiont was trying to merge with Lusamine. Lillie warned her mother that the Ultra Beast would turn her into a weak puppet. Her voice reached Lusamine who broke free and returned home.

Faba opened a wormhole to the UB realm.

Lusamine was taken by the Symbiont.

Ash was amazed when Nebby evolved into Solgaleo.

ASH'S DREAM

It was the Aether Foundation scientists who first realized the importance of "Nebby," and that it was an Ultra Beast of some kind. The whole incredible saga began with Ash's mysterious dream, in which he and Pikachu were exploring the ancient ruins of the Altar of the Sunne on Poni Island. This was the site of a mythical battle between Legendary Pokémon and Ultra Beasts. In the dream, two wormholes opened and Solgaleo and Lunala appeared. Ash made them a promise that he could not remember when he woke up. The next day, while walking in the forest, Ash discovered a tiny, nebula-like, creature, unknown to Rotomdex's database. Now he remembered he had promised to find this creature. Lillie called the creature Nebby. Ash did not then know that Nebby was in fact Cosmog, the early form of Solgaleo, and he had a baby legend in his hands.

LEGENDARY BATTLE

The knowledge of the Aether Foundation was crucial in the crisis at the time of the Total Eclipse, when The Blinding One, also known as the Legendary Pokémon Necrozma, came to Alola, seeking energy. An Ultra Wormhole appeared in the sky and the Legendary Pokémon, Lunala came through, pursued by Necrozma. When it attacked, Lunala responded with Phantom Force. It emerged that Necrozma could shatter into pieces then surround an opponent to drain their energy. When Solgaleo came to help Lunala, Necrozma drained Solgaleo's power before vanishing back through the wormhole. With the resources of the Aether Foundation, the Ultra Guardians managed to revive Lunala. Traveling through the wormhole to rescue Solgaleo, the Guardians learned from the Ultra Beast Naganadel that they had to share energy with Necrozma, to restore his power as the Blinding One and save their realm.

ULTRA BEASTS: EARLY ENCOUNTERS

BUZZWOLE

The first wave of Ultra Beasts provided many surprises for Ash and the Ultra Guardians. Buzzwole showed incredible strength when it tangled with Bewear, who took Team 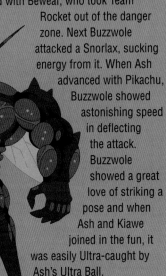 Rocket out of the danger zone. Next Buzzwole attacked a Snorlax, sucking energy from it. When Ash advanced with Pikachu, Buzzwole showed astonishing speed in deflecting the attack. Buzzwole showed a great love of striking a pose and when Ash and Kiawe joined in the fun, it was easily Ultra-caught by Ash's Ultra Ball.

STAKATAKA

A building development by Ash's old enemy Mr. Greedy-Creep (that's Viren to everyone else) was the site of another Ultra Beast event. Stakataka, with its wall-like appearance was mistaken for a plinth by some of Viren's workers, and they put his statue on it. Big mistake! Stakataka hates anything being put on top of it. Ash managed to tame the Ultra Beast by riding it out, like a bucking bronco.

POIPOLE

This creature was a source of great mystery when it first arrived in Alola and was befriended by Pikachu. Team Rocket tried to steal it, as James classified it as super-duper rare. Although pink and twirly, Poipole proved a dangerous opponent with the poison it could squirt from its tail. Rowlet had to be revived with Full Restore spray by Lillie, after Poipole mistook it for an enemy. Even Rotomdex had no data on it. Lusamine soon revealed that Poipole was an Ultra Beast and called it a Poison Pin Pokémon. Poipole loves pranks like pulling an Exeggutor's tail, or popping a Dewpider's bubble.

CELESTEELA

Sophocles stumbled across this rocket-like creature while in the forest. He believed that like the moon-being Celeste in his favorite fairy tale, it just wanted to get home. Lusamine revealed that Celesteela was a Launch- and Flying-type Ultra Beast. As it was a rocket, Team Rocket tried to catch it, but its blast-power on takeoff was too much for them.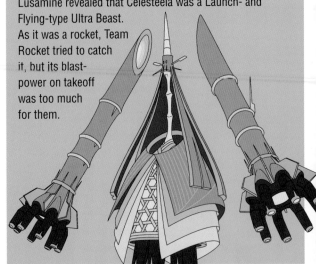

REALM OF THE ULTRA BEASTS

On the other side of the wormhole is a cold, dark realm filled with unusual creatures like the UB Symbionts and Poipole. This place of barren rocks, dark chasms, and bleak crags, was once a beautiful and fertile land, filled with flowers and trees, all basking in the light of the Blinding One. Then one dark day, a meteor struck Necrozma and it fell, damaged, to the ground. The Ultra Beasts were forced to live on the little light that remained, hoping that one day the Blinding One would rise again. Thanks to the Ultra Guardians and all the people of Alola, that day finally arrived.

ULTRA WORMHOLES

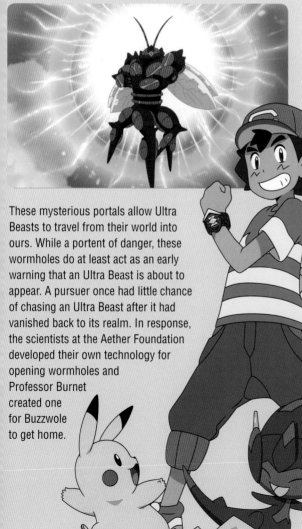

These mysterious portals allow Ultra Beasts to travel from their world into ours. While a portent of danger, these wormholes do at least act as an early warning that an Ultra Beast is about to appear. A pursuer once had little chance of chasing an Ultra Beast after it had vanished back to its realm. In response, the scientists at the Aether Foundation developed their own technology for opening wormholes and Professor Burnet created one for Buzzwole to get home.

ASH AND POIPOLE

This little Ultra Beast was a puzzle to Ash and his friends as its story slowly unfolded. Poipole was a flighty creature, very affectionate to Pikachu, but often playing tricks on others. It seemed grumpy once when Ash refused to let it have his Z-Ring. No one understood its strange moods. One talent it had was that of painting, and it showed by the cool images it created just how much it loved its new home. But there was a troubled side to Poipole. One night it had a dark dream and the next day created a big painting of the Blinding One on a ceiling at the school. When the local artist, Mina, saw Poipole's pictures she said they revealed that it was sad and carrying a big mission. Later, when Necrozma appeared, it could be seen that a symbol on the Legendary Pokémon was the same as one in Poipole's paintings. The little Ultra Beast was connected to the great myths of Alola! Ash and the gang later learned that Poipole was sent by one of its evolved form, Naganadel, from the land of the Ultra Beasts to seek help in the realm of Alola, as the home of the Ultra Beasts was dying.

THE ULTRA GUARDIANS

The menace from the Ultra Beasts became more serious when Lusamine was taken into their realm by the UB Symbiont, and had to be rescued by Ash and his friends. After this, Lusamine asked the gang to become Ultra Guardians. This gave them a new task, to be ready to race into action at any moment and protect Alola from Ultra Beasts.

ULTRA GEAR

The Aether Foundation provides the team with all they need. Sleek costumes, each in a signature color, appear when the team descend into the base. Ash, of course, likes to keep his favorite cap! Beast Balls have been developed to catch Ultra Beasts, and the spray, Full Restore, is ready to heal and revive. All guardians must say 'Ult-roger!' in response to commands.

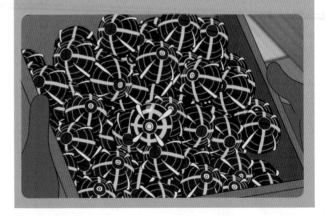

ULTRA BASE

To make the Ultra Guardians' operation as efficient as possible, the Aether Foundation partnered with the school to create a secret base beneath the school site. The high-tech headquarters contains a communications hub with a central screen for speaking to Lusamine in an emergency. There are also resources for keeping and studying Ultra Beasts, like the lab where they helped heal Lunala after the battle with Necrozma, and Z-Ring power restored the Legendary Pokémon to life.

RIDE POKÉMON

In the Alola region, all transport is carried out by Ride Pokémon, as Ash discovered when he was on vacation at the start of his stay, cruising through the waves on his personal watercraft, Sharpedo. The Ultra Guardians are all given their own Ride Pokémon to fly them into action whenever an Ultra Beast appears. Ash rides Garchomp, Lillie has Altaria, Sophocles rides Metang, Mallow's steed is Flygon, and Lana has Dragonair. These creatures are incredibly brave and will take their rider into any battle no matter how dangerous.

The Aether Foundation truly values the service of these Pokémon, and sent them to the Pokémon Paradise resort for rest and recuperation in the hot springs after many stressful adventures. At the resort, sneaky Team Rocket tried to catch the Ride Pokémon, but the creatures showed their worth by fighting back as a team and foiling Jessie and James. The Pokémon and their riders celebrated the victory with a luxurious flower bath.

Fully restored, these steeds also showed their bravery in the dramatic battle between the Legendary Pokémon, Solgaleo and Lunala, with Necrozma. In this battle, Lillie fell from Altaria, but was saved by Lunala. The Ride Pokémon took the Ultra Guardians through a wormhole into the realm of the Ultra Beasts when the time came to save Solgaleo and solve the mystery of the Blinding One.

THE ECLIPSE

The Ultra Guardians' greatest challenge came at the time of the first total solar eclipse in twenty-one years. This gave rise to a ceremony of thanksgiving, the Manola festival, which means "you and I, living here together." The Alolan kahunas visited the ruins on their islands to show gratitude to the Legendary Pokémon that created Alola. At this time, all adults grew mysteriously tired, as the Ultra-aura around the islands weakened, with the coming of Necrozma.

POKÉ SPORTS

The Alola region is known for its love of sports, with Pokémon joining in everything from wrestling to baseball. These events create sports heroes who are famous across the region. Ash and his pals are quick to join in and make quite an impression on the athletic scene.

POKÉBASE

When Ash saw baseball played with Pokémon on TV he was excited to give it a try. The top team in the Pro League were the Magikings, and their top batter, Oluolu, was from Alola. The class was thrilled when Oluolu came to teach the sport, using a special three-a-side team game.

WRESTLING

The Battle Royal Dome is the place to see wrestling contests. Alola's top star is The Masked Royal, with his Pokémon partner, Incineroar. They are seen in battles against foes like Mad Magmar, and the team that like to bend the rules, The Revengers. Ash has become a star, too, with Litten, who also evolved into Incineroar, as his partner. The Masked Royal named his young ally "Ash Royal," but Ash never guessed the Masked Royal was Professor Kukui!

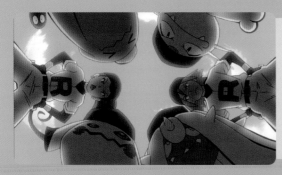

Match between the school and Team Rocket

When team Rocket showed up, Ash assumed they were there to steal Pokémon. In fact, Jessie announced they were in fact there to get Uloulo's autograph, as she was a mega fan. Ash and his friends had their eyes on that, too, so Uloulo suggested a match to decide who won the prize. He helped the school team, with his Pokémon, Snorlax.

Pulling out the Pokémon base pepper

The match turned out to be a thrilling one, as Meowth had a hidden talent as a baseball pitcher. Also, Team Rocket saw a great advantage in that fact that Uloulo's Pokémon did not seem at all motivated, and, in fact, barely moved at all. In a crucial final play, Uloulo used his Z-Ring to produce Snorlax's Pulverizing Pancake move and crash safely home, winning the game. Kindly Uloulo let Team Rocket have his autograph anyway.

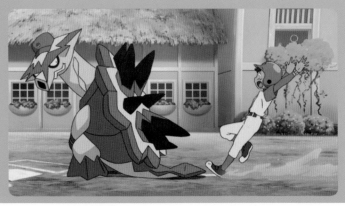

CHARJABUG RACES

Sophocles is crazy about Charjabug racing, and he wanted to enter the 25th Annual Koko Cup at the vast race stadium. Three were needed for the team, so Sophocles was director, Kiawé was mechanic, and Ash was support runner.

The race took place over three terrains: rock, desert, and ice. Team Rocket entered, but were disqualified when it emerged their Charjabug was Meowth in disguise. The Sophocles Lab team defeated the arrogant team Red Comet when they used String Shot to get traction on the ice, and left their rivals standing.

POKÉMON SLED JUMPING

Ash and his pals entered the PokéSled Jump Tournament when they visited the highest peak in Alola, Mount Lanakila on Ula'ula Island. They were invited by top Sled Jumper, Cerah, who almost injured Lillie while practicing on the slopes. Cerah's Pokémon, Ninetales, saved Lillie from harm, and there was great interest in Ninetales' Aurora Veil move. On the day of the tournament, Cerah performed an exhibition jump, Ash broke the record for going backward and the winner was Kahuna Hala with Crabominable. Lillie and Snowy did not win but performed a perfect Aurora Veil.

ENTERTAINMENT

As well as sports, there is plenty of entertainment in Alola with pop concerts like the popular DJ Leo and Dugtrio, who just happen to be great friends with Prof Kukui. Poké Dance is a fun activity which is also studied at the school, where it helps develop the bond between Trainer and Pokémon. There are also cultural events like the Bread Festival and the Fire Festival.

The top TV show in Alola is Detective Laki, filmed at the TV studios on Melemele Island. This show is so compulsive it makes Rotomdex want to be a private eye and he often wears his Laki wig!

ALOLA LEGENDARY POKÉMON

SOLGALEO • (SOUL-gah-LAY-oh)

Height	11'02" (3.4 m)	Category	Sunne
Weight	507.1 lbs (230.0 kg)	Type	Psychic-Steel

Myth states that when the Blinding One created the islands of Alola the sun and moon became flesh—the sun becoming Solgaleo. This Pokémon is said to have torn open the sky to battle with Ultra Beasts at the Altar of the Sunne. Solgaleo appears first as a small Pokémon called Nebby, seeming as helpless as a baby.

LUNALA • (loo-NAH-luh)

Height	13'01" (4.0 m)	Category	Moone
Weight	264.6 lbs (120.0 kg)	Type	Psychic-Ghost

Just as Solgaleo is the sun, ancient legend says that Lunala is the moon made flesh. Its appearance embodies the beauty of the night. Like Solgaleo, Lunala can create Ultra Wormholes to travel from the realm of Ultra Beasts to the Alola region. A counterpart to Solgaleo, the pair work together to bring harmony and protect all living things.

NECROZMA • (neh-KROHZ-muh)
THE BLINDING ONE

Height	7'10" (2.4 m)	Category	Prism
Weight	507.1 lbs (230.0 kg)	Type	Psychic-Dragon

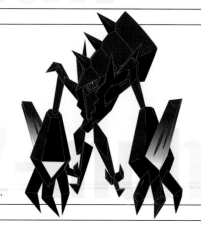

Known in Alolan legend as The Blinding One, Necrozma appeared in a time of darkness to bring light and life to the Alola region. With Solgaleo and Lunala it shone for days across land and sea. When Necrozma returned to Alola, draining power from Solgaleo, it was mistaken for an enemy. For a time it was known as "UB Black." Soon Ash and his friends realized that they should be helping it, not fighting it.

TYPE: NULL

Height	6'03" (1.9 m)	Category	Synthetic
Weight	265.7 lbs (120.5 kg)	Type	Null

Type: Null is a Synthetic Pokémon, created by the scientists at the Aether Foundation to combat the threat of Ultra Beasts. Its headgear restrains its power. When Faba kept it in chains, it was rescued by Gladion and evolved into Silvally.

Stats for Island Guardians on page 267

SILVALLY • (sill-VAL-lie)

Height	7'07" (2.3 m)	Category	Synthetic
Weight	221.6 lbs (100.5 kg)	Type	Normal

This Synthetic Pokémon was trained by Gladion to fight Ultra Beasts and proved effective against the UB Symbiont, Kommo-o and others. When Type: Null bonds with a loyal Trainer it destroys its own headgear to unleash more speed and power.

COSMOG • (KOZ-mog)

Height	0'08" (0.2 m)	Category	Nebula
Weight	0.2 lbs (0.1 kg)	Type	Psychic

Known as "Nebby" to Ash and his friends, this cute Pokémon turned out to be the unevolved form of Cosmoem and ultimately Solgaleo. In this form, Cosmog could teleport people to places they were thinking about.

ALOLA MYTHICAL POKÉMON

ZERAORA
• (ZEH-rah-OH-rah)

Height	4'11" (1.5 m)
Weight	98.1 lbs (44.5 kg)
Category	Thunderclap
Type	Electric

Any opponent faces a storm of power when Zeraora charges its claws with electricity. Its attack is lightning-fast and even the flying sparks it generates can shock you into submission.

MAGEARNA
• (muh-GEER-nuh)

Height	3'03" (1.0 m)
Weight	177.5 lbs (80.5 kg)
Category	Artificial
Type	Steel-Fairy

This Pokémon was constructed many centuries ago by a human scientist, giving it a mechanical body to house its Soul-Heart. It understands not just speech but also the ways of human emotion.

MARSHADOW
• (Mar-SHAD-oh)

Height	2'04" (0.7 m)
Weight	48.9 lbs (22.2 kg)
Category	Gloomdweller
Type	Fighting-Ghost

Slipping into the shadows of people and Pokémon, it is able to understand them. Starting out by mimicking others, it may grow to surpass them in power. Like most other Mythicals it cannot evolve.

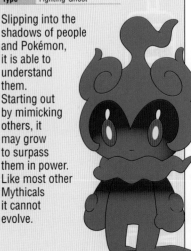

ABRA

Height: 2'11" (0.9 m)
Weight: 43.0 lbs. (19.5 kg)

PSYCHIC

ABSOL

Height: 3'11" (1.2 m)
Weight: 103.6 lbs. (47.0 kg)

DARK

AERODACTYL

Height: 5'11" (1.8 m)
Weight: 130.1 lbs. (59.0 kg)

ROCK | FLYING

AIPOM

Height: 2'07" (0.8 m)
Weight: 25.4 lbs. (11.5 kg)

NORMAL

ALAKAZAM

Height: 4'11" (1.5 m)
Weight: 105.8 lbs. (48.0 kg)

PSYCHIC

ALOLAN DIGLETT

Height: 0'08" (0.2 m)
Weight: 2.2 lbs. (1.0 kg)

GROUND | STEEL

ALOLAN DUGTRIO

Height: 2'04" (0.7 m)
Weight: 146.8 lbs. (66.6 kg)

GROUND | STEEL

ALOLAN EXEGGUTOR

Height: 35'09" (10.9 m)
Weight: 916.2 lbs. (415.6 kg)

GRASS | DRAGON

ALOLAN GEODUDE

Height: 1'04" (0.4 m)
Weight: 44.8 lbs. (20.3 kg)

ROCK | ELECTRIC

ALOLAN GOLEM

Height: 5'07" (1.7 m)
Weight: 661.4 lbs. (316.0 kg)

ROCK | ELECTRIC

ALOLAN GRAVELER

Height: 3'03" (1.0 m)
Weight: 242.5 lbs. (110.0 kg)

ROCK | ELECTRIC

ALOLAN GRIMER

Height: 2'04" (0.7 m)
Weight: 92.6 lbs. (42.0 kg)

POISON | DARK

ALOLAN MAROWAK

Height: 3'03" (1.0 m)
Weight: 75.0 lbs. (34.0 kg)

FIRE | GHOST

ALOLAN MEOWTH

Height: 1'04" (0.4 m)
Weight: 9.3 lbs. (4.2 kg)

DARK

ALOLAN MUK

Height: 3'03" (1.0 m)
Weight: 114.6 lbs. (52.0 kg)

POISON | DARK

ALOLAN NINETALES

Height: 3'07" (1.1 m)
Weight: 43.9 lbs. (19.9 kg)

ICE | FAIRY

ALOLAN PERSIAN

Height: 3'07" (1.1 m)
Weight: 72.8 lbs. (33.0 kg)

DARK

ALOLAN RAICHU

Height: 2'04" (0.7 m)
Weight: 46.3 lbs. (21.0 kg)

ELECTRIC | PSYCHIC

ALOLAN RATICATE

Height: 2'04" (0.7 m)
Weight: 56.2 lbs. (25.5 kg)

DARK | NORMAL

ALOLAN RATTATA

Height: 1'00" (0.3 m)
Weight: 8.4 lbs. (3.8 kg)

DARK | NORMAL

ALOLAN SANDSHREW

Height: 2'04" (0.7 m)
Weight: 88.2 lbs. (40.0 kg)

ICE | STEEL

ALOLAN SANDSLASH

Height: 3'11" (1.2 m)
Weight: 121.3 lbs. (55.0 kg)

ICE | STEEL

ALOLAN VULPIX

Height: 2'00" (0.6 m)
Weight: 21.8 lbs. (9.9 kg)

ICE

ALOMOMOLA

Height: 3'11" (1.2 m)
Weight: 69.7 lbs. (31.6 kg)

WATER

AMAURA

Height: 4'03" (1.3 m)
Weight: 55.6 lbs. (25.2 kg)

ROCK | ICE

AMBIPOM

Height: 3'11" (1.2 m)
Weight: 44.8 lbs. (20.3 kg)
NORMAL

AMPHAROS

Height: 4'07'' (1.4 m)
Weight: 135.6 lbs. (61.5 kg)
ELECTRIC

ANORITH

Height: 2'04" (0.7 m)
Weight: 27.6 lbs. (12.5 kg)
ROCK | BUG

ARAQUANID
Height: 5'11" (1.8 m)
Weight: 180.8 lbs. (82.0 kg)
WATER | BUG

ARBOK

Height: 11'06" (3.5 m)
Weight: 143.3 lbs. (65.0 kg)
POISON

ARCANINE

Height: 6'03" (1.9 m)
Weight: 341.7 lbs. (155.0 kg)
FIRE

ARCHEN

Height: 1'08" (0.5 m)
Weight: 20.9 lbs. (9.5 kg)
ROCK | FLYING

ARCHEOPS

Height: 4'07" (1.4 m)
Weight: 70.5 lbs. (32.0 kg)
ROCK | FLYING

ARIADOS
Height: 3'07" (1.1 m)
Weight: 73.9 lbs. (33.5 kg)
BUG | POISON

ARMALDO

Height: 4' 11" (1.5 m)
Weight: 150.4 lbs. (68.2 kg)
ROCK | BUG

AURORUS

Height: 8'10" (2.7 m)
Weight: 496.0 lbs. (225.0 kg)
ROCK | ICE

BAGON

Height: 2'00" (0.6 m)
Weight: 92.8 lbs. (42.1 kg)
DRAGON

BALTOY

Height: 1'08" (0.5 m)
Weight: 47.4 lbs. (21.5 kg)
GROUND | PSYCHIC

BANETTE

Height: 3'07" (1.1 m)
Weight: 27.6 lbs. (12.5 kg)
GHOST

BARBOACH

Height: 1'04" (0.4 m)
Weight: 4.2 lbs. (1.9 kg)
WATER | GROUND

BASCULIN
Height: 3'03" (1.0 m)
Weight: 39.7 lbs. (18.0 kg)
WATER

BASTIODON
Height: 4'03" (1.3 m)
Weight: 329.6 lbs. (149.5 kg)
ROCK | STEEL

BEHEEYEM
Height: 3'03" (1.0 m)
Weight: 76.1 lbs. (34.5 kg)
PSYCHIC

BELDUM
Height: 2'00" (0.6 m)
Weight: 209.9 lbs. (95.2 kg)
STEEL | PSYCHIC

BEWEAR
Height: 6'11" (2.1 m)
Weight: 297.6 lbs. (135.0 kg)
NORMAL | FIGHTING

BISHARP

Height: 5'03" (1.6 m)
Weight: 154.3 lbs. (70.0 kg)
DARK | STEEL

BLACEPHALON

Height: 5'11" (1.8 m)
Weight: 28.7 lbs. (13.0 kg)
FIRE | GHOST

BLISSEY

Height: 4'11" (1.5 m)
Weight: 103.2 lbs. (46.8 kg)
NORMAL

BOLDORE

Height: 2'11" (0.9 m)
Weight: 224.9 lbs. (102.0 kg)
ROCK

BONSLY

Height: 1'08" (0.5 m)
Weight: 33.1 lbs. (15.0 kg)
ROCK

BOUNSWEET

Height: 1'00" (0.3 m)
Weight: 7.1 lbs. (3.2 kg)

GRASS

BRAVIARY

Height: 4'11" (1.5 m)
Weight: 90.4 lbs. (41.0 kg)

NORMAL   FLYING

BRIONNE

Height: 2'00" (0.6 m)
Weight: 38.6 lbs. (17.5 kg)

WATER

BRUXISH

Height: 2'11" (0.9 m)
Weight: 41.9 lbs. (19.0 kg)

WATER   PSYCHIC

BUNEARY

Height: 1'04" (0.4 m)
Weight: 12.1 lbs. (5.5 kg)

NORMAL

BUTTERFREE

Height: 3'07" (1.1 m)
Weight: 70.5 lbs. (32.0 kg)

BUG   FLYING

BUZZWOLE

Height: 7'10" (2.4 m)
Weight: 735.5 lbs. (333.6 kg)

BUG   FIGHTING

CARBINK

Height: 1'00" (0.3 m)
Weight: 12.6 lbs. (5.7 kg)

ROCK   FAIRY

CARRACOSTA

Height: 3'11" (1.2 m)
Weight: 178.6 lbs. (81.0 kg)

WATER   ROCK

CARVANHA

Height: 2'07" (0.8 m)
Weight: 45.9 lbs. (20.8 kg)

WATER   DARK

CASTFORM

Height: 1'00" (0.3 m)
Weight: 1.8 lbs. (0.8 kg)

NORMAL

CATERPIE

Height: 1'00" (0.3 m)
Weight: 6.4 lbs. (2.9 kg)

BUG

CELESTEELA

Height: 30'02" (9.2 m)
Weight: 2204.4 lbs. (999.9 kg)

STEEL   FLYING

CHANSEY

Height: 3'07" (1.1 m)
Weight: 76.3 lbs. (34.6 kg)

NORMAL

CHARJABUG

Height: 1'08" (0.5 m)
Weight: 23.1 lbs. (10.5 kg)

BUG   ELECTRIC

CHINCHOU

Height: 1'08" (0.5 m)
Weight: 26.5 lbs. (12.0 kg)

WATER   ELECTRIC

CINCCINO

Height: 1'08" (0.5 m)
Weight: 16.5 lbs. (7.5 kg)

NORMAL

CLAMPERL

Height: 1'04" (0.4 m)
Weight: 115.7 lbs. (52.5 kg)

WATER

CLAUNCHER

Height: 1'08" (0.5 m)
Weight: 18.3 lbs. (8.3 kg)

WATER

CLAWITZER

Height: 4'03" (1.3 m)
Weight: 77.8 lbs. (35.3 kg)

WATER

CLAYDOL

Height: 4'11" (1.5 m)
Weight: 238.1 lbs. (108.0 kg)

GROUND   PSYCHIC

CLEFABLE

Height: 4'03" (1.3 m)
Weight: 88.2 lbs. (40.0 kg)

FAIRY

CLEFAIRY

Height: 2'00" (0.6 m)
Weight: 16.5 lbs. (7.5 kg)

FAIRY

CLEFFA

Height: 1'00" (0.3 m)
Weight: 6.6 lbs. (3.0 kg)

FAIRY

CLOYSTER

Height: 4'11" (1.5 m)
Weight: 292.1 lbs. (132.5 kg)

WATER   ICE

COMFEY

Height: 0'04" (0.1 m)
Weight: 0.7 lbs. (0.3 kg)

FAIRY

CORPHISH

Height: 2'00" (0.6 m)
Weight: 25.4 lbs. (11.5 kg)

WATER

CORSOLA

Height: 2'00" (0.6 m)
Weight: 11.0 lbs. (5.0 kg)

WATER   ROCK

COSMOEM

Height: 0'04" (0.1 m)
Weight: 2204.4 lbs. (999.9 kg)

PSYCHIC

COSMOG

Height: 0'08" (0.2 m)
Weight: 0.2 lbs. (0.1 kg)

PSYCHIC

COTTONEE

Height: 1'00" (0.3 m)
Weight: 1.3 lbs. (0.6 kg)

GRASS   FAIRY

CRABOMINABLE

Height: 5'07" (1.7 m)
Weight: 396.8 lbs. (180.0 kg)

FIGHTING   ICE

CRABRAWLER

Height: 2'00" (0.6 m)
Weight: 15.4 lbs. (7.0 kg)

FIGHTING

CRADILY

Height: 4'11" (1.5 m)
Weight: 133.2 lbs. (60.4 kg)

ROCK   GRASS

CRANIDOS
Height: 2'11" (0.9 m)
Weight: 69.4 lbs. (31.5 kg)

ROCK

CRAWDAUNT

Height: 3'07" (1.1 m)
Weight: 72.3 lbs. (32.8 kg)

WATER   DARK

CROBAT

Height: 5'11" (1.8 m)
Weight: 165.3 lbs. (75.0 kg)

POISON   FLYING

CUBONE

Height: 1'04" (0.4 m)
Weight: 14.3 lbs. (6.5 kg)

GROUND

CUTIEFLY

Height: 0'04" (0.1 m)
Weight: 0.4 lbs. (0.2 kg)

BUG   FAIRY

DARTRIX

Height: 2'04" (0.7 m)
Weight: 35.3 lbs. (16.0 kg)

GRASS   FLYING

DECIDUEYE

Height: 5'03" (1.6 m)
Weight: 80.7 lbs. (36.6 kg)

GRASS   GHOST

DEDENNE

Height: 0'08" (0.2 m)
Weight: 4.9 lbs. (2.2 kg)

ELECTRIC   FAIRY

DELIBIRD

Height: 2'11" (0.9 m)
Weight: 35.3 lbs. (16.0 kg)

ICE   FLYING

DEWGONG

Height: 5'07" (1.7 m)
Weight: 264.6 lbs. (120.0 kg)

WATER   ICE

DEWPIDER

Height: 1'00" (0.3 m)
Weight: 8.8 lbs. (4.0 kg)

WATER   BUG

DHELMISE

Height: 12'10" (3.9 m)
Weight: 463.0 lbs. (210.0 kg)

GHOST   GRASS

DITTO

Height: 1'00" (0.3 m)
Weight: 8.8 lbs. (4.0 kg)

NORMAL

DRAGALGE

Height: 5'11" (1.8 m)
Weight: 179.7 lbs. (81.5 kg)

POISON   DRAGON

DRAGONAIR
Height: 13'01" (4.0 m)
Weight: 36.4 lbs. (16.5 kg)

DRAGON

DRAGONITE

Height: 7'03" (2.2 m)
Weight: 463.0 lbs. (210.0 kg)

DRAGON   FLYING

DRAMPA

Height: 9'10" (3.0 m)
Weight: 407.9 lbs. (185.0 kg)

NORMAL   DRAGON

DRATINI

Height: 5'11" (1.8 m)
Weight: 7.3 lbs. (3.3 kg)

DRAGON

DRIFBLIM

Height: 3'11" (1.2 m)
Weight: 33.1 lbs. (15.0 kg)

GHOST   FLYING

DRIFLOON

Height: 1'04" (0.4 m)
Weight: 2.6 lbs. (1.2 kg)

GHOST   FLYING

DROWZEE

Height: 3'03" (1.0 m)
Weight: 71.4 lbs. (32.4 kg)

PSYCHIC

DRUDDIGON

Height: 5'03" (1.6 m)
Weight: 306.4 lbs. (139.0 kg)

DRAGON

DUNSPARCE

Height: 4'11" (1.5 m)
Weight: 30.9 lbs. (14.0 kg)

NORMAL

EEVEE

Height: 1'00" (0.3 m)
Weight: 14.3 lbs. (6.5 kg)

NORMAL

EKANS

Height: 6'07" (2.0 m)
Weight: 15.2 lbs. (6.9 kg)

POISON

ELECTABUZZ

Height: 3'07" (1.1 m)
Weight: 66.1 lbs. (30.0 kg)

ELECTRIC

ELECTIVIRE

Height: 5'11" (1.8 m)
Weight: 305.6 lbs. (138.6 kg)

ELECTRIC

ELECTRIKE

Height: 2' 00'' (0.6 m)
Weight: 33.5 lbs. (15.2 kg)

ELECTRIC

ELEKID

Height: 2'00" (0.6 m)
Weight: 51.8 lbs. (23.5 kg)

ELECTRIC

ELGYEM

Height: 1'08" (0.5 m)
Weight: 19.8 lbs. (9.0 kg)

PSYCHIC

EMOLGA

Height: 1'04'' (0.4 m)
Weight: 11.0 lbs. (5.0 kg)

ELECTRIC   FLYING

ESPEON

Height: 2'11" (0.9 m)
Weight: 58.4 lbs. (26.5 kg)

PSYCHIC

EXEGGCUTE

Height: 1'04" (0.4 m)
Weight: 5.5 lbs. (2.5 kg)

GRASS   PSYCHIC

EXEGGUTOR

Height: 6'07" (2.0 m)
Weight: 264.6 lbs. (120.0 kg)

GRASS   PSYCHIC

FEAROW

Height: 3'11" (1.2 m)
Weight: 83.8 lbs. (38.0 kg)

NORMAL   FLYING

FEEBAS

Height: 2'00" (0.6 m)
Weight: 16.3 lbs. (7.4 kg)

WATER

FINNEON

Height: 1'04" (0.4 m)
Weight: 15.4 lbs. (7.0 kg)

WATER

FLAAFFY

Height: 2'07" (0.8 m)
Weight: 29.3 lbs. (13.3 kg)

ELECTRIC

FLABÉBÉ

Height: 0'04" (0.1 m)
Weight: 0.2 lbs. (0.1 kg)

FAIRY

FLAREON

Height: 2'11" (0.9 m)
Weight: 55.1 lbs. (25.0 kg)

FIRE

FLETCHINDER

Height: 2'04" (0.7 m)
Weight: 35.3 lbs. (16.0 kg)

FIRE   FLYING

FLETCHLING

Height: 1'00" (0.3 m)
Weight: 3.7 lbs. (1.7 kg)

NORMAL   FLYING

FLOETTE

Height: 0'08" (0.2 m)
Weight: 2.0 lbs. (0.9 kg)

FAIRY

FLORGES

Height: 3'07" (1.1 m)
Weight: 22.0 lbs. (10.0 kg)

FAIRY

FLYGON

Height: 6'07" (2.0 m)
Weight: 180.8 lbs. (82.0 kg)

GROUND   DRAGON

FOMANTIS

Height: 1'00" (0.3 m)
Weight: 3.3 lbs. (1.5 kg)

GRASS

FORRETRESS

Height: 3'11" (1.2 m)
Weight: 277.3 lbs. (125.8 kg)

BUG   STEEL

FRILLISH

Height: 3'11" (1.2 m)
Weight: 72.8 lbs. (33.0 kg)

WATER   GHOST

FROSLASS

Height: 4'03" (1.3 m)
Weight: 58.6 lbs. (26.6 kg)

ICE   GHOST

FURFROU

Height: 3'11" (1.2 m)
Weight: 61.7 lbs. (28.0 kg)

NORMAL

GABITE

Height: 4'07" (1.4 m)
Weight: 123.5 lbs. (56.0 kg)

DRAGON   GROUND

GARBODOR

Height: 6'03" (1.9 m)
Weight: 236.6 lbs. (107.3 kg)

POISON

GARCHOMP

Height: 6'03'' (1.9 m)
Weight: 209.4 lbs. (95.0 kg)

DRAGON   GROUND

GASTLY

Height: 4'03" (1.3 m)
Weight: 0.2 lbs. (0.1 kg)

GHOST   POISON

GASTRODON

Height: 2'11" (0.9 m)
Weight: 65.9 lbs. (29.9 kg)

WATER   GROUND

GENGAR

Height: 4'11" (1.5 m)
Weight: 89.3 lbs. (40.5 kg)

GHOST   POISON

GIBLE

Height: 2'04" (0.7 m)
Weight: 45.2 lbs. (20.5 kg)

DRAGON   GROUND

GIGALITH

Height: 5'07" (1.7 m)
Weight: 573.2 lbs. (260.0 kg)

ROCK

GLACEON

Height: 2'07" (0.8 m)
Weight: 57.1 lbs. (25.9 kg)

ICE

GLALIE

Height: 4'11" (1.5 m)
Weight: 565.5 lbs. (256.5 kg)

ICE

GOLBAT

Height: 5'03" (1.6 m)
Weight: 121.3 lbs. (55.0 kg)

POISON   FLYING

GOLDEEN

Height: 2'00" (0.6 m)
Weight: 33.1 lbs. (15.0 kg)

WATER

GOLDUCK

Height: 5'07" (1.7 m)
Weight: 168.9 lbs. (76.6 kg)

WATER

GOLETT

Height: 3'03" (1.0 m)
Weight: 202.8 lbs. (92.0 kg)

GROUND   GHOST

GOLISOPOD

Height: 6'07" (2.0 m)
Weight: 238.1 lbs. (108.0 kg)

BUG   WATER

GOLURK
Height: 9'02" (2.8 m)
Weight: 727.5 lbs. (330.0 kg)

GROUND   GHOST

GOODRA

Height: 6'07" (2.0 m)
Weight: 331.8 lbs. (150.5 kg)
DRAGON

GOOMY

Height: 1'00" (0.3 m)
Weight: 6.2 lbs. (2.8 kg)
DRAGON

GOREBYSS

Height: 5'11" (1.8 m)
Weight: 49.8 lbs. (22.6 kg)
WATER

GRANBULL

Height: 4'07" (1.4 m)
Weight: 107.4 lbs. (48.7 kg)
FAIRY

GROWLITHE

Height: 2'04" (0.7 m)
Weight: 41.9 lbs. (19.0 kg)
FIRE

GRUBBIN

Height: 1'04" (0.4 m)
Weight: 9.7 lbs. (4.4 kg)
BUG

GUMSHOOS

Height: 2'04" (0.7 m)
Weight: 31.3 lbs. (14.2 kg)
NORMAL

GUZZLORD

Height: 18'01" (5.5 m)
Weight: 1957.7 lbs. (888.0 kg)
DARK   DRAGON

GYARADOS

Height: 21'04" (6.5 m)
Weight: 518.1 lbs. (235.0 kg)
WATER   FLYING

HAKAMO-O

Height: 3'11" (1.2 m)
Weight: 103.6 lbs. (47.0 kg)
DRAGON   FIGHTING

HAPPINY

Height: 2'00" (0.6 m)
Weight: 53.8 lbs. 24.4 kg)
NORMAL

HARIYAMA

Height: 7'07" (2.3 m)
Weight: 559.5 lbs. (253.8 kg)
FIGHTING

HAUNTER

Height: 5'03" (1.6 m)
Weight: 0.2 lbs. (0.1 kg)
GHOST   POISON

HAWLUCHA

Height: 2'07" (0.8 m)
Weight: 47.4 lbs. (21.5 kg)
FIGHTING   FLYING

HERACROSS

Height: 4'11" (1.5 m)
Weight: 119.0 lbs. (54.0 kg)
BUG   FIGHTING

HERDIER

Height: 2'11" (0.9 m)
Weight: 32.4 lbs. (14.7 kg)
NORMAL

HONCHKROW

Height: 2'11" (0.9 m)
Weight: 60.2 lbs. (27.3 kg)
DARK   FLYING

HOOTHOOT

Height: 2'04" (0.7 m)
Weight: 46.7 lbs. (21.2 kg)
NORMAL   FLYING

HOUNDOOM

Height: 4'07" (1.4 m)
Weight: 77.2 lbs. (35.0 kg)
DARK   FIRE

HOUNDOUR

Height: 2'00" (0.6 m)
Weight: 23.8 lbs. (10.8 kg)
DARK   FIRE

HUNTAIL

Height: 5'07" (1.7 m)
Weight: 59.5 lbs. (27.0 kg)
WATER

HYPNO

Height: 5'03" (1.6 m)
Weight: 166.7 lbs. (75.6 kg)
PSYCHIC

IGGLYBUFF

Height: 1'00" (0.3 m)
Weight: 2.2 lbs. (1.0 kg)
NORMAL   FAIRY

INCINEROAR

Height: 5'11" (1.8 m)
Weight: 183.0 lbs. (83.0 kg)
FIRE   DARK

INKAY

Height: 1'04" (0.4 m)
Weight: 7.7 lbs. (3.5 kg)
DARK   PSYCHIC

JANGMO-O

Height: 2'00" (0.6 m)
Weight: 65.5 lbs. (29.7 kg)

DRAGON

JELLICENT

Height: 7'03" (2.2 m)
Weight: 297.6 lbs. (135.0 kg)

WATER GHOST

JIGGLYPUFF

Height: 1'08" (0.5 m)
Weight: 12.1 lbs. (5.5 kg)

NORMAL FAIRY

JOLTEON

Height: 2'07" (0.8 m)
Weight: 54.0 lbs. (24.5 kg)

ELECTRIC

JYNX

Height: 4'07" (1.4 m)
Weight: 89.5 lbs. (40.6 kg)

ICE PSYCHIC

KABUTO

Height: 1'08" (0.5 m)
Weight: 25.4 lbs. (11.5 kg)

ROCK WATER

KABUTOPS

Height: 4'03" (1.3 m)
Weight: 89.3 lbs. (40.5 kg)

ROCK WATER

KADABRA

Height: 4'03" (1.3 m)
Weight: 124.6 lbs. (56.5 kg)

PSYCHIC

KANGASKHAN

Height: 7'03" (2.2 m)
Weight: 176.4 lbs. (80.0 kg)

NORMAL

KARTANA

Height: 1'00" (0.3 m)
Weight: 0.2 lbs. (0.1 kg)

GRASS STEEL

KECLEON

Height: 3'03" (1.0 m)
Weight: 48.5 lbs. (22.0 kg)

NORMAL

KLEFKI

Height: 0'08" (0.2 m)
Weight: 6.6 lbs. (3.0 kg)

STEEL FAIRY

KOMALA

Height: 1'04" (0.4 m)
Weight: 43.9 lbs. (19.9 kg)

NORMAL

KOMMO-O

Height: 5'03" (1.6 m)
Weight: 172.4 lbs. (78.2 kg)

DRAGON FIGHTING

KROKOROK

Height: 3'03" (1.0 m)
Weight: 73.6 lbs. (33.4 kg)

GROUND DARK

KROOKODILE

Height: 4'11" (1.5 m)
Weight: 212.3 lbs. (96.3 kg)

GROUND DARK

LANTURN

Height: 3'11" (1.2 m)
Weight: 49.6 lbs. (22.5 kg)

WATER ELECTRIC

LAPRAS

Height: 8'02" (2.5 m)
Weight: 485.0 lbs. (220.0 kg)

WATER ICE

LARVESTA

Height: 3'07" (1.1 m)
Weight: 63.5 lbs. (28.8 kg)

BUG FIRE

LARVITAR

Height: 2'00" (0.6 m)
Weight: 158.7 lbs. (72.0 kg)

ROCK GROUND

LEAFEON

Height: 3'03" (1.0 m)
Weight: 56.2 lbs. (25.5 kg)

GRASS

LEDIAN

Height: 4'07" (1.4 m)
Weight: 78.5 lbs. (35.6 kg)

BUG FLYING

LEDYBA

Height: 3'03" (1.0 m)
Weight: 23.8 lbs. (10.8 kg)

BUG FLYING

LICKILICKY

Height: 5'07" (1.7 m)
Weight: 308.6 lbs. (140.0 kg)

NORMAL

LICKITUNG

Height: 3'11" (1.2 m)
Weight: 144.4 lbs. (65.5 kg)

NORMAL

LILEEP

Height: 3'03" (1.0 m)
Weight: 52.5 lbs. (23.8 kg)

ROCK   GRASS

LILLIGANT

Height: 3'07" (1.1 m)
Weight: 35.9 lbs. (16.3 kg)

GRASS

LILLIPUP

Height: 1'04" (0.4 m)
Weight: 9.0 lbs. (4.1 kg)

NORMAL

LITLEO

Height: 2'00" (0.6 m)
Weight: 29.8 lbs. (13.5 kg)

FIRE   NORMAL

LITTEN

Height: 1'04" (0.4 m)
Weight: 9.5 lbs. (4.3 kg)

FIRE

LOPUNNY

Height: 3'11" (1.2 m)
Weight: 73.4 lbs. (33.3 kg)

NORMAL

LUCARIO

Height: 3'11" (1.2 m)
Weight: 119.0 lbs. (54.0 kg)

FIGHTING   STEEL

LUMINEON

Height: 3'11" (1.2 m)
Weight: 52.9 lbs. (24.0 kg

WATER

LUNALA

Height: 13'01" (4.0 m)
Weight: 264.6 lbs. (120.0 kg)

PSYCHIC   GHOST

LURANTIS

Height: 2'11" (0.9 m)
Weight: 40.8 lbs. (18.5 kg)

GRASS

LUVDISC

Height: 2'00" (0.6 m)
Weight: 19.2 lbs. (8.7 kg)

WATER

LYCANROC

Height: 2'07" (0.8 m)
Weight: 55.1 lbs. (25.0 kg)

ROCK

MACHAMP

Height: 5'03" (1.6 m)
Weight: 286.6 lbs. (130.0 kg)

FIGHTING

MACHOKE

Height: 4'11" (1.5 m)
Weight: 155.4 lbs. (70.5 kg)

FIGHTING

MACHOP

Height: 2'07" (0.8 m)
Weight: 43.0 lbs. (19.5 kg)

FIGHTING

MAGBY

Height: 2'04" (0.7 m)
Weight: 47.2 lbs. (21.4 kg)

FIRE

MAGEARNA

Height: 3'03" (1.0 m)
Weight: 177.5 lbs. (80.5 kg)

STEEL   FAIRY

MAGIKARP

Height: 2'11" (0.9 m)
Weight: 22.0 lbs. (10.0 kg)

WATER

MAGMAR

Height: 4'03" (1.3 m)
Weight: 98.1 lbs. (44.5 kg)

FIRE

MAGMORTAR

Height: 5'03" (1.6 m)
Weight: 149.9 lbs. (68.0 kg)

FIRE

MAGNEMITE

Height: 1'00" (0.3 m)
Weight: 13.2 lbs. (6.0 kg)

ELECTRIC   STEEL

MAGNETON

Height: 3'03" (1.0 m)
Weight: 132.3 lbs. (60.0 kg)

ELECTRIC   STEEL

MAGNEZONE

Height: 3'11" (1.2 m)
Weight: 396.8 lbs. (180.0 kg)

ELECTRIC   STEEL

MAKUHITA

Height: 3'03" (1.0 m)
Weight: 190.5 lbs. (86.4 kg)

FIGHTING

MALAMAR

Height: 4'11" (1.5 m)
Weight: 103.6 lbs. (47.0 kg)

DARK   PSYCHIC

MANDIBUZZ

Height: 3'11" (1.2 m)
Weight: 87.1 lbs. (39.5 kg)

DARK | FLYING

MANECTRIC

Height: 4'11" (1.5 m)
Weight: 88.6 lbs. (40.2 kg)

ELECTRIC

MANKEY

Height: 1'08" (0.5 m)
Weight: 61.7 lbs. (28.0 kg)

FIGHTING

MANTINE

Height: 6'11" (2.1 m)
Weight: 485.0 lbs. (220.0 kg)

WATER | FLYING

MANTYKE

Height: 3'03" (1.0 m)
Weight: 143.3 lbs. (65.0 kg)

WATER | FLYING

MAREANIE

Height: 1'04" (0.4 m)
Weight: 17.6 lbs. (8.0 kg)

POISON | WATER

MAREEP

Height: 2'00" (0.6 m)
Weight: 17.2 lbs. (7.8 kg)

ELECTRIC

MARSHADOW

Height: 2'04" (0.7 m)
Weight: 48.9 lbs. (22.2 kg)

FIGHTING | GHOST

MASQUERAIN

Height: 2'07" (0.8 m)
Weight: 7.9 lbs. (3.6 kg)

BUG | FLYING

MAWILE

Height: 2'00" (0.6 m)
Weight: 25.4 lbs. (11.5 kg)

STEEL | FAIRY

METAGROSS

Height: 5'03" (1.6 m)
Weight: 1212.5 lbs. (550.0 kg)

STEEL | PSYCHIC

METANG

Height: 3'11" (1.2 m)
Weight: 446.4 lbs. (202.5 kg)

STEEL | PSYCHIC

METAPOD

Height: 2'04" (0.7 m)
Weight: 21.8 lbs. (9.9 kg)

BUG

MIENFOO

Height: 2'11" (0.9 m)
Weight: 44.1 lbs. (20.0 kg)

FIGHTING

MIENSHAO

Height: 4'07" (1.4 m)
Weight: 78.3 lbs. (35.5 kg)

FIGHTING

MILOTIC

Height: 20'04" (6.2 m)
Weight: 357.1 lbs. (162.0 kg)

WATER

MILTANK

Height: 3'11" (1.2 m)
Weight: 166.4 lbs. (75.5 kg)

NORMAL

MIME JR.

Height: 2'00" (0.6 m)
Weight: 28.7 lbs. (13.0 kg)

PSYCHIC | FAIRY

MIMIKYU

Height: 0'08" (0.2 m)
Weight: 1.5 lbs. (0.7 kg)

GHOST | FAIRY

MINCCINO

Height: 1'04" (0.4 m)
Weight: 12.8 lbs. (5.8 kg)

NORMAL

MINIOR

Height: 1'00" (0.3 m)
Weight: 88.2 lbs. (40.0 kg)

ROCK | FLYING

MISDREAVUS

Height: 2'04" (0.7 m)
Weight: 2.2 lbs. (1.0 kg)

GHOST

MISMAGIUS

Height: 2'11" (0.9 m)
Weight: 9.7 lbs. (4.4 kg)

GHOST

MORELULL

Height: 0'08" (0.2 m)
Weight: 3.3 lbs. (1.5 kg)

GRASS | FAIRY

MR. MIME

Height: 4'03" (1.3 m)
Weight: 120.1 lbs. (54.5 kg)

PSYCHIC | FAIRY

MUDBRAY

Height: 3'03" (1.0 m)
Weight: 242.5 lbs. (110.0 kg)

GROUND

MUDSDALE

Height: 8'02" (2.5 m)
Weight: 2028.3 lbs. (920.0 kg)

GROUND

MUNCHLAX

Height: 2'00" (0.6 m)
Weight: 231.5 lbs. (105.0 kg)

NORMAL

MURKROW

Height: 1'08" (0.5 m)
Weight: 4.6 lbs. (2.1 kg)

DARK   FLYING

NAGANADEL

Height: 11'10" (3.6 m)
Weight: 330.7 lbs. (150.0 kg)

POISON   DRAGON

NATU

Height: 0'08" (0.2 m)
Weight: 4.4 lbs. (2.0 kg)

PSYCHIC   FLYING

NECROZMA

Height: 7'10" (2.4 m)
Weight: 507.1 lbs. (230.0 kg)

PSYCHIC

NIHILEGO

Height: 3'11" (1.2 m)
Weight: 122.4 lbs. (55.5 kg)

ROCK   POISON

NOCTOWL

Height: 5'03" (1.6 m)
Weight: 89.9 lbs. (40.8 kg)

NORMAL   FLYING

NOIBAT

Height: 1'08" (0.5 m)
Weight: 17.6 lbs. (8.0 kg)

FLYING   DRAGON

NOIVERN

Height: 4'11" (1.5 m)
Weight: 187.4 lbs. (85.0 kg)

FLYING   DRAGON

NOSEPASS

Height: 3'03" (1.0 m)
Weight: 213.8 lbs. (97.0 kg)

ROCK

OCTILLERY

Height: 2'11" (0.9 m)
Weight: 62.8 lbs. (28.5 kg)

WATER

OMANYTE

Height: 1'04" (0.4 m)
Weight: 16.5 lbs. (7.5 kg)

ROCK   WATER

OMASTAR

Height: 3'03" (1.0 m)
Weight: 77.2 lbs. (35.0 kg)

ROCK   WATER

ORANGURU

Height: 4'11" (1.5 m)
Weight: 167.6 lbs. (76.0 kg)

NORMAL   PSYCHIC

ORICORIO

Height: 2'00" (0.6 m)
Weight: 7.5 lbs. (3.4 kg)

FIRE   FLYING

PALOSSAND

Height: 4'03" (1.3 m)
Weight: 551.2 lbs. (250.0 kg)

GHOST   GROUND

PANCHAM

Height: 2'00" (0.6 m)
Weight: 17.6 lbs. (8.0 kg)

FIGHTING

PANGORO

Height: 6'11" (2.1 m)
Weight: 299.8 lbs. (136.0 kg)

FIGHTING   DARK

PARAS

Height: 1'00" (0.3 m)
Weight: 11.9 lbs. (5.4 kg)

BUG   GRASS

PARASECT

Height: 3'03" (1.0 m)
Weight: 65.0 lbs. (29.5 kg)

BUG   GRASS

PASSIMIAN

Height: 6'07" (2.0 m)
Weight: 182.5 lbs. (82.8 kg)

FIGHTING

PAWNIARD

Height: 1'08" (0.5 m)
Weight: 22.5 lbs. (10.2 kg)

DARK   STEEL

PELIPPER

Height: 3'11" (1.2 m)
Weight: 61.7 lbs. (28.0 kg)

WATER   FLYING

PETILIL

Height: 1'08" (0.5 m)
Weight: 14.6 lbs. (6.6 kg)

GRASS

PHANTUMP

Height: 1'04" (0.4 m)
Weight: 15.4 lbs. (7.0 kg)

GHOST GRASS

PHEROMOSA

Height: 5'11" (1.8 m)
Weight: 55.1 lbs. (25.0 kg)

BUG FIGHTING

PICHU

Height: 1'00" (0.3 m)
Weight: 4.4 lbs. (2.0 kg)

ELECTRIC

PIKACHU

Height: 1'04" (0.4 m)
Weight: 13.2 lbs. (6.0 kg)

ELECTRIC

PIKIPEK

Height: 1'00" (0.3 m)
Weight: 2.6 lbs. (1.2 kg)

NORMAL FLYING

PINECO

Height: 2'00" (0.6 m)
Weight: 15.9 lbs. (7.2 kg)

BUG

PINSIR

Height: 4'11" (1.5 m)
Weight: 121.3 lbs. (55.0 kg)

BUG

POIPOLE

Height: 2'00" (0.6 m)
Weight: 4.0 lbs. (1.8 kg)

POISON

POLITOED

Height: 3'07" (1.1 m)
Weight: 74.7 lbs. (33.9 kg)

WATER

POLIWAG

Height: 2'00" (0.6 m)
Weight: 27.3 lbs. (12.4 kg)

WATER

POLIWHIRL

Height: 3'03" (1.0 m)
Weight: 44.1 lbs. (20.0 kg)

WATER

POLIWRATH

Height: 4'03" (1.3 m)
Weight: 119.0 lbs. (54.0 kg)

WATER FIGHTING

POPPLIO

Height: 1'04" (0.4 m)
Weight: 16.5 lbs. (7.5 kg)

WATER

PORYGON

Height: 2'07" (0.8 m)
Weight: 80.5 lbs. (36.5 kg)

NORMAL

PORYGON-Z

Height: 2'11" (0.9 m)
Weight: 75.0 lbs. (34.0 kg)

NORMAL

PORYGON2

Height: 2'00" (0.6 m)
Weight: 71.6 lbs. (32.5 kg)

NORMAL

PRIMARINA

Height: 5'11" (1.8 m)
Weight: 97.0 lbs. (44.0 kg)

WATER FAIRY

PRIMEAPE

Height: 3'03" (1.0 m)
Weight: 70.5 lbs. (32.0 kg)

FIGHTING

PROBOPASS

Height: 4'07" (1.4 m)
Weight: 749.6 lbs. (340.0 kg)

ROCK STEEL

PSYDUCK

Height: 2'07" (0.8 m)
Weight: 43.2 lbs. (19.6 kg)

WATER

PUPITAR

Height: 3'11" (1.2 m)
Weight: 335.1 lbs. (152.0 kg)

ROCK GROUND

PYROAR

Height: 4'11" (1.5 m)
Weight: 179.7 lbs. (81.5 kg)

FIRE NORMAL

PYUKUMUKU

Height: 1'00" (0.3 m)
Weight: 2.6 lbs. (1.2 kg)

WATER

RAMPARDOS

Height: 5'03" (1.6 m)
Weight: 226.0 lbs. (102.5 kg)

ROCK

RELICANTH

Height: 3'03" (1.0 m)
Weight: 51.6 lbs. (23.4 kg)

WATER	ROCK

REMORAID

Height: 2'00" (0.6 m)
Weight: 26.5 lbs. (12.0 kg)

WATER

RIBOMBEE

Height: 0'08" (0.2 m)
Weight: 1.1 lbs. (0.5 kg)

BUG	FAIRY

RIOLU

Height: 2'04" (0.7 m)
Weight: 44.5 lbs. (20.2 kg)

FIGHTING

ROCKRUFF

Height: 1'08" (0.5 m)
Weight: 20.3 lbs. (9.2 kg)

ROCK

ROGGENROLA

Height: 1'04" (0.4 m)
Weight: 39.7 lbs. (18.0 kg)

ROCK

ROWLET

Height: 1'00" (0.3 m)
Weight: 3.3 lbs. (1.5 kg)

GRASS	FLYING

RUFFLET

Height: 1'08" (0.5 m)
Weight: 23.1 lbs. (10.5 kg)

NORMAL	FLYING

SABLEYE

Height: 1'08" (0.5 m)
Weight: 24.3 lbs. (11.0 kg)

DARK	GHOST

SALAMENCE

Height: 4'11'' (1.5 m)
Weight: 226.2 lbs. (102.6 kg)

DRAGON	FLYING

SALANDIT

Height: 2'00" (0.6 m)
Weight: 10.6 lbs. (4.8 kg)

POISON	FIRE

SALAZZLE

Height: 3'11" (1.2 m)
Weight: 48.9 lbs. (22.2 kg)

POISON	FIRE

SANDILE

Height: 2'04" (0.7 m)
Weight: 33.5 lbs. (15.2 kg)

GROUND	DARK

SANDYGAST

Height: 1'08" (0.5 m)
Weight: 154.3 lbs. (70.0 kg)

GHOST	GROUND

SCIZOR

Height: 5'11" (1.8 m)
Weight: 260.1 lbs. (118.0 kg)

BUG	STEEL

SCRAFTY

Height: 3'07" (1.1 m)
Weight: 66.1 lbs. (30.0 kg)

DARK	FIGHTING

SCRAGGY

Height: 2'00'' (0.6 m)
Weight: 26.0 lbs. (11.8 kg)

DARK	FIGHTING

SCYTHER

Height: 4'11" (1.5 m)
Weight: 123.5 lbs. (56.0 kg)

BUG	FLYING

SEAKING

Height: 4'03" (1.3 m)
Weight: 86.0 lbs. (39.0 kg)

WATER

SEEL

Height: 3'07" (1.1 m)
Weight: 198.4 lbs. (90.0 kg)

WATER

SHARPEDO

Height: 5'11" (1.8 m)
Weight: 195.8 lbs. (88.8 kg)

WATER	DARK

SHELGON

Height: 3'07" (1.1 m)
Weight: 243.6 lbs. (110.5 kg)

DRAGON

SHELLDER

Height: 1'00" (0.3 m)
Weight: 8.8 lbs. (4.0 kg)

WATER

SHELLOS

Height: 1'00" (0.3 m)
Weight: 13.9 lbs. (6.3 kg)

WATER

SHIELDON

Height: 1'08" (0.5 m)
Weight: 125.7 lbs. (57.0 kg)

ROCK	STEEL

SHIINOTIC

Height: 3'03" (1.0 m)
Weight: 25.4 lbs. (11.5 kg)

GRASS | FAIRY

SHUPPET

Height: 2'00" (0.6 m)
Weight: 5.1 lbs. (2.3 kg)

GHOST

SILVALLY

Height: 7'07" (2.3 m)
Weight: 221.6 lbs. (100.5 kg)

NORMAL

SKARMORY

Height: 5'07" (1.7 m)
Weight: 111.3 lbs. (50.5 kg)

STEEL | FLYING

SKRELP

Height: 1'08" (0.5 m)
Weight: 16.1 lbs. (7.3 kg)

POISON | WATER

SLIGGOO

Height: 2'07" (0.8 m)
Weight: 38.6 lbs. (17.5 kg)

DRAGON

SLOWBRO

Height: 5'03" (1.6 m)
Weight: 173.1 lbs. (78.5 kg)

WATER | PSYCHIC

SLOWKING

Height: 6'07" (2.0 m)
Weight: 175.3 lbs. (79.5 kg)

WATER | PSYCHIC

SLOWPOKE

Height: 3'11" (1.2 m)
Weight: 79.4 lbs. (36.0 kg)

WATER | PSYCHIC

SMEARGLE
Height: 3'11" (1.2 m)
Weight: 127.9 lbs. (58.0 kg)

NORMAL

SMOOCHUM

Height: 1'04" (0.4 m)
Weight: 13.2 lbs. (6.0 kg)

ICE | PSYCHIC

SNEASEL

Height: 2'11" (0.9 m)
Weight: 61.7 lbs. (28.0 kg)

DARK | ICE

SNORLAX

Height: 6'11" (2.1 m)
Weight: 1014.1 lbs. (460.0 kg)

NORMAL

SNORUNT

Height: 2'04" (0.7 m)
Weight: 37.0 lbs. (16.8 kg)

ICE

SNUBBULL

Height: 2'00" (0.6 m)
Weight: 17.2 lbs. (7.8 kg)

FAIRY

SOLGALEO

Height: 11'02" (3.4 m)
Weight: 507.1 lbs. (230.0 kg)

PSYCHIC | STEEL

SPEAROW

Height: 1'00" (0.3 m)
Weight: 4.4 lbs. (2.0 kg)

NORMAL | FLYING

SPINARAK

Height: 1'08" (0.5 m)
Weight: 18.7 lbs. (8.5 kg)

BUG | POISON

SPINDA

Height: 3'07" (1.1 m)
Weight: 11.0 lbs. (5.0 kg)

NORMAL

STAKATAKA

Height: 18'01" (5.5 m)
Weight: 1807.8 lbs. (820.0 kg)

ROCK | STEEL

STARMIE

Height: 3'07" (1.1 m)
Weight: 176.4 lbs. (80.0 kg)

WATER | PSYCHIC

STARYU

Height: 2'07" (0.8 m)
Weight: 76.1 lbs. (34.5 kg)

WATER

STEENEE

Height: 2'04" (0.7 m)
Weight: 18.1 lbs. (8.2 kg)

GRASS

STOUTLAND

Height: 3'11" (1.2 m)
Weight: 134.5 lbs. (61.0 kg)

NORMAL

STUFFUL

Height: 1'08" (0.5 m)
Weight: 15.0 lbs. (6.8 kg)

NORMAL | FIGHTING

SUDOWOODO

Height: 3'11" (1.2 m)
Weight: 83.8 lbs. (38.0 kg)

`ROCK`

SURSKIT

Height: 1'08" (0.5 m)
Weight: 3.7 lbs. (1.7 kg)

`BUG` `WATER`

SYLVEON

Height: 3'03" (1.0 m)
Weight: 51.8 lbs. (23.5 kg)

`FAIRY`

TALONFLAME

Height: 3'11" (1.2 m)
Weight: 54.0 lbs. (24.5 kg)

`FIRE` `FLYING`

TAPU BULU

Height: 6'03" (1.9 m)
Weight: 100.3 lbs. (45.5 kg)

`GRASS` `FAIRY`

TAPU FINI

Height: 4'03" (1.3 m)
Weight: 46.7 lbs. (21.2 kg)

`WATER` `FAIRY`

TAPU KOKO

Height: 5'11" (1.8 m)
Weight: 45.2 lbs. (20.5 kg)

`ELECTRIC` `FAIRY`

TAPU LELE

Height: 3'11" (1.2 m)
Weight: 41.0 lbs. (18.6 kg)

`PSYCHIC` `FAIRY`

TAUROS

Height: 4'07" (1.4 m)
Weight: 194.9 lbs. (88.4 kg)

`NORMAL`

TENTACOOL

Height: 2'11" (0.9 m)
Weight: 100.3 lbs. (45.5 kg)

`WATER` `POISON`

TENTACRUEL

Height: 5'03" (1.6 m)
Weight: 121.3 lbs. (55.0 kg)

`WATER` `POISON`

TIRTOUGA

Height: 2'04" (0.7 m)
Weight: 36.4 lbs. (16.5 kg)

`WATER` `ROCK`

TOGEDEMARU

Height: 1'00" (0.3 m)
Weight: 7.3 lbs. (3.3 kg)

`ELECTRIC` `STEEL`

TORKOAL

Height: 1'08" (0.5 m)
Weight: 177.2 lbs. (80.4 kg)

`FIRE`

TORRACAT

Height: 2'04" (0.7 m)
Weight: 55.1 lbs. (25.0 kg)

`FIRE`

TOUCANNON

Height: 3'07" (1.1 m)
Weight: 57.3 lbs. (26.0 kg)

`NORMAL` `FLYING`

TOXAPEX

Height: 2'04" (0.7 m)
Weight: 32.0 lbs. (14.5 kg)

`POISON` `WATER`

TRAPINCH

Height: 2'04" (0.7 m)
Weight: 33.1 lbs. (15.0 kg)

`GROUND`

TREVENANT

Height: 4'11" (1.5 m)
Weight: 156.5 lbs. (71.0 kg)

`GHOST` `GRASS`

TROPIUS

Height: 6'07" (2.0 m)
Weight: 220.5 lbs. (100.0 kg)

`GRASS` `FLYING`

TRUBBISH

Height: 2'00" (0.6 m)
Weight: 68.3 lbs. (31.0 kg)

`POISON`

TRUMBEAK

Height: 2'00" (0.6 m)
Weight: 32.6 lbs. (14.8 kg)

`NORMAL` `FLYING`

TSAREENA

Height: 3'11" (1.2 m)
Weight: 47.2 lbs. (21.4 kg)

`GRASS`

TURTONATOR

Height: 6'07" (2.0 m)
Weight: 467.4 lbs. (212.0 kg)

`FIRE` `DRAGON`

TYPE: NULL

Height: 6'03" (1.9 m)
Weight: 265.7 lbs. (120.5 kg)

`NORMAL`

TYRANITAR

Height: 6'07" (2.0 m)
Weight: 445.3 lbs. (202.0 kg)

`ROCK` `DARK`

TYRANTRUM

Height: 8'02" (2.5 m)
Weight: 595.2 lbs. (270.0 kg)

ROCK | DRAGON

TYRUNT

Height: 2'07" (0.8 m)
Weight: 57.3 lbs. (26.0 kg)

ROCK | DRAGON

UMBREON

Height: 3'03" (1.0 m)
Weight: 59.5 lbs. (27.0 kg)

DARK

VANILLISH

Height: 3'07" (1.1 m)
Weight: 90.4 lbs. (41.0 kg)

ICE

VANILLITE

Height: 1'04" (0.4 m)
Weight: 12.6 lbs. (5.7 kg)

ICE

VANILLUXE

Height: 4'03" (1.3 m)
Weight: 126.8 lbs. (57.5 kg)

ICE

VAPOREON

Height: 3'03" (1.0 m)
Weight: 63.9 lbs. (29.0 kg)

WATER

VIBRAVA

Height: 3'07" (1.1 m)
Weight: 33.7 lbs. (15.3 kg)

GROUND | DRAGON

VIKAVOLT

Height: 4'11" (1.5 m)
Weight: 99.2 lbs. (45.0 kg)

BUG | ELECTRIC

VOLCARONA

Height: 5'03" (1.6 m)
Weight: 101.4 lbs. (46.0 kg)

BUG | FIRE

VULLABY

Height: 1'08" (0.5 m)
Weight: 19.8 lbs. (9.0 kg)

DARK | FLYING

WAILMER

Height: 6'07" (2.0 m)
Weight: 286.6 lbs. (130.0 kg)

WATER

WAILORD

Height: 47'07" (14.5 m)
Weight: 877.4 lbs. (398.0 kg)

WATER

WEAVILE

Height: 3'07" (1.1 m)
Weight: 75.0 lbs. (34.0 kg)

DARK | ICE

WHIMSICOTT

Height: 2'04" (0.7 m)
Weight: 14.6 lbs. (6.6 kg)

GRASS | FAIRY

WHISCASH

Height: 2'11" (0.9 m)
Weight: 52.0 lbs. (23.6 kg)

WATER | GROUND

WIGGLYTUFF

Height: 3'03" (1.0 m)
Weight: 26.5 lbs. (12.0 kg)

NORMAL | FAIRY

WIMPOD
Height: 1'08" (0.5 m)
Weight: 26.5 lbs. (12.0 kg)

BUG | WATER

WINGULL
Height: 2'00" (0.6 m)
Weight: 20.9 lbs. (9.5 kg)

WATER | FLYING

WISHIWASHI
Height: 0'08" (0.2 m)
Weight: 0.7 lbs. (0.3 kg)

WATER

XATU
Height: 4'11" (1.5 m)
Weight: 33.1 lbs. (15.0 kg)

PSYCHIC | FLYING

XURKITREE
Height: 12'06" (3.8 m)
Weight: 220.5 lbs. (100.0 kg)

ELECTRIC

YUNGOOS

Height: 1'04" (0.4 m)
Weight: 13.2 lbs. (6.0 kg)

NORMAL

ZOROARK

Height: 5'03" (1.6 m)
Weight: 178.8 lbs. (81.1 kg)

DARK

ZORUA

Height: 2'04" (0.7 m)
Weight: 27.6 lbs. (12.5 kg)

DARK

ZUBAT

Height: 2'07" (0.8 m)
Weight: 16.5 lbs. (7.5 kg)

POISON | FLYING

ZYGARDE

Height: 16'05" (5.0 m)
Weight: 672.4 lbs. (305.0 kg)

DRAGON | GROUND

ZYGARDE COMPLETE
Height: 16'05" (5.0 m)
Weight: 672.4 lbs. (305.0 kg)

DRAGON | GROUND

GALAR

A whole new world of Pokémon opens up for Ash as his journey continues into the Galar region. This exciting destination has its own unique Pokémon as well as intriguing Galarian forms of the many creatures already discovered. Get ready for new challenges and creatures that range from delightful to diabolical!

NEW FRIENDS

It's time for Ash and Pikachu to make new friends and fight duels like never before with the amazing creatures in store for them in the Galar region. Meet Grookey, a Grass-type, Chimp Pokémon. Then there's Scorbunny the Fire-type Rabbit Pokémon, and Sobble the Water-type Water Lizard Pokémon!

SCORBUNNY

Height	1'00" (0.3 m)	Category	Rabbit Pokémon
Weight	9.9 lbs (4.5 kg)	Type	Fire

GROOKEY

SCORBUNNY

SOBBLE

GROOKEY

Height	1'00" (0.3 m)	Category	Chimp Pokémon
Weight	11 lbs (5.0 kg)	Type	Grass

SOBBLE

Height	1'00" (0.3 m)	Category	Lizard Pokémon
Weight	8.8 lbs (4.0 kg)	Type	Water

RECENTLY DISCOVERED LEGENDARIES

ZACIAN

Height	9'02" (2.8 m)	Category	Warrior
Weight	242.5 lbs (110.0 kg)	Type	Fairy

Now armed with a weapon it used in ancient times, this Pokémon needs only a single strike to fell even Gigantamax Pokémon.

ZAMAZENTA

Height	9'06" (2.9 m)
Weight	463.0 lbs (210.0 kg)
Category	Warrior
Type	Fighting

Its ability to deflect any attack led to it being known as the Fighting Master's Shield. It was feared and respected by all.

LIFE LESSONS

Pokémon is full of diverse characters and amazing storylines, but one question remains: What is it all about? Is it simply a young boy's coming-of-age story? Is it a story of unending friendship? Is it about the responsibility of putting your faith in your friends? Or is it, as so many claim, all of the above?

FRIENDSHIP

Ash has an incredible bond with Pikachu, and that bond is based on mutual respect, the ability to know what your limitations are, and love for someone who depends on you and on whom you depend. It is a relationship based upon mutual sacrifice. From the beginning, Ash has proven his willingness to sacrifice his time, energy, and health for the protection and betterment of Pikachu. With a friendship like that, it is no wonder why Pikachu never gives up when battling another Pokémon.

KINDNESS

Treat your friends and your Pokémon the way you want to be treated and you'll live a happy and fulfilling life. Ash constantly challenges those who are abusive, be it with their Pokémon, or other humans. He often finds himself sticking up for the underprivileged and weak. What Ash doesn't do is lord over those he considers beneath him, even if they are outmatched. He may trash-talk, but he never bullies.

NATURE

Time and time again, the after-effects of fooling with the natural order of life is very bad. Most memorable is Team Aqua and Team Magma's insistence that their land mass/water mass ideology is better, with disastrous results. Taking a Pokémon out of its natural modus operandi and forcing it to your will is also going to bring retribution. Nature will find its balance with you or without you.

SPORTSMANSHIP

Simply stated, Ash wants to catch 'em all and he wants to win them all, but winning isn't everything. His style of taking on any challengers or stepping up to seemingly insurmountable odds may be impressive, but it doesn't always work out in his favor. Ash did not win his first tournament, placing in the top sixteen. He has lost numerous battles…

NEVER GIVE UP

… but he has also never given up, even when faced with defeat. His plucky determination has slightly changed over the years, and now Ash battles with less bravado and more strategy—and he's been winning more, too!

POKÉMON PAGE NUMBER INDEX

DK | Penguin Random House

Third Edition
Project Editor Lisa Stock
Project Art Editor Stefan Georgiou
Designer Thelma-Jane Robb
Cover Designer James McKeag
Production Editor Siu Chan
Production Controller Lloyd Robertson
Managing Editor Paula Regan
Managing Art Editor Jo Connor
Art Director Lisa Lanzarini
Publisher Julie Ferris
Publishing Director Mark Searle

This American Edition, 2020
First American Edition, 2016
Published in the United States by DK Publishing
1450 Broadway, Suite 801, New York, NY 10018

A catalog record for this book is available from the Library of Congress.
ISBN 978-0-7440-2197-4

DK books are available at special discounts when purchased in bulk for
sales promotions, premiums, fund-raising, or educational use.
For details, contact: DK Publishing Special Markets,
1450 Broadway, Suite 801, New York, NY 10018. SpecialSales@dk.com

DK would like to thank Hank Woon and the rest of the team at
The Pokémon Company International. Thanks also to Mike Degler,
Tim Fitzpatrick, Tracy Wehmeyer, Jennifer Sims, Brent Gann,
Dan Caparo, Tim Amrhein, Areva, and Beth Guzman for their
work on the 1st and 2nd editions, and to Megan Douglass
for proofreading.

Printed and bound in China

For the curious

www.dk.com